Servicing and Supporting IBM PCs and Compatibles

Julian Moss

SIGMA PRESS
Wilmslow, England

Copyright © 1992, Julian Moss

All rights reserved. No part of this publication may be reproduced, stored in a retrieval system or transmitted in any form or by any means, electronic, mechanical, photocopying, recording or otherwise, without prior written permission of the publisher.

In this book, many of the designations used by manufacturers and sellers to distinguish their products may be claimed as trademarks. Due acknowledgment is hereby made of all legal protection.

Typeset and Designed by Sigma Hi-Tech Services Ltd, Wilmslow, UK

Cover Design by Design House, Marple Bridge.

First published in 1992
Sigma Press, 1 South Oak Lane, Wilmslow, Cheshire SK9 6AR, UK

First printed 1992

ISBN: 1-85058-243-2

British Library Cataloguing in Publication Data
A CIP catalogue record for this book is available from the British Library

Printed by: Interprint Ltd, Malta

Foreword

I know what you're thinking: *"Another book about PCs. Aren't there enough already?"*. Certainly, there is a whole stack of books which cover almost every conceivable – and some inconceivable – aspects of the IBM Personal Computer, its branches and its descendants. However, books should change with changing markets and there ain't nuthin' that changes as fast as the PC market. This book seeks to address a particular aspect of today's market.

One of the favourite comparisons used about the Personal Computer market is the parallel with the development of the car industry at the beginning of the century. Well, here's another one. In the early days of the car, drivers had to be their own mechanics as the expertise needed to repair these temperamental machines was rare. As the number of cars grew, specialist repair shops grew up where you could take your ailing automobile.

However, taking your car to the garage for repair is an expensive business – even the insurance for such a visit is not cheap. Hence there has been a boom in do-it-yourself car repair manuals and courses to enable the budget conscious driver to avoid expensive garage bills with a little judicious home maintenance.

So it is with the PC business. In the earliest days – ten years ago or so – most personal computers were bought by hobbyists who didn't mind – in fact positively enjoyed – tinkering about with the innards of their PCs. Gradually, these people were replaced in importance by the large organisations who had specialist departments to deal with the halt and the lame amongst the company PCs. Ordinary users didn't need to know what happened under the lid but relied on the 'experts' in technical support. They just turned them on and they went.

Meanwhile, as the inexorable economics of the computer business ground on, Personal

Computers became affordable not just by the large corporation and the well heeled but by everyone who needed some computer power whether at home or at work. However, they still couldn't afford the fancy maintenance contracts offered by third party companies or go to a specialist dealer who provided support. Rather they went to their High Street store which, in order to remain competitive, could not afford the overhead of specialist support staff.

But, even within the large corporation or support centre, someone has to know what is going on. Spare a thought for the poor support staff. They are confronted daily by a battery of calls from people with a wide range of experience. These vary from users who know nothing about what might be wrong apart from the fact that it's dead, to callers who are having problems with some fancy new peripheral card interfering with the expanded memory driver and could you kindly tell them (in hex) what the offending address might be.

This book is aimed at anyone who might be called upon to 'support' a personal computer, whether their own or somebody else's. As the personal computer becomes more and more of a commodity, the less and less help people will get in setting up, maintaining and enhancing their computers. The rapid growth of the mail order business means that many people now buy PCs without actually seeing anyone at all!

As a result people will need to know more about how their computer works in order to enhance and customise it to their needs. Meanwhile the support staff within companies have to run flat out to stay ahead of the power users within the organisation.

Unfortunately, despite its claims to user-friendliness, the PC business often seems to be surrounded by a wall of jargon. Non-professionals often suspect that this is some secret language designed to keep outsiders out. The truth is that it is a shorthand, and like any shorthand seems to be gibberish to anyone unfamiliar with it.

This book is designed – with the minimum of jargon – to take the reader on a step by step journey through their personal computer, its peripherals (there I go with the jargon, I mean printers and other bits you attach to a PC) and anything else liable to affect the day to day happiness of your personal computer.

By the end you should be able to advance on your computer clutching a screwdriver with the conviction that you know what you are doing. In my experience, knowing what you are doing before you start is a good philosophy in any area of life.

Steve Malone

Preface

IBM compatible personal computers are by far the most popular type of microcomputer for home or business use. Over sixty million of them, from over a thousand different manufacturers, are in use today. Walk into an office anywhere in the world and the chances are, if there's a computer there, it will be a PC.

PCs may not be technically the most advanced micros you can buy, but they have several big advantages. There's a lot of competition in the marketplace, so they're cheap. There's a stupendous choice of software available for them, tens of thousands of programs ranging from freeware to premium priced commercial packages. They're reliable, because the hardware is based around industry standard, tried and tested components. And when they do go wrong, the straightforward design and use of standard parts means that they are easy to repair.

If you want to learn how PCs work, and how to fix them when they go wrong, this book is for you. It covers all aspects of servicing and supporting IBM compatible personal computers. Servicing is, of course, about maintaining machines and repairing hardware faults. Support is a more nebulous term. As far as this book is concerned, it means the ancillary tasks of installing, configuring and tuning PCs to get the best out of them, and solving problems that are not hardware-related, such as computer viruses.

When, back in 1981, IBM introduced the PC, they created a standard for personal microcomputers. Over the years that standard has been developed, refined, extended and greatly improved, but every PC compatible made today inherits much of its design from that original IBM machine. Software written when the PC first came out will still run - considerably faster! - on today's hot 50MHz 80486 box. Hardware add-ins designed to conform to the notional IBM standard will work in almost any PC compatible no matter who the manufacturer.

Since all PC compatibles closely conform to an unwritten 'standard', what's true of one machine is also true of many others. Descriptions of how things work, or the likely causes of a particular fault symptom, are valid for any PC. Fault-finding knowledge gained on one make can be applied equally well to another. Standardisation can impede the adoption of new technology, but it does make the job of support and maintenance much easier. It's this standardisation that makes this book possible.

About this book

This book is aimed at anyone who has an interest in looking after PCs. Whether it's your job, or whether you simply want to be able to upgrade and maintain your own personal machine, there should be plenty of interest within these pages.

If you want to find faults or swap cards in and out and know what you're doing, you need a level of technical knowledge that extends beyond what even an advanced user would have. If you aren't familiar with electronics, have never studied computer science at college, and have never programmed PCs at a low level, then you probably don't have that knowledge.

Chapter 1 will remedy that omission. It describes the basic components that are the building blocks of a modern personal computer. After you've read it, you won't be able to go out and design your own PC, but you'll at least understand most of the terminology used in the later chapters and in the technical manuals that accompany many PC peripherals and boards. You'll also understand some concepts that occasionally confuse *experts*, such as the difference between interrupts and IRQs, or between expanded and extended memory.

In Chapter 2 we look at the mechanics and thought processes involved in troubleshooting. You'll discover how to follow a logical process of elimination to pinpoint a faulty part from several possible alternatives, and how to use diagnostic aids to help identify a fault. Many of the later chapters include diagnostic routines written specially for this book in BASIC.

Chapters 3 to 11 explain in more detail the various parts of IBM PC compatible computers and common peripherals. Each chapter begins by describing the theory and practice of how each device works. We highlight particular problem areas, and the reasons why they occur.

Each chapter closes with a list of common problems, and probable solutions. However, though some faults are common, PCs can play up in an infinite variety of ways. It just isn't possible to list every conceivable fault with a surefire solution to it. That's why throughout the book, explanations are given of how things work and how you should go about finding a fault. The intention is to teach you to be an effective troubleshooter. With practice, you'll instinctively know where to start looking when a problem occurs.

Chapter 12 looks at the tools you'll need to carry out repairs and upgrades to PCs. It also shows how to use some things that you may not have used before: a test meter, chip inserters and extractors and a soldering iron.

Chapter 13 goes into the ways in which the operating environment of a computer can affect its reliability and eventual life. Many factors - some of which are difficult to determine, like the quality of the mains supply - can adversely affect the performance of a PC. In the real world, few PCs will have a perfect environment. However, awareness of the possible problems will help you avoid them.

Preventive maintenance can be beneficial to the health of a computer or peripheral. Chapter 14 looks at setting up a preventive maintenance programme. If the checks are scheduled too frequently, and the list of things to do is too long, then preventive maintenance just won't get done. There's a good old saying: *If it ain't broke, don't fix it!* This chapter proposes a simple procedure that should only take a few minutes per machine, every few months.

Every PC user wants more speed out of his or her machine. Incorrect set-up or configuration is a common cause of poor performance and unexplained system crashes. Chapter 15 examines various ways in which PCs can be configured and tuned to get the best possible performance.

Chapter 16 looks at the increasingly prevalent problem of computer viruses. There's a lot of myth and mystique about this subject. Many companies make a lot of money selling software that they claim will eliminate the problem. But there is a great deal that can be done simply by using good housekeeping procedures and some low-cost virus checking software to banish these nuisance programs once and for all.

Networking is a complex and fast-moving area, and merits an entire book to itself. Chapter 17 provides a brief introduction to the subject. It's one which anyone involved in supporting personal computers in a business environment will need to know about sooner or later. Finally, in Chapter 18 we sum up by looking at what you can do to develop and improve your PC troubleshooting skills.

At the back of the book are several Appendices containing reference material which you'll find useful when dealing with PC problems. Appendix 1 is a glossary of the main technical terms used in the book, for those who haven't encountered them before. Appendix 2 lists the error codes that many older PCs give when the power-on tests find a fault. Fortunately, most modern machines now give error messages in plain English.

Appendix 3 will be one of the most useful. It gives details of the PC memory map, and lists the IRQ line, I/O port and DMA channel usages which have been defined as *standard*. Appendix 4 lists the characteristics of many hard disks. It isn't exhaustive; there are literally thousands of types. This list includes many of the best-known manufacturers' products.

Appendix 5 lists some current suppliers of parts, which will be useful to the PC repairer. Appendix 6 gives some information about the most common PC viruses. Lastly, Appendix 7 gives details of a disk containing the BASIC diagnostics listings and some of the shareware and public domain utilities that are referred to in the text. Most of these utilities are available from bulletin boards. However, for those who don't have a modem, the disks may be purchased from the publishers.

This book is a distillation of the knowledge gained from several years' experience in programming, supporting and troubleshooting IBM compatible personal computers. Writing it has been an enjoyable experience. I hope you, the reader, find it equally enjoyable as well as useful.

Julian V Moss

Acknowledgements

When IBM designed the PC, they didn't just make a computer, they created a way of life. All of us whose livelihood depends on the existence of the PC industry should acknowledge the contributions of two men who were responsible for making the PC such a success: Bill Lowe, the man who got the project off the ground, and Don Estridge, tragically killed in an air crash on August 5th, 1985, who brought it to completion. Their story is outstandingly told in *Blue Magic* by James Chposky and Ted Leonsis, published by Grafton Books. It is a true story told in the manner of a novel; the story of the people, the power and the politics behind the desk-top computers we now take for granted.

Over the years, many people have helped me in my quest for knowledge about PCs. Without their help, this book would not have been possible. I owe a debt of gratitude to two people who, unknowingly, taught me the basics of how PCs and PC software work. They are Peter Norton and Ray Duncan. Peter's highly readable *Programmer's Guide to the IBM PC* and Ray's *Advanced MSDOS Programming* – both published by Microsoft Press – answered many of my questions, put to rest a few misconceptions, and laid the foundations for my knowledge of the inner workings of IBM compatible personal computers.

Many companies helped me in the preparation of this book by sending technical information about their products. I would particularly like to thank Karen Atkins of Western Digital, who must have spent most of an afternoon at the photocopier in order to provide me with an immense pack of information about their hard disks, controllers, display adapters and network cards. Thanks are also due to James Eades of Seagate Technology Europe, who sent information about his company's wide range of disk drives, and more beautiful photographs of hard disks than there was space to use. I have found both these companies to be equally helpful when it comes to technical support, a point perhaps to bear in mind when deciding whose products to buy.

I want to thank to Larry Polyak of MicroSystems Development who sent me a free copy of the commercial version of his diskette diagnostic program Test Drive to evaluate. By the time you read this, Larry may also have available a product which tests serial and parallel ports. Thanks also to Richard Talbot of CompuServe's UK office who enabled me to explore the world's largest information service. My telephone bill will never be the same again!

Finally, I'd like to thank Larry Goldstein and Phil Croucher for their comments on the first draft. They've helped me to write a better book.

Within the book, many company, product and trade names have been mentioned. Use of these names, which include those given below, is hereby acknowledged:

IBM, PC/XT, PC/AT, PC jr, PS/2, PC DOS, Micro Channel, MCA are trademarks of International Business Machines Corporation.

Microsoft, MS, MS-DOS, OS/2, Windows are trademarks of Microsoft Corporation.

LIM 4.0, Expanded Memory Specification are copyright Lotus Development Corp., Intel Corp. and Microsoft Corp.

123 is copyright Lotus Development Corporation.

Amstrad is a registered trademark of Amstrad plc.

Check It is a registered trademark of TouchStone Software Inc.

Compaq, Deskpro are trademarks of Compaq Computer Corporation.

DesQview and QEMM are trademarks of Quarterdeck Office Systems.

Digital Research, DR DOS and Concurrent DOS 386 and Multiuser DOS are trademarks of Digital Research Inc.

Intel, 386, 386sx, 486 are trademarks of Intel Corporation.

Landmark, AlignIt and PC Probe are trademarks of Landmark Research International Corp.

LANsmart is a trademark of D-Link.

LANtastic is a trademark of Artisoft.

Microcom Networking Protocol, MNP are trademarks of Microcom Inc.

Mouse Systems is a trademark of Mouse Systems Corp.

Novell, NetWare are trademarks of Novell Corp.

Seagate, Seagate Technology and the Seagate logo are registered trademarks of Seagate Technology, Inc.

The Norton Utilities is a registered trademark of Symantec Corp.

Test Drive is a trademark of Microsystems Development.

CONTENTS

1. Hardware Basics 1
1.1 Hardware Components. 2
1.2 The Processor. 4
1.3 Memory. 4
1.4 Memory Addressing 6
1.5 Types of Memory 8
1.6 Memory Speed and Wait States 8
1.7 Memory Access 9
1.8 Input/Output Ports. 9
1.9 The System Bus 10
1.10 Interrupt Requests 12
1.11 The Clock. 13
1.12 The Timer. 14
1.13 Direct Memory Access. 14
1.14 AT Compatibles and the 80286 Processor. 15
1.15 The 80386 and 80486 Processors. 16
1.16 Memory map 16
1.17 Expanded Memory. 18
1.18 Extended Memory. 19
1.19 DOS Extenders. 19
1.20 The High Memory Area. 20
1.21 The MCA Bus. 21
1.22 The EISA Bus. 21

2. Problem Solving 23
2.1 Is it Hardware or Software? 23
2.2 Diagnosing a Problem 25

2.3 Power-On Self Test..26
2.4 Diagnostic Software...28
2.5 IBM Advanced Diagnostics.....................................29
2.6 Third-Party Software...31
2.7 Public Domain and Shareware Diagnostics.....................33
2.8 BASIC Diagnostics..37
Summary...38

3. The Power Supply 39
3.1 Power Supply Basics..40
3.2 Power Requirements...41
3.3 Testing the Power Supply.....................................43
3.4 Diagnosing Problems..45
3.5 Power Supply Removal...47
3.5 Power Supply Replacement.....................................48
Summary...48

4. The Motherboard and Expansion Bus 49
4.1 Motherboard Construction.....................................50
4.2 Motherboard Components.......................................51
4.3 Memory Parity..52
4.4 Memory Banks...52
4.5 Chip Sets..53
4.6 Motherboard Connectors.......................................53
4.7 Motherboard Configuration....................................56
4.8 Memory Configuration...59
4.9 CMOS Setup for AT Compatibles................................60
4.10 ROM Shadowing...64
4.11 Fitting Expansion Cards.....................................65
4.12 Card Conflicts..66
4.13 Upgrading Memory..73
4.14 Performance Enhancement.....................................74
4.15 Diagnosing Problems...75
4.16 Motherboard Repair or Replacement...........................78
4.17 Removing the Motherboard....................................78
4.18 Replacing the Motherboard...................................79

5. The Keyboard 81
5.1 Keyboard Basics..81
5.2 XT and AT Keyboards..83
5.3 Diagnosing Problems..84
5.4 Dismantling and Reassembly...................................88

6. The Display ... 91
- 6.1 Monitor Basics ... 91
- 6.2 Digital and Analogue Monitors ... 94
- 6.3 Laptop Displays ... 95
- 6.4 Monitor Selection ... 96
- 6.5 Testing Monitors ... 97
- 6.6 Display Adapters ... 100
- 6.7 Two-monitor Systems ... 106
- 6.8 Display Problems ... 107

7. Diskette Drives ... 113
- 7.1 Diskette Basics ... 114
- 7.2 Types of Diskette ... 115
- 7.3 Diskette Drives ... 116
- 7.4 Drive Configuration ... 118
- 7.5 The Diskette Drive Controller ... 120
- 7.6 Diagnosing Problems ... 120
- 7.7 Drive Misalignment ... 121
- 7.8 Servicing Drives ... 124
- 7.9 Drive Failure ... 125
- 7.10 Diskette Change-line Problems ... 126
- 7.11 Problems Reading Diskettes Written by Other Machines ... 126
- 7.12 Diskette Problems – Checklist ... 128
- 7.13 Diskette Drive Installation ... 129
- 7.14 Diskette Drive Removal ... 130
- 7.15 3.5inch Drives ... 130
- 7.16 External Diskette Drives ... 131

8. Hard Disks ... 133
- 8.1 Hard Disk Basics ... 133
- 8.2 Recording Media ... 135
- 8.3 Head Actuators ... 136
- 8.4 Head Parking ... 137
- 8.5 Recording Methods ... 138
- 8.6 Hard Disk Interfaces ... 140
- 8.7 Hard Disk Controllers ... 143
- 8.8 Drive Types ... 145
- 8.9 Cylinder Wraparound ... 147
- 8.10 Hard Disk Cards ... 148
- 8.11 Low-level Formatting ... 149
- 8.12 Interleave ... 151
- 8.13 Skew ... 152

8.14 Disk Optimisation	153
8.15 Removing a Hard Disk	156
8.16 Installing a Hard Disk	156
8.17 Preparing a Hard Disk	158
8.18 Dealing with Bad Sectors	160
8.19 File Recovery	161
8.20 Hard Disk Problems	165

9. Serial Ports *167*

9.1 Serial Port Basics	167
9.2 Synchronous and Asynchronous Communication	169
9.3 Serial Port Hardware	171
9.4 Driving Serial Ports	172
9.5 Handshaking	173
9.6 Software Handshaking	174
9.7 Hardware Handshaking	174
9.8 Diagnosing Problems	175
9.9 Break out Box	178
9.10 Serial Port Problems	1801

10. Modems and Other Serial Devices *183*

10.1 Printers	183
10.2 Plotters	184
10.3 Mice	185
10.4 Mouse Operation	186
10.5 Cleaning a Mouse	187
10.6 Mouse Problems	188
10.7 Modems	188
10.8 External Modems	190
10.9 Internal Modems	192
10.10 Communications Terminology	193
10.11 Error Correction and Data Compression	194
10.12 Making a Connection	195
10.13 Modem Problems	196
10.14 Null Modems	1990

11. Parallel Ports and Printers *201*

11.1 The Parallel Port	201
11.2 Types of Printer	203
11.3 Dot-matrix Printers	204
11.4 Ink jet Printers	205
11.5 Laser Printers	206

11.6 Daisywheel Printers..207
11.7 Thermal Transfer Printers.....................................207
11.8 Preventive Maintenance.......................................208
11.9 Parallel Printer Problems....................................210
11.10 Serial Printer Problems.....................................213
11.11 Printer Configuration Problems..............................214
11.12 The Pound Sign Problem......................................215
11.13 Other Problems..215
11.14 Diagnosing Problems...216

12. Tools and Techniques 219
12.1 The Technician's Toolkit.....................................219
12.2 Software Tools...222
12.3 Test Meters..223
12.4 Chip Removal and Replacement.................................225
12.5 Soldering..227
12.6 Replacing Soldered-in Components.............................229
12.7 Spares...229
12.8 When to Call in the Professionals............................230
12.9 Types of Maintenance Cover...................................231

13. Installation and Use................................ 233
13.1 The Operating Environment....................................233
13.2 Ambient Temperature..234
13.3 Humidity...235
13.4 Dirt and Dust..236
13.5 Shock and Vibration..237
13.6 Static Electricity...238
13.7 Mains Supply...239
13.8 Voltage Spikes...239
13.9 Noise and Distortion...241
13.10 Low or High Voltage...241
13.11 Dealing with Supply Problems................................242
13.12 Wear and Tear...243
13.13 The Importance of Backups...................................244

14. Preventive Maintenance 247
14.1 Weekly Maintenance...248
14.2 Six-monthly Maintenance......................................249
14.3 Backup Batteries...252
14.4 Reformatting Hard Disks......................................252
14.5 Printers...253

15. Configuration and Tuning 255
15.1 Booting the System 255
15.2 Optimising CONFIG.SYS. 256
15.3 Device Drivers 259
     ANSI.SYS 260
     RAMDRIVE.SYS 260
     DRIVER.SYS 261
15.4 DOS 4.0 and Expanded memory 261
15.5 Optimising AUTOEXEC.BAT 262
15.6 Keyboard Utilities 264
15.7 Using Expanded Memory 266
15.8 High and Upper Memory 267
15.9 DOS 5 Memory Management 268
15.10 Managing TSRs. 269
15.11 Disk Partitioning 270
15.12 Directory Structure. 271
15.13 Defragmentation 271
15.14 Disk Caches 272
15.15 BUFFERS and FASTOPEN 274
15.16 Mathematics Coprocessors 274
15.17 ROM Shadowing. 275
15.18 Configuration Problems 276

16. Computer Viruses. 279
16.1 What is a Virus? 280
16.2 Trojans and Logic Bombs. 280
16.3 Virus Prevention 281
16.4 Network Security. 283
16.5 Virus Symptoms 284
16.6 Virus Detection 284
16.7 Dealing with a Virus Attack 286
16.8 Virus Removal 288
16.9 Virus Removal on Networks. 289
16.10 Backups: The Ultimate Safeguard 289

17. Networking 291
17.1 Determining the Requirements 291
17.2 Types of LAN. 292
17.3 Server-based LANs 292
17.4 Peer-to-peer LANs. 293
17.5 Zero Slot LANs. 294
17.6 Multi-user DOS. 294

17.7 LAN Topologies 295
17.8 Ethernet 296
17.9 IBM Token Ring 297
17.10 Unshielded Twisted Pair 299
17.11 Fibre Optics 299
17.12 Installing LAN Cards 299

18. Developing Your Expertise 301
18.1 Building a Toolkit 301
18.2 Making a Hardware Record 302
18.3 Improving your Knowledge 302
18.4 Going Online 302

Glossary of Terms 307

Power On Self-Test Error Codes 317

PC Resources 320

Hard Disk Data 324

Directory of Suppliers 328

Common PC Viruses 332

Diagnostics and Utilities 333

PC Support Utilities Disks: Ordering Information

A useful selection of utility programs for PC support is available direct from:

Sigma Press, 1 South Oak Lane, Wilmslow, Cheshire SK9 6AR, UK.

Phone: 0625 - 531035   Fax: 0625 - 536800

The current price (at June 1992) is £10 in the UK; add £1 in Europe (outside UK) or £3 (airmail elsewhere). Specify 5.25 inch (two 360 Kb disks) or 3.5 inch (one 720 Kb).

Cheques payable to Sigma Press

Access and Visa welcome – quote card number, expiry date, cardholder name and address, and delivery adddress if different

Further details of the utility programs are on pages 333 and 334 of this book.

1

Hardware Basics

Before you can begin troubleshooting and repairing PCs, you must have a basic understanding of how a PC works. You'll need to know what each component of a PC does, and how they all fit together. If your experience of PCs up to now has been as a user, or even as a programmer, you probably don't have that knowledge. You won't have needed it. Don't worry. If you're ignorant of what goes on inside the box, this book will explain all.

All microcomputers consist of the same basic 'building blocks'. What distinguishes them from each other is the precise way in which individual components work, and how they are connected. For example, different machines may use different microprocessors. All microprocessors do basically the same job, but they do it in different ways. The instruction set – the primitive commands which the microprocessor obeys – will be different. The way in which memory is used may be different. So may be the way in which programs access disk drives, or the display. What this means is that different software is usually needed to run on different machines. You can't run a Macintosh program on a PC, for example.

The choice of components used in a computer, and the way in which they fit together, is determined by its *architecture*. The PC architecture uses microprocessors in the Intel 80x86 family. Other Intel components are used in other parts of the system. The way system memory is used is unique to the PC. (It's also somewhat eccentric, as we shall see later.) Computers built to conform to the PC architecture, even if they are made by different manufacturers, should all run the same software, and produce the same results. This is known as *PC compatibility*.

In this chapter, you'll find a description of the basic components and the architecture used in PC compatible computers. If you're already an electronics whiz and hardware hacker, you can skip on to Chapter 2.

1.1 Hardware Components

A personal computer is made up of many separate items. From the user's point of view, there is the system unit, the keyboard and the monitor. Once the cover's off, though, several more parts become visible.

In most PC compatibles the power supply is positioned at the rear right hand side of the system unit. It's a metal-encased box, with cooling slots punched out of the casing. There are usually stickers on it to warn you about the high voltages found inside. The job of the power supply is to convert the raw AC mains to the stabilised DC voltages at plus and minus 5 and 12 volts needed by the electronics of the PC.

The diskette drives are of course readily identifiable. The hard disk, if present, may sometimes be visible from the outside. More often, it is hidden away inside the machine. All that can usually be seen of it is a die-cast metal casing, attached to which is a small circuit board, with two or three cables leading from it.

Sitting at the bottom of the case is a large circuit board which holds the expansion slots into which other circuit boards fit. This is known as the system board, or motherboard. On most PCs the motherboard contains the CPU, the main memory, and other circuits described later in this chapter. Many motherboards on the latest PCs contain serial and parallel I/O ports, and even the disk controller and video display adapter circuitry. The advantage of this is that the motherboard can then have fewer expansion slots, since add-in circuit boards are not needed for these things. This allows the manufacturer to build a smaller computer.

Some PC designs have a passive backplane, which is essentially just a board containing expansion slots. The system board proper – the CPU, memory and logic – are on a separate board which plugs into one of the slots. The advantage of this approach is that the manufacturer can make one basic design. He can then offer a range of different CPUs for different levels of performance, simply by plugging in a different system board.

The black, square or rectangular components mounted on the motherboard and expansion cards are integrated circuits (ICs). Each IC is made up of thousands – often hundreds of thousands – of transistors, all etched on to a single wafer or *chip* of silicon. The small, oblong ICs with seven or eight metal 'legs' on each of the long sides, are known as *dual-inline* (DIL) or *dual-inline-package* (DIP) ICs. These are the basic building blocks of a computer. Only a few years ago, computers were constructed entirely using this type of integrated circuit.

Advances in technology have made it possible to build larger, more complex circuits on a single chip. This technique is called *large-scale integration* (LSI). The microprocessors used in the latest high-performance PC compatibles – the 80386 and 80486 – are all state-of-the-art examples of LSI technology.

It is now possible to build all the logic of the original IBM PC, which used several dozen discrete ICs, onto a couple of LSI chips. This gives many advantages. The system board can be made smaller, reducing the overall size of the computer itself. Since the board requires fewer components it is quicker and cheaper to manufacture. Power consumption and heat dissipation are lower. This, together with the reduced component count, gives better reliability.

On the latest board designs you will probably see many small components soldered directly to the board. These are known as *surface-mounted devices* (SMDs). SMDs have become popular in the last couple of years. They lend themselves extremely well to automated production lines, and therefore reduce the cost of board manufacture. The disadvantage is that they are well nigh impossible to un-solder and replace by hand. This just about rules out attempts at repairing faulty boards.

If you're unfamiliar with electronics, the purpose of all the parts on a circuit board is probably a complete mystery. Figure 1.1 shows some common types of electronic component, as an aid to identification.

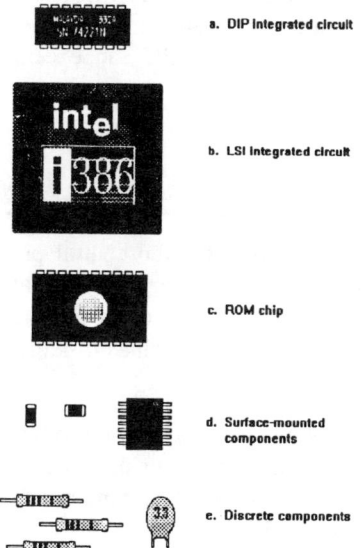

Modern electronics is so reliable that component failures are rare. Most problems are caused by mechanical parts and electrical interconnections. As far as circuit boards are concerned, we have reached the stage where they must be treated as a single unit, to be discarded as a whole if a fault occurs. Since most boards run forever without a fault, this is not necessarily as wasteful as it seems. It is also a factor that makes it feasible to service and repair PCs without needing a high level of electronics skills.

Figure 1.1: Some typical electronic components

1.2 The Processor

The central processing unit is the part that makes a computer useful. It's the bit that does most of the work. It reads the bytes of program instructions held in memory and obeys them, faithfully and very, very fast. The term *central processing unit* originated in the days of mainframes, when it described a very large box containing a lot of complex circuitry. In a microcomputer like the PC, the CPU is a single integrated circuit chip containing a lot of complex circuitry. This chip called a *microprocessor*.

In the original IBM PC and XT, and the cheapest, slowest compatibles, the microprocessor used is an Intel 8088 or 8086. In later, faster models, more powerful microprocessors from the same Intel family are used. These are, in order of power, the 80286, 80386sx, 80386dx, 80486sx and 80486dx. Each of these chips runs all the instructions of its less powerful predecessors, but is faster, and adds new features of its own. However, when a PC is running DOS, it runs even the fastest 80486 just like a superfast 8088, ignoring all its extra capabilities.

Typically, program instructions tell the CPU to move some data from one memory location to another, or to load data into one of its registers and add, subtract, multiply or divide that data with the contents of another location. Or they may tell it to load some data into a register, and then jump to a different part of the program if the value is less than, greater than or equal to some other value. These instructions – called *machine code* – are very primitive. For example, it takes dozens of instructions just to display a single character on the screen. But because the CPU can execute these simple instructions very quickly – often millions every second – even complex tasks take very little time.

1.3 Memory

The two most important components in a microcomputer are the central processing unit (CPU) and the memory. The CPU does the work. The memory is its 'scratch pad' or work area. Every other part of the computer is there simply to get information to and from these two main components, the non-volatile storage such as disk drives, and the outside world.

Memory is arranged as a linear array of 8-bit bytes, which may be used to hold either machine code instructions for the microprocessor – programs – or data. Each byte of memory has a unique address by which it may be accessed at random, and it is consequently known as *random access memory*, or RAM.

Each byte of RAM can hold a positive integer value in the range 0 to 255, a signed value in the range -128 to +127, or a single character in the extended ASCII character set. In the IBM PC family the character set includes the digits 0 to 9, all the letters of the alphabet (in both upper and lower case), punctuation, 32 control characters, and 128 special characters which include fractions, foreign alphabet symbols, and line graphics for box drawing.

Two bytes together – known as a *word* – can be used to hold a positive integer in the range 0 to 65535, or a signed integer in the range –32768 to +32767. Larger groups of bytes may be used to represent larger numbers, including fractional or *floating-point* numbers.

Machine code instructions for an Intel microprocessor may be one or more bytes in length. The instruction type is usually one or two bytes. This may be followed by up to four bytes which are the data, or *operand*, for the instruction. This might be a constant value for use in a calculation or comparison, or the address of a location in memory from which data is to be read or written.

In the IBM PC architecture, there is no differentiation between memory used for storing program instructions and that used to hold data. Data and program can be freely mixed in the same area of memory. It is up to the programmer to ensure that a program does not overwrite parts of itself with data, and that the CPU will never find itself trying to interpret bytes of data as program instructions. Figure 1.2 presents a very simple program, in which the bytes of memory are shown as hexadecimal, ASCII and machine instructions. Program instructions look like rubbish when viewed as text, and vice-versa.

```
Address  Hex bytes      ASCII            Program instructions

0100     BA 09 01       ||..     Main:   MOV   DX, 0109h    ;Set address of msg
0103     B4 09          ↑.               MOV   AH, 09h      ;Set function number
0105     CD 21          =!               INT   21h          ;Print message
0107     CD 20          =                INT   20h          ;Terminate program

0109     48 65 6C 6C    Hell             DEC   AX           ;Text of message
                                         ???                ;is nonsense if
                                         INSB               ;interpreted as
                                         INSB               ;instructions
010D     6F 2C 20 77    o, w             OUTSW
                                         SUB   AL, 20h
0111     6F 72 6C 64    orld             ... etc ...
0115     21 24          !$
```

Figure 1.2: Bytes in memory can represent numbers, text or program instructions

A common program error occurs when a block of data that is larger than expected overflows the area reserved for it and writes over adjoining program instructions. When the processor comes to execute these instructions, the result is usually disastrous. More sophisticated computer architectures separate the data from the instructions, so that this sort of problem can't occur.

1.4 Memory Addressing

Early microprocessors such as the Intel 8080 and Zilog Z80 used a 16-bit address bus, which allowed them to access up to 64k (65,536) bytes of memory. One of the original uses for microprocessor chips was in process control applications such as automated machine tools, washing machine controllers and the like. The control software for this type of job was typically only a few kilobytes in size. So 64k seemed like plenty of memory at the time.

The 8086 was designed to be upwardly compatible with the 8080 and Z80, so that any computer that used it could make use of existing software. Also, the 8086 introduced 16-bit instructions and access to more memory, for the benefit of more sophisticated software which would be developed later. The 8086 can access up to 1Mb of memory, which again seemed like more than anyone would ever need, and would have in itself cost as much as a complete IBM PC at the time the chip was introduced.

Sixteen bits can be stored in two bytes, and can be manipulated readily in the 8086's 16-bit registers. Therefore the 8086 handles addresses internally as 16-bit values. To achieve full 20-bit addressability using only 16-bit registers, the microprocessor uses *segmented addressing*.

The 8086 has a set of registers called *segment registers*. The values held in each of these registers point to memory locations, the address of which is an exact multiple of 16. In other words, the segment start address is found by multiplying the segment register contents by 16 or, in computer terms, shifting it left four bits. Memory locations are referenced by treating every address in a program as an offset relative to the start of a segment register. This is illustrated in Figure 1.3.

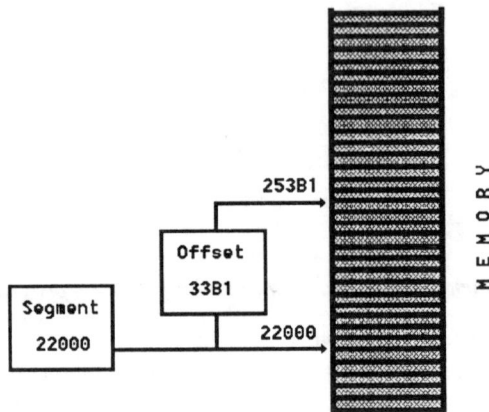

Figure 1.3: Segmented memory addressing

The 8086 has four segment registers:

❑ CS – the code segment

❑ DS – the data segment

❑ ES – the extra segment, and

❑ SS – the stack segment.

While programmers need to know the precise function of each of these registers, it isn't essential knowledge for support and repair people. However, it is useful to be able to understand the addressing notation used, since the configuration instructions for many add-in cards may refer to memory addresses using this notation.

If an expansion card uses 32k bytes of memory starting at location D000:0000, what does this mean? The number in front of the colon is the segment address. The number after the colon is the offset. Memory addresses are usually written in hexadecimal – base 16 – in which the letters A to F are used to represent the decimal values 10 – 15. To convert an address in segment:offset notation to an absolute 20-bit address, simply append a zero to the segment address, and add the offset (remembering that this is hexadecimal), so:

```
    Segment:   D0000   +
    Offset:    0000
                -----
    Address:   D0000
                -----
```

To find the upper limit, note that 32k is 8000 hex. Since we are counting from 0, the highest location is 32k – 1 or 7FFF hex, so:

```
    Segment:   D0000   +
    Offset:    7FFF
                -----
    Address:   D7FFF
                -----
```

In this example, the expansion card requires memory addresses D0000 to D7FFF for its own use, so no other card which uses memory in that range should be present in the system.

The segment:offset notation is useful for programmers, since programs handle segments and offsets as separate quantities. However, for support purposes, it is a good idea always to work in absolute addresses. One reason is that many segment:offset combinations equate to the same absolute location. For example, D000:3FFF, D300:0FFF and D180:27FF all represent the same byte of memory. Using absolute addresses eliminates this ambiguity.

1.5 Types of Memory

The random access memory most commonly used in IBM PCs and compatibles, and in almost all modern computers, is *dynamic RAM* (DRAM). This is because DRAM is the cheapest type of memory, consumes the least power, and has the greatest capacity per chip.

If you were asked to design a memory chip, you'd probably make it so that, once the binary pattern of 0s and 1s that represented your data was stored, it would be retained for as long as power was applied to the chip. Memory which is made like this is called *static RAM* (SRAM). It is very fast, but requires several transistors for each bit, so the chips are relatively large for their capacity, consume more power, and are expensive.

Dynamic RAM uses a simpler design in which each bit needs just a single transistor. Each bit must be periodically *refreshed* to make it retain the correct value. This, and other factors, mean that DRAM is not as fast as SRAM. However, dynamic RAM lends itself to the incorporation of massive numbers of memory cells on a single chip. One Megabit chips are commonplace, 4 Megabit chips are available and 16 Megabit chips are currently being developed.

Another type of memory you'll encounter is *read-only memory* or ROM. This type of chip has program instructions built into it during manufacture, so that they are not lost when power is removed. It is never possible to overwrite these instructions, they may only be read. ROM chips are used to hold program instructions that are a permanent part of the computer's design, such as the BIOS code. We will look at the BIOS later.

1.6 Memory Speed and Wait States

Dynamic RAM is used for main memory in PCs because of its high capacity and low cost. However, it has one disadvantage: It's slow. A period has to be allowed after each access for the memory cells to recharge, before they can be accessed again. This restricts the speed at which the processor can transfer information to and from memory.

Memory chips are rated by their manufacturers in terms of their *access time*. For a read access, this is the length of time it takes for the data to appear on the data bus, after the address has been specified on the address bus. The access time is measured in nanoseconds (ns). For a particular memory chip, it can be determined from the number that appears as a suffix to the part number printed on the chip. This gives the access time in units of 10 nanoseconds. For example: an NEC D421000C-10 is a one megabit

DRAM with an access time of 100ns. The minimum time that may be allowed between two successive memory accesses is equal to the access time plus the recharge time. For practical purposes you can assume that this is almost double the access time.

With the arrival of faster processors, memory speed is becoming a bottleneck. A memory access may typically take two processor cycles, so for a 16MHz processor, which has a 62.5ns cycle time, this would be 2 x 62.5ns = 125ns. With 100ns memory chips, a memory cycle would be around 190ns. To slow the processor down to the speed of the memory, a *wait state* must be inserted – an extra processor cycle during which the CPU does nothing but wait for the data it has requested. Wait states waste time – and hence power – so they should be avoided. That's why faster machines need faster memory, and even use techniques like cacheing memory in SRAM, to keep the processor waiting as little as possible.

1.7 Memory Access

The most common type of memory access is to transfer data to and from the CPU. The microprocessor obtains a byte of data from memory as follows. First, the address of the memory location required is placed on the address bus. A signal is then sent on the MEMR line of the control bus. This tells the hardware to copy the contents of that memory location on to the data bus so that it can be read into one of the microprocessor registers.

A byte is written to memory in a similar way. The address is placed on the address bus, and the byte of data is placed on the data bus. A MEMW signal is sent, and the hardware then stores the data value in the memory location specified, overwriting the previous contents. Each read or write is known as a *memory cycle*.

1.8 Input/Output Ports

I/O ports are a little like memory addresses. However, they can be read from or written to not only by the CPU, but also by devices which interface with the outside world. They are used to communicate with things like the keyboard, or the serial port. I/O ports aren't just used to get data into and out of the system, though. They are also used to set up and control parts of the hardware, and get information about its status.

For example, a serial port has one I/O address which is used to read and write data, and another that is used to set up the speed, word length, parity and other characteristics. Others are used to obtain information about things like whether there is a device at the other end of the cable, or whether a character has been received. Normally, this is all taken care of by the low level software – such as that contained in the system BIOS – which handles the serial port. All the user has to do is to read from or write to the device.

I/O ports are read from and written to in much the same way as memory. For output, the address is placed on the address bus, and then the byte of data to be written is placed on the data bus. The microprocessor then sets the IOW status line to show that it is writing to an I/O port rather than a memory location. A similar process is followed for input.

A common support problem occurs when two expansion cards in a PC are configured to use the same I/O port addresses. Usually, the result is that neither expansion card works. The standard devices like serial ports and disk controllers have standard I/O addresses reserved for them by IBM. However, things like tape streamers and SCSI adapters weren't envisaged when the IBM PC was designed. If you have one of these devices in your system, you must set it up to use addresses which aren't reserved, or are reserved for another device that isn't present. A table of I/O addresses and their normal usage is given in Appendix 3(c).

1.9 The System Bus

The main components of the microcomputer – CPU, memory, control logic and input-output (I/O) devices – are linked together by means of the system *bus*. Like its road-going namesake, the bus is simply a means of conveying something – in this case digital information – from one place to another.

Figure 1.4 shows a simplified block diagram of a PC. The system bus can be viewed as three distinct parts: the *address bus*, the *data bus*, and the *control bus*, which convey address, data and control signals between the CPU, memory and other devices.

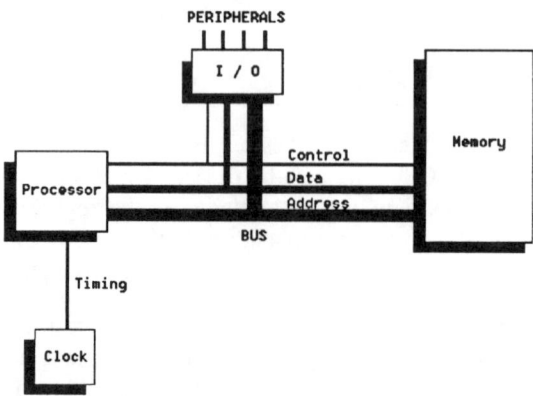

Figure 1.4: The PC system architecture

Memory is basically an array of 8-bit wide locations, each of which can be uniquely addressed. The 8086 and 8088 microprocessors used in the basic PC can address up to 1 Megabyte (Mb) – just over a million bytes – of memory. Twenty bits are needed to represent a million unique addresses, so these computers have an address bus 20 bits wide. This means that there are 20 address lines, A0 to A19. The data bus of a PC is one byte – eight bits – wide, and therefore has eight data lines, D0 to D7.

The control bus is a collection of signals, each of which is a message from one part of the hardware to another. One example, as we've already seen, is the way the microprocessor tells the memory whether it wants to read from or write to the location specified on the address bus. Two signal lines are used. One, called MEMR, is used when the processor wants to read from memory. When it wishes to write to memory, it uses the signal MEMW. Other signals on the control bus include *interrupt requests* (IRQs) – signals to the microprocessor from external devices – and the *system clock*.

If the CPU and all the other devices were allowed access to the bus whenever they wanted, the result would be anarchy. Nothing would work. In practice, the address and data buses only hold meaningful information at certain times, so control signals are needed to show when the addresses and data are valid. Other devices, such as interface cards, also need to access the bus, and must only be allowed to do so at times when they would not disrupt other activities.

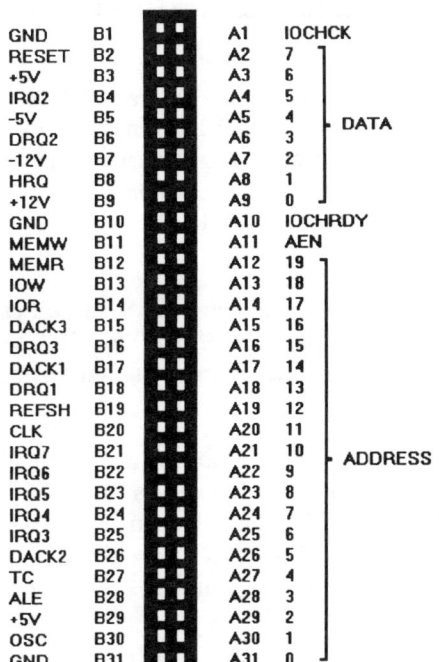

Figure 1.5: PC expansion slot connections

Management of the bus is handled by a device called the *bus controller*. This controls access to the bus, following status signals put out by the microprocessor. It takes care of the fact that the address lines may show the address of an I/O port rather than a memory location, or that the eight data lines on an 8088 microprocessor use the same physical pins as the first eight address lines (though at different times). However, these complications need not concern us.

All the address, data and control signals, as well as power for the expansion cards, are accessible using the expansion sockets. A diagram of the PC expansion socket connector is shown in Figure 1.5.

1.10 Interrupt Requests

Interrupt requests (IRQs) are signals generated by devices on the bus to request that some action is taken. An example would be the serial port that has received a character from an attached modem. The serial port has no buffering, so it can only hold one character at a time. The processor must read the character, and place it in a buffer in memory, otherwise it will be overwritten by the next one to be received. As in this example, interrupts often need to be dealt with quickly, or data is lost.

In the PC architecture, interrupts are handled by a chip called the *programmable interrupt controller* (PIC). This receives interrupt request signals from devices, and issues interrupts to the CPU, dependent upon the priority that has been assigned to each device.

When the CPU receives an interrupt, it responds by saving information about what it is currently doing, and jumping to a special interrupt service routine (ISR). Each device has its own ISR. This may be provided by the BIOS, as is true of the keyboard, or by an application such as a tape backup program, which would provide its own routine to service the tape streamer. After the ISR has been completed, the CPU uses the saved information to resume what it was doing before the interrupt occurred.

An interrupt request from one device can be received while an ISR for another is being processed. If this occurs, the PIC holds on to it until the CPU informs it that the earlier interrupt has been dealt with. The interrupt controller is programmed at start-up with priorities for the different interrupt requests, which affect the order in which it deals with them. If a program incorrectly modifies these priorities, then it is likely that the system will malfunction.

Some confusion can arise over the use of the term *interrupt*. The Intel 80x86 series CPUs can deal with up to 256 different interrupt types, numbered from 0 to 255. The start addresses for each ISR – called *interrupt vectors*, and each occupying four bytes – are stored in the first 1024 bytes of system memory.

Interrupts may be generated within software, by issuing an *int N* instruction, where *N* is the interrupt number. For example, *int 33* (or 21 in hexadecimal) is the way in which PC programs call an MS-DOS operating system function. Alternatively, as has been described, an interrupt can be generated by the hardware. Here, the device requests an interrupt and the PIC supplies the CPU with the value of *N* so that it knows the correct ISR to jump to.

Hardware on the system bus which requires interrupt processing must generate an interrupt request signal. A PC XT has eight IRQ lines numbered IRQ0 to IRQ7, of which two are used by the system. Programmers are sometimes confused by the fact that the number of the interrupt service routine for each device is not the same as the

IRQ number. The value 8 is added to the IRQ number, so that for example, the keyboard controller, which generates IRQ1, is serviced by interrupt 09h. AT compatibles have a further eight IRQ lines, IRQ8 to IRQ15, and these are serviced by interrupts 70h to 77h.

A list of the interrupts and IRQs used in the IBM PC, XT and AT computers is included in Appendix 3.

1.11 The Clock

The circuitry of a microprocessor is very complex. It contains hundreds of thousands of individual transistors, each of which has a specific function to perform. The clock is needed, essentially, to beat time and ensure that the microprocessor, the memory and other parts of the computer's logic work together harmoniously, each doing its job at the appropriate moment.

The performance of the computer is related to the speed of the clock. Clock speeds are measured in millions of cycles (or *ticks*) per second. The unit of cycles per second is the *Hertz* (Hz); a million cycles per second is one Megahertz (MHz). The IBM PC used a clock of 4.77MHz, while the PC AT had a 6MHz clock. Later PCs and compatibles use speeds of 8, 10, 12, 16, 20, 25, 33, 40 and 50MHz. CPU chips are rated for use at up to a certain speed. This limit can be determined by looking at the suffix to the part number. For example, an 8088 that can work at up to 8MHz would bear the marking *8088-8*. Some cheap PC clones run the CPU at a greater speed than the manufacturer intended. This can be the cause of obscure system crashes, and is a practice which is not recommended.

Another way of expressing processor speed is in terms of its *cycle time*. This is calculated by dividing 1 by the clock speed, so a 16MHz CPU would have a cycle time of 62.5 nanoseconds (billionths of a second). A NOP (no operation, i.e., do nothing) instruction would take a single clock cycle to perform. However, most machine code program instructions that do something useful, take at least two clock cycles to execute. The average number of instructions per second that the microprocessor can execute is therefore only a fraction of the clock rate.

The later microprocessor chips in the 8086 family, such as the 80286, 80386 and 80486, take fewer clock cycles to carry out the same instructions as their older brethren. So clock speed alone is not an indicator of the overall performance of a computer.

One performance measurement often seen in advertisements is the *Landmark speed*. This is expressed in Megahertz. It is always faster than the actual clock rate of the computer. Consequently, it is very popular with less scrupulous PC vendors, since it allows them to quote a higher speed for their machines than is actually the case. The

Landmark speed is an approximation of the clock rate at which the 8088 processor in an IBM PC would have to run to match the performance of the computer being tested. It is a very poor measure of actual performance, though, and should be treated with suspicion.

1.12 The Timer

The PC has a *programmable timer*. This is quite distinct from the system clock. The clock provides the synchronisation pulses for the whole system. The timer chip derives from these a timing frequency of 1.19MHz, and then uses this frequency to generate timing pulses, at a rate selected by software.

The timer has three programmable outputs. Timer 0 is tied to IRQ0, and is programmed to cause an interrupt at 1.19MHz divided by 65536 or about 18.2 times a second. IRQ0 is passed on to the processor as interrupt 8 where it can be harnessed by the system for such purposes as updating the date and time used by DOS.

Timer 1 is used to generate memory refresh cycles for the dynamic RAM chips. It is programmed by the BIOS at start-up with a value appropriate for the type of memory chip used in the system. Timer 2 provides the loudspeaker tone. Applications programs can load different values into it so as to generate different audio frequencies.

1.13 Direct Memory Access

If the only way that data could get to and from memory was through the CPU, the processor would spend more time servicing external devices like the disk drives or the display than running the user's programs. The PC is designed to be expandable, and has the potential to interface with peripherals that can transfer data at very high rates. In order that performance is not impaired during data transfers, the PC has a direct memory access (DMA) controller. This provides four direct data channels – seven on AT class systems – between a device such as a hard disk controller, tape streamer or network card, and the memory. DMA may also be used to transfer blocks of data from one part of memory to another.

The DMA controller can be programmed by a device wishing to transfer data into or out of memory. In simple terms, the device supplies a start address and a word count. The DMA controller will then automatically transfer the required number of bytes into the specified memory locations without any intervention by the CPU.

A list of the DMA channels available on XT and AT class machines is given in Appendix 3(d).

1.14 AT Compatibles and the 80286 Processor

So far in this chapter, we've looked at the basic PC architecture as defined by IBM's original PC. When IBM introduced a much improved model, the Personal Computer AT, it contained several improvements over the PC and XT, while remaining compatible with the earlier machines. Most PCs sold today are AT compatibles, so it is important to understand what the differences are.

When it was introduced, the most important feature of the AT was that it used the Intel 80286 processor. The 80286 can run in one of two modes:

❑ Real Address Mode

❑ Protected Virtual Address Mode.

These modes are more commonly known simply as *real mode* and *protected mode*. In real mode, the 80286 is upwardly compatible with the 8088 used in earlier models of PCs. All PC software will run in this mode without modification. Intel introduced a few new machine code instructions with the 80286. These are not used by PC software developers, since their inclusion would make programs impossible to run on 8088 and 8086-based PCs.

In protected mode, the 80286 has much greater capabilities. It has a more sophisticated memory addressing mechanism. This gives it a 24-bit addressing range, allowing access to up to 16 megabytes of RAM (although a hardware limitation of the earliest IBM ATs restricts this in practice to 4Mb). The new method of memory addressing provides access control to memory segments. This enables code and data to be kept apart. It also allows code to be protected from corruption by other programs. This is necessary in a multi-tasking operating system, so that an error in one program cannot affect other tasks or crash the entire system.

In an AT compatible running under DOS, the 80286 operates in real mode simply as a faster 8086. Real mode software will not run properly in protected mode, nor will the ROM BIOS routines work. Consequently it is not possible to exploit the possibilities that protected mode offers and still maintain full PC compatibility.

The 80286's extended addressing capability makes it possible for memory above 1Mb to be fitted. This memory is called *extended memory*. However, it is not possible to run DOS programs in this memory, as it can only be accessed using the 24-bit addressing available in protected mode.

The 80286 has a 16-bit data bus, unlike the 8088 used in the PC and XT. This means that 16-bit – two byte – values can be read from or written to memory in a single memory cycle, which is obviously faster. The AT also provides an extra seven hardware interrupt request lines, and three more DMA channels which allow full 16-bit memory access. Consequently, both the performance and expansion potential of the AT is improved. The AT expansion slots include an extra edge connector socket so that cards can access the extra data, address and IRQ lines and DMA channels.

1.15 The 80386 and 80486 Processors

The Intel 80386 first appeared in PC compatible computers in 1986. The 80386 is a 32-bit processor – i.e. it has a 32-bit data bus, 32-bit registers and an instruction set that allows 32-bit (4 byte) values to be manipulated in a single instruction. This gives significant performance benefits when working with large numbers.

Like the 80286 before it, the 80386 retains downward compatibility with the 8086 and 8088 processors. It has a real mode, in which it operates simply as a fast 8086, offering improvements both in the clock speed and in the number of clock cycles needed for each instruction over the earlier processors. It also has a protected mode, which offers similar facilities to the protected mode of the 80286, but has some significant improvements which enable it to multi-task more efficiently. Finally, the 80386 has a *virtual 8086* mode, which enables real mode applications to be run within a protected mode environment. This feature is used by Microsoft Windows 3 to enable multi-tasking of standard DOS programs.

Later microprocessors produced by Intel are derivatives of the 80386. The 80386sx is functionally identical to the original 80386 – now known as the 80386dx – but has only a 16-bit data bus, so that 32-bit data items must be read from or written to memory in two chunks. This brings performance down closer to 80286 levels, but significantly reduces the complexity and hence cost of the associated hardware. The 80386sx offers all the memory management and multi-tasking benefits of its older brother, for only a little more cost than an equivalent 80286-based system.

The 80486 processor is more of an improved 80386 than a new processor in its own right. The chip is functionally equivalent to an 80386 and its mathematics co-processor – the 80387 – on a single chip. Performance gains arise out of a reduction in the number of clock cycles needed to perform many instructions, closer integration between the CPU and the maths processor, an on-chip memory cache, and a new fast access method to external memory called *burst mode*. The 80486sx processor is simply an 80486 without the co-processor.

1.16 Memory map

In real mode, the PC processor can address up to 1Mb of memory. However, not all of that space is available for RAM chips to be installed. The memory map is allocated in a way peculiar to the PC architecture. Nobody would design a computer like this today. The reason PCs still use the same way of allocating memory, despite the problems it causes, is to maintain compatibility with software written to run on the IBM PC of a decade ago.

Early IBM PCs had just 64Kb of RAM. This was installed at the base of the address space, in locations 00000 to 0FFFF (hex). The machines also had a ROM containing the basic input/output system (BIOS). This is a set of routines for dealing with input/output devices such as the keyboard, the display and the serial and parallel ports. Programs can access these devices by calling the BIOS routines, and so do not need to be aware of differences between machines that could affect the way input/output is carried out. The BIOS ROM lives at the top of the 1Mb address space, typically in the region FC000 to FFFFF hex.

When the IBM PC was designed, protected mode had not even been thought of. A megabyte of memory seemed like more than anyone would ever need. So IBM reserved the whole of the address space from A0000 to FFFFF (hex) for system use. That means that no matter how much memory is installed, DOS on a PC will only be able to use the area from 00000 to 9FFFF – the first 640Kb.

Sections of the address space above 640Kb are reserved for specific purposes. Locations A0000 to BFFFF are reserved for video adapter memory. C0000 to CFFFF are used for additional BIOS ROMs such as those needed by EGA or VGA display adapters or hard disk controllers. D0000 to EFFFF are reserved for special I/O cards and plug-in ROM cartridges. A diagram of the PC memory map is given in Figure 1.6. The 640Kb memory barrier has proved to be a major restriction for software in recent years. It is worth noting that it exists because of IBM's design, not a limitation of DOS.

In the years since the PC was designed, manufacturers have come up with all kinds of add-ins. The reserved address space has been used for things that IBM never even envisaged. As users' requirements become more sophisticated, memory management

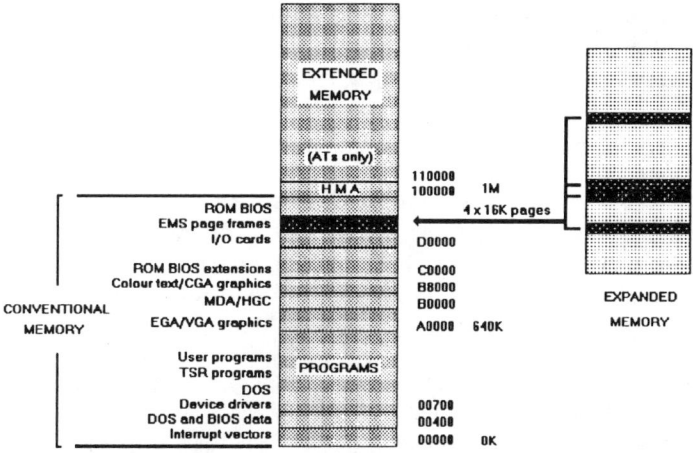

Figure 1.6: The PC memory map

has become increasingly complex. Whole books have been written on this subject alone. Address conflicts – programs competing for the same area of memory – can be a major source of support problems, so this is an area that is well worth taking the trouble to understand.

1.17 Expanded Memory

When the IBM PC was introduced, 640Kb of memory seemed more than ample for anyone's needs. However, as people began to use PCs for more complex tasks, like manipulating huge spreadsheets with Lotus 1-2-3, they started to need even more memory. To solve this problem, Lotus got together with Intel and Microsoft and produced a specification for providing *expanded memory* in a PC. The hardware that implemented this specification was the Intel AboveBoard.

Because the 8086 and 8088 could physically address a maximum of only 1Mb of memory, and since the area above 640Kb was reserved by IBM for use by other things, what Lotus and Intel did was design a board that provided the additional memory outside the PC memory map. The memory is accessed using a 64K buffer area called a *page frame*, which is located within the reserved area at an address configurable by the user. The page frame is like a window on the expanded memory, through which it can be accessed by the DOS program, as shown in Figure 1.6. A software device driver called an *Expanded Memory Manager* (EMM) provides a mechanism for programs to swap 16Kb *pages* of data in and out of the page frame. Since the page frame is located within the 1Mb address space of the 8086/8, data held there can be manipulated just like any other data in memory. However, only four 16Kb pages can be kept there and accessed directly at any one time.

Expanded memory was originally designed simply to provide space for the storage of data such as large spreadsheets. However, software such as Quarterdeck's Desqview was developed which allowed it to be used to swap whole programs in and out of memory, a form of multi-tasking. Later versions of the Lotus, Intel and Microsoft expanded memory specification added improvements to give greater flexibility and performance, but the principles of operation remain the same.

When expanded memory is installed in a PC, it is the user's responsibility to find an unused 64Kb of address space in the reserved memory area. This can sometimes be difficult. If the area selected isn't actually unused, problems will occur. If it happens to be used by a display adapter, ROM, network card or whatever, then corrupted data or system crashes are likely to result.

Expanded memory is the only type of extra memory that can be fitted to 8088 or 8086-powered machines. It is not really random access memory at all. The expanded memory board is more like a peripheral, and data is read from and written to it in blocks.

1.18 Extended Memory

As we have seen, ATs and compatibles can have *extended* memory, addressable memory that extends beyond the 1Mb boundary. However, it is all but inaccessible to programs running under DOS. When running DOS, the CPU runs in real mode, in which it emulates an 8086 and is subject to the same address space restrictions as that processor. The ability to address extended memory can only be gained while running in protected mode.

One way to use extended memory is to use it to emulate expanded memory. Some 80286-based systems are unable to do this. The 80286 needs an enhanced logic chip set which gives the hardware some extra help. It must also run a machine-specific memory manager provided by the manufacturer. 80386s and above can achieve the same result using the memory management features inherent in the CPU architecture, so generic 80386 memory managers are possible. The most common – EMM386.SYS – is included with many versions of DOS.

When an expanded memory emulator is used, what happens is as follows. When a DOS real mode program requests a page of data from expanded memory, the memory manager disables interrupts, switches the processor into protected mode, copies the data from extended memory into the appropriate page frame, switches back to real mode, re-enables interrupts and then returns to the calling program. This can then access the data in the page frame in exactly the same way as if it was running on an XT with an expanded memory card.

Interrupts must be disabled while the processor is in protected mode because the interrupt routines in the BIOS, DOS or other user-installed programs, are designed only to be run in real mode. They would not save the processor status correctly if an interrupt caused them to be executed while it was in protected mode. Because interrupts are turned off while a program – such as a disk cache – accesses extended memory, they may be lost altogether. This can often be a cause of problems with serial communications at speeds of more than 9600bps, and other devices which generate a lot of interrupts.

1.19 DOS Extenders

More recently, new techniques have been developed that allow DOS programs to run in protected mode and thereby have access to all the memory installed in an AT compatible. These techniques are known as *DOS Extenders*. They overcome the problem that DOS and BIOS functions will not run in protected mode, by switching into real mode whenever a function needs to be executed.

When an interrupt call is made, the DOS extender copies the relevant data from extended memory to conventional memory – below 1Mb – where it is accessible in real mode. It then switches the CPU into real mode and reissues the function call. On return from the function call, the CPU is switched back into protected mode, the data is copied back into extended memory, and control is returned to the application. DOS extenders also provide a range of functions for the protected mode application to use to manage extended memory.

DOS extenders are usually sold as code libraries which application builders can incorporate into their software packages. So the DOS extender comes as part of a software package. It isn't provided by the operating system. Problems arise if users try to run two or more programs using incompatible DOS extenders under a multi-tasking system such as Desqview. As a result, two of the major players in the market, Phar Lap Software and Quarterdeck Office Systems, got together to produce a standard for DOS extenders – the *Virtual Control Program Interface* (VCPI).

When Microsoft introduced Windows 3, they created a new and incompatible standard – the *DOS Protected Mode Interface* (DPMI). Because of the overwhelming success of Windows 3, DPMI seems set to be the DOS extender standard for the 1990s.

1.20 The High Memory Area

The 8088 and 8086 processors with their 20 address lines can access memory in the range 00000 to FFFFF. The topmost location in this range can be represented in the segment:offset notation as FFFF:000F. What happens if the offset value in this example is increased by 1? If we do the arithmetic:

```
    Segment:   FFFF +
    Offset:    0010
               -----
    Address:   100000
               -----
```

The resulting address, 100000 hex, would require a 21st address line in order to be generated by the hardware. On an 8088 or 8086, this 21st line doesn't exist. The address is truncated to 20 bits, and maps on to location 00000, at the very bottom of system memory.

AT class machines use the 80286 or later processors which have 24 address lines, and so it is possible for a 21-bit address to be generated. To maintain compatibility with the PC and XT, a device called the *A20 gate* is used. This disables A20 – the 21st address line – and ensures that attempts to access memory above 1Mb are mapped into the bottom of the address range as they would be by an 8088 or 8086. However, it is possible for the A20 gate to be turned off. If this is done, processors in AT class machines can access 65520 locations of memory which are above the 1 megabyte limit of the 8088/8086, while remaining in real mode. This facility is exploited by memory management software such as 386 to the Max, HIMEM.SYS and both Microsoft and Digital Research's DOS 5 operating systems, which include utilities that can load device drivers and utilities into the high memory area. Use of these utilities will release space within the 640K base memory available to DOS, for use by applications programs.

1.21 The MCA Bus

In April 1987, IBM officially discontinued the PC, XT and AT and introduced a new range of personal computers, the Personal System 2 (PS/2). These machines are quite different from the PC or its clones, both in appearance and design. Undoubtedly the most significant difference is that the more powerful models used a new high-performance bus that was incompatible with the old PC bus. IBM gave the new bus the name *Micro Channel Architecture* (MCA).

MCA was intended to overcome many of the limitations of the ISA bus. It was designed for greater performance; the ISA bus as implemented by IBM in the AT ran at 8MHz. This was becoming a limitation as processor speeds increased. MCA was also designed to give greater reliability. Expansion boards and the bus interact in a different way, so that instances of certain boards not working in particular machines or even particular slots in one machine should be a thing of the past. Finally, all MCA boards use a switchless set-up procedure called Programmable Option Selection (POS). This eliminates DIP switches. Boards are configured using a special set-up program supplied by the manufacturer. This enables boards to be reconfigured without taking the lid off the box, though it raises the question of what to do if the disk containing the set-up program is lost!

1.22 The EISA Bus

The Extended Industry Standard Architecture (EISA) bus is an attempt to solve the same problems that MCA intended to do, but it goes about it in a slightly different way. MCA has several disadvantages: it is completely incompatible with the ISA bus; its technically advanced features make board design much more complex than for ISA; and, it uses proprietary IBM technology, for which royalties must be paid to IBM.

A group of nine computer manufacturers led by Compaq got together to develop the EISA bus. This offers similar benefits to MCA: higher performance, switchless set-up and so on. However, by clever design, the bus slots can also accept standard ISA expansion cards. Consequently, purchasers of EISA machines can continue to use their older cards if required.

EISA machines only began to appear during 1990, and the number of EISA expansion cards is still very limited. However, benchmarking by respected testing authorities has shown that there is little to choose between EISA and MCA in terms of practical performance, and that the benefits of either of them are unlikely to be realised in normal stand-alone PC applications. ISA will continue to be useful for some time yet.

Since EISA offers backward compatibility with ISA cards, EISA machines are true PC compatibles. At present, EISA is only used in top-end 80386 and 80486-based systems, where the benefits are most likely to be needed, while MCA is available on 80286-based systems. However, the ISA compatibility makes EISA a good choice for new PC purchases, with the option to use existing expansion cards, and upgrade to EISA cards as they become available and performance needs demand them.

Summary

In this chapter we examined the main components of a PC compatible microcomputer system, how they fit together and how they work. Among the most important parts of the system are the CPU, the memory and the I/O ports. Data is conveyed between one part of the system and another using the bus. Interrupts are used so that I/O devices can inform the CPU that they need some urgent attention. Direct memory access is provided so that devices can transfer data to and from memory without needing the CPU's intervention.

We looked at the way the first 1Mb of memory is used in a PC compatible system. The upper limit of memory which DOS on a PC is able to access is 640Kb, because IBM reserved the top 384Kb for use by other things. Expanded memory provides a way for PC applications to use more than 640Kb of RAM, but this memory can only be used to store data, not run programs. 80286 and later processors can address extended memory beyond 1Mb, but only when running in protected mode. They cannot access this memory when running DOS, unless they use it to emulate expanded memory, or are using a DOS extender.

Finally, we looked briefly at the two new designs of bus – EISA and MCA – which are available on some modern computers. Between them, they have only a small fraction of the market, and only a few expansion cards are made which can use them. We will not consider either of these buses in detail later on in the book. It remains to be seen whether they will become more popular in the future. Benchmark testing has shown that their benefits are minimal for the vast majority of PC applications. Given the limited choice of expansion cards, and the higher cost of both cards and computers, it is hardly surprising that most buyers have opted to stick with the existing standard – ISA – for the time being.

Hardware design is a very complex area. This chapter has given just an overview of the subject. You'll find this knowledge helpful when diagnosing faults and understanding why they occur.

2

Problem Solving

In the previous chapter, we looked at the basic principles underlying the design of an IBM compatible PC – its architecture. It certainly helps to understand how things are supposed to work when you're trying to figure out why they won't. But it's by no means all you need to know. Fault finding is a skill you can learn. It's the application of both knowledge and logic; performing tests, and drawing conclusions from them; using tools – such as diagnostic programs – to help pinpoint the cause of a problem.

In this chapter we look at problem solving. First, you'll learn how to tell whether a problem is caused by hardware or software. Next we'll discuss fault diagnosis – the techniques used to trace a fault. Finally, we'll look at diagnostics – both those that are built into the PC, and other programs specifically written to help locate a fault.

2.1 Is it Hardware or Software?

To non-technical computer users, the distinction between hardware and software isn't clear. To them, the computer together with the software application they are using is just a tool to enable them to carry out a particular task. If something fails to work as they think it should, then the computer has *broken down*. The possibility that they may at some point have hit the wrong key, or that a change may have been made to the software configuration, or the disk is full, is unlikely to occur to them. As a troubleshooter, you should always bear in mind that most users have a limited understanding of the hardware and software. You should never make the assumption that obvious, elementary points have already been checked.

A couple of real-life examples may help emphasise the point. One morning I received a phone call from a user. He complained that his monitor had gone wrong. His PC had been left on overnight running a long database update, and in the morning when he came in, the screen was completely blank.

I went up to the user's office and soon spotted the cause of the problem. The monitor power switch was off! Now, I could have asked him to check the power switch over the telephone. But I didn't. I'd made an unwarranted assumption. I'd assumed that, since the screen had been on and working when he went home, it would still have been switched on the following morning. I'd also assumed that something as obvious as the power switch being off would have been noticed by the user. I had therefore – wrongly – suspected a more serious fault.

On another occasion, a secretary telephoned to say that her PC, which she used for word processing, was very slow. Someone went along to her office, dismantled the case, reseated all the boards and cables, checked the processor clock speed and ran Norton's Speed Disk to de-fragment the files on the hard disk. Still the machine was slow. After further examination, he found that there was no CONFIG.SYS in the root directory. This meant that the system was running with a default of BUFFERS = 2 and FILES = 8. With BUFFERS = 2, the machine couldn't keep more than two blocks of disk in memory at one time, so it was having to reread the data from the disk almost every time it accessed a file. Creating a CONFIG.SYS file with BUFFERS = 20 and FILES = 20 immediately restored the performance to normal.

There's a lesson to be learned from this. Never overlook the obvious. That may seem an obvious statement, but it's something we all do. Somebody once said that a man with a hammer will tend to view every problem as a nail. There is an irresistible tendency to look for a solution in terms of the things we understand best. Wheel in a networking expert to look at your PC fault, and he will be convinced that it's a network problem. Bring along a hardware hacker, and he'll probably think it's some obscure BIOS incompatibility with the VGA card. The actual fault will probably turn out to be something silly, like not setting a vital environment string in AUTOEXEC.BAT.

So use some logic. Look for simple explanations of a fault before you start investigating the complicated ones. If something isn't working that was working perfectly the day before, it's as likely to be a blown fuse or a faulty cable, as it is to be a component failure. If a PC is working normally, except when a particular application is run, it's probable that the fault relates only to that application. It might be a user error or a software configuration error. If a PC plays up after something in the system has been changed then, no matter how convinced you are, or the user is, that the thing that was changed has nothing at all to do with the problem being experienced, it should still be the prime suspect.

If an item of hardware isn't functioning at all, check that it is switched on. Is the power light on? If not, is the device switched on, both at its own switch and at the wall socket? Is the plug which you believe to be the one for this piece of equipment actually connected to it? Is the cable pushed right in to the sockets at both ends? If there is still no joy, test the fuse.

If a peripheral like a printer is powered up but not working then check if it will self-test. Is the data cable properly connected at each end? Are you sure that it is connected to the right port on the PC? If the sockets are not labelled, check the manual. Frequently, the explanation for a non-working printer has turned out to be that the data cable was plugged into an identical, but incorrect, port on the PC.

If the hardware connections all appear to be OK then the software configuration should be checked. Can you output to the device using a different package? For a printer, try a DOS command like DIR >PRN. If you can write to a printer from DOS, but not from a software package, it could be that the package has been set up to use a different type of printer, or a different port. Check the configuration; don't accept an assurance from the user that it hasn't been changed. Someone else may have come along and changed it. The configuration file may have been accidentally overwritten or erased. Look at its directory entry and check the date it was created. If it is recent, then it has probably been altered. If the problems started after that date, you've almost certainly found the fault.

Don't overlook the basics. Examine CONFIG.SYS. Check that all the normal parameters are present: FILES, BUFFERS, COUNTRY and so on, and that they have the appropriate parameters. Look for any unusual additions, such as device drivers, which might be affecting the operation of the system.

Examine AUTOEXEC.BAT. Check that no terminate-and-stay-resident (TSR) utilities such as Sidekick have been installed. These could conflict with other software, and cause the problem that you are trying to solve. If there is any doubt, remove the TSRs. Edit the batch file to place a colon in front of the name of each utility, making it into a label instead of a command. Then reboot the machine. If the problem vanishes, you can bring each TSR back one by one until the culprit is found.

When attempting to solve a PC problem, the important thing is to proceed methodically. Treat anything you're told about what happened or what has been done with scepticism, unless you can see it for yourself. Assume nothing about either the competence of the user or the state of the machine. Check everything. Most problems are caused by something obvious. The reason many faults take much longer to solve than they should is simply that the obvious is often overlooked!

2.2 Diagnosing a Problem

Fault diagnosis is a matter of observing the symptoms, making logical deductions from them, and performing tests to check out your deductions. If you have insufficient evidence to pinpoint the cause of a problem, perform tests to eliminate some of the possibilities or generate further information.

Take the example of a PC monitor being apparently dead. The fact that the power LED is not illuminated shows that no power is present. If the monitor power switch is on, the next step is clearly to check the mains supply. If the mains socket switch is on, the cable or fuse are the next most likely suspects. You should check that the cable is fully pushed home in its socket. If that isn't the problem, the next step would be to check the fuse, or swap the cable with one from another machine that is known to be working. Another good idea would be to plug the cable into a different wall socket, in case the first one is faulty. If, after all these tests, the monitor is still dead, the problem is probably either the monitor's power supply, the switch or an internal fuse.

Note the cycle of observe, deduce, test. Observe the monitor is dead, deduce that there might be no power, check that the switch is on. Observe that with the switch on there is still no power, deduce that the problem could be with the cable or fuse, test the cable and fuse. Having checked all these, note that the wall socket is still untested, so eliminate that as a possibility by testing the cable in another socket known to be working.

In this example the fault is obvious and the tests easy to carry out. However, it illustrates the approach. Trying a cable from another machine is an effective and quick way of ruling out the possibility of a faulty cable or fuse. Substitution of a suspect part with a known good one is an excellent fault finding technique, which will either solve a problem or eliminate one of the possible causes of it.

Not all problems will be as easy to resolve, of course; if a hard disk is refusing to work then a substitute controller card or hard disk may not be to hand. This is where experience plays its part – the knowledge of which of the possible causes of a problem are the most likely, and which are improbable. But experience will only come with practice.

If you're inexperienced at fault finding then it's a good idea to make a written record of what you've done. First, write down the symptoms of the fault. Then write down all the possible causes that occur to you. Now proceed to eliminate them one by one, starting with those that are the easiest to check. Cross out the suggestions which have been eliminated, and make a note of the reason. Write down other possibilities as they occur to you. This will help you to approach the diagnosis in a logical way. It also means that you'll have a record of what you have and have not tried. If the solution proves to be elusive then you can show the notes to someone else, who can see what you've done, and maybe suggest some other things to try. Finally, a record of the problem and its eventual solution can be useful for reference, either by yourself or someone else, should the same fault ever recur in the future.

2.3 Power-On Self Test

A PC is a complex device. Not all faults have an obvious solution. Nor is it always easy to verify a particular diagnosis by substituting the suspect part for a known good one. The tendency towards large scale integration and building more on to the motherboard – I/O ports, display adapters, disk controllers and so on – makes substitution of components even more difficult. Often additional help, in the form of diagnostic software, is needed to get to the root cause of a problem.

Every PC comes with some basic diagnostic software, the Power-On Self Test (POST) routines which are part of the system BIOS ROM. These tests are executed every time the PC is started up. Their main purpose is to find out what is in the system: how much memory, what hard and floppy disks, what display adapter and so on, so the tests performed are not very thorough. However, the routines check all the standard devices for basic functionality. Often the first indication of a fault will be after the system has been switched on, when the POST routines report an error.

When a PC is powered up, the system unit normally gives a short beep. This beep is a report from the POST procedure, and shows that all is well. If two or more beeps are heard, or none at all, then the POST is telling you that it has found a fault.

The PC uses the speaker to convey the message because, if the fault condition is serious, it's possible that the display won't be working. If no beep is heard, then – assuming that the loudspeaker is connected – it's probable that the CPU is failing to execute the POST routines. Power may not be reaching vital system board components. Two short beeps mean that the display adapter is working, and an error message will appear on the screen. A continuous beeping indicates that there is a serious power fault and that the system should be turned off as quickly as possible. This probably would be the instinctive reaction of the operator.

Combinations of long and short beeps may also be used to give other error messages. For the definitive explanations, you should refer to the operations manual for the machine in question. However, the beep codes given by some popular machines are shown in Appendix 2. Generally, more than two short beeps indicate a display-related problem; the display adapter configuration may be incorrect, or it may be conflicting with another expansion board. However, if one long and one short beep is heard on an IBM system and possibly others, it indicates a problem with the motherboard.

If the PC display is working then the POST routines are able to display an error message. The format of this message varies from machine to machine. On a true IBM PC the error message consists of a numeric code. On other systems, a message such as *POST ERROR nnnn* may be displayed. Many non-IBM systems which display a POST error code still adhere to the codes used by IBM. These are also listed in Appendix 2.

Most modern PC compatibles made by manufacturers other than IBM do not use the POST error codes. Later systems tend to have larger ROMs that can accommodate error messages written in English. Some reportedly include the error *KEYBOARD NOT PRESENT, PRESS F1 TO CONTINUE*. If one of these error messages appears, the action needed to remedy the problem should be obvious.

2.4 Diagnostic Software

If the system fails one of the POST error checks, the fault is usually something fairly major, like being unable to boot from the hard disk, or a lack of response from the keyboard. However, there are many other types of fault that can occur, and go undetected by the POST. These include faults which only appear once the system has fully warmed up, and intermittent faults such as memory parity failures. The latter may occur infrequently, and seemingly at random, but usually halt the machine. Faults such as these require something more thorough than the POST to show them up. This is the job of the diagnostics program.

Most new computer systems come with a diskette labelled *Diagnostics*. This usually contains several different utilities. For AT class systems, there is normally a program called SETUP, which is used to enter and update the system configuration details in the battery-backed CMOS RAM. There is often a utility for parking the heads of the hard disk prior to transporting the system; this may be called PARK, HDPARK, SHIP or something along those lines. Finally there is a program for carrying out diagnostic tests on the hardware and low-level formats of the hard disk. This is often called DIAGNOSE or DIAG. Sometimes all these functions will be integrated into a single program, with the various options selectable from a menu.

Many expansion cards, particularly those from third-party manufacturers, come with their own diagnostics diskette. This is especially true of display adapters. Display circuitry is one of the least standardised areas of PC compatible hardware, particularly since the advent of VGA, so there is little that non hardware-specific test programs can do other than display test patterns using the standard display modes and ask the user to observe the results.

Some PCs, such as those with a BIOS from A.M.I. or a Phoenix ROM BIOS Plus, have their diagnostics built into the system ROM. This has certain advantages. Since diagnostics are not run all that often, it is not uncommon to discover that the diagnostics disk has been lost just at the time that it is most needed. If they are in ROM, you can't lose them!

The effectiveness of the standard system diagnostics varies from machine to machine. Thorough tests take time. In the case of disk drives, they will involve writing to and reading from the disk, which will destroy any data stored there. The standard diagnostics supplied with a machine are intended to be run by relatively untutored users. Consequently, the range of tests they will perform is usually limited. ROM-based diagnostics suffer from the additional limitation that the size of the program – and hence the range of tests offered – is restricted to the available space in the ROM.

2.5 IBM Advanced Diagnostics

IBM produce Advanced Diagnostics disks for the PC, XT and AT. These can be used to carry out hardware tests on those systems. When the diagnostics are run, a menu appears as shown in Figure 2.1.

```
            The IBM Personal Computer AT
            ADVANCED DIAGNOSTICS
            Version 2.06
            (c)Copyright IBM Corp. 1981, 1986

            SELECT AN OPTION

            0 - SYSTEM CHECKOUT
            1 - FORMAT DISKETTE
            2 - COPY DISKETTE
            3 - PREPARE SYSTEM FOR MOVING
            4 - SETUP
            9 - END DIAGNOSTICS

            SELECT THE ACTION REQUIRED
            ?
```

Figure 2.1: IBM Advanced Diagnostics initial menu

If the first option – System Checkout – is selected, then the program checks to see what adapters are installed in the system, and displays a list of what it has found. This should look like Figure 2.2. You are then asked whether the list is correct. If you answer 'No', items may be added to or deleted from the list. Once you're satisfied that the list is correct, each item may be individually tested.

Items 1 and 2 on the Advanced Diagnostics menu are intended for preparing copies of the diagnostic diskette, since you should never run software from the original master copy. Option 3 parks the hard disk heads so that the machine may be safely moved. Option 4 is used to enter configuration details into the CMOS memory. The Advanced Diagnostics for the IBM XT has a similar menu but without option 4.

The IBM Advanced Diagnostics are very useful if you have a PC made by IBM. Because they were written specifically for the IBM hardware, they are often able to identify the precise component that is at fault when a problem is detected. Of course, they are unable to do this for PCs from other manufacturers. However, whether or not the IBM diagnostics will run on a clone is a very good test of PC compatibility.

```
THE INSTALLED DEVICES ARE

1  - SYSTEM BOARD
2  - 640KB MEMORY
3  - KEYBOARD
4  - MONOCHROME AND PRINTER ADAPTER
6  - 2 DISKETTE DRIVE(S) AND ADAPTER
9  - SERIAL/PARALLEL ADAPTER - PARALLEL PORT
11 - SERIAL/PARALLEL ADAPTER - SERIAL PORT
17 - 1 FIXED DISK DROVE(S) AND ADAPTER

IS THIS LIST CORRECT (Y/N)
```

Figure 2.2: IBM Advanced Diagnostics Installed Devices menu

Most non-IBM PCs come with a diagnostics program of their own. AMI diagnostics are supplied with systems having an AMI BIOS. They are either in ROM, or on a separate diskette. AMIDIAGS can perform a number of tests on all parts of the system. They can also be used to format disks. The disk-based version allows the PC manufacturer to set up a file specifying the type of memory chips used and their layout on the system board, so that the memory tests can identify a faulty chip.

The initial menu of the diskette-based AMI Diagnostics is shown in Figure 2.3. This program performs a number of tests on the system at quite a low level. System board components, including the arithmetic co-processor (if fitted), DMA controller, interrupt controller, timer and real-time clock are all tested. So are protected mode operation, CPU speed and the validity of the CMOS setup information. The Memory tests include checks for parity, addressing and refresh operation.

Selecting the Hard Disk option produces a menu containing several choices. These include formatting the disk, selecting the interleave, testing the performance, performing a media analysis, and recording bad tracks. Choosing Floppy gives a menu from which you can format a disk, carry out read/write tests, check the rotation speed of the drive, and test the operation of the drive change line.

The Keyboard test displays a picture of a keyboard. As you press each key, the scan code and ASCII character code are displayed. The Video option performs several tests in 40 x 25 and 80 x 25 text modes, and 320 x 200, 640 x 200 and 640 x 480 resolution graphics modes. The Miscellaneous option tests the parallel and serial ports. A specially wired loop-back plug is needed for the serial port tests.

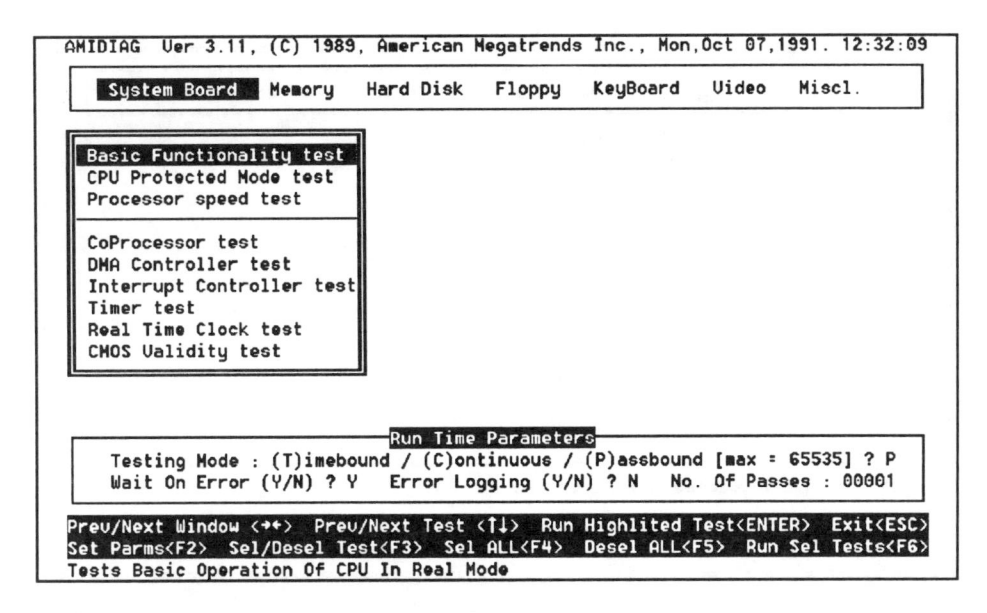

```
AMIDIAG Uer 3.11, (C) 1989, American Megatrends Inc., Mon,Oct 07,1991. 12:32:09
   System Board   Memory   Hard Disk   Floppy   KeyBoard   Uideo   Miscl.

   Basic Functionality test
   CPU Protected Mode test
   Processor speed test

   CoProcessor test
   DMA Controller test
   Interrupt Controller test
   Timer test
   Real Time Clock test
   CMOS Validity test

                           Run Time Parameters
   Testing Mode : (T)imebound / (C)ontinuous / (P)assbound [max = 65535] ? P
   Wait On Error (Y/N) ? Y   Error Logging (Y/N) ? N   No. Of Passes : 00001

   Prev/Next Window <→←>  Prev/Next Test <↑↓>  Run Highlited Test<ENTER>  Exit<ESC>
   Set Parms<F2>  Sel/Desel Test<F3>  Sel ALL<F4>  Desel ALL<F5>  Run Sel Tests<F6>
   Tests Basic Operation Of CPU In Real Mode
```

Figure 2.3: AMI Diagnostics initial menu

Well-known PC manufacturers can supply advanced diagnostic programs specific to the machine, often at extra cost. With systems from the smaller manufacturers, however, especially those which O.E.M. hardware from obscure Far Eastern manufacturers, the likelihood of diagnostic software being supplied is small. To fault-find on these machines, you'll need to rely on experience and trial-and-error, or use third-party diagnostics.

2.6 Third-Party Software

The supplied diagnostics for non-IBM PCs are variable in effectiveness, if they are available at all. If your job is to support and maintain many PCs from different manufacturers there's an additional problem, that of maintaining a set of diagnostic diskettes for each machine. Consequently, a demand has arisen for general-purpose diagnostic software that can be used on any PC compatible computer.

One of the most comprehensive general-purpose diagnostic programs is Check It, from TouchStone Software Corporation. This includes tests for the CPU, memory (base, extended and expanded), hard and floppy disk drives, display adapters, serial and parallel ports, printers, keyboards, mice and joysticks. The Check It menu, displaying the range of tests available, is shown in Figure 2.4. Check It will provide information about the software installed on a machine, including IRQ assignments, DOS device drivers and CMOS setup information. This can help you decide whether a problem is caused by the software configuration of a system.

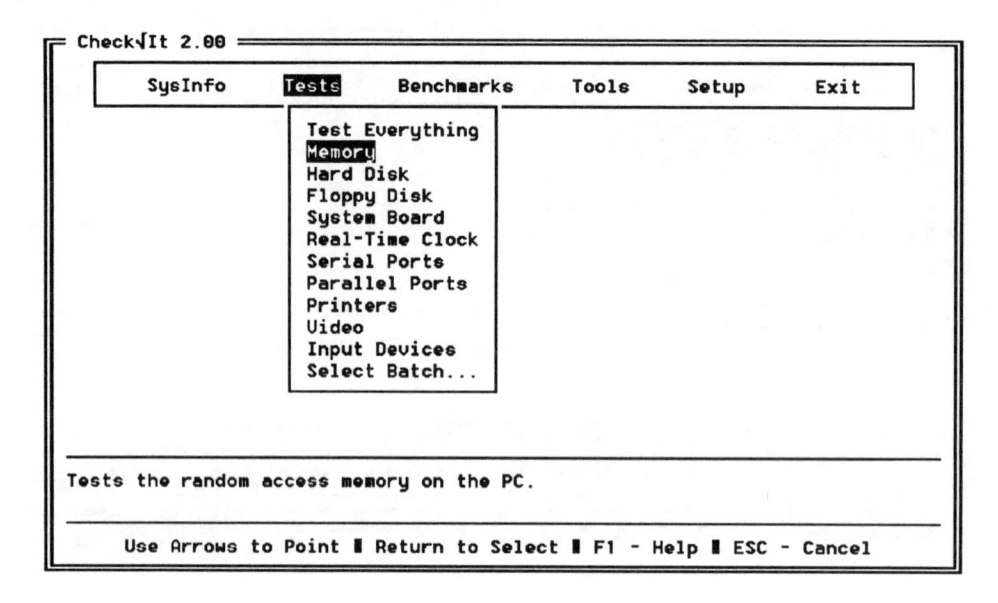

```
┌─ Check√It 2.00 ═══════════════════════════════════════════════════════
│         SysInfo    Tests    Benchmarks    Tools    Setup    Exit
│                    ┌─────────────────┐
│                    │ Test Everything │
│                    │ Memory          │
│                    │ Hard Disk       │
│                    │ Floppy Disk     │
│                    │ System Board    │
│                    │ Real-Time Clock │
│                    │ Serial Ports    │
│                    │ Parallel Ports  │
│                    │ Printers        │
│                    │ Video           │
│                    │ Input Devices   │
│                    │ Select Batch... │
│                    └─────────────────┘
│
│  ─────────────────────────────────────────────────────────────────
│  Tests the random access memory on the PC.
│  ─────────────────────────────────────────────────────────────────
│    Use Arrows to Point ▌ Return to Select ▌ F1 - Help ▌ ESC - Cancel
└───────────────────────────────────────────────────────────────────────
```

Figure 2.4: Check It diagnostic menu

Intermittent faults are among the most difficult problems to track down. Check It will allow tests to be run repeatedly, overnight if necessary, logging the results to disk or to a printer, so that this type of problem can be flushed out.

Another product which helps to diagnose PC problems is PC Probe by Landmark Research International. Like Check It, this tests system board, RAM, video board and display, serial and parallel ports, disk controllers and drives. It can also check hard disks for optimum interleave, and reformat and re-interleave them on the fly.

Landmark produce a range of diagnostic toolkits, including special diagnostic cards that fit in an expansion slot and can show you what's wrong even if the display isn't working. These toolkits aren't cheap, compared with software-only products. But if you're serious about servicing, and have to support a large number of PCs, they could soon pay for themselves in time saved.

For maintenance and alignment of diskette drives, Dysan Interrogator or Landmark's AlignIt may be used. These products work with a special diskette called a Digital Diagnostics Diskette (DDD). They can be used to test and correct many aspects of a diskette drive's alignment and performance.

Several programs are specifically intended for testing and optimising hard disks. Their primary purpose is performance improvement rather than fault diagnosis. SpinRite and Optune will perform surface analysis – thorough testing of the disk media for read/write reliability. They can also change the interleave factor of a hard disk to give optimum performance. Optune can de-fragment the files on the disk.

Disk Technician Advanced, by Prime Solutions, is designed to look after hard disks by predicting problems and taking appropriate action before they occur. It is preventive maintenance for disk drives. Disk Technician Advanced tests the entire drive. If any problems – even minor ones – are encountered, it moves any data on that area of the disk out of the way, low-level formats it and retests it, and then moves the data back. A log is kept of the results. Disk Technician Advanced will also check the interleave of a disk drive, and optimise it for best performance.

Many commercially available packages, while not marketed specifically as diagnostics, perform some of the functions of the programs mentioned above. The best-known of these are PC Tools and Norton's Utilities.

The Norton Advanced Utilities include several programs that are useful for fault diagnosis and rectification. SYSINFO gives an in-depth report on the configuration of the machine, including memory utilisation, disk characteristics, I/O devices installed, display adapter configuration, IRQ assignments, CMOS setup information, TSR programs and device drivers installed. Examples of the information provided by SYSINFO are shown in Figures 2.5, 2.6 and 2.7.

CALIBRATE, another of the Norton Utilities, is a program that will report on the hard disk characteristics and perform a surface analysis. It has daily, weekly and monthly test options – getting progressively more thorough – which like Disk Technician Advanced can be used to highlight problem areas before they become too serious. CALIBRATE can low-level format a disk, and automatically select the optimum interleave factor, without destroying any data.

Norton Disk Doctor can perform surface analysis on a disk, and remap any bad sectors discovered. It can also repair corrupted file allocation tables and boot sectors. Together with DISKEDIT, UNFORMAT, UNERASE and several other useful programs, the Norton Utilities are an indispensable tool for dealing with disk problems.

System Sleuth, by Dariana Technology Inc. is another utility that can provide a lot of data about a system's configuration. Menu options enable information about the system resources, including the disk subsystem, memory, display and I/O cards to be displayed. The results can be output to a file as a report if required.

2.7 Public Domain and Shareware Diagnostics

There are many utilities in the public domain or available as shareware which would make useful additions to a diagnostic toolkit. However, before looking at some of them, it is worth pointing out the potential pitfalls. Diagnostic software has to interact closely with the PC hardware to do its job. This makes it vulnerable to differences in the hardware design between PCs from different manufacturers.

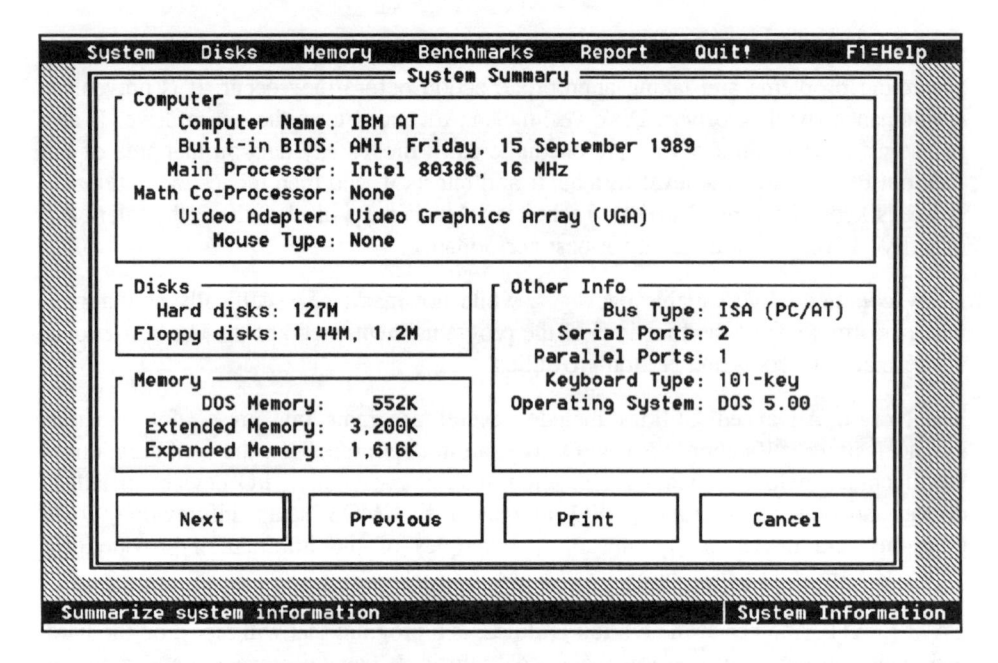

```
   System      Disks     Memory     Benchmarks     Report      Quit!        F1=Help
                              ══ System Summary ══
   ┌ Computer ─────────────────────────────────────────────────────────────┐
   │     Computer Name: IBM AT                                             │
   │     Built-in BIOS: AMI, Friday, 15 September 1989                     │
   │    Main Processor: Intel 80386, 16 MHz                                │
   │  Math Co-Processor: None                                              │
   │     Video Adapter: Video Graphics Array (VGA)                         │
   │        Mouse Type: None                                               │
   └───────────────────────────────────────────────────────────────────────┘
   ┌ Disks ──────────────────────┐  ┌ Other Info ────────────────────────┐
   │   Hard disks: 127M          │  │       Bus Type: ISA (PC/AT)        │
   │ Floppy disks: 1.44M, 1.2M   │  │    Serial Ports: 2                 │
   └─────────────────────────────┘  │  Parallel Ports: 1                 │
   ┌ Memory ─────────────────────┐  │   Keyboard Type: 101-key           │
   │     DOS Memory:    552K     │  │ Operating System: DOS 5.00         │
   │ Extended Memory:  3,200K    │  └────────────────────────────────────┘
   │ Expanded Memory:  1,616K    │
   └─────────────────────────────┘

        Next            Previous            Print            Cancel

   Summarize system information                             System Information
```

Figure 2.5: Norton SYSINFO system information summary

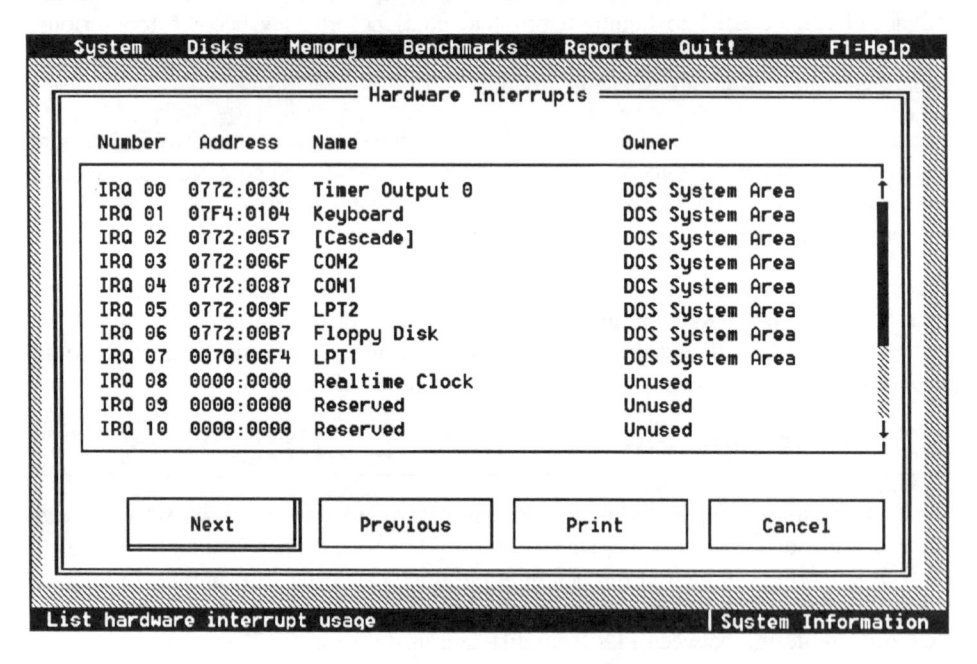

```
   System      Disks     Memory     Benchmarks     Report      Quit!        F1=Help
                             ══ Hardware Interrupts ══

      Number    Address      Name                    Owner

      IRQ 00   0772:003C    Timer Output 0          DOS System Area
      IRQ 01   07F4:0104    Keyboard                DOS System Area
      IRQ 02   0772:0057    [Cascade]               DOS System Area
      IRQ 03   0772:006F    COM2                    DOS System Area
      IRQ 04   0772:0087    COM1                    DOS System Area
      IRQ 05   0772:009F    LPT2                    DOS System Area
      IRQ 06   0772:00B7    Floppy Disk             DOS System Area
      IRQ 07   0070:06F4    LPT1                    DOS System Area
      IRQ 08   0000:0000    Realtime Clock          Unused
      IRQ 09   0000:0000    Reserved                Unused
      IRQ 10   0000:0000    Reserved                Unused

         Next            Previous            Print            Cancel

   List hardware interrupt usage                            System Information
```

Figure 2.6: Norton SYSINFO hardware interrupt usage report

```
  System    Disks   Memory    Benchmarks   Report    Quit!      F1=Help
 ┌──────────────────────── Disk Characteristics ────────────────────────┐
 │ ┌─ Logical Characteristics ──────────────────────────────┐  A: ↑     │
 │ │ Bytes per sector:    512    Sectors per cluster: 4    │  B:        │
 │ │ Number of clusters: 20,475                             │  C:        │
 │ │ Number of FAT's:     2      FAT type: 16-bit           │  D:        │
 │ │ Media Descriptor Byte: F8 Hex                          │  E: ↓     │
 │ │                                                        │            │
 │ │ FAT start sector:        1    Sectors Occupied 160     │ ┌ Size ┐  │
 │ │ Root Dir start sector: 161    Sectors Occupied 32      │ │       │  │
 │ │ Data start sector:     193    Sectors Occupied 81,900  │ │ 41M   │  │
 │ └────────────────────────────────────────────────────────┘ └───────┘  │
 │ ┌─ Physical Characteristics ────────────────────────────┐             │
 │ │ Sides: 15    Tracks: 322    Sectors per track: 17     │             │
 │ │ Drive number: 80 Hex                                   │             │
 │ └────────────────────────────────────────────────────────┘             │
 │      [  Next  ]    [  Previous  ]    [  Print  ]    [  Cancel  ]      │
 └──────────────────────────────────────────────────────────────────────┘
  Show high and low level information about a disk  │ System Information
```

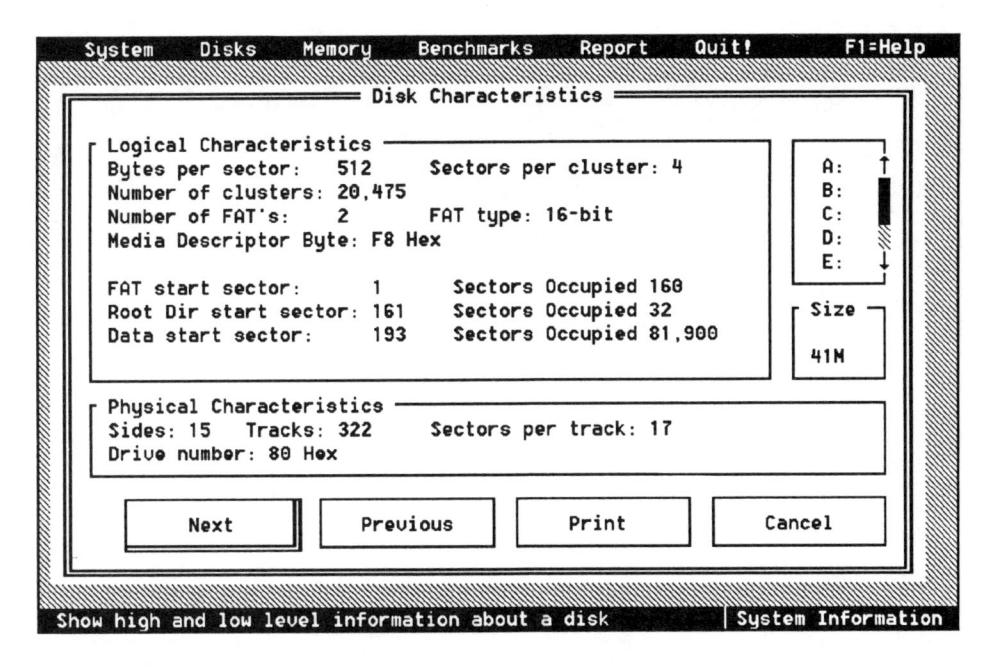

Figure 2.7: Norton SYSINFO Disk Characteristics report

Many public domain (PD) utilities are written by PC enthusiasts, who do not have the opportunity to test their creations on a range of machines. Some of the programs found in software libraries and on bulletin boards are also quite old. Many were written at a time when an IBM AT was state of the art, and all hard disks used MFM and ST-506 disk controllers, so a few of these programs will not work on modern hardware. The operating system in use may also cause problems. Some older utilities give incorrect results or crash when run under MS-DOS 4 and above or DR-DOS.

The risks involved in using hard disk utilities of doubtful reliability should not need spelling out. As you'll see in a later chapter, PCs may use one of several different types of hard disk controller. The newer types were rarely encountered before 1989. An old disk utility may work successfully with one of these new hard disk controllers. But it may not work at all or, worse, it may completely corrupt the hard disk. So it is wise to be careful. Unless a disk utility is of recent origin, appears to have been tested on a variety of machines, and is still supported by its author, it is best avoided.

There are several PD utilities that report on the system configuration in a similar way to Check It, Sleuth and Norton's SYSINFO. Two of the more comprehensive ones are SHOW by Arend van der Brug and MACHINFO by AME. Example displays from these two utilities are shown in Figures 2.8 and 2.9. While these are not strictly diagnostic programs, they do provide some useful information about the system that can help you sort out certain types of problem.

```
C:\UTILS\MISC>>show system
             SHOW [v3.14] - Show DOS 5.00 system information
-------------------------------------------------------


CPU-type    (MHz) | PrefetchQ | Coprocessor  (MHz)
------------------+-----------+--------------------
Intel 80386 ( 0.1) |  14 bytes |     none


HDisk | Disk | COM | LPT | Game
------+------+-----+-----+------
  1   |  2   |  2  |  1  |  0


Memory size | Free memory | Type
------------+-------------+-------------------------------
   552 KB   |    508 KB   | Normal (DOS)
   256 KB   |      0 KB   | VGA Video (CGA simulation), High res. monitor
  1616 KB   |    608 KB   | Expanded (EMS 4.0)
  3200 KB   |      0 KB   | Extended

C:\UTILS\MISC>>_
```

Figure 2.8: SHOW system information report

RAMTEST by Brown Bag Software is a program that tests the conventional, extended and expanded memory in a PC. It is a useful program to run if memory errors have been experienced. Older versions of this program, and all the PD memory test utilities I tried, failed when run on the latest PC hardware. However, the most recent version of RAMTEST has been tested on several 80386s and seems to work well.

Test Drive from Microsystems Development is a disk drive diagnostic tool similar to the Dysan Interrogator. It will test several adjustments on a 5.25in, 360Kb diskette drive including the rotation speed, head alignment, hub centring and general read/write performance. A Digital Diagnostic Disk is required for some of these tests. This program is shareware, and registration includes the cost of a DDD. The shareware version does not support 3.5in, or high density drives, although the rotation speed and read/write tests did work, using only the first 40 tracks of the disk.

HDTEST by P. R. Fletcher is a package that can do a thorough surface analysis of hard disks. It can also recover data from damaged parts of a disk. The program is functionally similar to Norton's NDD. It has been tested on many different equipment configurations. The package includes a utility called FIXFAT. As you would expect, this is intended to recover from a situation when one copy of the disk File Allocation Table is damaged. HDTEST is user-supported shareware; its author is a member of the Association of Shareware Professionals.

HDTEST is very much a techie's tool. Unlike Norton, there are no colourful screens and helpful menus, just terse messages in black and white. There is a 36-page manual stored as a text file on disk. This contains a good deal of information about the program, and about disk operation in general, including a detailed description of the 19 command line parameters.

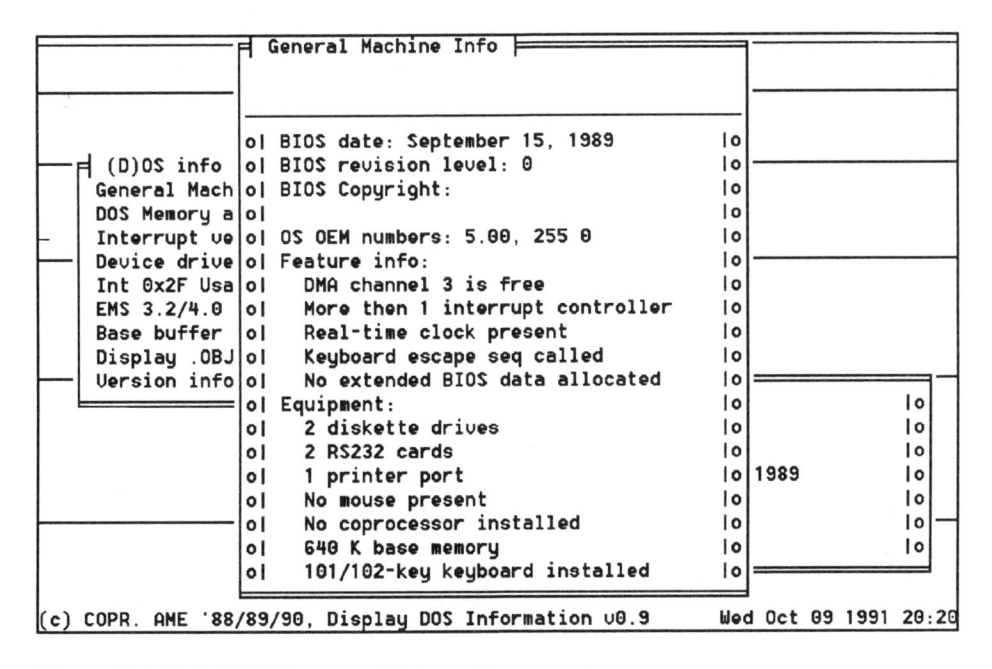

```
                          ╡ General Machine Info ╞
  ┌─────────────────────┐
  │                     │ o│ BIOS date: September 15, 1989      │o│
  ├─╡ (D)OS info        │ o│ BIOS revision level: 0             │o│
  │   General Mach      │ o│ BIOS Copyright:                    │o│
  │   DOS Memory a      │ o│                                    │o│
  └─  Interrupt ve      │ o│ OS OEM numbers: 5.00, 255 0        │o│
      Device drive      │ o│ Feature info:                      │o│
      Int 0x2F Usa      │ o│   DMA channel 3 is free            │o│
      EMS 3.2/4.0       │ o│   More then 1 interrupt controller │o│
      Base buffer       │ o│   Real-time clock present          │o│
      Display .OBJ      │ o│   Keyboard escape seq called       │o│
      Version info      │ o│   No extended BIOS data allocated  │o│
  ├─────────────────────┤ o│ Equipment:                         │o│         │o│
                          o│   2 diskette drives                │o│         │o│
                          o│   2 RS232 cards                    │o│         │o│
                          o│   1 printer port                   │o│ 1989    │o│
                          o│   No mouse present                 │o│         │o│
                          o│   No coprocessor installed         │o│         │o│
                          o│   640 K base memory                │o│         │o│
                          o│   101/102-key keyboard installed   │o│
 (c) COPR. AME '88/89/90, Display DOS Information v0.9    Wed Oct 09 1991 20:20
```

Figure 2.9: MACHINFO general information report

Despite its apparent complexity, HDTEST is a worthwhile addition to the diagnostic toolkit. It tests the disk surface much more thoroughly than most other diagnostic packages, and tries much harder to recover data from damaged sectors. It found and mapped out troublesome bad sectors which a low-level format, a DOS format, Check It and NDD had all failed to find. However, HDTEST takes much longer to run than most general-purpose disk test programs – often several hours.

2.8 BASIC Diagnostics

If you are trying to find a fault on a system with no diagnostic software to help you, it can be a little like looking for a needle in a haystack in the dark. Sometimes, even a simple test program can be a big help. Where possible, I've included test and diagnostic programs written in BASIC in the appropriate chapters of the book.

BASIC isn't the ideal language for writing diagnostic software. Many of the low-level functions needed to test a system component simply cannot be accessed. However, it has two big advantages over other languages such as C, Pascal or assembler. It is easy to read and type in, and every PC compatible comes with a BASIC interpreter.

On an IBM PC, XT or AT, the BASIC interpreter is called BASICA. The letter A stands for Advanced BASIC. It's held in ROM, so you don't need to be able to boot up the system from a DOS disk to use it. On most clones using Microsoft MS-DOS version 4 or earlier, the interpreter is called GWBASIC. MS-DOS 5 has a new BASIC interpreter called QBASIC. The program listings in this book were tested under GWBASIC version 3.22, which is shipped with MS-DOS version 3.3. However, they should work under the other versions without difficulty.

Each of the program listings is self-contained, and uses a unique range of statement numbers. This means that you could load all the test programs into a single file, and add a simple front end to allow individual tests to be selected from a menu. More experienced readers may wish to modify the tests, and even add new ones of their own.

Summary

In this chapter we looked at basic problem solving techniques, and some of the software aids available to help with fault diagnosis. It is vital to adopt a methodical approach to problem solving. You should never overlook the obvious, nor look for a complicated explanation for a problem when the simpler possibilities have not been checked out.

The power-on tests which a PC carries out when it is first switched on are often the first indication of a problem. For more obscure or intermittent faults, the diagnostic program supplied by the PC manufacturer may be a help in finding the solution. However, the tests it performs are often not very thorough. Some of the cheaper systems may not be supplied with any diagnostics at all.

If you want to be able to troubleshoot any PC effectively, third-party diagnostics, including popular commercial products like the Norton Advanced Utilities, are essential. Useful programs can also be found in public domain and shareware libraries. However, older PD utilities often don't work correctly on modern hardware, and should be treated with caution. Simple test routines written in BASIC can often be used. Listings of BASIC test programs are included in later chapters of the book.

3

The Power Supply

Power is the life-blood of a microcomputer, and the power supply is its heart. If the power is cut off or the power supply stops working then the system dies. So the power supply is a good place to begin our in-depth look at the various parts that go to make up a PC.

Computer power supplies are generally pretty reliable. Some makes seem more prone to power supply failures than others. This is probably due to poor design or the use of under-specified components. Failures can also be caused by a poor quality mains supply. With most PCs, though, the power supply is something that just keeps on working.

The job of the power supply is to take the raw mains and turn it into the smooth, regulated, harmless, low DC voltages needed by the electronic circuits within the PC. But beware! Mains electricity is dangerous. Touch it and it can kill you. Though what comes out of the power supply may be harmless, there are dangerous mains voltages present inside. So never open up a power supply or poke around inside it while power is applied.

This chapter looks at how power supplies work, how to test them, and the problems that can occur if they are faulty or overloaded. It does *not* describe how to repair broken power supplies. The repair of equipment which operates at mains voltages is a job for a qualified electrical engineer working with the proper tools in a safe workshop environment. It is not a job for someone working at an office desk or the kitchen table. The power supply in a PC is completely encased in a metal enclosure. It should be treated as a replaceable sealed unit. Replacement power supplies are not, by and large, expensive, and the cost in time spent troubleshooting and repairing a faulty unit will usually exceed the cost of a new replacement.

3.1 Power Supply Basics

Most domestic electrical equipment is powered by a conventional transformer-based power supply. A simple example is shown in Figure 3.1. The transformer converts the input from the AC supply to a low voltage, and provides isolation. The rectifier turns the alternating current into direct current, and together with the regulator and filter produces a smooth DC voltage output.

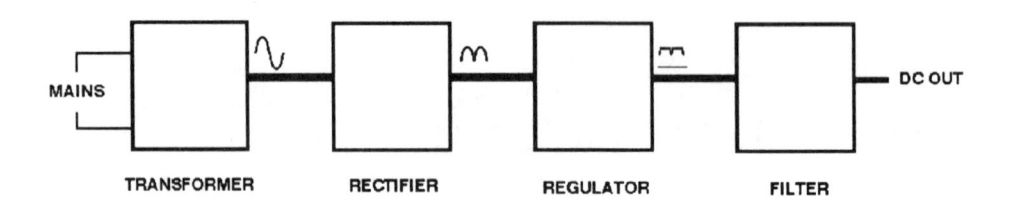

Figure 3.1: Transformer power supply

Computer power supplies employ switching regulators, and do not use transformers at all. They are known as *switched-mode* power supplies. A basic switching regulator circuit is shown in Figure 3.2. The mains input voltage is rectified and then applied directly to a switching device – this could be a high-voltage transistor. This is switched on and off at a high frequency, so that the filtered output voltage is kept constant. The length of time for which the switching device is turned on is controlled by the switching pulses. These pulses vary the on/off ratio to ensure that the output voltage is constant, whatever the load. A practical switched-mode power supply is, of course, far more complex than this, because the circuitry to monitor the output voltage and generate the switching waveform has been omitted. Since in a switched-mode power supply there is no transformer to provide isolation from the mains, it must also provide additional fail-safe circuits to protect against overload and failure of the switching devices.

Although the switched-mode power supply is more complex than a transformer-based unit, it has many advantages. These are:

❏ Higher efficiency – power is not wasted as heat in the regulator or the transformer

❏ much reduced weight and smaller size due to the absence of the transformer and large heat sink of a conventional power supply.

These benefits are very significant. A fully-expanded PC consumes a fair amount of power, and the power supply must be adequately rated to cope with this. Many AT compatibles have 200W supplies. If the AT power supply was transformer-based it would weigh 20 – 25lbs, require a powerful and noisy fan and be almost as large as a typical PC system box.

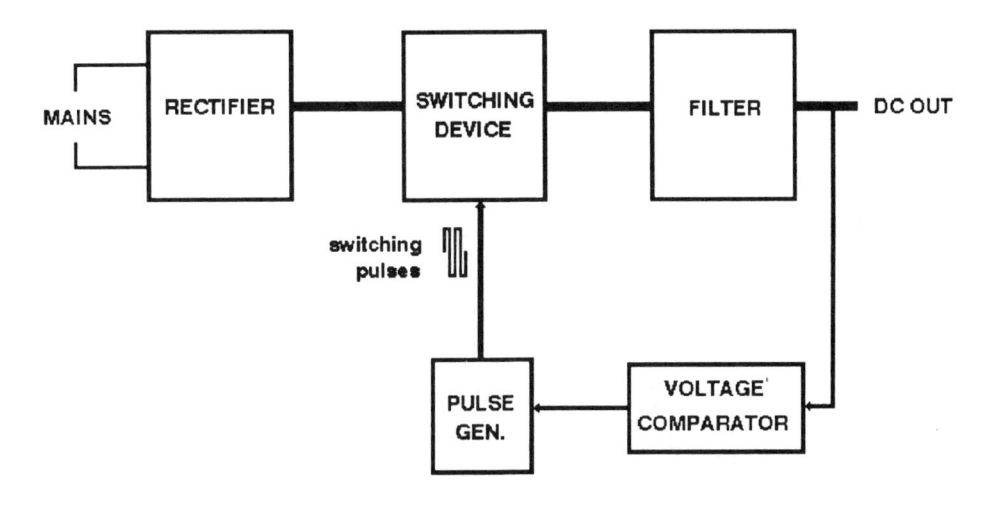

Figure 3.2: Switched mode power supply

3.2 Power Requirements

Before looking at power supply problems and their solutions, let's consider just what it is that a computer power supply is required to do when it is working normally.

A PC needs power at two different voltage levels and both positive and negative polarities: +5VDC, +12VDC, -5VDC and -12VDC. The power supply has to provide power at all these four voltages. Most power is needed at +5VDC. This is the voltage needed by most of the electronic circuitry. A fair amount of power is also required at +12VDC. Some electronic circuits operate at this voltage, but mostly it is needed to operate the disk drive motors. Only a small amount of power is needed at -5VDC and -12VDC, in case certain specialised components are present. The -12VDC is primarily used by the RS-232 serial ports.

The total power requirements of a PC depend upon the components within it. Each component will draw a certain quantity of current at each of the supply voltages it uses. Some components will draw different amounts of current depending on what they are doing. For example, a diskette drive will draw more current when the motor is running, and when the heads are moving.

Table 3.1: Power consumption of PC system components

Power Consumption

	Current drawn (amps)			
	+5V	+12V	-5V	-12V
System board, 1M RAM	3.0	0.05	–	0.05
Fan	–	0.25	–	–
Display adapter	0.5	–	–	–
I/O card	0.25	0.1	–	0.1
Disk controller	0.5	–	–	–
Internal modem	0.8	–	0.1	–
Diskette drive	0.5	0.8	–	–
Hard disk 5.25in (spin up)	1.2	4.0	–	–
(half height) (operating)	1.2	1.3	–	–
Hard disk 3.5in (spin up)	1.2	2.5	–	–
(half height) (operating)	1.2	1.2	–	–
Network card (Ethernet)	1.0	0.1	–	–

Table 3.1 lists typical current requirements for various PC system components. Note, however, that in practice the average current drawn will vary widely between similar components of different types. A 33MHz 80386 system board will draw more current than an 8MHz 8086. Older systems will draw more current than comparable new ones, since they tend to use many more discrete components. High capacity disk drives having several platters and heads will draw more current than lower capacity ones with few, or those designed for power-conscious systems such as laptops.

If a PC power supply is running hot, or the machine is intermittently malfunctioning, it's a good idea to do a power audit. This is simple to do. List all the boards and devices inside the system unit. Then add up the current requirements determined from Table 3.1. Now compare the result with the current ratings for the appropriate type of power supply shown in Table 3.2.

If any of the figures exceed – or come close to – the maximum current for that voltage, it's likely that, under certain conditions, the rating is being exceeded. At best this would mean that the power supply components are being put under excessive strain. At worst, the overload protection could trip or a component could fail. The danger period is at start-up, when all the parts of the PC will draw a surge of current for a second or two.

Table 3.2: Typical PC power supply ratings

Type Of Power Supply

Voltage	PC (65W) Current(A) Min	Max	XT (130W) Current(A) Min	Max	AT (200W) Current(A) Min	Max
+5 (+/- 5%)	1.5	7.0	2.5	15.0	7.0	19.8
+12 (+/- 5%)	0.3	2.0	1.0	4.2	0.5	7.3
-5 (+/- 10%)	0.06	0.3	–	0.3	–	0.3
-12 (+/- 10%)	0.06	0.3	–	0.3	–	0.3

If a PC has been heavily upgraded, with several disk drives and most of the expansion slots filled, it's quite possible for the power requirements to exceed the capacity of the power supply. This is particularly likely with low-cost small footprint machines. Such machines aren't designed to take much expansion. If you're getting close to, or exceeding, the ratings, you should fit a higher capacity power supply.

If your system is an IBM, or uses an XT or AT pattern power supply, higher capacity replacements are readily available, at low cost, from a variety of manufacturers. If the PC is a *name brand* model, and has its own design of power supply, this may not be the case. That's why power supply capacity and expansion potential should always be considered when choosing a machine.

3.3 Testing the Power Supply

If a power problem is suspected, you'll need to test the power supply. To do this, you'll need a volt-ohm meter. You'll be testing to see if a voltage is present, and if it's within the permitted limits.

On IBM PCs and many clones, power is supplied to the system board by two special 6-way non-reversible connectors. These connectors are usually labelled P1 and P2 (on ATs it's P8 and P9), and are wired as shown in Table 3.3. Pin 1 is the *power good* signal. This is generated by the power supply when all the output voltages are correct. If this signal isn't present, the PC will not boot up. The remaining pins are used to deliver the power to the system board.

Table 3.3: IBM AT system board power connector voltages

Connector	Pin	Colour	Nominal	Min	Max
P8	1		pwr gd	+2.4	+5.25
P8	2		+5	+4.75	+5.25
P8	3		+12	+11.4	+12.6
P8	4		-12	-10.8	-13.2
P8	5	Black	gnd	–	–
P8	6	Black	gnd	–	–
P8	7	Black	gnd	–	–
P8	8	Black	gnd	–	–
P9	9		-5	-4.5	-5.5
P9	10		+5	+4.75	+5.25
P9	11		+5	+4.75	+5.25
P9	12		+5	+4.75	+5.25

Table 3.3 also shows the nominal and permissible voltages at each power connector pin, with respect to ground. These can be measured using the test points provided. With the volt-ohm meter set to the 12VDC range, attach the negative test probe to pin 6. Then measure the voltage at each of pins 1, 2, 3, 4 and 12. Check, by referring to the table, that the voltages are within the limits specified.

Power supply voltages should never be checked with the supply disconnected from the system board. If you refer to Table 3.2 you'll see that there is a minimum current that should be drawn for most of the output voltages generated. No current at all will be drawn if the power supply is not connected to a load. If you need to test a power supply while it is out of the system box, you'll need to make up a special test load. Wire-wound resistors or lamp bulbs of an appropriate wattage may be used to make a suitable load.

The purpose of the power good signal is to ensure that the system won't run if the power supplied to it is not within specification. The processor is halted when the power good signal is at zero volts, and a cold boot is performed as soon as it goes high (i.e., a nominal +5V). If any of the output voltages from the supply are close to the limits, or if the power good sensing circuit is over-sensitive, slight fluctuations in the mains supply could cause the signal to drop momentarily to zero. This will cause the PC to reboot. So if a PC develops a habit of occasionally rebooting itself, check the voltage levels.

3.4 Diagnosing Problems

In this section, we'll look at some power-related problems and list the tests that should be carried out. As far as possible, these tests are listed in a logical order, with the most likely causes, and the easiest things to check, given first.

If a test gives more information about the cause of the problem, then use common sense in deciding what to try next. The test procedures could have been presented as flowcharts. However, that would have taken a lot of space, and if you followed the flowcharts blindly, you wouldn't learn anything. It's also hard to draw up a flowchart which covers every possible eventuality. The object of this book is to help you learn about how PCs work, and how to solve problems for yourself. The tests suggested here will give you ideas for things to try. They'll help to ensure that obvious things are not overlooked. But as you gain more experience, you'll find yourself automatically separating the likely from the improbable, and quickly homing in on the cause of a fault.

System appears completely dead:

❏ Check input voltage selector is set correctly.

❏ Check mains supply by checking operation of pilot lights, fan, monitor (if plugged into same socket).

❏ Check power cable plugged in fully.

❏ Test fuse and cable continuity.

❏ Check operation of switch (mechanically, by inspection; electrically, by disconnecting from mains and then measuring the resistance across the live and neutral terminals of mains plug while operating the switch – the resistance should be high with the switch off, low with it on).

❏ Check output voltages and *power good* signal from power supply using volt-ohm meter.

❏ Remove expansion cards and disconnect power connectors from disk drives and check output voltages and *power good* signal again, in case overload cut-out is being triggered. Replace power supply if there is still no power.

❏ If power is now present, calculate power requirements from figures in Table 3.1 to see if power supply is adequately rated for the job. Replace if necessary. Otherwise replace expansion cards and peripheral power connectors one by one until the component drawing excessive power is discovered.

System comes on momentarily, then dies:

❏ Check mains cable is pushed fully into socket.

❏ Check input voltage selector is set correctly.

❏ Check operation of switch, as described above. The switch mechanism may not be latching **on**. Check switch can move freely to both extremes of its travel.

❏ Check output voltages and *power good* signal from power supply using volt-ohm meter.

❏ Remove expansion cards and disconnect power connectors from disk drives and check output voltages and *power good* signal again, in case overload cut-out is being triggered.

❏ If power is now present, calculate power requirements from figures in Table 3.1 to see if power supply is adequately rated for the job. Replace if necessary. Otherwise replace expansion cards and peripheral power connectors one by one until the component that is drawing excessive power is discovered.

System cuts out after a period of operation:

Early model Amstrad PC1512s suffered from this problem, which was caused by an over-sensitive overload cut-out. It was cured by a power supply modification. Many un-modified machines may still be in existence; check with your dealer if this is thought to be the cause.

❏ Check mains cable is pushed fully into socket.

❏ Check operating temperature. Increase fan speed if possible (see your system manual) if temperature seems excessive.

❏ Calculate power requirements from figures in Table 3.1 to see if power supply is adequately rated for the job. Replace with an uprated unit if necessary.

❏ Check output voltages from power supply using volt-ohm meter. Replace power supply if voltages are close to limits.

System locks up:

This is usually a software problem. However, if this happens during normal DOS operations, or the machine seems to have locked after being left unattended for a period, it could be due to static electricity, or voltage *spikes* on the mains.

❏ Check keyboard lock!

- ❏ Check mains supply. Temporarily fit a power conditioner to see if this cures the problem.

- ❏ Swap the PC with one in another location, to see if the problem is within the PC, or connected with its location.

System reboots itself:

This could be a software problem. However, if it happens during normal DOS use or in a well-tested application, it could be due to voltage fluctuations.

- ❏ Check output voltages from power supply using volt-ohm meter. Replace power supply if voltages are close to limits.

- ❏ Check mains supply. Fit an uninterruptible power supply to see if this cures the problem.

- ❏ Swap the PC with one in another location, to see if the problem is within the PC, or connected with its location.

3.5 Power Supply Removal

On most systems, it's a simple job to replace a power supply. The ones used by IBM have an integral switch accessible at the rear of the system unit. You can buy direct replacements for these units from a variety of sources. Many PC compatibles, particularly older models, use a power supply that conforms to the same pattern. Finding a replacement unit for such machines is neither difficult nor expensive. If your machine uses a unique design of power supply, however, your only option may be to purchase a replacement from the original manufacturer.

The exact procedure for replacing a PC power supply will depend on the make and model. A few machines, such as Amstrad's PC1512 and PC1640, have the power supply inside the monitor casing. Because of the high voltages found inside a CRT monitor, power supply replacement for such machines is best left to a qualified engineer.

For other models, the procedure is as follows:

- ❏ First, switch off the machine and disconnect it from the mains

- ❏ Remove the system unit cover

- ❏ Disconnect the power cables from all the drives

- ❏ Disconnect the power connectors from the system board

- ❏ If there is a remote on/off switch, this must also be disconnected

- ❏ Remove the power supply retaining screws: typically there are four, or two if the power supply is also retained by lugs that slide into holes in the chassis

- ❏ You should now be able to lift the power supply out of the case.

3.5 Power Supply Replacement

- ❏ First, check that the voltage selector is set for the correct mains input voltage

- ❏ Fit the power supply into the case, and secure with the retaining screws

- ❏ Connect the remote on/off switch, if fitted

- ❏ Fit the two 6-way power connectors to the system board, noting that the two ground wires on each connector (usually coloured black) adjoin

- ❏ Connect the power leads to all the drives

- ❏ Replace the cover

- ❏ Connect the mains cable

- ❏ The system should now be ready for use.

Summary

In this chapter, we saw that personal computers use switched mode power supplies because they are smaller, lighter and more efficient than conventional power supplies. They provide current at four different voltages, which are needed by the PC electronics and the disk drives. The power capacity of a power supply varies from model to model. The power requirements depend on the equipment fitted inside the PC. We explained how the power requirements may be estimated. We listed a variety of fault symptoms that could be caused by power problems, and outlined tests which should be carried out to isolate the fault. Finally, we described the removal and replacement of a power supply.

4

The Motherboard and Expansion Bus

If the power supply is the heart of a PC then the motherboard represents the arteries, the central nervous system and the brain. Generally, it contains the CPU chip, the ROM BIOS, memory, the bus and the logic chips.

Motherboards vary greatly from machine to machine. In a few PCs, the motherboard is simply a backplane containing the bus connectors and a few logic chips. The main circuitry – the CPU, memory and so on – is contained on a separate system board which plugs into one of these connectors. The advantage of building a PC this way is that it is can be upgraded to a faster processor simply by replacing the system board. At the other extreme, modern PCs, particularly slimline, compact machines, put everything on to the motherboard, including parallel and serial ports, disk drive controllers and a video adapter. A typical motherboard layout is shown in Figure 4.1.

A section of the motherboard is normally used to hold the memory. In the earliest PCs, designed when 64K memory chips were the norm, the amount of memory that could be held on the motherboard was limited. Expansion cards had to be used if additional memory was needed. However, with 1Mbit and 4Mbit chips now commonplace, it is not unusual to find motherboards able to accommodate 8Mb or more of RAM.

This chapter will describe those system components that form the essentials of a PC compatible system, and which are usually found on the motherboard. We'll look at the problems that can occur with the board itself, the CPU and the memory. Then we'll look at setting-up the motherboard and fitting expansion cards. Though serial and parallel ports and display adapters are often built into the motherboards of modern PCs, we'll look at those in later chapters.

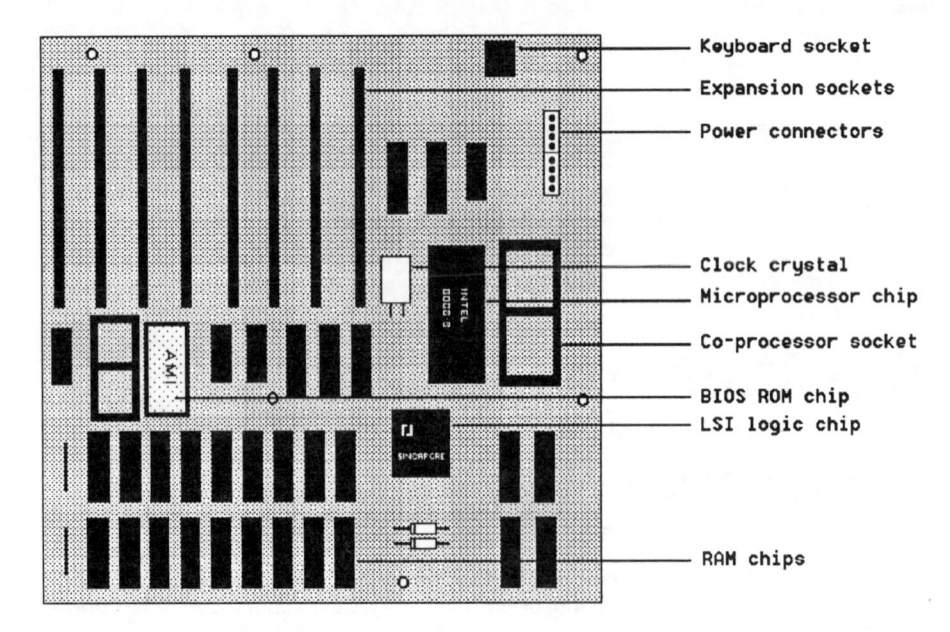

Figure 4.1: A typical PC motherboard layout

4.1 Motherboard Construction

The motherboard is the largest component inside a personal computer. It contains the CPU; possibly an arithmetic co-processor; the system clock; the ROM containing the system BIOS routines; RAM which will be used to hold DOS and user programs; the keyboard controller; and logic circuits that control access to the system bus and deal with I/O, interrupt and DMA processing. There's a lot of electronics on a motherboard, and the interconnections between the various parts are complex.

The printed circuit boards (PCBs) used in PCs are made out of fibreglass. The connections between the various components are formed by thin copper tracks. The circuit boards in a modern PC contain a great many tracks, and are expensive to manufacture. Whereas a PCB in an item of consumer electronics, such as a hi-fi amplifier, may have copper tracks on one or perhaps both sides of the board, a PC motherboard will also have layers of tracks sandwiched within its 2.5mm thickness. The board must be manufactured to close tolerances, so that the tracks all line up at the component holes. These holes are plated through with copper, so as to make an electrical connection to each layer.

Many of the copper tracks on the motherboard are very fine. Consequently you should never put too much pressure on the board when inserting or removing cards or chips. If you do, you could cause the board to bend excessively and break one of the tracks. A good quality motherboard is very robust. However, once a track is broken, it is almost impossible to trace and repair. The motherboard is often the most expensive component in a PC, so it's worth taking a little care with it.

If you're evaluating PCs prior to buying a number of them, the quality of the motherboard is something you should consider. However this isn't easy if you haven't had much experience of electronics. One point to look out for is the thickness of the board itself. Some of the cheaper circuit boards of oriental origin are quite thin. While they may work perfectly well, and represent good value for money, they should not be expected to withstand much careless handling or frequent insertion and removal of expansion cards.

Other points to consider are the quality of the soldering – joints should be bright silver – and the absence of *blue-wiring* – the thin wires sometimes found laid on top of the circuit board, interconnecting various parts. They are usually the result of afterthoughts or omissions in the design.

The method used for mounting the motherboard can vary from machine to machine. On IBM systems and many clones, it is seated on several plastic stand-off pillars, and held in place by two screws. These locate into metal ground posts. Electrical connections to the board from the power supply, loudspeaker and so on are made using push-on connectors.

On many motherboards, the positioning of the mounting screws and pillars is the same as that used by IBM. The connectors used for the electrical connections and the position of the keyboard socket are also standard. This is because many motherboards are sold as direct replacements and upgrades for the old, slow IBM XT and AT. Removal and replacement of the motherboard is described later in this chapter.

4.2 Motherboard Components

A conventional PC motherboard contains dozens of individual components. The microprocessor, maths co-processor (if present), RAM and ROM BIOS chips are usually fitted in IC sockets. Memory chips, as well as the older CPUs, are usually DIL components – black plastic packages with a row of legs on each of the two longest sides. Later processors and LSI chips are square PLCC devices with contacts on all four sides; these fit into special square sockets. Removal of PLCC devices from their sockets is not easy, and requires a special tool. Fortunately this should rarely be necessary. Smaller chips are usually soldered in place. On modern boards, many of these are surface-mounted devices – legless components soldered directly to the board.

The CPU, like other chips, has several identifying markings printed on it. One of these is the part number, which is followed by the speed rating in MHz. For example, an 80386 rated at 25MHz would have the marking *80386-25*. The speed rating of the CPU should match the clock speed of the computer.

Some less reputable PC manufacturers try to save money by installing a CPU that has a manufacturer's rating which is lower than the clock speed. You should avoid such machines. When Intel manufacture CPUs, they test the chips at various operating speeds. The rating given to a chip is the highest speed at which it satisfactorily completed all the tests. So the implication of the speed rating is that the chip failed a test at a higher speed. The CPU may actually work at a higher speed most of the time. However, if an unexplained error should occur, you'll never be sure that it wasn't caused by exceeding the chip's speed rating.

4.3 Memory Parity

Memory chips are usually arranged on the motherboard in rows of nine. This is because each chip usually holds a single bit for each addressable byte of memory. For example, a 256K x 1 memory chip will hold one bit of data for each of 256K (262,144) separate locations. Eight such chips are needed to store 256K bytes. The ninth chip is used for parity. When a value is written to memory, the PC hardware writes an additional 1 or a 0 to the parity chip, so that the total number of binary ones is even. Whenever the location is accessed, the hardware checks that the number of ones is still even. If the value of a single bit has changed due to a fault, the system logic will detect this and cause the machine to halt with a parity error.

Some cheap PCs save money by not including a parity chip. This may seem a reasonable economy. These days, memory is very reliable. Competition at the bottom end of the PC market is very intense. The saving obtained by omitting the parity chips and their associated circuitry helps the manufacturer to keep down the cost. Only you, the purchaser, can decide whether you'd wish to entrust important data to a machine that couldn't warn you if a memory error occurred.

4.4 Memory Banks

XT compatibles, which use an 8088 processor, have an 8-bit data bus. On these machines, data is transferred to and from memory one byte at a time. AT compatibles using the 80286 or 80386sx processors have a 16-bit data bus, so they must have the capability to read from and write to memory 16 bits – two bytes – at a time. When a 16-bit memory access takes place, the two bytes being read occupy adjacent locations.

The way that memory is addressed makes it impossible to access two locations stored on the same chip at the same time. Therefore, on ATs, memory is arranged in banks of two rows of chips. One row holds the even-numbered bytes, the other holds the odd-numbered bytes. Then, whenever a 16-bit item of data is read from or written to memory, the two bytes will always be stored on different rows of chips and can consequently be accessed simultaneously.

Because an AT has separate rows for odd and even bytes, memory must be added in increments of two rows of chips. In other words, if 256K x 1 chips are used, memory may only be increased in increments of 512K. Thirty two-bit systems – those that use the 80386dx or 80486 processors – must use banks of four rows of chips for the same reason.

4.5 Chip Sets

Besides the processor and memory, the motherboard contains controller chips and other logic whose job is to bind everything together into a functioning microcomputer. All PC compatibles are essentially similar at the hardware level. This is what PC compatibility is about. However, the actual physical design varies from machine to machine. The IBM PC, XT and AT used standard Intel chips that were intended for use in any computer built around an Intel CPU. This, plus the fact that the memory chips available at the time had a low capacity, meant that there were a lot of ICs on the motherboard – over 100 in a PC XT, for example. Modern developments in electronics have led to the production of large scale integrated circuits. Now, a set of two or three chips can have the same functionality as a couple of dozen discrete components.

Several manufacturers produce LSI chip sets. There are various versions to suit the speed and type of processor used. Intel themselves produce the High Integration Chipset. Faraday, a division of Western Digital, manufacture the FE 3600 System Logic chip set which integrates the logic for an IBM AT compatible on to four LSI ICs. Chips and Technologies manufacture the well known New Enhanced AT (NEAT) chip set, which offers enhanced memory management functionality. Most of these chip sets support the use of ROM shadowing and the relocation of RAM memory above 640K for use as extended memory.

LSI, together with high capacity memory chips, have enabled a dramatic reduction in the number of components on a PC motherboard to be achieved. A typical system board contains everything needed for a working system, including one parallel and two serial ports, floppy and hard disk controllers and a VGA display adapter. For the purchaser and end-user, the benefits are a smaller system unit that takes up less desk space, and greater reliability as there are fewer parts to go wrong.

4.6 Motherboard Connectors

If you look inside a PC, you'll see several flying leads plugged into connectors on the motherboard. On IBM systems, the pin assignments for these connectors are standardised. The connections for an IBM AT are listed in Table 4.1. However, other models may use different connectors or pin assignments. If the flying leads have to be removed for any reason, take care to note down the correct position and orientation of each one. The pin assignments for motherboards sold as upgrades for old systems are usually listed in the manual that accompanies each board.

Table 4.1: IBM AT motherboard external connections

Connector	Pin	Function
Speaker	1	Data
	2	Key (no pin)
	3	Ground
	4	+5V DC
Keyboard	1	Keyboard clock
	2	Keyboard data
	3	not used
	4	Ground
	5	+5V DC
Power LED and Keylock	1	LED Power
	2	Key (no pin)
	3	Ground
	4	Keyboard inhibit
	5	Ground
Backup Battery (IBM AT)	1	Ground
	2	not used
	3	not used
	4	+6V DC

Power is supplied to the motherboard using two 6-way non-reversible connectors and heavy gauge wires. This was discussed in the previous chapter. The point to remember about these two connectors, if you're in doubt which way round they should go, is that the two black ground wires on each connector must be fitted so that they are next to each other.

The flying lead connections carry low current signals and use light, twisted wire leads. The loudspeaker is connected using a four-way socket with the outer two pins – 1 and 4 – used. In many system units, pin 2 on the plug is removed, and the corresponding hole in the connector blanked off. This acts as a key so that the connector cannot be fitted the wrong way round. However on some cheaper clones, this may not have been done. The loudspeaker is a non-polarised device, so it should not matter which way round it is connected.

On an AT or compatible, a five-way connector is used to attach the lead for the keyboard lock and power-on indicator lamp. The lamp is connected to pins 1 and 3 of the connector, and the switch to pins 4 and 5, pin 2 being the key. On IBM ATs and some other systems, an external lithium battery is used to maintain the data in the CMOS RAM. This is attached using a four-way connector. The positive voltage goes to pin 1, with pins 3 and 4 both being connected to ground. Pin 2 is again the key. Some AT compatibles have a back-up battery on the motherboard itself, and so do not require this connection.

The keyboard connector is a 5-pin DIN socket mounted towards the rear right of the motherboard. The pin assignment for this socket is shown in Figure 4.2. Some machines have a front-panel keyboard socket, and an alternative connector for this may be provided on the motherboard.

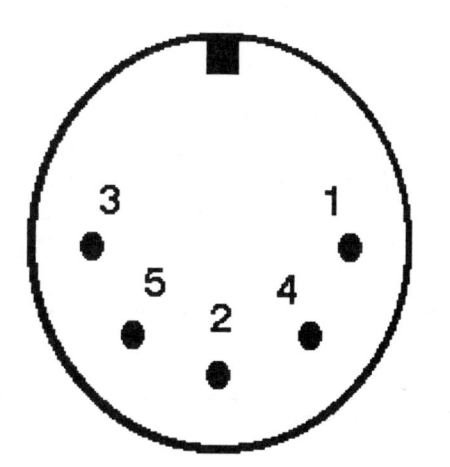

1. Keyboard Clock
2. Keyboard Data
3. No connection
4. Keyboard Ground
5. +5V DC

Figure 4.2: Keyboard connector pin assignments

Many PC compatibles provide a hardware reset button. Often, there is also a switch to enable the processor speed to be selected; this is usually known as the *turbo* switch. The reset button uses a two-pin connector. Pin 1 is the reset line and pin 2 is ground. The two pins are linked together when the switch is pushed in. The polarisation is therefore unimportant. The turbo switch is not a standard fitment, and the pin assignments may vary between different motherboards. If there is ambiguity about the way in which it is connected, the system manual should be consulted, though it is unlikely that any harm would be caused if the connector were incorrectly fitted. The turbo indicator LED is polarity sensitive and will only illuminate if it is connected the right way round.

4.7 Motherboard Configuration

A typical PC motherboard will have several options that must be set up correctly for the particular hardware configuration. Some of these options may be set using jumpers or switches on the board. More commonly, they are stored in the CMOS RAM and set using the SETUP utility. An incorrectly set up motherboard can be the cause of system malfunctions.

A good start when working on any computer is to find out what the current configuration is, and what devices the system itself thinks are installed. If your PC has an AMI BIOS, it will display this information for a few seconds at start-up. Otherwise, there are many utilities that provide the same data. Some were discussed in Chapter 2. They include commercial programs like Norton SYSINFO and TouchStone Check It, and many public domain utilities. A simple BASIC program that will provide some useful information about the system is given in Listing 4.1. An example of the output is shown in Figure 4.3. This program gets its information from data held by the ROM BIOS. If you have some devices installed which aren't shown by the program, you'll probably need special device drivers to access them.

The program obtains the BIOS ROM locations by scanning the reserved area of high memory for a BIOS *signature*. This is the two-byte value 55AA (hex), occurring at a memory address that is an exact multiple of 4K bytes. Every ROM contains these bytes in its first two locations. At start-up, the ROM BIOS routines use this characteristic to detect the presence of other ROMs in the system. Typical values which will appear are: C000:0 – EGA or VGA; C800:0 – XT hard disk controller configured as drive 0 (C:); CA00:0 – XT hard disk controller configured as drive 1 (D:).

```
Type of system:              PC/AT or compatible
Arithmetic Co-processor:     None
Base memory available:        552 k bytes.
Extended memory installed:   3200 k bytes.
Number of diskette drives:   2
Number of hard disks:        1
Number of serial ports:      2
Number of parallel ports:    1
Number of game ports:        0
Current video mode:          80x25 colour (CGA/EGA/VGA)
Type of keyboard:            101/102 keys
BIOS ROM locations:          C000:0
Ok
```

Figure 4.3: Example display from Listing 4.1

```
1000 REM ==== LISTING 8.1 - GET EQUIPMENT DETAILS ====
1005 DEF SEG=&HF000: E0%=PEEK(&HFFFE)
1007 PRINT "Type of system:",
1010 IF E0%=248 THEN PRINT "PS/2 Model 80": E0%=0: AT%=1
1011 IF E0%=249 THEN PRINT "PC Convertible": E0%=0
1012 IF E0%=250 THEN PRINT "PS/2 Model 30": E0%=0
1013 IF E0%=251 THEN PRINT "PC/XT or compatible": E0%=0
1014 IF E0%=252 THEN PRINT "PC/AT or compatible": E0%=0: AT%=1
1015 IF E0%=253 THEN PRINT "IBM PC jr": E0%=0
1016 IF E0%=254 THEN PRINT "PC/XT or compatible": E0%=0
1017 IF E0%=255 THEN PRINT "IBM PC or XT": E0%=0
1019 IF E0%<>0 THEN PRINT "Unknown - ID byte = ";HEX$(E0%);"H"
1020 DEF SEG=&H0: E0%=PEEK(&H410): E1%=PEEK(&H411): D0%=PEEK(&H475)
1021 PRINT "Arithmetic Co-processor:",
1022 E2%=INT(E0%/2)-INT(E0%/4)*2
1023 IF E2%=0 THEN PRINT "None" ELSE PRINT "Installed"
1025 PRINT "Base memory available:",PEEK(&H413)+PEEK(&H414)*256;"k
bytes."
1026 IF AT%=0 THEN 1030
1027 OUT 112,&H30: M%=INP(113): OUT 112,&H31: M%=M%+INP(113)*256
1028 PRINT "Extended memory installed:",M%;"k bytes."
1030 PRINT "Number of diskette drives:",INT(E0%/64)+(E0%-(INT(E0%/2)*2))
1032 PRINT "Number of hard disks:",D0%
1034 PRINT "Number of serial ports:",INT(E1%/2)-INT(E1%/16)*8
1036 PRINT "Number of parallel ports:",INT(E1%/64)
1040 PRINT "Number of game ports:",INT(E1%/16)-INT(E1%/32)*2
1050 E0%=PEEK(&H449): PRINT "Current video mode:",
1051 IF E0%=0 THEN PRINT "40x25 mono (CGA/EGA/VGA)"
1052 IF E0%=1 THEN PRINT "40x25 colour (CGA/EGA/VGA)"
1053 IF E0%=2 THEN PRINT "80x25 mono (CGA/EGA/VGA)"
1054 IF E0%=3 THEN PRINT "80x25 colour (CGA/EGA/VGA)"
1055 IF E0%=7 THEN PRINT "80x25 mono (MDA/Hercules)"
1057 IF E0%>7 THEN PRINT E0%
1060 E0%=PEEK(&H496): E0%=INT(E0%/16)-INT(E0%/32)*2
1062 PRINT "Type of keyboard:",
1064 IF E0%=0 THEN PRINT "84 keys" ELSE PRINT "101/102 keys"
1070 REM ==== Get ROM BIOS locations ====
1071 PRINT "BIOS ROM locations:",
1072 FOR I=49152! TO 64000! STEP 256
1073 DEF SEG=I
1074 IF PEEK(0)=&H55 AND PEEK(1)=&HAA THEN PRINT HEX$(I);":0",
1075 NEXT I
1078 PRINT
1095 END
```

The IBM PC design is to a certain extent self-configuring. Often, all you need to do plug a card into an expansion slot, power up the system, and it will recognise the new device and use it. As we've already seen, IBM set standards for the I/O ports, interrupt lines, BIOS signatures and so on, and this allows the system to test automatically for the presence of many devices. However, there are still many things that require manual configuration.

There are three methods that may be used for configuring a motherboard or, indeed, any PC board. One is to use DIP switches. These are small banks of four or eight switches, about the size of an integrated circuit, as shown in Figure 4.4 (a). Each switch is numbered – e.g., SW3. The function of these switches varies from machine to machine, and is described in the manual that accompanies the system.

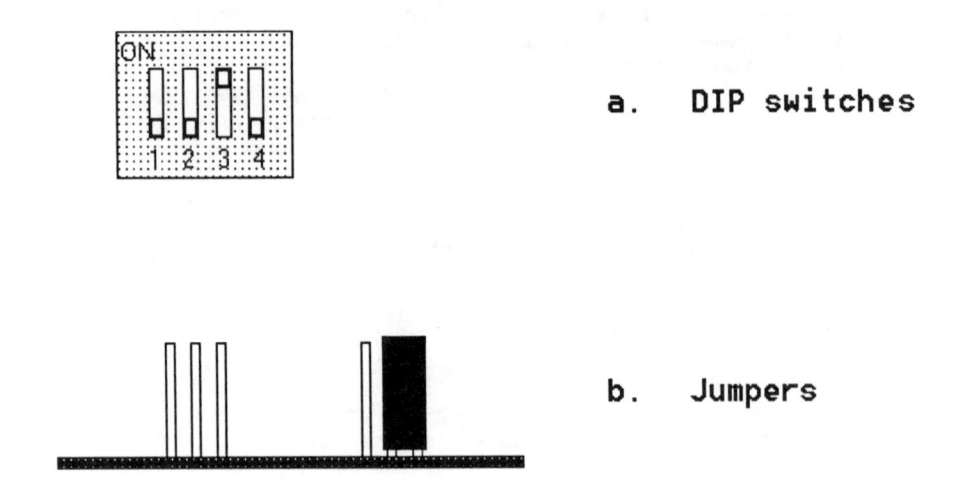

a. DIP switches

b. Jumpers

Figure 4.4: Jumpers and DIP switches

The second configuration method is to use jumpers, pictured in Figure 4.4 (b). Most boards have these clusters of pins which stick up from the circuit board. They also are numbered – e.g., J3. The jumper itself is a small black sleeve. Configuration is accomplished by fitting the jumper over two of the pins, linking them together. Again, the system manual may need to be consulted, but some boards may have the setting printed alongside the appropriate pair of pins. The third method of configuration is to store the settings in CMOS RAM, and use the SETUP utility to change them. This option is only available on AT compatibles, of course.

A motherboard will usually have some, if not all, of the following configuration options:

Monitor type: Specifies whether the primary monitor – the one to use by default – is monochrome or colour. In most systems, of course, there will only be one monitor. Note that a monochrome monitor driven by a CGA adapter is a colour monitor as far as the system is concerned. However, EGA or VGA cards may be used either as monochrome or colour adapters. VGA adapters can determine the monitor type automatically, whereas EGA cards must be configured manually using jumpers or DIP switches.

Clock speed: For PC compatibles that operate at a higher speed than the original IBM XT or AT, there is usually an option to run the processor at a reduced speed, in case the higher speed causes problems with some boards or software. This is rare, so the high speed setting should normally be used.

Bus speed: PC compatibles that run at a faster speed than the IBM equivalent usually run the bus at a higher speed as well. This may cause compatibility problems. Some expansion cards won't work at high bus speeds, so a switch or jumper is usually provided to reduce the speed of the bus, typically by adding wait states.

Memory fitted: A group of switches or jumpers may be used to inform the system of how much memory is installed. Many modern systems find this for themselves.

Memory type: Some systems may have jumpers which must be set depending on the type or speed of the memory chips installed.

ROM size: Some motherboards may have the option of being supplied with different size ROMs. This should not be changed from the factory setting without good reason.

A motherboard that has on-board I/O ports, video adapter or disk controllers will probably have additional jumpers associated with these devices. The purpose of these is to disable the on-board device so that it does not conflict with another similar one mounted on an expansion card. You'll often need to disable a serial port so that a modem card – which looks to the system like another serial port – can be added. Sometimes you may want to disable an on-board video controller so that one with a higher specification can be fitted.

4.8 Memory Configuration

Setting the memory configuration on a PC compatible system can often be a source of confusion. It's impossible to give specific guidance here, as there are almost as many ways of setting up memory in a computer as there are PC manufacturers. However, a couple of points are worthy of note.

Many AT compatibles have 1Mb of RAM in two banks of 512Kb. DOS can only use 640Kb of this 1Mb, and users frequently ask if they can use the 384Kb which is unused as extended memory. Older ATs can't map blocks of RAM into different areas of the address space. Many such machines have a jumper to set whether the second 512Kb is used as base or extended memory. If it is used as base memory, only 128Kb of that memory can be used, to make the base memory up to 640Kb. The rest occupies address space which overlaps that reserved for use by video adapters, ROMs and so on, and is inaccessible to the system. If the jumper setting is changed to map the whole of that 512Kb into the extended memory area, only 512Kb of base memory will be available. This frustrating inability to use the RAM in the system to its best advantage is a characteristic of older AT compatibles which the introduction of new enhanced logic chip sets has now overcome.

Some PCs use jumpers to tell the system how much system board memory is present. An error will occur if this is set to a higher figure than the actual memory installed. While it might seem silly to set the jumpers to *less* than the memory installed, in some circumstances there is a very good reason for this. If an expanded memory board is fitted, it can be used for multi-tasking by a software package such as Desqview. Programs can be swapped into base memory – where they can run, from expanded memory – where they are stored. If as much motherboard memory as possible is disabled, the expanded memory board can be used instead to *backfill* the base memory area up to the limit of 640Kb. This lets the hardware on the expanded memory board swap in and out large blocks of base memory, which improves multi-tasking performance.

4.9 CMOS Setup for AT Compatibles

The IBM AT and compatibles have a real-time clock fitted on the motherboard as standard. This is different from the real-time clock often provided in many XT compatibles. The AT clock uses a Motorola MC146818 chip. Besides the clock, this chip contains 64 bytes of RAM. The MC146818 is a *complementary metal oxide semiconductor* (CMOS) chip, which takes just a few microamps of current. This enables it to run for years on a single battery. Consequently, it can keep time and retain information stored in its RAM, even while the machine is switched off.

Ten bytes of the CMOS RAM are used to hold the current date and time and an alarm time. The remaining bytes are used to hold information about the system, such as the amount of memory present and the type of disk drives fitted. This information is usually entered using the Setup or Diagnostics program provided with the machine. The PC uses a checksum to ensure that the data in the CMOS RAM is valid. If the data is invalid, or has become corrupt, the system will not run. The PC will only recognise the existence of disk drives or memory if they are correctly specified in CMOS.

Normally, you'll need to set up the CMOS RAM the first time a machine is used, whenever a change to the configuration is made, or after the back-up battery has been replaced. Occasionally, a machine loses its CMOS configuration for no obvious reason. A power fluctuation or static electricity spike is frequently blamed. When this happens, you'll see a warning message on boot-up saying that the equipment installed does not match the details held in CMOS RAM, and that the Setup program should be run.

On some PCs, no error will be reported, but the system won't recognise the existence of the hard disk or any extended memory. When this happens, it's a nuisance. Often, you can't remember how much memory the machine has, or what the hard disk type number is. Much time and effort is wasted solving what should be a trivial problem.

```
1200 REM ==== LISTING 4.2 - CMOS SETUP UTILITY ====
1205 DIM C%(64)
1210 GOSUB 1600: REM get current setup
1220 GOSUB 1800: REM display it
1230 GOSUB 1500: REM display menu
1240 IF A$="E" OR A$="e" THEN GOSUB 1400: GOTO 1220
1242 IF A$="R" OR A$="r" THEN GOSUB 1700: GOTO 1220
1246 IF A$="S" OR A$="s" THEN GOSUB 1650: GOTO 1220
1248 IF A$="W" OR A$="w" THEN GOSUB 1750: GOTO 1210
1250 END
1400 REM ==== Edit date/time ====
1403 LOCATE 22,1: INPUT "Enter time - HH:",A$
1406 C%(5)=VAL("&H"+A$)
1408 LOCATE 22,21: INPUT " MM:",A$
1410 C%(3)=VAL("&H"+A$)
1412 LOCATE 22,29: INPUT " SS:",A$
1414 C%(1)=VAL("&H"+A$)
1420 LOCATE 23,1: INPUT "Enter date - DD:",A$
1422 C%(8)=VAL("&H"+A$)
1424 LOCATE 23,21: INPUT " MM:",A$
1426 C%(9)=VAL("&H"+A$)
1428 LOCATE 23,29: INPUT " YY:",A$
1430 C%(10)=VAL("&H"+A$)
1432 S%=0
1434 RETURN
1500 REM ==== Display menu ====
1510 LOCATE 25, 1
1520 PRINT "[R]ead from disk  [S]ave to disk  [W]rite to CMOS  [E]dit date/time  e[X]it";
1534 A$=INKEY$: IF A$="" THEN 1534
1536 IF A$="E" OR A$="R" OR A$="S" OR A$="W" OR A$="X" THEN 1550
1538 IF A$="e" OR A$="r" OR A$="s" OR A$="w" OR A$="x" THEN 1550
1540 GOTO 1534
1550 RETURN
1600 REM ==== Get CMOS contents ====
1610 C$="Current CMOS settings": S%=10
1620 FOR I%=0 TO 63: OUT 112,I%: C%(I%+1)=INP(113): NEXT I%
1630 RETURN
1650 REM ==== Save CMOS contents ====
1652 LOCATE 22, 1
1655 INPUT "Enter filename   : ",F$
1660 INPUT "Enter description: ",C$
```

```
1665 OPEN F$ FOR OUTPUT AS #1
1670 PRINT #1,C$
1675 FOR I%=0 TO 63: PRINT #1,C%(I%+1): NEXT I%
1680 CLOSE #1
1690 RETURN
1700 REM ==== Load data from file ====
1702 ON ERROR GOTO 1730: S%=10
1705 LOCATE 22, 1: INPUT "Enter filename    : ",F$
1710 OPEN F$ FOR INPUT AS #1
1715 INPUT #1,C$
1720 FOR I%=0 TO 63: INPUT #1,C%(I%+1): NEXT I%
1725 FOR I%=1 TO 6: C%(I%)=0: NEXT I%
1728 GOTO 1740
1730 PRINT "File not found. Press any key"
1732 C$=INKEY$: IF C$="" THEN 1732
1735 RESUME 1745
1740 ON ERROR GOTO 0
1742 CLOSE #1
1745 RETURN
1750 REM ==== Write data to CMOS ====
1760 FOR I%=S% TO 63: OUT 112,I%: OUT 113,C%(I%+1): NEXT I%
1770 RETURN
1800 REM ==== Display CMOS contents ====
1810 I%=C%(1): GOSUB 1950: SS%=I%: REM Time (seconds)
1811 I%=C%(3): GOSUB 1950: MM%=I%: REM Time (minutes)
1812 I%=C%(5): GOSUB 1950: HH%=I%: REM Time (hours)
1813 I%=C%(8): GOSUB 1950: DD%=I%: REM Date (day)
1814 I%=C%(9): GOSUB 1950: MN%=I%: REM Date (month)
1815 I%=C%(10): GOSUB 1950: YY%=I%: REM Date (year)
1820 MB%=C%(22)+C%(23)*256
1821 MX%=C%(24)+C%(25)*256
1825 DA%=INT(C%(17)/16): DB%=C%(17)-DA%*16: REM Diskettes A: and B:
1830 D0%=C%(26): REM Hard drive 0
1831 D1%=C%(27): REM Hard drive 1
1840 CLS
1841 PRINT ,"AT CMOS Setup Utility": PRINT
1842 PRINT ,C$: PRINT
1850 PRINT " Time:",,RIGHT$(STR$(HH%+100),2);":";RIGHT$(STR$(MM%+100),2);
":";RIGHT$(STR$(SS%+100),2)
1852 PRINT " Date:",,RIGHT$(STR$(DD%+100),2);"/
";RIGHT$(STR$(MN%+100),2);"/";RIGHT$(STR$(YY%+100),2)
1854 PRINT " Base memory size:",MB%;"K bytes"
1856 PRINT " Extended memory size:",MX%;"K bytes"
1858 PRINT " Diskette drive A:",: I%=DA%: GOSUB 1990
1860 PRINT " Diskette drive B:",: I%=DB%: GOSUB 1990
1862 PRINT " Hard disk 0:",,: I%=D0%: GOSUB 1980
1864 PRINT " Hard disk 1:",,: I%=D1%: GOSUB 1980
1880 RETURN
1950 REM == Convert BCD to decimal ===
1952 I%=I%-INT(I%/16)*16+INT(I%/16)*10
1954 RETURN
```

```
1980 REM == Print hard disk type ==
1981 IF I%=0 THEN PRINT "Not installed" ELSE PRINT I%
1989 RETURN
1990 REM == Print diskette type ==
1991 IF I%=0 THEN PRINT "Not installed"
1992 IF I%=1 THEN PRINT "5$^1/_4$' 360Kb DS/DD"
1993 IF I%=2 THEN PRINT "5$^1/_2$' 1.2Mb DS/HD"
1994 IF I%=3 THEN PRINT "3$^1/_2$' 720Kb DS/DD"
1995 IF I%=4 THEN PRINT "3$^1/_2$' 1.44Mb DS/HD"
1996 IF I%>4 THEN PRINT "unknown"
1998 RETURN
```

A solution to this problem is provided by the program in Listing 4.2. It's a simple utility that allows the setup data to be read from the non-volatile RAM and saved to a disk file. If the CMOS has an attack of amnesia, the settings can be retrieved from the disk file and restored to the system.

```
              AT CMOS Setup Utility

              Current CMOS settings

Time:                 20:47:27
Date:                 09/10/91
Base memory size:     640 K bytes
Extended memory size: 3200 K bytes
Diskette drive A:     3½' 1.44Mb DS/HD
Diskette drive B:     5¼' 1.2Mb DS/HD
Hard disk 0:          47
Hard disk 1:          Not installed




[R]ead from disk  [S]ave to disk  [W]rite to CMOS  [E]dit date/time  e[X]it
```

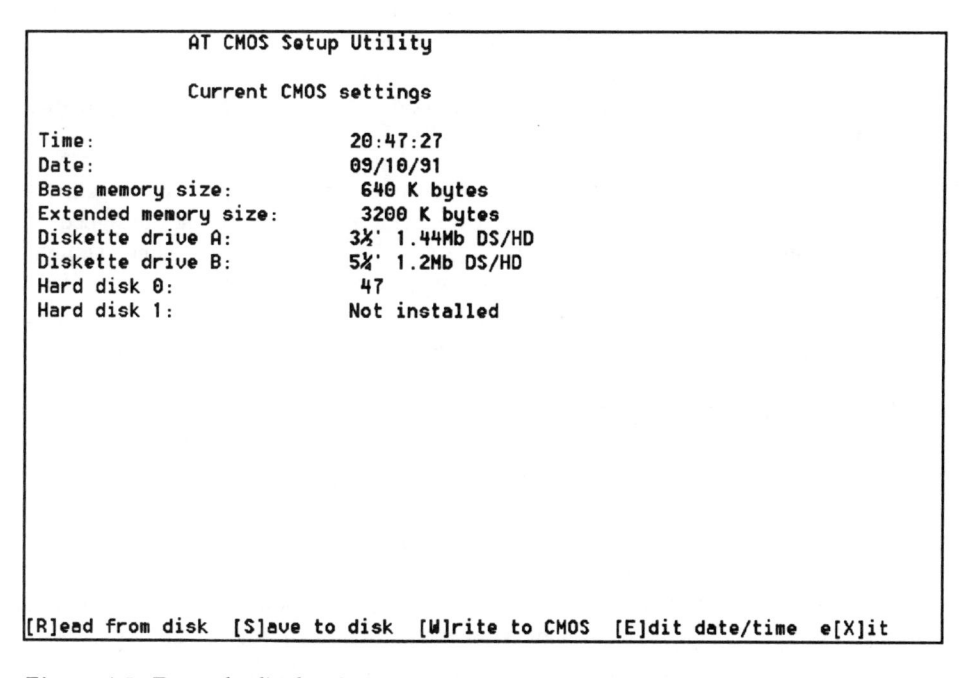

Figure 4.5: Example display from Listing 4.2

When the program is loaded, the current CMOS contents are displayed, as in the example in Figure 4.5. The date and time shown are correct at the instant the program was loaded. A menu containing five options is displayed at the foot of the screen.

If S is selected, the CMOS contents are saved to a disk file. You are prompted for a filename, which should be a full pathname. You can also enter a description. This will be useful if CMOS backups for several different machines are held on the same disk. You should store the files, the program and GWBASIC.EXE on diskette, not the hard disk, since if the contents of the CMOS are lost, the hard disk will be inaccessible.

If R is chosen, you are prompted for a filename, and the data is then loaded from the specified file. The time is zeroed, but the date shown is that when the file was written. This should help you tell if the data is still valid. You may have added extra memory, for example, and not updated the CMOS backup.

The E option is used to set the date and time. The program will prompt for the hours, minutes and seconds, and the day, month and year. The Enter key should be pressed after each one. To write the data into the CMOS RAM, use the W option. After updating the CMOS configuration, reboot the system so the new values can come into effect.

If a PC which has a built-in SETUP in ROM loses its configuration, the machine may insist that SETUP is entered when an error is found. In this situation, the built-in routine can be used to tell the machine that it has a single floppy drive and some base memory. Then reboot it from diskette, run Listing 4.2, and load the full configuration settings from the backup file.

If you use the manufacturer's setup disk to reconfigure or restore the CMOS settings of a PC that has data on its hard disk, be careful. Some setup disks are designed to give a fully automatic set-up of a new machine. I've found several that launch straight into formatting and partitioning the hard drive after the CMOS has been set. This process is usually controlled by an AUTOEXEC.BAT file on the disk itself. So check, and if necessary, delete the batch file to avoid the chance of accidents occurring.

4.10 ROM Shadowing

Most of the latest chip sets support the ability to shadow the system ROMs. This is usually an option in SETUP. Shadowing means that the contents of the ROM are copied into RAM at start-up and then run from there. The reason is one of speed. Read-only memory has a much slower access time than random-access memory. Consequently, when the system is running code in ROM – such as the BIOS routines – the processor must execute extra wait states while the system fetches the instructions and places them on the data bus. If ROM shadowing is used, whenever the CPU executes a routine held in ROM, the instructions are read from RAM instead. This means that the CPU receives the instructions at the speed of RAM, rather than the slower ROM.

Whether the increase in performance is noticeable depends very much on what the system is doing. RAM is typically twice as fast as ROM, so the execution speed of BIOS routines – including the EGA or VGA BIOS – may be doubled. However in most applications, only a tiny fraction of the total processing time is spent in BIOS functions. For many users, the only noticeable effects of ROM shadowing are to make DIR listings scroll up the screen too quickly to read, and to reduce the length of the PC's beep!

If you shadow your ROM, you are reducing the RAM available for extended memory. On some machines, that can cause some confusion the first time you select the option. If you have an A.M.I. BIOS, the SETUP routine will automatically subtract the RAM used to shadow the ROM from the amount allocated to extended memory.

The Phoenix BIOS SETUP doesn't do this. Not only that, but it doesn't tell you how much RAM you've used to shadow the ROM, so you can't do the sum yourself. What usually happens is that you exit SETUP, the system reboots, and almost immediately reports a memory size error. If this happens to you, don't worry. Go straight back into SETUP and the system will reset the memory size to the amount of memory it found. Exit SETUP again, and this time, when the system reboots, the memory size will be correct.

4.11 Fitting Expansion Cards

Adding a device to a PC compatible usually entails fitting an expansion card into a slot on the motherboard. There are two things to be considered when fitting a card: physical constraints and hardware conflicts.

Generally, a card will work in any of the expansion slots, though a 16-bit card must be placed in a 16-bit slot. However, older cards may cause problems. One is the size of the mounting bracket. The original IBM PC had only five expansion slots. The spacing between them was much wider than that used in the XT, AT and compatible systems. Cards intended for use in a PC have brackets almost a quarter of an inch wider than those used on all present-day cards. Consequently, an IBM PC expansion card will not fit into an XT, AT or compatible unless the bracket is changed for a later, narrower type.

Expansion slot 8 on an IBM XT – the one nearest the power supply – cannot be used unless the expansion card is able to provide a *card selected* signal, and adheres to stricter timing standards. This slot was designed for a special card in a model called the IBM 3270 PC. The installation instructions supplied with many adapter cards may state that they cannot be used in this slot. The restriction does not apply to the PC AT or other manufacturer's PC compatibles.

The IBM AT had a taller case than the PC and XT, and some expansion cards designed for it extend about 2cm above the top of the mounting bracket. Most compatible systems do not have this extra height above the expansion slots, and so are not able to accept such expansion cards.

Some cards, such as modems or hardcards, have a casing that takes up much more space on either side of the slot than a standard card would need. Others have connectors which may foul an adjacent card. Disk controllers and others must be fitted where the cables can reach the disk drives. All these considerations affect the slot in which a card may be located. If you're fitting a hardcard in a position which is a bit of a tight squeeze, check that the sharp ends of component leads on the solder side of an expansion card do not short out on the hardcard's metal casing. Neither should ribbon cables be placed where they may chafe against sharp objects. In time, this could cut through the insulation, causing a short circuit and probable malfunction of the equipment.

Some 8-bit cards extend below the level of the expansion connector in the area beyond the edge connector itself. This would foul on the additional connector of a 16-bit slot, and precludes its fitting in such a slot. It is also possible that the card could foul other components on the motherboard.

A 16-bit expansion card – one that has an additional, shorter edge connector beyond the standard one – should normally only be fitted in an AT class system, and should occupy a 16-bit slot. There are exceptions, however. Many 16-bit VGA display adapters can detect which type of slot they are in, and will work in 8-bit mode if necessary. Such cards may therefore be used in XT class machines, or in 8-bit slots in an AT. There are sometimes valid reasons for doing this, as we shall see later.

4.12 Card Conflicts

Before you install an expansion card in a PC compatible, you should check that none of the I/O port addresses, hardware IRQ lines, DMA channels and memory-mapped regions it needs are used by other devices in the system. It is impossible for two devices to be active in the system and both use the same resource. In fact, unless the card is designed in a certain way, two should not even be installed at the same time if they are configured to use the same resource. Since it's easy to forget what's inside a box after a while, it's a good idea to maintain a configuration record sheet. This is a form on which is recorded details of how the machine is set up, what expansion cards are present and what resources they use. An example of a configuration record is shown in Figure 4.6.

If you don't have a configuration record, you'll need to check out each expansion card individually, to see what resources are being used. Software utilities such as Machinfo, Check It, System Sleuth and Norton SYSINFO can often help here. An example of the output from Machinfo, showing an interrupt vector map, is shown in Figure 4.7. If you don't have any suitable utilities, you can use the two BASIC programs presented in Listings 4.3 and 4.4. These will help identify the IRQ lines and I/O ports that are used.

The Motherboard and Expansion Bus 67

```
╔══════════════════════════════════════════════════════════════╗
║              P C   C o n f i g u r a t i o n   R e c o r d   ║
╚══════════════════════════════════════════════════════════════╝
```

User Name:	Location:
Make/Model:	Serial Number:
Processor: Speed: MHz	Memory - Base: Ext: Exp:
Diskette drives:	Monitor type:
Hard disk: Mb DOS version:	Partitions - C: D: E: F:
Model: Type: MFM/RLL/IDE/ESDI/SCSI [Bad tracks recorded overleaf]		
Low level info: Cyl: Hd: SPT: WPC: RWC: LZ:		

I/O and Expansion Details

Maths Co-processor:

COM1:   COM2:   COM3:   COM4:

LPT1:   LPT2:   LPT3:

Resource Utilisation

MEMORY MAP	IRQ	Usage
1000	2	
	3	
	4	
	5	
	6	
F000	7	
	10	
	11	
E000	12	
	13	
	14	
	15	
D000		

I/O Ports

```
200-207  208-20F  300-307  308-30F
210-217  218-21F  310-317  318-31F
220-227  228-22F  320-327  328-32F
230-237  238-23F  330-337  338-33F
240-247  248-24F  340-347  348-34F
250-257  258-25F  350-357  358-35F
260-267  268-26F  360-367  368-36F
270-277  278-27F  370-377  378-37F
280-287  288-28F  380-387  388-38F
290-297  298-29F  390-397  398-39F
2A0-2A7  2A8-2AF  3A0-3A7  3A8-3AF
2B0-2B7  2B8-2BF  3B0-3B7  3B8-3BF
2C0-2C7  2C8-2CF  3C0-3C7  3C8-3CF
2D0-2D7  2D8-2DF  3D0-3D7  3D8-3DF
2E0-2E7  2E8-2EF  3E0-3E7  3E8-3EF
2F0-2F7  2F8-2FF  3F0-3F7  3F8-3FF
```

Memory	DMA	Usage
C000	1	
	2	Diskette Ctrller
	3	
B000	5	
	6	
	7	
A000		

Notes

Figure 4.6: A PC configuration record sheet

```
┌─ Interrupt vector table ─────────────────────────────────────────────┐
│                                                                      │
│  Interrupt                                                           │
│  Nr   Address     Description             Owner                     │
│                                                                      │
│  00   13A7:0110   Divide by Zero          A:\PCINFO\DOSINFO.EXE     │
│  01   0070:06F4   Single Step                                        │
│  02   0772:0016   Nonmaskable (NMI)       IBMDOS.COM/MSDOS.SYS      │
│  03   0070:06F4   Breakpoint trap                                    │
│  04   0070:06F4   Overflow trap                                      │
│  05   08CD:01B5   Print Screen            C:\UTILS\MISC\PINCH.COM   │
│  06   F000:EB52   Reserved                BIOS                       │
│  07   F000:EAA6   Reserved                BIOS                       │
│  08   0772:003C   IRQ0 Timer Tick         IBMDOS.COM/MSDOS.SYS      │
│  09   07F4:0104   IRQ1 Keyboard           Unknown owner              │
│  0A   0772:0057   IRQ2 I/O channel        IBMDOS.COM/MSDOS.SYS      │
│  0B   0772:006F   IRQ3 Com2               IBMDOS.COM/MSDOS.SYS      │
│  0C   0772:0087   IRQ4 Com1               IBMDOS.COM/MSDOS.SYS      │
│  0D   0772:009F   IRQ5 Fixed disk         IBMDOS.COM/MSDOS.SYS      │
│  0E   0772:00B7   IRQ6 Diskette           IBMDOS.COM/MSDOS.SYS      │
│  0F   0070:06F4   IRQ7 Printer                                       │
│                                                                      │
│  <esc>=exit                                               <PageDwn>  │
├──────────────────────────────────────────────────────────────────────┤
│ (c) COPR. AME '88/89/90, Display DOS Information v0.9  Wed Oct 09 1991 20:21 │
└──────────────────────────────────────────────────────────────────────┘
```

Figure 4.7: MACHINFO display showing interrupt vector map

```
IRQ 0  - System Timer         - Active
IRQ 1  - Keyboard             - Active
IRQ 2  - Slave PIC            - Active
IRQ 3  - Serial COM2          - Inactive
IRQ 4  - Serial COM1          - Inactive
IRQ 5  - Parallel LPT2        - Inactive
IRQ 6  - Diskette             - Active
IRQ 7  - Parallel LPT1        - Inactive
IRQ 8  - Real-time clock      - Inactive
IRQ 9  - Redirected IRQ2      - Active
IRQ 10 - (Reserved)           - Inactive
IRQ 11 - (Reserved)           - Inactive
IRQ 12 - (Reserved)           - Inactive
IRQ 13 - Maths coprocessor    - Inactive
IRQ 14 - Hard disk            - Active
IRQ 15 - (Reserved)           - Inactive
Ok
─
```

Figure 4.8: Example display from Listing 4.3

```
1100 REM ==== LISTING 4.3 - TEST IRQ ACTIVATION ====
1105 DEF SEG=&HF000: E0%=PEEK(&HFFFE): AT%=0
1107 IF E0%=248 THEN AT%=1
1108 IF E0%=252 THEN AT%=1
1120 I%=INP(&H21)
1130 FOR N%=0 TO 7
1131 PRINT "IRQ";N%;" - ";
1132 J%=INT(I%/2)
1133 GOSUB 1160
1134 I%=J%
1135 NEXT N%
1138 IF AT%=0 THEN 1158
1140 I%=INP(&HA1)
1150 FOR N%=8 TO 15
1151 PRINT "IRQ";N%;" - ";
1152 J%=INT(I%/2)
1153 GOSUB 1160
1154 I%=J%
1155 NEXT N%
1158 END
1160 IF N%=0 THEN PRINT "System Timer",
1161 IF N%=1 THEN PRINT "Keyboard",
1162 IF N%=2 THEN IF AT%=0 THEN PRINT "(Reserved)", ELSE PRINT "Slave
PIC",
1163 IF N%=3 THEN PRINT "Serial COM2",
1164 IF N%=4 THEN PRINT "Serial COM1",
1165 IF N%=5 THEN IF AT%=0 THEN PRINT "Hard Disk", ELSE PRINT "Parallel
LPT2",
1166 IF N%=6 THEN PRINT "Diskette",
1167 IF N%=7 THEN PRINT "Parallel LPT1",
1168 IF N%=8 THEN PRINT "Real-time clock",
1169 IF N%=9 THEN PRINT "Redirected IRQ2",
1170 IF N%=10 THEN PRINT "(Reserved)",
1171 IF N%=11 THEN PRINT "(Reserved)",
1172 IF N%=12 THEN PRINT "(Reserved)",
1173 IF N%=13 THEN PRINT "Maths coprocessor",
1174 IF N%=14 THEN PRINT "Hard disk",
1175 IF N%=15 THEN PRINT "(Reserved)",
1176 IF I%=J%+J% THEN PRINT "- Active" ELSE PRINT "- Inactive"
1178 RETURN
```

Listing 4.3 shows the IRQ lines which are active – a sample output is shown in Figure 4.8. It works by examining the contents of the interrupt controller's interrupt mask register to see what interrupts are currently enabled. There is a flaw in this approach – which affects all such diagnostic programs – that can result in some IRQs going undetected.

Hardware interrupts that aren't used by DOS are not enabled when the system is started up. Also, well-behaved programs which enable interrupts when they are loaded should disable them again when they terminate. So the IRQ line used by a network card whose driver is permanently loaded will be detected by Listing 4.3. However, a tape streamer that is only activated when the back-up software is run may not show up in the listing.

It's only possible for software to tell if an interrupt is used if it is actually enabled. If your backup software or whatever has a shell-to-DOS facility, you can try running the BASIC program from within the shell. Any interrupts enabled by that software should then be visible. Otherwise, you'll have no choice but to take the covers off and check manually what is inside the machine.

```
2000 REM ==== LISTING 4.4 - TEST I/O PORTS ====
2002 DIM R(4)
2004 GOSUB 2070
2010 FOR I%=256 TO 1023 STEP 8
2012 L%=0
2014 FOR J%=0 TO 7
2015 K%=INP(I%+J%)
2016 IF K%<>R(1) AND K%<>R(2) AND K%<>R(3) AND K%<>R(4) THEN L%=1
2018 NEXT J%
2020 IF L%=0 THEN 2028
2022 PRINT "Range ";HEX$(I%);" to ";HEX$(I%+7);" used - ";
2024 GOSUB 2040
2028 NEXT I%
2030 END
2040 IF I%=496 THEN PRINT "AT hard disk controller": GOTO 2060
2041 IF I%=512 THEN PRINT "Game port": GOTO 2060
2042 IF I%=632 THEN PRINT "Parallel port 2": GOTO 2060
2043 IF I%>=688 AND I%<736 THEN PRINT "EGA/VGA adapter (alternate)": GOTO 2060
2044 IF I%=760 THEN PRINT "Serial port 2": GOTO 2060
2045 IF I%=800 THEN PRINT "XT hard disk controller": GOTO 2060
2046 IF I%=888 THEN PRINT "Parallel port 1": GOTO 2060
2047 IF I%=896 OR I%=928 THEN PRINT "Bisynchronous comms": GOTO 2060
2048 IF I%=944 THEN PRINT "MDA adapter": GOTO 2060
2049 IF I%=952 THEN PRINT "Parallel port": GOTO 2060
2050 IF I%>=960 AND I%<976 THEN PRINT "EGA or VGA adapter": GOTO 2060
2051 IF I%>=976 AND I%<992 THEN PRINT "CGA or VGA adapter": GOTO 2060
2052 IF I%=1008 THEN PRINT "Diskette controller": GOTO 2060
2053 IF I%=1016 THEN PRINT "Serial port 1": GOTO 2060
2059 PRINT "(unknown)"
2060 RETURN
2070 REM == test values returned from unused locations ==
2072 FOR I%=0 TO 3
2073 R(I%+1)=INP(&H120 + I%): REM assume ports 120 -123 unused
2074 NEXT I%
2075 RETURN
```

Listing 4.4 is a program that displays the I/O ports that are present in a system. It relies on the fact that if a non-existent port is read then a constant value – usually FF (hex) – is returned. I've found that some systems occasionally return different values when an unused port is read.

The program reads four locations at 120 – 123 (hex) – which are normally unused – to see what values are obtained. The I/O port area from 100 to 3FF (hex) is then tested, and any addresses that return a value different from those found at 120 – 123 are assumed to be actual I/O ports. The program prints each block of eight addresses in which one or more ports appear to be used, together with a description of the standard device that usually occupies that location. An example display is shown in Figure 4.9. This shows the ports used by a scanner (at 270 – 277 hex) and a tape streamer (at 300 to 307 hex) besides the standard devices found in most systems.

```
Range 1F0 to 1F7 used - AT hard disk controller
Range 200 to 207 used - Game port
Range 270 to 277 used - (unknown)
Range 2F8 to 2FF used - Serial port 2
Range 300 to 307 used - (unknown)
Range 378 to 37F used - Parallel port 1
Range 3B0 to 3B7 used - MDA adapter
Range 3B8 to 3BF used - Parallel port
Range 3C0 to 3C7 used - EGA or VGA adapter
Range 3C8 to 3CF used - EGA or VGA adapter
Range 3D0 to 3D7 used - CGA or VGA adapter
Range 3D8 to 3DF used - CGA or VGA adapter
Range 3F0 to 3F7 used - Diskette controller
Range 3F8 to 3FF used - Serial port 1
Ok
```

Figure 4.9: Example display from Listing 4.4

Listing 4.4 may not work reliably on all systems. If large numbers of *unknown* devices are reported then suspect the program, not the PC. And if all I/O ports in a block of eight return the same value as a non-existent port, the block will remain undetected by the program. Reading from an I/O port can sometimes alter its contents, so there's a slight chance that if the program is run while a network connection or other background I/O process is active, an error may occur.

If two cards try to use the same IRQ line, I/O port or DMA channel the system will probably crash and you'll have to cold boot it to restart. Cards which use an area of memory above 640Kb can also be a problem. The memory areas used by display adapters are well documented but communications and network cards may also occupy an area of the memory map, and there is not a great range of free space to choose from.

Conflicts can occur with other cards, with the system – which may have a ROM in that part of the memory map – or with a memory manager, which may be using the area for EMS page frames. In one case where such a conflict occurred, a network card was using an area of memory that was also being used by an expanded memory manager. The network connection functioned quite happily, but parts of the user's spreadsheet were being corrupted.

A more subtle type of conflict can occur if both 8- and 16-bit cards are present in a machine. Since AT class machines may contain either type of card, the bus controller has to decide, for every bus I/O operation, whether a 16-bit data transfer is appropriate or not. When a memory access is about to take place, the bus controller sends an advance warning of which area of memory the data transfer is intended for. If a 16-bit card is resident in that area, it signals its presence, so that the system knows to handle the transfer 16 bits at a time, rather than 8.

The problem is that the advance warning only specifies the memory area to the nearest 128K bytes. In terms of the memory map above 640K, this means that there are only three distinguishable regions: segments A000 – BFFF, C000 – DFFF and E000 to FFFF. The area from A000 to BFFF is taken up by display adapter memory, the EGA or VGA adapter ROM occupies the start of the second area, while the system ROM BIOS resides within the region E000 to FFFF.

To see what happens, consider the situation in which a 16-bit VGA card has a ROM in the area C000 – C7FF, and an 8-bit network card uses an area D000 – D3FF. When the system wishes to transfer some data to the network card, it signals that it is about to address the 128K segment C000 – DFFF. The VGA adapter, unable to tell that the data is not destined for it, signals that it would like a 16-bit data transfer, please. The bus then sends out the data 16 bits at a time, The network card can't deal with this, and so the system crashes.

This scenario is a potential problem in any situation where 8- and 16-bit cards have ROM or RAM that co-resides in the same 128K byte segment of memory. Many VGA cards have an auto-sensing function. They will try to avoid this problem by switching to 8-bit operation if a conflict is detected. However, auto-sensing is not infallible. If this type of conflict is causing a problem, try manually configuring the VGA card to 8-bit operation using a jumper (if provided), or else try installing it in an 8-bit expansion slot.

The other thing you should consider if an expansion card won't work in a particular

PC is bus compatibility. This is not, strictly speaking, a problem of conflicts. Most PC compatibles run the CPU at a higher clock speed than the 8MHz used in the IBM AT. Many older, poorly designed clones run the bus at the same speed. Some expansion cards simply won't work at the higher speed. The solution here is to reduce the clock speed; a jumper or DIP switch is usually provided. This problem is less common today as modern PC designs run the bus at the *standard* speed independent of the clock rate of the CPU.

4.13 Upgrading Memory

A PC or compatible can have up to 640Kb of base memory directly accessible under DOS. Beyond that, there are two ways in which extra memory may be fitted. You can add expanded memory, using an expanded memory board that plugs into an expansion slot. Alternatively if the machine is an AT, you can add extended memory. You can do this either by installing additional memory chips on the motherboard or, if no memory sockets are provided, by using an extended memory board. The extended memory on many ATs can be accessed as expanded memory using a software driver, as explained in Chapter 1.

Increasing the memory on the motherboard is the simplest method of upgrading a system's memory if there are empty sockets on the board. Memory chips come in a few basic sizes. Equivalent parts to those recommended by the system board manufacturer are available from several manufacturers. For example, the following parts are 256K x 1 bit DIP chips: Fujitsu MB81256-10, Hitachi HM50256P-12, Mitsubishi M5M4256AP-10. The part number usually gives a clue to the capacity, while the suffix number is the access time in tens of nanoseconds. Don't ever use a slower speed than those recommended for – or already fitted to – the machine. If you've never installed IC chips before, the procedure is described in Chapter 12.

Some motherboards will accept a choice of chip sizes. Many ATs are supplied with 1Mb of RAM, in four rows of 256Kb chips. Special sockets allow the 16-pin 256Kbit chips to be replaced by 18-pin 1Mbit chips. If your system has these sockets then you can have 4Mb of RAM on the motherboard. The same may often be done with systems using single in-line memory modules (SIMMS). However, not all systems can be upgraded in this way. Check with the manufacturer, if in doubt, because motherboards are not all built the same way.

If extra memory is fitted, you may well have to alter some jumper settings on the motherboard. The exact nature of these settings will vary between different machines. Some systems allow different banks of memory to use different capacity chips. Others insist that all the memory chips on the board are of the same type. Whatever the case, all the chips in a memory bank (two rows of nine on a 286 or 386sx system, four rows on a 386dx or 486) must be of the same type.

Once you've installed the new memory and set the jumpers, the system can be powered up. On ATs, you'll need to run the Setup utility to change the CMOS configuration to show the new memory size. Otherwise, you won't be able to use the new memory. Once the PC is up and running again, it's a good idea to run some memory tests using a diagnostic program such as Check It, to test fully the new RAM.

Where to purchase your extra memory is a contentious issue. Currently, DRAM is cheap, but many PC manufacturers charge anything up to 10 times the price of the basic chips for memory bought through their dealers. You can save a great deal of money by shopping around. A few PC vendors attempt to prevent users from buying memory upgrades from other sources, by requiring an additional chip to be fitted, which is included as part of the official upgrade kit. However, third-party memory retailers are aware of what chips are needed to upgrade most types of PC. They can even supply detailed fitting instructions in many cases. If you specify what machine the memory is for when ordering, there is really nothing to worry about.

4.14 Performance Enhancement

As PC software becomes more sophisticated, it needs more memory and more processor power. This has led users to demand ways of upgrading the performance of their otherwise perfectly serviceable PCs. One solution is to use a speed-up card. This is a small card that plugs into the expansion bus, and has a plug on a flying lead which fits the CPU socket. This effectively replaces the existing CPU with a faster one.

These cards can be tricky to fit, because the location of the CPU on the motherboard varies, and in some machines expansion cards, disk drives and so on can get in the way. The cards are usually designed to fit an IBM XT or AT, and the fitting instructions are written accordingly. You'll probably have to improvise a little if your machine was made by someone else. Speed-up boards are not a satisfactory way of upgrading a PC since there are too many compromises, the most significant being that the system bus remains an 8-bit bus.

A better solution is to replace the complete motherboard. As component prices have fallen, this is a realistic and cost-effective option. There is a thriving market in *bare* motherboards. Almost all are manufactured in the Far East, and sold as replacements or upgrades for existing machines. Motherboards are generally sold with no memory fitted, so the cost of this should also be added. For XT clones, it is more cost-effective to replace a motherboard than to repair it if a fault develops.

Replacing a PC or XT motherboard with an 80286 or 80386 AT board not only gets you a faster processor, but faster memory, and a 16-bit AT bus as well. You can retain the existing XT peripherals, but they'll spoil the performance to some extent. Many new motherboards have serial and parallel ports built into them, but if not, the existing ports may be used without problems. The display adapter will also function quite happily in an AT, although some performance benefit could be gained by replacing it with a 16-bit card. The diskette controller can be used with no problems. The biggest performance bottleneck will be the old XT hard disk and its controller.

Using an XT hard disk – including hard cards – in an AT system is not a good idea, except as a temporary measure. For a start, the drives used in XTs are not generally all that fast. Also, the controller will of necessity be an 8-bit card. It will only be able to transfer data on to the bus one byte at a time, so data transfer rates will be much slower than they could be.

The setup procedure for the system will also be different. XT disk controllers have their own BIOS, since the system BIOS on a PC or XT does not contain the routines necessary to support a hard disk. The ROM for an XT hard disk controller usually resides at address C800:0. AT systems have hard disk support built into the system ROM, and information about the hard disk characteristics are stored in the battery-backed CMOS RAM.

You should only enter into the CMOS RAM details of hard disks that will be driven by the AT hard disk controller. Since the XT hard disk must be driven by the XT controller, its details must not be included. The CMOS entry for the drive should be set to zero, as if no hard disk is present. If it isn't, when the system is switched on, it will spend a long time waiting for a response from the non-existent AT drive, before the POST routines report a hard disk error.

4.15 Diagnosing Problems

If a PC displays error symptoms that aren't obviously attributable to a specific device, it's possible that there could be a fault in one of the system components on the motherboard. First, you should check that it isn't a configuration problem; that all expansion cards are set to unique interrupt, I/O and DMA settings and there are no conflicts. The software configuration should also be checked. If a fault occurs randomly while different programs are being run, the problem is more likely to be a hardware fault. However, don't overlook the possibility that a badly behaved TSR utility could be causing the system to crash. Temporarily clear all TSRs out of the AUTOEXEC.BAT, remove any non-essential device drivers from CONFIG.SYS, then reboot and see if the problem recurs.

Next, check that the basic physical condition of the system is healthy. Socketed ICs can gradually *creep* out of their sockets due to the action of thermal expansion and contraction. In time this can lead to intermittent contacts. All socketed chips should be firmly pressed into their sockets. This procedure should be part of preventive maintenance, and is described in Chapter 14. Also, you should ensure that all the internal cables are connected, and the expansion cards are correctly seated in the bus connectors.

If the fault is still present you'll need to run some diagnostics to try to establish the cause. If you get a POST error, this may be sufficient to identify the fault. If the machine can boot up and display a DOS prompt, run Advanced Diagnostics or a third-party product such as Check It to identify the problem.

Memory errors are one of the most common motherboard faults. Diagnostic programs check out memory by writing and then reading back different patterns of bits to each memory location. If a discrepancy is found, the address of the faulty location is displayed. IBM's Advanced Diagnostics, and some third-party products, can even identify the actual chip at fault.

Unlike IBM's diagnostics, programs like Check It are intended to be run on a variety of PC compatibles having different motherboard layouts. For it to be able to identify a faulty memory chip, Check It must be told the word length – 8-bit for an XT, 16-bit for an AT – the size of the chips used, whether the rows run from top to bottom or left to right, and at which end of each row is the parity chip. The program will then display a diagram of the RAM layout, like that shown in Figure 4.10. The diagram will not be correct for all types of PC. Some use a combination of DIP and SIMM memory.

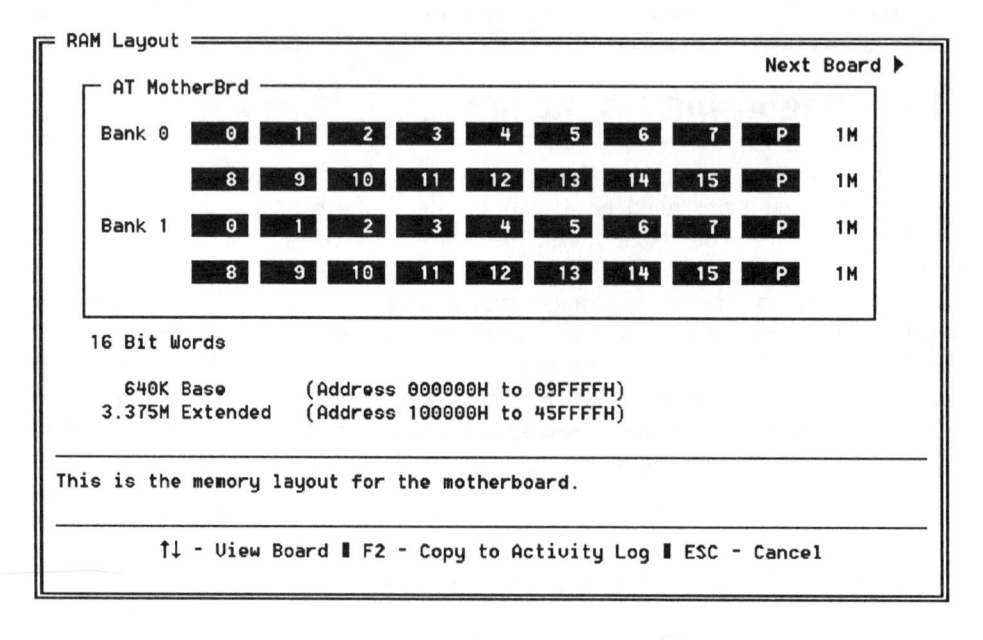

Figure 4.10: Check It RAM layout screen

Check It can test either or both base and extended memory. It can do either a quick test, or a longer one which tries several different test patterns. If required, it will run the tests repeatedly, and log the results to a disk or a printer. This is very useful for tracking down occasional, intermittent faults. The program will give the memory address of any locations in which an error is found, and will identify the chip pictorially.

When a memory error is found, you can confirm the faulty chip by swapping it with another to see if the position of the fault also changes. Sometimes a memory error can be caused by one of the IC sockets, which may have a whisker of metal or a fragment of wire that intermittently makes contact between two pins. The fault could also be in the addressing or bus control circuitry. A parity error might be due to a fault in the parity detection circuit. Swapping over two chips will help eliminate these possibilities.

Once you've identified a faulty memory chip, you'll need to replace it. If spare replacement chips aren't available, a temporary solution would be to swap the faulty chip with one taken from the highest-numbered memory bank on the board. If you do this, you'll have to reconfigure the memory allocation jumpers and memory size stored in CMOS to exclude the highest bank from use.

System faults that are possible motherboard problems are listed below. If further investigation shows that the problem may lie elsewhere in the system, you should refer to the relevant chapter for further guidance.

PC only beeps or displays POST error on power-up:

❑ Check POST message and rectify problem if possible.

❑ Check seating of socketed chips.

❑ Temporarily remove non-essential add-ins (e.g., streamer or network cards). Remove and reseat essential expansion cards, and check all interconnecting cables. If the problem is cured, replace other cards one by one, testing for correct operation each time.

System crashes:

❑ Determine circumstances of crashing: is it always with the same software? Remove unnecessary TSRs and device drivers.

❑ Check for card conflicts: IRQs, I/O ports, DMA channels, memory locations. Reconfigure if any are found.

❑ Remove and reseat expansion cards and interconnection cables.

- ❏ Run diagnostics, repeatedly if necessary, to identify hardware fault.
- ❏ Try reducing processor/bus clock speed.

System fails with Parity Error

- ❏ Run Advanced Diagnostics (or third-party diagnostics) to establish fault.
- ❏ Identify and replace faulty chip(s).

4.16 Motherboard Repair or Replacement

If you have a motherboard fault that isn't a simple memory chip replacement, curing the problem can be difficult. The diagnostics may not identify the specific component at fault, and specialised test equipment may be needed to do so. The replacement of surface-mounted components is beyond the ability of the amateur technician, so if your diagnostics identify one of these components as being at fault, you still have a problem.

If you're faced with a motherboard fault you can't repair, you have two choices. If the PC is from a good quality manufacturer, you can probably get an exchange motherboard for it. This is the solution which most professional service engineers would adopt. However, replacement motherboards can be expensive, so before ordering one, it's wise to make doubly sure that it really is the cause of the problem.

If the PC is perhaps three or more years old, the cost of an exchange motherboard may not be justified. In this case, a more practical solution would be to fit a cheap Taiwanese motherboard in its place. If you decide to adopt this approach, you must check beforehand that the chassis mounting holes, keyboard socket position, power supply connectors and other internal connections will match the replacement board. This won't be a problem with IBM XTs and ATs and most Far Eastern clones. However, some of the more up market PC compatibles won't take an alternative motherboard without a lot of extra work.

4.17 Removing the Motherboard

These are the steps you should follow to remove a motherboard from a PC:

- ❏ Power off the system.
- ❏ Remove the system unit cover.
- ❏ Remove all expansion cards, making a clear note of the location and orientation of all attached cables.

- ❏ Disconnect all flying cables from the motherboard, making a note of their location and orientation. These may include: power supply, keyboard, loudspeaker, backup battery, keylock, CPU speed switch, CPU reset switch, various front panel LEDs.
- ❏ Locate the position of the retaining screws and remove these, noting the presence of fibre insulating washers, if any.
- ❏ Slide the motherboard to the left (when viewed from the front) away from the power supply, until the stand-off pillars are free of their locating slots, then lift the board out of the system unit.

4.18 Replacing the Motherboard

These steps should be followed when replacing a motherboard:

- ❏ Place the motherboard into the system unit as far to the left as it will go. When the stand-off pillars are located in their slots, slide the board to the right. Take care to ensure that the pillars are correctly located. Do not use excessive pressure or bend the board while trying to locate the slots.
- ❏ Insert and tighten the retaining screws, using fibre insulating washers if these were originally installed.
- ❏ Attach the flying leads to their terminals on the board, checking that they are correctly oriented.
- ❏ Replace the expansion cards and attach any data cables, taking care to check that they are correctly located and oriented.
- ❏ Check that any jumpers on the board are correctly configured. For ATs, the CMOS data will need to be re-entered, if the backup battery was disconnected when the motherboard was removed.

Summary

The motherboard contains the processor and memory – the brains of the system – and the bus and associated logic which transfers data between the different parts of the system and makes them work together. Motherboards differ widely in their construction, but all carry out the same functions. Modern ones are more compact, because they use LSI chip sets. Besides reducing the component count, these chip sets often provide extra features – such as memory management – which weren't available on IBM's original machines. Many motherboards also contain peripherals such as serial and parallel ports and display adapters, which take up expansion slots on older systems.

Motherboards often require some setting-up or configuration. This is usually done using on-board jumpers. In addition, AT class systems have battery-backed CMOS memory. This is used to hold certain information about the system. The configuration must be correct or the machine will not work.

When expansion cards are fitted, you must ensure that they do not attempt to use resources used by other cards. This is a frequent cause of system malfunctions.

Extra memory may be added to a system either by fitting extra RAM chips to the motherboard, or by adding an expansion card. The memory chips must be of the correct type, and the jumper and CMOS settings may need changing to reflect the amount of memory installed.

Motherboard faults may sometimes be diagnosed by the POST routines, but diagnostics will usually be needed. If the fault is not easily repairable, it may be cheaper to replace the entire board. Many replacement motherboards are made that are compatible with IBM's even down to the mounting holes and external connections used. These low-cost boards can be used either as replacement parts or performance upgrades for older machines.

5

The Keyboard

Keyboards probably suffer more wear and tear than any other part of a PC. Though they contain some electronics, this is rarely the cause of failures. Most often, keyboard problems are caused by jammed keys. These may be the result of broken springs or dirt or sticky substances impeding their free movement. Care of the keyboard, and regular preventive maintenance, will help to prevent problems from occurring.

In this chapter, you'll learn about the two different types of PC keyboard and how they work. You'll also find out how to deal with the most common keyboard faults.

5.1 Keyboard Basics

IBM PCs and compatibles are supplied with one of two main styles of keyboard. Older models, and some later XT clones, have an 83- or 84-key keyboard, with a layout like that shown in Figure 5.1.

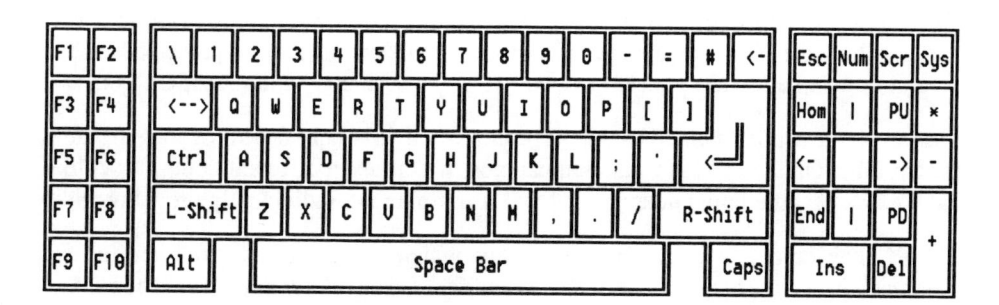

Figure 5.1: 84-key standard keyboard layout

These keyboards have the function keys in two columns at the left-hand side. Later machines have a 101- or 102-key layout, with a separate cursor key pad, and a row of function keys along the top. This layout is shown in Figure 5.2.

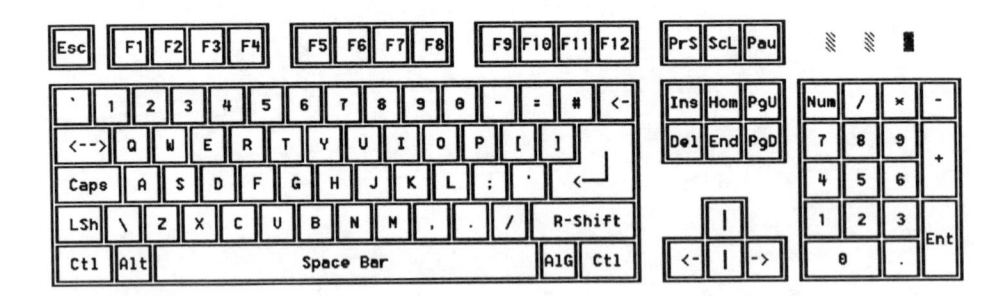

Figure 5.2: 102-key enhanced keyboard layout

The IBM PC keyboard is a sophisticated device. It has a controller chip, an Intel 8048, which watches for key movements. When one is pressed, it sends a *scan code* – a byte which identifies the position of the key – to the computer. When a key is released, a second scan code, with a value 128 greater than the original, is sent. The controller also generates an interrupt request IRQ1 with each scan code. This informs the system that a scan code has been sent, so that it can deal with it straight away. The interrupt controller translates the IRQ into interrupt 9, which is serviced by a routine in the BIOS.

The scan code identifies the actual key that was pressed, but not the ASCII value of the character generated. PC keyboards vary depending on the country in which the machine is sold. The BIOS holds a look-up table that is used to convert from the scan code number to the ASCII character value generated by that key on an American keyboard. Both numbers – the scan code and the ASCII code – are passed to the user program. Function, cursor and control keys do not have an ASCII code, so for those only the scan code is presented. The BIOS maintains a 32-byte circular type-ahead buffer, which can be used to store up to 15 key-strokes ready to be processed by the program. Each key-stroke consists of two bytes: the scan code and the ASCII code.

The keyboard is programmed to auto-repeat a key if it is held down for longer than a certain time. On the IBM AT and compatibles, which use a different controller chip – the Intel 8042 – the initial delay period and repeat rate are individually programmable.

The PC keyboard is implemented in a way which makes it easy to cater for the different key layouts used in different countries. Users of foreign – i.e., non-US – keyboards must load the program KEYB.COM or a similar utility supplied by the manufacturer. This replaces the BIOS interrupt 9 routine and ensures that the correct ASCII codes are generated for the keyboard in use.

Table 5.1: Differences between US and UK keyboards

Shift Status	Scan code	U.S. key	U.K. key
Unshifted	29h	\	#
	2Bh	'	\
Shifted	03h	@	"
	04h	#	£
	28h	"	@
	29h	|	~
	2Bh	~	|

The differences between US and UK keyboards are shown in Table 5.1. The most significant difference is the absence of the pound symbol on the US model. Keyboards intended for use in other countries – such as France and Germany – have different arrangements of the alphabetic keys, which will cause some irritation to anyone familiar with the US or UK layout.

5.2 XT and AT Keyboards

A common misconception is that keyboards with 12 function keys and a separate cursor pad are only for use with IBM ATs and compatibles, and 10 function key keyboards are for XTs. In fact, the main difference is the controller chip. XT keyboards use the 8048 chip, while those intended for use with ATs have an 8042.

An XT compatible computer will not work with an AT style keyboard, because it cannot drive the 8042 chip. However a 101-key keyboard was produced by IBM as a replacement unit for XTs. IBM ATs and compatibles may have either 84- or 102-key keyboards, although the smaller units are rare nowadays. Even laptop keyboards, which rarely have more than 84 keys, look like 102-key keyboards to the system.

Most currently produced keyboards have a slide switch that can be used to make them emulate either an XT or an AT keyboard. This must be correctly set, or an error will be reported by the system during the power-on self test routines.

Many XTs and some early AT clones may not recognise the existence of the extra function keys F11 and F12. The reason is that support for these keys was not built into the BIOS. Generally, it is possible to tell if the BIOS will support the enhanced keyboard because the system automatically turns on Num Lock when it is started up. If an enhanced keyboard is not detected, or not supported, Num Lock will be left off.

5.3 Diagnosing Problems

Keyboard problems generally fall into one of two areas: non-operation, and broken or stuck keys. The first of these faults may be caused either by a break in the connection between the keyboard and the system unit, or by a problem with the keyboard itself.

Most AT compatibles, and many more recent XTs, have a lock that disables the keyboard. This is frequently the cause of apparently failed keyboards. Either the user forgets that the system was locked, or the key has been moved so that it is not fully in the unlocked position. More unusually, a connector may have come adrift inside the case, either at the key-lock or on the motherboard.

A dead keyboard can also be caused by the switch which is used to select the XT or AT mode of operation, if this is fitted. If the switch has been moved to the incorrect position it will result in an apparent failure of the keyboard. At boot-up time, this will generate a POST error message.

The socket into which the keyboard plugs is often subject to a lot of wear and tear. Usually, this is a 5-pin DIN plug mounted directly on to the motherboard. The connections were shown in the previous chapter in Figure 4.2. Age and careless handling can result in the contacts within the DIN plug making intermittent contact with the pins of the plug. This will lead to keyboard errors being reported.

The keyboard cable should also be checked. Each wire should be tested for continuity using a volt-ohm meter and the cable replaced if suspect. If it has been subjected to undue strain, a wire may have broken away from one of the connectors. On the older IBM keyboards, a grip is used to clamp the cable where it enters the keyboard. If this has been pulled free, you'll need to remove the case and resecure it. Later keyboards use a modular jack plug like a telephone plug which fits into a socket on the case.

If all the above points have been checked, and the keyboard still doesn't work, the problem could be a fault in the keyboard itself. You can eliminate this possibility by substituting another keyboard that you know works. If this doesn't cure the problem, the fault is almost certainly within the PC system unit.

Faults which result in the non-operation of one or a group of keys are rare with the PC keyboard. If this is experienced, it could be due to a failure in the logic that decodes the row and column numbers of the keys pressed. With non-US keyboards, it could also be caused by corruption of the software keyboard driver.

The Keyboard

```
9000 REM ==== LISTING 5.1 - KEYBOARD TEST PROGRAM ====
9100 REM ==== Display scan code and character ====
9110 PRINT "Keyboard test: press Ctrl/Break to terminate"
9120 K%=INP(96): IF K%=0 OR K%>127 THEN 9120
9130 K$=INKEY$
9140 PRINT "Scan:";RIGHT$("0"+HEX$(K%),2);
9150 IF K%>53 OR K$="" THEN PRINT " Numeric/Function/Cursor key": GOTO
          9180
9160 IF ASC(K$)>=32 THEN PRINT " Character: ";K$: GOTO 9180
9170 IF ASC(K$)>1 THEN PRINT " ASCII code:";ASC(K$): GOTO 9180
9180 K$=INKEY$: L%=INP(96): IF L%=K% THEN 9180
9185 PRINT "Scan:";RIGHT$("0"+HEX$(L%),2)
9190 GOTO 9120
```

Listing 5.1 is a program that can be used to test the keyboard. It displays the scan code of a key when it is pressed, together with the ASCII value or character code, if applicable. If you run it, note that even the Shift, Alt and Control keys have scan code values of their own. Although these keys are normally only used in conjunction with other keys, this is simply the way the BIOS handles them. To exit the program, press Ctrl/Break.

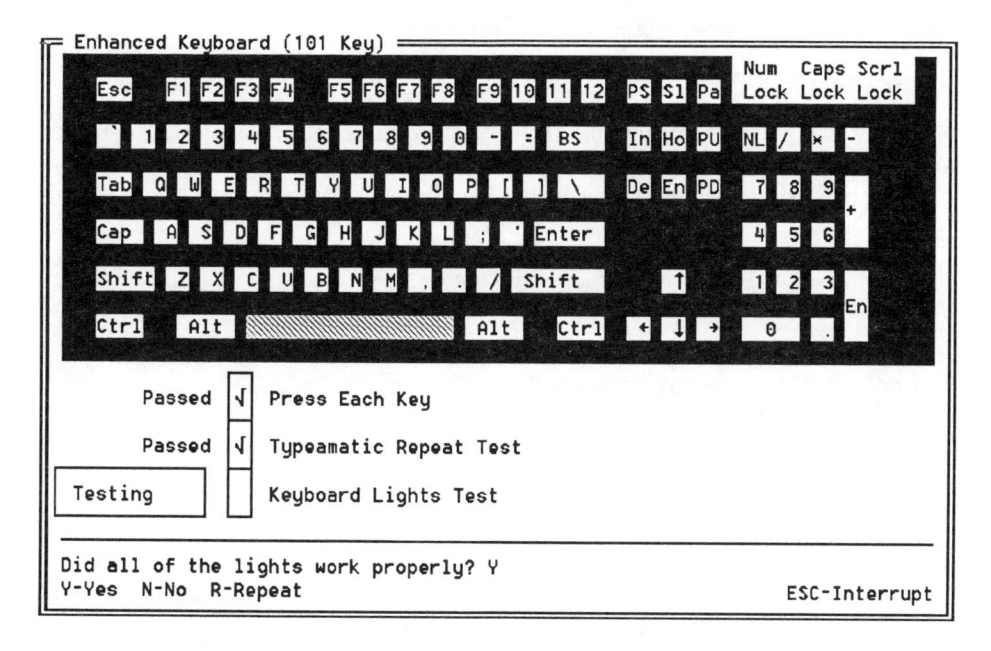

Figure 5.3: Check It keyboard test screen

Diagnostic utilities also provide routines for checking the operation of the keyboard. Check It is typical. A diagram of the keyboard is displayed on the screen, as shown in

Figure 5.3. The user must press each key in turn. The position of each key on the diagram is highlighted as it is pressed. These diagnostics can sometimes be confusing, as the layout of many keyboards differs slightly from the standard IBM US keyboard layout displayed by the program.

```
9200 REM ==== LISTING 5.2 ====
9205 REM ==== Display shift key status ====
9210 CLS: PRINT "Shift key test: press Ctrl/Break to terminate"
9220 DEF SEG=&H0
9230 K%=PEEK(&H417)
9235 LOCATE 3, 1
9240 PRINT "Right Shift  : ";: GOSUB 9250
9241 PRINT "Left Shift   : ";: GOSUB 9250
9242 PRINT "Control key  : ";: GOSUB 9250
9243 PRINT "Alt key      : ";: GOSUB 9250
9244 PRINT "Scroll Lock  : ";: GOSUB 9250
9245 PRINT "Num Lock     : ";: GOSUB 9250
9246 PRINT "Caps Lock    : ";: GOSUB 9250
9247 PRINT "Insert       : ";: GOSUB 9250
9248 GOTO 9230
9250 L%=INT(K%/2): K%=K%-(L%+L%)
9252 IF K%=0 THEN PRINT "OFF" ELSE PRINT "ON "
9254 K%=L%
9256 RETURN
```

Listing 5.2 is a program to show the status of the various shift keys on the keyboard. Run the program and then press the keys listed on the screen. The program will show on or off, pressed or released, for each shift key. Press Ctrl/Break to exit the program.

```
9300 REM ==== LISTING 5.3 ====
9305 REM ==== Test keyboard indicator lights ====
9310 CLS: PRINT "Indicator light test: press Esc to terminate"
9320 FOR I%=0 TO 7
9325 OUT 96, 237: OUT 96, I%
9330 FOR J%=0 TO 2000: NEXT J%
9332 K$=INKEY$
9335 IF K$<>"" THEN IF ASC(K$)=27 THEN 9345
9340 NEXT I%
9342 GOTO 9320
9345 OUT 96, 237: OUT 96, 0
9348 END
```

Listing 5.3 is a program that will test the LEDs on an AT style keyboard. The program will cyclically flash the LEDs on and off. Press Escape to exit this program.

Stuck or broken keys are probably the most common keyboard problem. Each key is held in the *off* position by a spring. The key switches used are designed for a life of more than 10 million operations. This is equivalent to the key being used 20 times a minute every working day for four years. Despite this, you're sure to encounter the occasional broken spring.

The usual solution for a broken keyboard is to buy a new one. Unless you're skilled at soldering, you won't be able to effect a repair. Replacement keyboards are not all that expensive anyway, compared to the time that it would take to find and repair a fault, so this is the preferred course of action for most people. Genuine IBM or Compaq keyboards are more expensive than most, but compatible Taiwanese or Korean-made units may be had from about £45 ($70 US). Some of these cheap keyboards do not have a particularly good *feel*, but it is not true that you must pay a lot to get one that is pleasant to use.

If you can solder, it is quite easy to repair keyboards with broken keys. The most difficult task is likely to be getting hold of a new part. There are dozens of different makes and models of keyboard, and the chances of finding a supplier of a key-switch that exactly matches the broken one are small. PC manufacturers treat a keyboard as a replaceable complete unit, so they won't sell you a spare part. The best source of spares, of course, is an old keyboard of a similar type. Never throw dud keyboards away.

To replace a key-switch, you'll first have to dismantle the keyboard, as described below, then remove the faulty switch. Most key-switches have six contacts soldered to the main circuit board. These should be un-soldered using the soldering iron and de-soldering braid or a solder sucker. The key-switch may then be worked loose and pulled away from the circuit board. Replacement is the reverse of this procedure. If a spare key-switch is not available, you can make an emergency repair by using the one from the Alt Gr key, which few people use.

If keys are sticking, it's probable that the movement is sticky as a result of an accumulation of dirt and spilt liquids. You'll have to clean the key-switches to restore free movement of the keys.

The diagnosis of keyboard faults is summarised below:

Non-operation of keyboard:

❑ Check key-lock.

❑ Check XT/AT switch, if present.

❑ Check keyboard cable, plugs and sockets.

❑ Check internal connections to key-lock and keyboard sockets.

❑ Check keyboard itself by substitution.

- ❏ Check system software: remove unnecessary TSRs.
- ❏ Check system unit: run diagnostics.

Intermittent or non-operation of some keys only:

- ❏ Check key-lock and cable connections.
- ❏ Check system software: remove unnecessary TSRs.
- ❏ Check keyboard using diagnostic software.
- ❏ Check keyboard by substitution.
- ❏ Possible corruption of non-US keyboard driver.

Broken or sticking keys:

- ❏ Clean or replace key-switch.
- ❏ Replace keyboard, retaining original for spares.

5.4 Dismantling and Reassembly

Dismantling the keyboard is one of the least pleasant tasks you'll ever have to carry out. The inside acts as a trap for all kinds of dust, dirt, biscuit crumbs, hair, you name it and it will all drop out when the case is opened. It's a good start, therefore, to cover the work surface with newspaper. Place the keyboard upside down on the newspaper, and undo the screws which hold the case together. You may find other screws that need to be removed to release the circuit board and key switch assembly from the base. Remove the key-tops from the individual keys. However, on IBM keyboards at least, reassembly of the space-bar is difficult, so it's best left intact. Now shake out the worst of the dust and dirt, and brush away the remainder from between the key-switches using a soft brush or mini vacuum cleaner.

If one or more keys are inclined to stick, they should be given a liberal application of electrical contact cleaner or WD-40. Work the key up and down rapidly, cleaning away any dissolved muck from the shaft and applying more lubricant if necessary. When the keys are operating reliably again, replace the key-tops and reassemble the case.

If liquid has been spilled over a keyboard, the main objective is to wash it away before it has a chance to dry and leave a sticky residue to gum up the moving parts. The recommended procedure is to wash the keyboard using copious supplies of distilled or de-mineralised water, then invert it over newspaper or a towel in a warm place and leave it for a day or so to dry out.

If you haven't got any distilled water, the question arises: should ordinary tap water be used? Strictly, the answer must be no. Tap water, particularly in hard water areas, contains impurities that could be harmful to electrical contacts. However, given the choice between leaving a keyboard covered in sticky coffee and washing it in tap water, I'd choose the latter. Use hot water from the tap, or from a kettle that has boiled and then cooled to no more than hand-hot. Dry the circuit board as quickly as possible afterwards. Allow a day or so for final drying out, as any water which seeps inside the key-switches will take longer to evaporate than that in exposed areas. Then give the whole thing a liberal application of WD-40. This is a water repellent, as well as a contact cleaner and lubricant, so it will drive out any remaining traces of damp, and clean and lubricate the key-switches.

Reassembly of the keyboard is the reverse of dismantling. Replace the key-tops, checking for free movement of all keys. Then reassemble the case, checking where appropriate that the cable is attached and secured in the cable grip.

Summary

There are two types of PC keyboard, the 83/84-key standard model with 10 function keys on the left hand side, and the 101/102-key enhanced model which has 12 along the top. However, the most important difference is the two types of keyboard controller used in XT and AT systems. They are not compatible, though many keyboards are switchable between the two.

Most keyboard faults are essentially mechanical, including broken or damaged cables and plugs. Replacement is usually the most cost-effective solution. Repair can be easy, but it is difficult to obtain new key-switches to replace broken ones. Old keyboards should therefore be retained as a source of spare parts.

6

The Display

A PC compatible display has two parts: the monitor and the display adapter. This chapter examines both these components. First, we'll look at the two main types of monitor, how they work and the faults that occur. We will also look at the different types of display adapter, what their characteristics are and the problems that may occur in use.

Over the years, several different display standards have been developed, offering a choice of monochrome or colour output, at a variety of resolutions. The modular design of the PC, with the display adapter on a plug-in card, means that the purchaser can choose the type of display that best suits his needs. Another benefit is that it is possible to upgrade older PCs to the latest specification displays. Many microcomputers that were popular at the time the IBM PC was introduced did not have that capability, which is perhaps one reason why the IBM PC design has stood the test of time.

6.1 Monitor Basics

A computer monitor contains a *cathode ray tube* (CRT), some electronics that control the CRT's electron beam, and a power supply. The principles of operation of the CRT are illustrated in Figure 6.1. It is an evacuated glass tube, roughly conical in shape, with a phosphor coating on the inside of the large, screen end, and an electron gun at the narrow end. The gun fires a narrow beam of electrons at the screen. When the beam hits the phosphor coating, light is given off.

Magnetic deflection coils, driven by the electronics inside the display, in response to signals received from the computer, cause the electron beam to scan across the phosphor-coated front of the display tube from left to right and top to bottom. This is known as *raster scanning*. The electron beam is switched on and off as it scans across the phosphor, so that it paints a pattern of dots on the screen. Each dot is called a *pixel*. The pattern of pixels makes up the image that you see on the screen.

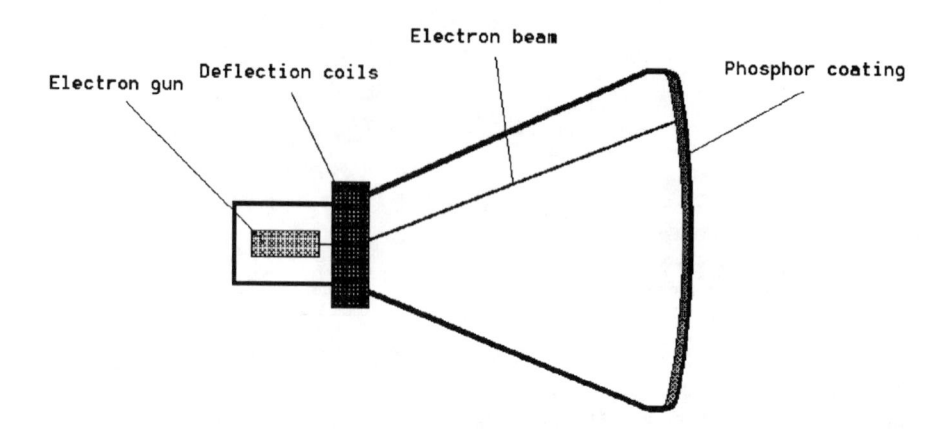

Figure 6.1: The cathode ray tube

On a standard monochrome monitor, the rate that the electron beam scans over the screen is such that the entire screen is repainted 50 times a second. The phosphor coating used has a characteristic called *persistence*, which means that it continues to radiate light after the electron beam has moved on. These two factors mean that the user sees a steady, flicker-free image on the screen.

A mono monitor needs to receive three signals to produce a display: horizontal synchronisation (HSYNC) to tell it when a scan line is about to begin, vertical synchronisation (VSYNC) to tell it when the display is going to start at the top of the screen, and VIDEO, which switches the electron beam on and off. In practice there is also a fourth signal – intensity – that selects whether the displayed dots are to be dim or bright. These signals are generated by the display adapter.

Colour monitors work on the same principles as monochrome monitors, except that there are three electron beams, one for each primary colour: red, green and blue. Because mixtures of the primary colours produce other colours – red and green will make yellow, blue and green will make cyan, all three primary colours together will make white – it is possible to produce the whole spectrum by combining varying amounts of red, green and blue.

The phosphor coating on a colour monitor consists of tiny dots of different phosphors which emit red, green or blue light when energised by the electron beams. A finely perforated metal grid called the *shadow mask* is placed just in front of the phosphor coating and ensures that the electrons from each of the three beams hit only the phosphor dots they are intended to hit, so the red electron beam only energises red phosphor dots and so on. The intensity of each of the three electron beams is separately controlled by signals from the display adapter.

Table 6.1: PC display mode characteristics

Standard	Max. Text/ (Chars)	Resolution Graphics (Pixels)	Horizontal Scan Rate (KHz)	Vertical Scan rate (Hz)	Monitor Type
MDA	80x25	-	18.432	50	TTL, Mono
HGC	80x25	720x348	18.432	50	TTL, Mono
CGA	80x25	640x200	15.750	60	TTL, Colour
EGA mono	80x43	640x350	18.430	50	TTL, Mono
EGA colour	80x43	640x350	21.850	60	TTL, Colour
VGA	80x50	640x480	31.500	60	TTL/Analogue
SuperVGA	100x40	800x600	35.200	56	Multisynch
8514/A	146x51	1024x768	35.500	43.5	Multi/Interlaced
8514/A	146x51	1024x768	56.100	70	Multisynch

The characteristics of the popular PC display modes are shown in Table 6.1. The maximum standard resolution is shown as the number of columns and rows in text mode, and the number of pixels (horizontally and vertically) in graphics mode. Note that some third-party EGA cards and most VGA cards provide higher resolutions than IBM's own display adapters. Many VGA cards can manage up to 1024 x 768 resolution.

Several factors determine whether a monitor is suitable for use with a particular display adapter. It must be capable of synchronising to the horizontal and vertical scan rates used by the adapter. The *horizontal scan rate* is the number of individual lines which the electron beam can scan in a second. The higher the resolution of the display the greater the number of scan lines that are needed to make up a complete picture. The *vertical scan rate* is the number of complete sweeps of the screen per second, otherwise known as the *refresh rate*. If this is too low, the human eye can actually detect the refreshing of the screen as an irritating flicker, particularly when the picture displayed has a light-coloured background.

At high resolutions, some display adapters use a type of scanning known as *interlacing*. Monitors which can sustain a high enough horizontal scan rate to display a picture of, for example, 1024 x 768 pixels 50 times a second, are expensive. If a lower horizontal scan rate is used, it takes longer to display a complete picture, and hence the vertical refresh rate will also drop. This leads to unacceptable flicker. The hardware overcomes this by scanning alternate lines of the picture on the first pass, then going back and filling in the missing lines on the second pass. Although the complete picture is only refreshed perhaps 40 times a second, the illusion of an 80Hz refresh rate is created, and this greatly reduces the flicker.

Another important characteristic of colour monitors is the *dot pitch*. This is the distance between the individual phosphor dots, and it effectively decides the minimum pixel size that will appear sharply displayed on the screen. It is particularly relevant for VGA monitors, since so many VGA adapters are able to support higher resolutions than standard VGA, and the dot pitch will determine whether these resolutions will be usable. For a typical high quality 14 inch VGA colour monitor, a dot pitch of 0.28mm may be found. Cheaper monitors may use larger dots with a pitch of 0.32mm. Some cheaper units may be able to synchronise to the signal at the higher resolutions supported by a display adapter, but the picture definition will be poor. Characters will seem out of focus, and the display will be tiring on the eyes.

6.2 Digital and Analogue Monitors

There are two basic types of computer monitor: digital or TTL, and analogue. Digital monitors are so called because the electrical signals from the display adapter that control what appears on the screen are digital. In other words, each signal is either on or off. TTL stands for *transistor-transistor logic*. It's an electronic term that describes the type of technology used in the monitor electronics. This determines the digital voltage levels used in the interface between the computer and the monitor. Analogue monitors are controlled using infinitely variable voltages.

The advantage of using analogue signals to control a monitor is that you can have an infinitely variable range of colours, because the signal that controls each of the red, green and blue electron guns may itself be infinitely variable. With a digital monitor you can have combinations of the three primary colours each at three levels of intensity – high, low or off. This allows a maximum of only 16 different colours to be displayed. However, the electronics inside a digital monitor are simpler and hence cheaper than for an analogue model.

Monitors generally use a 9-way D-type male connector for the signal lead. Display adapters usually have a matching 9-way female socket for TTL output signals. The analogue output from VGA adapters normally uses a 15-way D-type female socket, although all the pins are not used. Fig 6.2 gives diagrams and pin assignments of these connectors. A 9- to 15-way converter is used to convert the analogue output from the display adapter to the 9-way plug of the monitor.

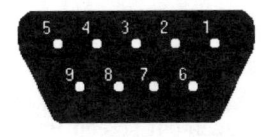

The Display 95

9-pin video connector

PIN	SIGNAL DESCRIPTION
1	Ground
2	Secondary Red
3	Primary Red
4	Primary Green
5	Primary Blue
6	Secondary Green / Intensity
7	Secondary Blue / Mono Video
8	Horizontal Sync
9	Vertical Sync

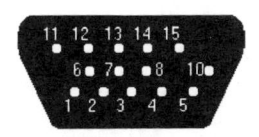

15-pin video connector

PIN	SIGNAL DESCRIPTION
1	Red Video
2	Green Video
3	Blue Video
4	Monitor ID bit 2 (not used)
5	Ground
6	Red return
7	Green return
8	Blue return
9	Key (no pin)
10	Sync return (ground)
11	Monitor ID bit 0 (not used)
12	Monitor ID bit 1 (not used)
13	Horizontal Sync
14	Vertical Sync
15	not used

Figure 6.2: Monitor connector pin assignments

6.3 Laptop Displays

The CRT monitor is too big and heavy, and consumes too much current for use in laptop computers. Instead, liquid crystal (LCD) or gas plasma displays are used. These are light, have a slim profile, and draw little current.

LCD displays are familiar for their use in digital watches and calculators. Each pixel of the display is an individual solid-state device, addressable by its row and column co-ordinates. When energised, the liquid crystal material becomes polarised (in the sense that it will only pass or reflect light of a certain polarity, like polarised spectacles) and appears dark in relation to its background. LCD displays are usually back-lit or edge-lit to improve contrast. Despite this, they are often difficult to read at an angle, or in bright sunlight.

Gas-plasma displays also use the principle of individually addressable pixels. Each pixel element is, in effect, a tiny fluorescent lamp containing a gas which glows when the cell is energised. Gas-plasma displays give a brighter and more contrasty picture than LCD, but the current needed to energise the display is much higher, and so they are most often seen in portable computers designed to be run off the mains, not batteries.

Being solid state, LCD and plasma displays are reliable and rugged. Sometimes a display driver fails. This results in one or more horizontal or vertical rows of pixels becoming either permanently dark or permanently light. A replacement screen is the only solution. Because they are so compact, and often use unorthodox construction methods, the dismantling and repair of laptops is not a task to be undertaken lightly. It is best left to a specialist.

6.4 Monitor Selection

Many monitors supplied with PCs are intended to operate at only the standard horizontal and vertical scan rates used by the display adapter in the machine. The horizontal scan rate of 15.75MHz used by the CGA was chosen because it was a standard for TV and computer monitors at the time the adapter was designed. IBM did not originally make a colour monitor, so a third-party one had to be used. The later EGA and VGA standards used special, higher frequency monitors. Many EGA monitors are switchable between 21.85MHz and 15.75MHz so that they may be used with either EGA or CGA cards. Most VGA monitors can only operate at the 31.5MHz scan rate required by the standard VGA display resolution.

To take advantage of the higher resolutions offered by most super-VGA cards, or those offering 8514/A or even XGA compatibility, a multi-synch monitor is needed. This is a monitor with more sophisticated electronics that are able to lock on to signals over a wide range of frequencies. These monitors can display a picture at a variety of resolutions. A typical example is the NEC MultiSync 3D, which will scan all frequencies between 15.5KHz and 36KHz (horizontal) and 50Hz to 100Hz (vertical). Slightly cheaper are multi-frequency monitors, which offer a choice of perhaps two or three fixed frequencies, rather than a true multi-synching capability.

The CRT in a colour monitor is by far the most expensive single component. To produce a tube with three precisely focussed electron guns, and red, green and blue phosphor dots accurately aligned with the shadow mask, requires much greater precision in manufacture. As in most things, you get what you pay for. The monitor market is very competitive. There are many low-cost models that claim multi-synch capability, and look like bargains. However, the savings are achieved at the expense of the CRT, which is of too poor a quality for the maximum resolution claimed. The video electronics may also have poor linearity, giving a display that is stretched or compressed at the extremes of the picture. If a monitor is to be used primarily for graphics work, it is a good idea to spend some time trying it out before deciding whether to buy it.

6.5 Testing Monitors

Computer monitors are usually pretty reliable. However, over a period the quality of the display may slowly deteriorate as the components age and some internal settings go out of adjustment. Even when new, there can be a wide variation in quality between monitors from different manufacturers. As already shown, this is largely a function of price.

```
8300 REM ==== LISTING 10.1 ====
8305 REM ==== MONITOR QUALITY TESTS ====
8306 C1$=CHR$(219): C10$=C1$+C1$+C1$+C1$+C1$+C1$+C1$+C1$+C1$
8307 C2$=CHR$(218): C3$=CHR$(196): C4$=CHR$(191): C5$=CHR$(179)
8308 C6$=CHR$(192): C7$=CHR$(217): C8$=CHR$(194): C9$=CHR$(193)
8309 C11$=CHR$(195): C12$=CHR$(197): C13$=CHR$(180)
8310 SCREEN 0,1: COLOR 7,0: CLS
8315 L%=23: REM Screen length less 1
8320 PRINT "Monitor Quality Tests": PRINT
8322 PRINT "1 - Colour purity test"
8324 PRINT "2 - Convergence test"
8326 PRINT "3 - EHT Regulation test"
8328 PRINT "9 - Exit": PRINT
8330 K$=INKEY$: IF K$="" THEN 8330
8331 IF K$="1" THEN GOSUB 8340
8332 IF K$="2" THEN GOSUB 8350
8333 IF K$="3" THEN GOSUB 8400
8334 IF K$="9" THEN END
8335 GOTO 8310
8340 REM ==== Colour purity test ====
8342 COLOR 15,0: CLS
8344 FOR I%=1 TO 2000: PRINT C1$;: NEXT I%
8346 COLOR 7,0: LOCATE L%,57: PRINT "Press any key to exit"
8348 K$=INKEY$: IF K$="" THEN 8348
8349 RETURN
8350 REM ==== Convergence test ====
8352 COLOR 15,0: CLS
8354 PRINT C2$;: FOR I%=1 TO 78: PRINT C8$;: NEXT I%: PRINT C4$;
8356 FOR J%=2 TO L%
8358 PRINT C11$;: FOR I%=1 TO 78: PRINT C12$;: NEXT I%: PRINT C13$;
8360 NEXT J%
8362 PRINT C6$;: FOR I%=1 TO 78: PRINT C9$;: NEXT I%: PRINT C7$;
8364 LOCATE L%,57: PRINT "Press any key to exit"
8366 K$=INKEY$: IF K$="" THEN 8366
8368 RETURN
8400 REM ==== Test EHT Regulation ====
8410 CLS
8420 PRINT C2$;: FOR I%=1 TO 78: PRINT C3$;: NEXT I%: PRINT C4$;
8422 FOR J%=2 TO L%
8424 PRINT C5$;: FOR I%=1 TO 78: PRINT " ";: NEXT I%: PRINT C5$;
8426 NEXT J%
```

```
8428 PRINT C6$;: FOR I%=1 TO 78: PRINT C3$;: NEXT I%: PRINT C7$;
8430 COLOR 31,0
8432 FOR J%=3 TO L%-2
8434 LOCATE J%,6
8436 FOR K%=1 TO 7: PRINT C10$;: NEXT K%
8438 NEXT J%
8440 COLOR 7,0
8445 LOCATE L%,57: PRINT "Press any key to exit"
8448 K$=INKEY$: IF K$="" THEN 8448
8450 CLS
8455 RETURN
8490 END
```

If you're buying a monitor, it may not be easy to test what the quality is really like. Listing 6.1 overcomes this problem. It's a BASIC program that can be used to test for colour purity, convergence and EHT regulation. The colour purity test checks the alignment of the shadow mask. A solid bright white box is displayed on the screen. Leave it there for two minutes. The box should remain a uniformly bright white. If the shadow mask is misaligned, or if any distortion occurs because of overheating, areas of discolouration will appear on the screen. If this effect is very noticeable, the CRT is of poor quality, and the monitor should be avoided.

The convergence test checks the alignment of the three electron beams in a colour CRT. It also tests the linearity of the display. The program displays a fine grid in bright white which covers the screen. If the beams are not perfectly aligned, then instead of being sharp white, the line will be fringed with red, green or blue. It may even change colour completely. If the effect is not too noticeable, it isn't all that serious. It's difficult to obtain perfect convergence over the whole area of the screen. Nevertheless, the fault will detract from the accuracy of displayed colours, and may make text seem blurred and indistinct. Linearity can be tested by observing how straight and evenly-spaced are the lines which make up the grid. This test will also show up how crisp is the focus on monochrome monitors.

The EHT regulation test draws a box around the edge of the screen. A solid bright white box is then flashed on and off in the centre of the screen. If the outer box moves in and out as the inner one flashes on and off, then the regulation of the monitor's EHT circuit is poor. It may be that the EHT supply is barely adequate for the CRT used; this could lead to premature component failure.

```
8000 REM ======== LISTING 6.2 ========
8005 REM ======== DISPLAY / MONITOR TESTS ========
8100 REM ==== Test Display Attributes ====
8105 DATA "Blue","Green","Cyan","Red","Magenta","Brown","White"
8110 SCREEN 0,1: COLOR 7,0: CLS
8120 PRINT "******** Display Attribute Test ********": PRINT
8130 COLOR 15,0: PRINT "This line should be bright white on black.": PRINT
```

The Display

```
8131 COLOR 23,0: PRINT "This line should be blinking.": PRINT
8132 COLOR 0,7 : PRINT "This line should be black on white.": PRINT
8133 FOR I%=1 TO 7
8134 READ K$: COLOR I%,0: PRINT "This line should be ";K$;".": PRINT
8135 NEXT I%
8190 COLOR 7,0: PRINT "Press any key ...";
8195 K$=INKEY$: IF K$="" THEN 8195


8000 REM ======== LISTING 6.3 ========
8005 REM ======== DISPLAY / MONITOR TESTS ========
8150 REM ==== Test Monochrome Display Attributes ====
8160 SCREEN 0,1: COLOR 7,0: CLS
8170 PRINT "******** Display Attribute Test ********": PRINT
8180 COLOR 15,0: PRINT "This line should be bright white on black.": PRINT
8181 COLOR 23,0: PRINT "This line should be blinking.": PRINT
8182 COLOR 0,7 : PRINT "This line should be black on white.": PRINT
8183 COLOR 1,0 : PRINT "This line should be underlined.": PRINT
8190 COLOR 7,0: LOCATE 24,1: PRINT "Press any key ...";
8195 K$=INKEY$: IF K$="" THEN 8195


8200 REM ==== LISTING 6.4 ====
8202 REM ==== Test Display Attributes ====
8205 DATA "Blue ","Green ","Cyan ","Red "
8206 DATA "Magenta ","Brown ","White ","Grey "
8207 DATA "Lt Blue ","Lt Grn ","Lt Cyan ","Lt Red "
8208 DATA "Lt Mgta ","Yellow ","Br White"
8210 SCREEN 0,1: COLOR 7,0: CLS
8220 REM === Foreground Colour Test ===
8225 FOR I%=1 TO 15
8230 COLOR I%,0: CLS: READ K$
8235 FOR J%=1 TO 250: PRINT K$;: NEXT J%
8240 COLOR 7,0: LOCATE 2,4: PRINT " Foreground Colour Test "
8245 FOR J%=1 TO 32000: NEXT J%
8248 NEXT I%
8250 REM === Background Colour Test ===
8252 RESTORE
8255 FOR I%=1 TO 7
8260 COLOR 0,I%: CLS: READ K$
8265 FOR J%=1 TO 250: PRINT K$;: NEXT J%
8270 COLOR 7,0: LOCATE 2,4: PRINT " Background Colour Test "
8275 FOR J%=1 TO 32000: NEXT J%
8278 NEXT I%
8280 REM === Border Colour Test ===
8282 RESTORE
8285 FOR I%=1 TO 7
8288 COLOR 7,0,I%: CLS: READ K$
8290 FOR J%=1 TO 250: PRINT K$;: NEXT J%
8292 COLOR 0,7: LOCATE 2,4: PRINT " Border Colour Test "
```

```
8294 FOR J%=1 TO 32000: NEXT J%
8296 NEXT I%
8298 COLOR 7,0,0: LOCATE 24,72: PRINT "Press any key ...";
8299 K$=INKEY$: IF K$="" THEN 8299
```

Listings 6.2, 6.3 and 6.4 test the different display attributes so that you can see how they appear on the screen. Listing 6.2 is a quick test that shows text in each of the available normal-intensity colours on a black background, as well as bright white, blinking and inverse video. Listing 6.3 is a similar test for the more restricted range of attributes available on monochrome monitors. Listing 6.4 is a more comprehensive test for colour displays that cycles through all the available foreground, background and border colours.

6.6 Display Adapters

While the monitor has the job of displaying the picture to the PC user, the function of generating the picture to be displayed is performed by the display adapter. This is usually a card that plugs in to the expansion bus, though on many recent machines the hardware is built on to the motherboard. A typical PC display adapter is pictured in Figure 6.3.

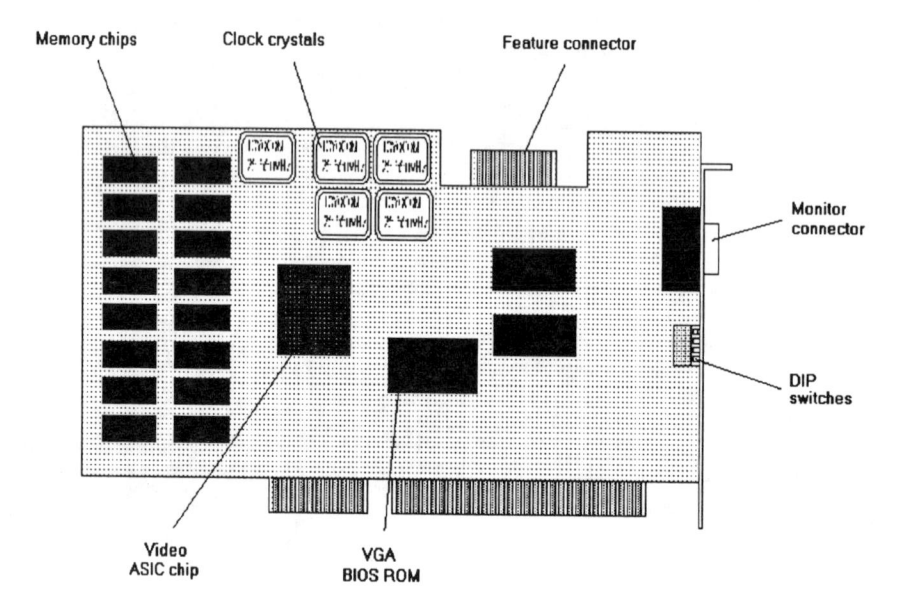

Figure 6.3: A typical display adapter

A variety of display standards have been introduced over the years. All PC display adapters are essentially similar in that they are memory-mapped. This means that an area of memory is reserved to hold a representation of what is to appear on the screen. The PC software writes bytes of data into this area of memory. These bytes may represent ASCII character codes, patterns of pixels forming part of a graphical image, or display attributes such as colour. The display adapter reads this data out of memory, and generates the appropriate signals to drive the monitor and create the desired picture on the screen.

As well as memory, display adapters have hardware I/O ports. Software writes to these I/O ports so as to do things like set the position and size of the cursor, or blank out the screen. It can also read information from these ports. For example, it can learn the current size of the cursor, or whether the CRT electron beam is doing a retrace. The latter, surprisingly, was once a useful piece of information for programmers. A hardware limitation of the IBM CGA card caused *snow* to appear on the screen if a program accessed the display memory while the adapter was reading from it. To avoid *snow*, programs had to update the display only during the retrace. Fortunately, the BIOS provides functions that take care of all this hardware-specific detail for programmers who don't wish to get involved in it.

Originally, the only display option available on the PC was the *Monochrome Display Adapter* (MDA). This works with a standard TTL green or amber screen monitor and produces a character-based text only display. Line graphics can be produced using special graphics characters, which have ASCII codes from 176 to 223. The MDA produces an excellent quality display, generating 25 lines of 80 characters, each of which is formed using a matrix of 9 x 14 dots.

In the display adapter memory, each character is represented by two bytes: the character code, and the display attribute. On the MDA, the attribute controls the foreground and background intensities (black, normal or bright), blinking and underlining. Four thousand bytes (25 x 80 x 2) are needed to store one complete screenful of information. The MDA has 16Kb of memory which can be used to hold four separate pages of information. However, most PC programs only use the first page – page 0. The display memory resides at locations B000:0 to B000:3FFF. The I/O port addresses are 3B0 – 3BF (hex).

The MDA works in a manner common to all PC display adapters in text mode. The video monitor is an unintelligent device, and has no knowledge of the shapes of the various characters. The display adapter therefore has a character generator ROM. This contains patterns of dots which represent the shape of each character. When it displays a character, the adapter's logic obtains the appropriate pattern from the ROM, and uses it to modulate the video signal in such a way as to display the pattern on the screen. This is illustrated in Figure 6.4.

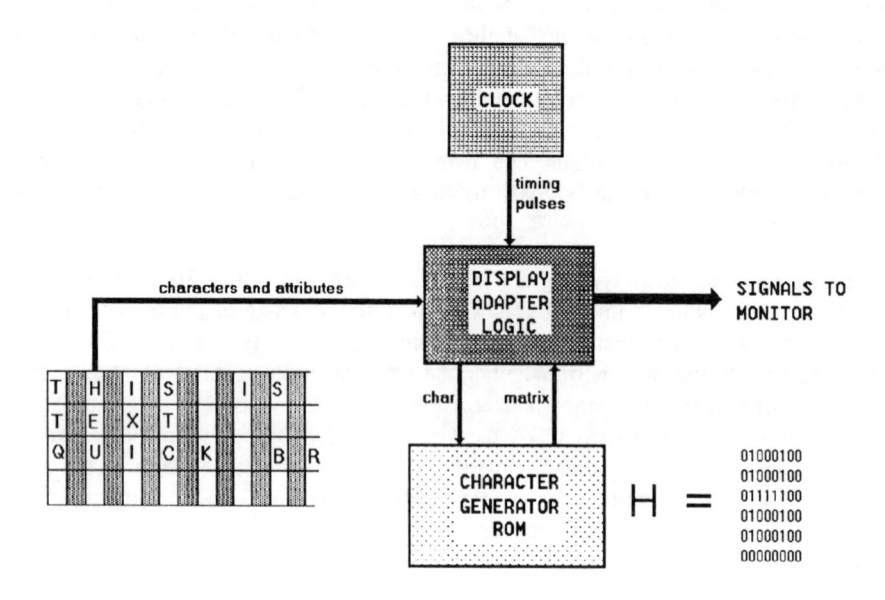

Figure 6.4: The display adapter

The *Colour Graphics Adapter* (CGA) was the result of a last-minute change of heart by IBM, who eventually gave in to the suggestion that prospective PC users might want to be able to display colour text and graphics. The adapter was designed to use a 15.75KHz horizontal scan rate. This meant that it could be used with existing TTL colour monitors and also, if an external video modulator was purchased, a standard colour TV. Two text modes were provided: 25 lines by 80 columns or 25 lines by 40 columns, each in 16 colours. The 40-column mode was needed because 80-column text would be unreadable on a standard TV screen. In graphics or *All Points Addressable* (APA) mode, two resolutions were provided: 320 x 200 pixels in four colours, or 640 x 200 in two.

In text mode the characters are stored in the same way as for the MDA, but in this case the attribute controls the foreground and background colours and blinking. Sixteen foreground and eight background colours may be specified, the backgrounds being limited to low-intensity hues. However, if the value 9 is written to I/O port 3D8 (hex), the blink attribute is disabled and bright backgrounds may be used instead. Underlining is not supported. Like the MDA, the CGA has 16K of memory. Four text pages (eight in 25 x 40 mode) are provided, starting at memory location B800:0. The I/O port addresses are at 3D0 – 3DF (hex).

In APA mode the resolution and the number of colours that can be used are limited by the 16K of memory on the adapter. In 640 x 200 x 2 colour mode, one bit is used to represent each pixel, having the value 0 or 1 depending on the colour used. In 320 x 200 mode, two bits are used for each pixel, which allows a choice of four colours. As graphics displays go, the CGA was quite poor. Its capabilities were limited by the design decision to allow the use of standard TV displays. In text mode the characters are formed using a chunky 8 x 8 dot matrix. The display flickers badly when text scrolls up the screen, and it is also prone to the problem of *snow* mentioned earlier.

Many older PC compatible systems were supplied with a display adapter based on the IBM CGA. For the original Compaq Portables and early Deskpros this is true even of those systems that have a green or amber monochrome monitor. Other machines such as the AT&T 6300, the Amstrad PC1512 and many Toshiba portables use an improved version of CGA with the vertical resolution increased to 400 lines. Special software drivers are needed to take advantage of the full resolution of these adapters in graphics mode; when running standard CGA software the display double scans each of the CGA's 200 lines. The Plantronics ColorPlus card is a CGA compatible card that offers 320 x 200 x 16 colours and 640 x 200 x 4 colours in graphics mode. Most third-party adapters are free from the flicker and snow problems that afflict the IBM card.

The *Hercules Graphics Card* (HGC) was introduced in 1983. This display adapter, like the MDA, uses standard TTL monochrome monitors. It provides 25 lines x 80 column text just like the MDA, and is hardware compatible with it, but in addition it provides APA graphics at a resolution of 720 x 348 pixels. At the time it was introduced there was a real need for a display adapter capable of producing high resolution graphics – the CGA being too poor for serious business use – so the HGC became a standard in its own right. Clones began to appear. You can now buy an HGC-compatible display card for about £30 ($50 US). A later version of the HGC is the *Hercules Graphics Card Plus*, which is upwardly compatible with the earlier card but has more memory and the ability to use customised screen fonts.

IBM introduced the *Enhanced Graphics Adapter* (EGA) in 1985. This can produce text and APA graphics on both colour and monochrome screens. It produces higher definition pictures, using an 8 x 14 dot matrix in 25 x 80 text modes (9 x 14 in monochrome) and adds a 43 line x 80 column mode using an 8 x 8 dot matrix. User-defined fonts may also be used giving character sizes of up to 8 x 32. In APA mode, the resolution is increased giving 640 x 350 pixels with a choice of 16 colours from a palette of 64. The IBM EGA card was supplied with 128Kb of memory, though 256Kb is needed to use the maximum resolution with 16 colours. Most third-party EGA compatible display cards are supplied with the full 256Kb.

The EGA is hardware compatible with both the MDA and the CGA. A DIP switch must be used to configure the adapter to work with either a monochrome or a colour monitor. In monochrome mode, it scans at 18.432KHz. The text pages (now increased to eight) begin at memory location B000:0 and the control I/O ports used are 3B0 – 3BF. In colour mode, it scans at either 15.75KHz if an ordinary CGA monitor is used, or 22KHz if an Enhanced Colour Display (ECD) is present. The text pages then start at B800:0 and the control ports are at 3D0 – 3DF.

In graphics mode, the display memory occupies the whole of the area from A000:0 to B000:FFFF. This area is 128Kb wide. The adapter enables the full 256Kb of display memory to be accessed by switching 64Kb segments into the addressable area.

EGA cards can use IRQ2 for something called the *vertical retrace interrupt*. Software which wished to avoid changing the screen display while the display adapter was in the middle of painting the picture could use this interrupt to tell when the CRT electron beam was retracing from the bottom of the screen to the top. This would then give a period of a couple of milliseconds during which the display information could be updated. This interrupt is not generally used by software packages. Many third-party EGA cards did not implement it correctly because of errors in IBM's published specification. Programs can find out the retrace status by reading from one of the I/O ports. The vertical retrace interrupt was dropped when VGA was introduced.

EGA saw the start of a trend by third-party manufacturers to offer compatible display cards with significant extra functionality. The Paradise EGA 480, a popular EGA card used in many PC compatibles, offers MDA or HGC emulation, as well as EGA mono operation, when used with a monochrome monitor. On a colour monitor, CGA and Plantronics emulation are available. If a multi-frequency monitor capable of synching at 30.5KHz is available, it offers 640 x 480 x 16 colour graphics – effectively VGA resolution.

The *Video Graphics Array* (VGA) was introduced along with the PS/2 series in April 1987. At the same time, IBM produced a card that could be used to upgrade older PCs to the same video standard. This was called the *PS/2 Display Adapter*. The VGA is similar in operation to the EGA, but offers further improvements in resolution, and more new BIOS functions. The standard resolution is increased up to 640 x 480 pixels by 16 colours, and uses a 9 x 16 character dot matrix in standard 25 x 80 text mode. A 50 lines x 80 columns display is possible using 8 x 8 characters. The VGA can display up to 256 out of a palette of 262,144 colours on-screen in lower resolutions if an analogue monitor is used. The standard memory supplied is 256Kb. The adapter senses whether a monochrome or a colour monitor is attached, and the video memory area and I/O port addresses used are consistent with those used by the EGA in either mono or colour display modes.

Soon after the arrival of VGA, third-party manufacturers started to bring out compatible cards offering a host of additional display resolutions. These often support the older standards, i.e., CGA, EGA, MDA and HGC, on present-day monitors, providing full hardware emulation of the old display adapters. An extra 256Kb of memory is sufficient to allow a 256 colour display at the standard 640 x 480 resolution. Higher resolutions of 800 x 600 pixels and text modes supporting up to 50 rows of 132 characters are commonly possible when the adapter is driving a multi-frequency or multi-synch monitor. VGA cards with 1Mb of RAM on board are also now commonplace. These offer many display resolutions for use with multi-synch monitors, up to 1024 x 768 pixels with 256 colours.

The problem with all these high resolutions is that they are non-standard. Each manufacturer has implemented them in a slightly different way. As a result, drivers specific to the display card are needed to enable software packages to take advantage of them. The card manufacturers supply drivers for the most common software packages such as Lotus 1-2-3, Symphony, Ventura Publisher and Microsoft Windows. However, if you are using other packages then unless special drivers are included in the package it is likely that you will only be able to use the standard VGA display modes.

The *8514/A Display Adapter* was introduced for PS/2 systems. It offers higher resolutions than the standard IBM VGA, and includes an on-board processor to give improved performance when running graphical applications. This display capability can be added to VGA-equipped PC compatibles using a card such as the *Paradise 8514/A Plus Card*. This is available with 512Kb or 1024Kb on-board memory. It supports 640 x 480 and 1024 x 768 pixel display resolutions, with 256 out of a palette of 262,144 colours, on 43.5Hz 8514 type interlaced or 60Hz or 70Hz non-interlaced monitors.

The 8514/A Plus Card is installed alongside an existing VGA display adapter, and is linked to it by means of a cable that attaches to the Feature Connector present on most VGA cards. This connector allows standard VGA signals to pass through and be displayed on the monitor attached to the 8514/A card. You can also have a dual monitor system, with a standard VGA monitor connected to the VGA card, and a multi-frequency monitor connected to the 8514/A card.

The *Extended Graphics Array* (XGA) was announced by IBM at the end of 1990. It is the display adapter for the 80486-based systems in the PS/2 range, and offers high performance through the use of a graphics co-processor chip. XGA has three modes of operation: standard VGA mode, an enhanced VGA 132-column text mode, and its own native XGA mode. In XGA mode the display resolutions are equivalent to those provided by the 8514/A, but offer 256 colours at 1024 x 768 and up to 65,536 colours at 640 x 480 resolution. However, XGA is incompatible with any previous PC display mode at the hardware level, so special drivers are needed.

XGA uses interlacing at 1024 x 768, and in that respect is inferior to many non-IBM 8514/A and super-VGA cards, which support a non-interlaced display at that resolution. However, its graphics co-processor makes it much faster at updating the display. True XGA cards for PC compatible systems have not yet appeared on the market. However, the specifications of the new standard have been made available to other manufacturers by IBM, and it is inevitable that they will appear in due course.

6.7 Two-monitor Systems

Because monochrome and colour display adapters use different memory map areas and different I/O port addresses, you can have two display adapters and two monitors in use simultaneously. This would typically be of use in a computer-aided design (CAD) system, where a monochrome text display is used to input commands to the software, and a high-resolution colour monitor is reserved for the display of graphical output.

In a dual monitor configuration, one display card must be an MDA or a CGA or an equivalent, the other may be any PC display adapter. One adapter must be configured as the primary (default) display. This is the function of a jumper on the motherboard. In the case of a VGA card, it must always be the primary display. EGA or VGA cards, which can operate in either monochrome or colour modes, are restricted to those display modes that do not conflict with those of the alternate display adapter. In other words, if an MDA is installed, the EGA or VGA may only be operated in colour display modes.

Table 6.2: EGA switch settings for dual monitor systems

Primary Adaptor	Secondary Adaptor	Monitor conn. to prim card	Monitor conn to sec card	Switch positions 0	1	2	3
EGA	MDA	40x25 col	Mono TTL	ON	OFF	OFF	ON
EGA	MDA	80x25 col	Mono TTL	OFF	OFF	OFF	ON
EGA	MDA	ECD normal	Mono TTL	ON	ON	ON	OFF
EGA	MDA	ECD enhanced	Mono TTL	OFF	ON	ON	OFF
EGA	CGA	Mono TTL	40x25 col	ON	OFF	ON	OFF
EGA	CGA	Mono TTL	80x25 col	OFF	OFF	ON	OFF
MDA	EGA	Mono TTL	40x25 col	ON	ON	ON	ON
MDA	EGA	Mono TTL	80x25 col	OFF	ON	ON	ON
MDA	EGA	Mono TTL	ECD normal	ON	OFF	ON	ON
MDA	EGA	Mono TTL	ECD enhanced	OFF	OFF	ON	ON
CGA	EGA	40x25 col	Mono TTL	ON	ON	OFF	ON
CGA	EGA	80x25 col	Mono TTL	OFF	ON	OFF	ON

The DIP switches on an EGA card must be set depending on what alternate display adapter is present and which of the two is the primary display. Table 6.2 shows the switch settings for an IBM EGA or compatible card. If a third-party EGA card with intelligent mode switching such as the Paradise EGA 480 is used, the mode switching should be turned off.

6.8 Display Problems

When faced with a problem that is affecting the display of a PC, the first step must be to decide whether the problem is due to incorrect configuration or a fault with the display adapter or the monitor. Display adapters are all solid-state; there are no mechanical parts in them and failures are rare. As a rule, PC monitors are also quite reliable. Sudden failures are unusual, but a gradual falling off in performance with age and the appearance of faults which can initially be overcome by adjustment of the external controls is not uncommon. However, many display-related problems are caused simply by an error in configuration: a switch being in the wrong position, or the wrong software drivers being used.

Most PC monitors draw their power from a mains outlet on the back of the system unit. They are switched on and off using the main PC power switch. One of the most common explanations for a monitor being reported faulty is that the its own power on/off switch has been turned off or the brightness has been turned down! The user, who never uses these controls, doesn't think of checking.

If the system sends a series of beeps at start-up, and the display is blank, the display adapter may not be properly seated in the expansion bus. The jumper for the primary display adapter might also be set incorrectly. ATs require the type of monitor to be specified during the SETUP routine, and stored in CMOS RAM.

If the display apparently revolves *out of synch*, the solution may depend on the type of monitor. Standard TTL monitors – typically those with green or amber screens – and the older colour monitors, have circuits that are no more sophisticated than the average domestic TV. This type of monitor has *vertical hold* and *horizontal hold* controls, usually on the back panel, which are used to fine tune the horizontal and vertical synchronisation frequencies until they lock on to the signal from the display adapter. Some monitors, particularly as they get older, will only lock when they are adjusted very close to the correct frequency. The problem is often that the frequency adjustment drifts as the monitor warms up. The display adapter output, being crystal controlled, is always accurate. If a monitor needs constant adjustment to hold a picture, the remedy is to have the unit serviced. Monitor alignment requires special equipment, and is not something you can attempt yourself.

Occasionally, a problem with synchronisation may be due to a monitor/display adapter incompatibility. In one case I experienced, a number of new PCs equipped with *clone* Hercules Graphics Cards had screens that would not stabilise in graphics mode when they were first switched on. Also, the picture would go out of synch when switching back from graphics to text mode, after they had warmed up. Older machines, which had genuine Hercules cards, did not suffer from the problem. The manufacturers of both the monitors and the display cards claimed that there was nothing wrong with their equipment, since they had both sold thousands of units with no similar problems being reported. Yet substituting real Hercules cards for the clones solved the problem. The SYNCH signal from the clone cards was probably not strong enough for these particular monitors to lock up reliably.

High quality monitors of the type used with EGA and VGA adapters very often don't have horizontal and vertical hold controls. The display electronics in these devices are much more sophisticated, and in the case of multi-synch monitors, will lock on to a very wide range of signals. A jumbled or un-synchronised picture is most likely to be caused by the software using an inappropriate driver, or a display mode that is unsupported either by the adapter or the monitor. For example, a fixed-frequency VGA monitor will only be able to display the standard 80-column text modes and 640 x 480 resolution graphics, although most non-IBM VGA adapters can be switched into other modes which the monitor will be unable to show.

Problems in which the display appears as a bright line or spot on the screen may be caused by a failure of the monitor's display electronics. Or it may be that the cable between the PC and the monitor is faulty or disconnected. If this happens, the monitor should be switched off rapidly, because the bright line or spot will permanently damage the phosphor coating of the CRT. If the cable plugs were not loose then the wiring of the cable should be checked for continuity using a volt-ohm meter. A different cable and monitor may be tried to eliminate the display adapter as the cause of the fault, but, to avoid damage, be ready to switch off the monitor quickly if the fault is still present.

If distorted or badly-formed characters are displayed the cause could be a faulty character-generator in the display adapter. Corruption of a graphics screen could be due to faulty display adapter memory. It could also be caused by software – such as a memory-resident utility – corrupting the video memory or attempting to write text to the screen while in graphics mode.

Blurred or badly-focussed text may be caused by convergence misalignment. The tests described earlier in the chapter may be carried out to check for this. Alternatively, the monitor may be unsuitable for the display resolution being employed. Interference patterns or side-to-side movement of the picture is usually caused by magnetic interference from a nearby power transformer. Another monitor, or other equipment such as a UPS may be the cause of this. The solution here is to move the offending device further away.

Although the EGA and VGA are upwardly compatible with the CGA, they do introduce a few new features that can sometimes be the cause of problems. Several new BIOS functions are provided, for things like loading and switching between different screen fonts. Programs can toggle the blink/background colour intensity attribute using a BIOS function rather than writing to a hardware register. Indeed, on some not-so-compatible display cards, writing to the register may not work. The new functions are implemented by providing an extra BIOS ROM as part of the display adapter. This usually starts at location C000:0. You can see the start of this ROM, which usually contains a copyright message, by using DEBUG, as shown in Fig. 6.5.

```
C:\>debug
-dC000:0
C000:0000  55 AA 30 EB 5B 54 68 69-73 20 69 73 20 6E 6F 74   U×0k[This is not
C000:0010  20 61 20 70 72 6F 64 75-63 74 20 6F 66 20 49 42    a product of IB
C000:0020  4D 20 20 28 49 42 4D 20-69 73 20 61 20 74 72 61   M  (IBM is a tra
C000:0030  64 65 6D 61 72 6B 20 6F-66 20 49 6E 74 65 72 6E   demark of Intern
C000:0040  61 74 69 6F 6E 61 6C 20-42 75 73 69 6E 65 73 73   ational Business
C000:0050  20 4D 61 63 68 69 6E 65-73 20 43 6F 72 70 2E 29    Machines Corp.)
C000:0060  EB 59 20 2A 20 43 6F 70-79 72 69 67 68 74 28 63   kY × Copyright(c
C000:0070  29 31 39 38 38 20 54 73-65 6E 67 20 4C 61 62 6F   )1988 Tseng Labo
-d
C000:0080  72 61 74 6F 72 69 65 73-2C 20 49 6E 63 2E 20 31   ratories, Inc. 1
C000:0090  31 2F 30 32 2F 38 39 20-56 38 2E 30 30 58 01 50   1/02/89 V8.00X.P
-q
C:\>
```

Figure 6.5: Finding the EGA/VGA BIOS details using DEBUG

The BIOS ROMs of third-party display adapters often contain a disclaimer that they are not IBM products. Some old PC software used to check for the existence of the characters *IBM* at the start of the ROM, and would only work if these were found. This disclaimer is the only way that other manufacturers could legitimately include the IBM name in their own ROM.

The PC BIOS provides a function for specifying the size of the cursor. With a CGA, which uses eight lines for each row of characters, lines 6 and 7 are used for the standard underline cursor. When the EGA was introduced, the standard character size was increased to 14 lines. However, the software available at the time assumed that if it was using a colour monitor then characters were eight scan lines high.

To overcome this, IBM provided a function called *cursor emulation*, which allowed software to set the cursor size as if it were on a CGA, but then translated the parameters into something suitable for the EGA's 14 line high text. However, the EGA and VGA can be programmed to display other character sizes. When this is done, cursor emulation can really mess things up. Software packages use all sorts of methods to set the cursor size, some of which may not work on certain not-quite-IBM-compatible display cards. Quite recently, I found a VGA card that would not display a cursor while running a well-known integrated software package.

So disappearing cursor problems may be caused by incompatibilities between the software and the display adapter.

As we have seen, there are many things that can cause display problems. The most common faults are summarised in the list below:

System beeps on power-up, no display:

❑ Motherboard jumper (mono/colour) incorrectly set.

❑ Display adapter not properly seated in expansion bus.

F1 CRT error or similar on AT compatible:

❑ CMOS data incorrect for type of display; run SETUP.

No picture:

❑ Check power to monitor.

❑ Check brightness control.

❑ Check cable attached to display adapter.

Display jumbled or out of lock:

❑ Vertical/horizontal hold out of adjustment.

❑ Monitor synchronisation circuits in need of adjustment.

❑ System using display mode not supported by monitor.

❑ Software using unsupported mode or incorrect drivers for display adapter.

Bright spot or line on screen:

(Warning: this can permanently damage the CRT)

❑ Monitor cable broken or not connected.

❑ Faulty monitor deflection circuits; try a substitute monitor;

❑ Faulty display adapter; try monitor on another PC.

Badly-formed characters on screen:

❑ Faulty display adapter.

Corrupted graphics display:

❑ Software interference with display adapter memory; remove device drivers and TSR utilities.

❑ Faulty display adapter memory.

Unsteady display, moving band on screen:

❑ Interference from nearby mains transformer.

No cursor:

❑ Faulty software.

❑ Display adapter not truly IBM-compatible.

Summary

Most PCs, except laptops, use CRT monitors. Monochrome monitors use a single electron beam to paint a picture on the green, amber or grey phosphor surface of the tube. Colour monitors have three beams, which individually energise phosphor dots of red, green and blue so as to create a range of hues by the process of colour addition. Digital monitors have only limited control of the intensity of the electron beam, which results in only a few possible colours. Analogue monitors can display an infinite range of colours.

The CRT is controlled by the display adapter. This determines the display resolution as well as the shape of characters in text mode. New and better display standards have been introduced every couple of years. Third-party manufacturers have produced display cards that support these new standards and offer additional higher resolution modes. However, special drivers are usually needed to take advantage of non-standard display modes. These are often not available for the less popular software packages.

As resolution of a display adapter increases, more expensive monitors are needed. Multi-synch monitors can operate at a variety of resolutions, and provide great flexibility for the user. Low cost monitors are available. However, the quality is likely to be inferior.

The most common display faults are errors in configuration – including use of the wrong software driver – and interference with the monitor's controls. Hardware faults should be left to a specialist to repair. Monitors have lethal voltages inside the case and anyway, the alignment of colour monitors requires specialised equipment.

7

Diskette Drives

Personal computer memory is completely volatile. Everything that you load into it is totally forgotten the instant the power is switched off. Without a method for permanently storing programs and data, and being able instantly to retrieve them, a PC would be almost useless. Magnetic disks are the most popular form of permanent data storage.

When the IBM PC was first introduced, diskette drives were expensive. Early PCs were equipped with a cassette port. This allowed users to save programs and data to an audio cassette recorder, just like a cheap home computer. All IBM PCs had BASIC in ROM, so it was quite possible to use them for something useful without booting up DOS from a diskette. Cassette tape didn't prove to be popular, however, so just about every PC ever made comes with at least one diskette drive.

The original diskettes used with the IBM PC were single-sided, double density and soft sectored, with eight sectors per track (these terms are explained later) and could hold 160Kb of data. Since then, higher capacity diskettes have been introduced, which use both sides of the disk, have nine sectors per track, and high density recording media that can hold double the number of tracks. The more rugged 3.5in. diskettes, which in high density versions increase the storage capacity to 1.44Mb, have now taken over from the old 5.25in. floppy as the most popular format.

We'll begin this chapter by looking at how diskettes and diskette drives work. Then we'll look at some problems that can occur, and how best to deal with them. Many of the principles and the terminology used also apply to hard disks, which are described in the following chapter.

7.1 Diskette Basics

A diskette consists essentially of two parts: the outer jacket and the inner recording medium. The function of the jacket is simply to protect the surface of the medium, and give the user something to hold on to. A 5.25in. diskette jacket has three apertures. The central, circular aperture is to allow the diskette medium to locate on the hub of the drive motor and be clamped there so that it can be turned by the motor. The elongated aperture is to allow the read/write heads of the diskette drive to get at the recording surface. The small circular hole lines up with a single small index hole in the medium when it is rotated into a particular position. It is used to locate the position of the first sector on every track. A notch in the edge of the jacket allows the diskette to be written to; when covered over with an adhesive tab, the disk is write-protected.

The 3.5in. diskettes are more rugged, having a jacket of stiff plastic. The read/write aperture is protected with a spring-loaded shutter. This makes it much more difficult to touch the recording surface accidentally. At one corner, the write-protect aperture has a plastic shutter, which should be moved to the open position to protect the disk. High-density diskettes have another aperture on the opposite side, which is used to enable the drive to distinguish them from low-density types.

The diskette recording medium is made of a flexible mylar film, coated on both sides with magnetic oxide. Information is written to the diskette by recording magnetic pulses on the oxide, in much the same way as music or speech is recorded on a conventional audio cassette. The diskette drive motor rotates the disk, and the read/write head can move in and out across the recording surface, so that the data is written in concentric circles called *tracks*. Each track can hold quite a lot of information, so for convenience the tracks are divided into smaller pieces called *sectors*. This is illustrated in Figure 7.1.

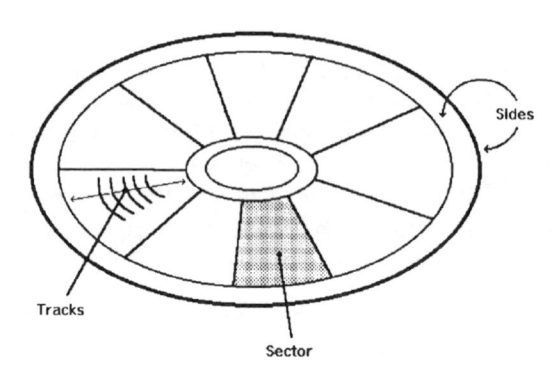

Figure 7.1: Structure of a diskette

Diskettes use a sector size of 512 bytes. A double-sided, double-density (DS/DD) 5.25in. diskette has two sides containing 40 tracks of 9 sectors each, so the total capacity is 512 x 40 x 9 x 2 = 368640 bytes. DOS reserves a number of bytes to hold the root directory and volume label, which is why the actual number of bytes available, as reported by the FORMAT utility, is always less than this. Table 7.1 gives the specifications of the types of diskette used with IBM PC compatible systems.

Table 7.1: Types of diskette used in IBM PCs

Storage Capacity	Physical size(in)	Sectors per trk	Bytes per sec	Tracks per side	Tracks per inch	Number of sides
160Kb	5.25	8	512	40	48	1
180Kb	5.25	9	512	40	48	1
320Kb	5.25	8	512	40	48	2
360Kb	5.25	9	512	40	48	2
1.2Mb	5.25	15	512	80	96	2
720Kb	3.5	9	512	80	135	2
1.44Mb	3.5	18	512	80	135	2

When a diskette is formatted, the sectors are written to the blank recording medium with zeros or another arbitrary filler character used where the data would be. Each sector contains some additional information as well as the data. There is a sector address – which identifies the individual sector to the system – and a Cyclic Redundancy Check (CRC) value. This is a number calculated by applying a mathematical function to each byte of data. Whenever the sector is read, the CRC is recalculated and compared with the original stored on the disk. If they disagree, then either a read error has occurred or the sector has become corrupted. The nature of the CRC is such that the chances of an error occurring and producing a CRC which matched the original is very small indeed.

7.2 Types of Diskette

Four different types of diskette are used in PC compatible computers. They are: 5.25in. double-sided, double-density; 5.25in. double-sided, high-density; 3.5in. double-sided, double density and 3.5in. double-sided, high density. Single-sided, double-density diskettes were used on the original IBM PCs, but it is unlikely that any of these are still in serious use. Double-sided, quadruple density 5.25in. diskettes are manufactured, and were used on some micros that ran MS-DOS, but they have never been used in PC compatibles. This type of media is not suitable for use in high density drives. If purchased, they may only be used as double-density 360Kb disks.

PC diskettes have a single index hole. They are known as *soft-sectored* diskettes, because the index hole merely marks the position of sector zero. The number and position of the sectors in each track is determined by the software. *Hard-sectored* diskettes have many index holes, one for each sector. They are intended for use in other types of computer and may not be used in a PC drive.

Though you can't see it, there's a big difference between double-density and high-density diskettes. The oxide recording medium is different. Magnetic objects have a tendency to magnetise things adjacent to them. High-density diskettes achieve their greater storage capacity by packing the magnetic dots – representing the data – more closely together. While the standard medium works perfectly well with double-density data, at higher recording densities, the magnetic dots would merge. This would make the dots difficult to read and result in errors.

To make a high-density diskette, manufacturers had to develop a new, *high coercivity* recording medium. The term high coercivity means that the material is harder to magnetise. To write to this medium, the read/write head of the diskette drive must generate a stronger magnetic field; the current through the head needs to be higher. However, because the medium is harder to magnetise, it eliminates the tendency of the magnetic dots to merge together.

Because of the differences in the recording medium used, the two types of diskette are not interchangeable. A high-density diskette cannot be successfully formatted as double-density, because in double-density mode, the drive uses a low write current, which creates too weak a signal to write properly to the high coercivity medium. A low-density diskette may be formatted as a high-density one, but will generate many errors, particularly towards the centre of the disk where the magnetic dots are closer together. Because the drive uses a high write current, it generates a strong magnetic field, which will further increase the tendency of the dots to merge. Double-density 3.5in. diskettes cannot usually be formatted as high-density, even in error, because the extra media identification hole that tells the drive it is a high density diskette is not present.

7.3 Diskette Drives

All diskette drives consist of the same basic components. An appreciation of what these components are and how they work, will help in understanding some of the problems that can occur.

The *drive motor* is used to spin the disk inside its jacket. The motor drives a *spindle*. When a diskette is inserted into the drive, the hub of the disk is clamped to the spindle, and the heads move into contact with the recording surface. The spindle rotates at 300 rpm (360 rpm for high-density 5.25in. diskettes). Early drives used a belt to turn the spindle, but modern ones use a direct-drive motor that turns the spindle directly.

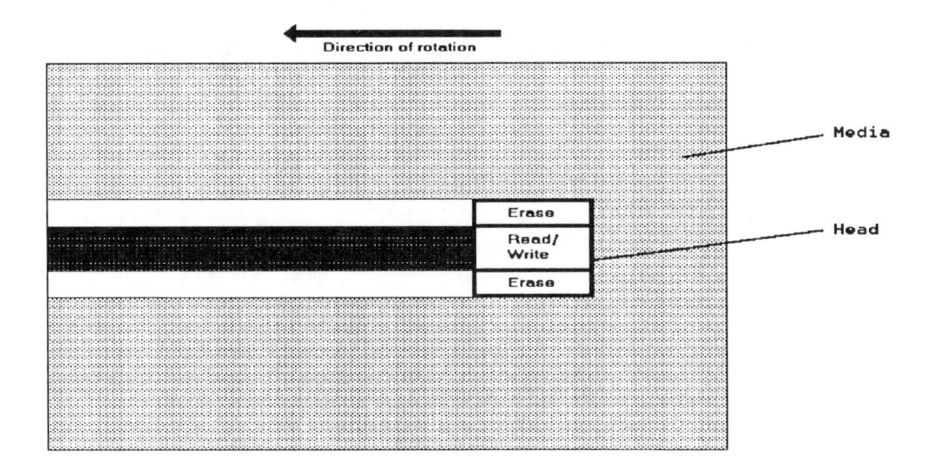

Figure 7.2: The diskette read/write head

A double-sided diskette drive has two *read/write heads*, one for each side of the disk. These function in much the same way as those in an audio cassette recorder, but differ in that they are flanked on each side by erase heads, as shown in Figure 7.2. When writing to the disk, the recording head overwrites anything that was previously recorded on the track. However, the new track may not line up precisely with the old one. The two erase heads remove any trace of the previous signal from either side of the recorded track, and eliminate the possibility of interference on playback.

The 40 or 80 tracks on the disk occupy a band just under an inch wide. The *head actuator* moves the read/write heads from track to track. This is done using a stepper motor, a special type of motor that moves in fixed steps, like the volume control on some hi-fi amplifiers. The position of the read/write head at each step of the motor determines the position of each track on the disk. The time taken for the heads to move from track to track is one factor that affects the speed with which data can be read from or written to the disk. This is known as the *average access time*. It is usually taken as the time to move a distance of half the total number of tracks. For most drives, this is of the order of 100ms.

Diskette drives contain several sensors. The *write protect sensor* is used to tell whether a diskette is write protected. It may be a micro-switch, physically sensing the presence of a write protect tab on 5.25in. disks, or an LED light source and photo-cell on the 3.5in. drives. Drives also have a *diskette sensor*, which determines whether a diskette is present. Finally, 3.5in. high density drives have a *media type sensor*, similar to the write protect sensor, used to detect whether the disk present is double density or high density.

Table 7.2: Diskette drive interface pin assignments

PIN	SIGNAL NAME	I/O
odd nos	Ground	
2	Reduced Write Current	O
4	Not used	
6	Not used	
8	Index	I
10	Motor Enable 1	O
12	Floppy Select 2	O
14	Floppy Select 1	O
16	Motor Enable 2	O
18	Direction (of head movement)	O
20	Step pulse	O
22	Write Data	O
24	Write Enable	O
26	Track 0	I
28	Write Protect	I
30	Read Data	I
32	Head Select	O
34	Diskette Change	I

The diskette drive contains quite a lot of electronics, on a printed circuit board known as a *logic board*. This controls the read/write and erase heads, the head actuator, the drive motor and the sensors, and provides a standardised interface to the rest of the system. The interface used is the Shugart Associates SA-450. This was invented by Al Shugart, founder of disk drive manufacturer Seagate, in the 1970s, and has subsequently become an industry standard. The interface connector is either a double-sided printed circuit edge connector (on 5.25in. drives) or a 34-way IDC connector on 3.5in. drives. The pin assignments of this connector are given in Table 7.2.

7.4 Drive Configuration

If you look at the logic board of a diskette drive, you'll notice several jumpers or slide switches. These are used to set various drive options. The designation of these jumpers or switches varies from drive to drive. Usually, they are identified by a cryptic combination of letters and numbers. If a data sheet for the drive is not available, then you'll have to make do with a combination of intuition and experience, or guesswork.

Drive select is used to set which drive number the drive should respond to. There are usually four settings, numbered DS0, DS1, DS2 and DS3, although on some drives they may be numbered 1 to 4 or even A to D. IBM and many other PC manufacturers use a drive cable with a twisted section between the connectors for the two drives. This swaps pins 10 and 16, and pins 12 and 14, and so dispenses with the need for drive select. If this type of cable is used, then both drives must be set to the second position.

Pin 34 of the Shugart connector was originally used to indicate *disk ready*; in other words, a disk is in the drive and ready for use. XT compatibles don't use this signal. ATs use the same pin to carry a signal called *disk changed*. This is used to speed up disk accesses, since the AT does not have to check that the same disk is still in the drive before every access. Newer drives have a jumper or switch to alter the use of pin 34, to suit the system in which it is being used. If this is incorrectly set, or if an old drive that only provides a disk ready signal is installed in an AT, the machine will be unable to detect that the disk has been changed. This can cause all sorts of problems, including corruption of data.

Some high density 3.5in. drives have a jumper that enables the media sensor. This is used so that the drive can tell whether it is writing to a double density, 720Kb disk, or a high density 1.44Mb one, and adjust the write current accordingly. The diskette controllers used in early ATs did not support the use of pin 2 of the diskette interface to control the write current. Later controllers do use pin 2, so drives used with them don't need this jumper.

Until recently, diskette drives contained a removable terminating resistor pack. This is usually located close to the data cable socket on the logic board. On IBM drives it is clearly labelled *T-RES* so that there can be no mistake in identification. The purpose of the terminating resistor is to ensure that electrical energy in the signals from the disk controller is absorbed at the far end of the cable. If it were not present, the surplus signal energy would be reflected back down the cable, causing interference and errors.

The diskette drive cable is a long flat ribbon cable. At one end, there is a connector which mates with a socket on the controller board. At the other end there are two connectors, one for each of the two drives that a PC supports. The A: drive must be attached to the socket at the far end of the cable. This is the drive that should have a terminating resistor in place. If present, the B: drive is attached to the intermediate connector, and should have its terminating resistor removed. The resistor should be retained, in case you should wish to reinstall the drive as drive A: at some time in the future.

In some drives, the terminating resistor is built into the logic board, and disabled using a set of DIP switches or jumpers. Others use a single switch, and employ diode switching to place the resistors in or out of circuit. The latest drives simplify things further by eliminating the terminating resistor altogether. These drives might cause problems with long data cables, such as would be used with an external drive, but in most situations they work perfectly well.

7.5 The Diskette Drive Controller

All PCs have a diskette controller. This takes instructions from the software within the PC – usually the BIOS – and converts them to the signals needed to control a standard PC drive with a Shugart interface. It also buffers the data, and reads or writes it serially to and from the drive. On some PCs, the diskette drive controller is a separate expansion card. More often, it shares a card with the hard disk controller. On the latest PCs it may be part of a multi-function card containing the hard disk controller, serial and parallel ports. Or it may be built on to the motherboard itself.

Whatever the type of machine, all diskette controllers operate in the same way. The software sends commands to the controller using I/O ports. The registers used are 3F2 – 3F7 (hex). Some controllers support a secondary set of addresses at 372 – 377 (hex), selectable by jumper. However, these are not normally used. The controller demands attention from the system using IRQ6. DMA channel 2 is used to transfer data between the controller and system memory.

The diskette drive controller does not generally require any configuration. Some may require a jumper to be set if the system uses dual speed drives. Since the layout of every controller card is different, you'll need to refer to the controller documentation for the location of this jumper.

7.6 Diagnosing Problems

The most common diskette problem is that of read/write errors. For example, DOS reports errors reading diskettes that can be read quite happily by another PC. Write errors may also occur, and large numbers of bad sectors may be reported when formatting disks.

There are several possible explanations for this type of problem. The obvious should not be overlooked. If the problems are confined to a particular diskette, it could simply be damaged or faulty. If they affect several diskettes of the same type and manufacture, they could simply be poor quality disks, or the wrong type – DS/QD being used as DS/HD, for instance. However, if the errors occur on a wide range of disks, and are occurring more frequently as time goes on, it is likely that the problem lies in the drive itself.

The first and simplest thing to do is to clean the read/write heads using a commercial head cleaning kit. Use of these kits is described in the chapter on preventive maintenance. Usually, they comprise a jacket containing a mildly abrasive and absorbent diskette, which is moistened with cleaning fluid and inserted into the drive.

The system is then made to seek on the diskette – causing the cleaner to rotate and the heads to move about – by repeatedly executing a DIR or CHKDSK command or running a special head cleaning utility program for about 30 seconds or so.

Since there is nothing at all recorded on the cleaning diskette, any DOS command that accesses it will cause the heads to seek around the area in which the system expects to find track zero, before eventually reporting a General Failure error. Consequently, only a single track of the cleaning diskette is used. Eventually, it will wear out; most head cleaners claim to be efficient for up to 15 cleanings. A head cleaning utility such as CLEAN (in the public domain) will extend the life of the head cleaner by moving the heads to a different track, so that a different part of the surface is used.

7.7 Drive Misalignment

If cleaning does not cure a drive of read/write errors, then it may be out of alignment. There are several drive adjustments that must be correct for the drive to work perfectly. A misalignment in one or more of these parameters will increase the chance of errors occurring when reading or writing diskettes. It may also result in diskettes being produced that cannot be read reliably on other drives.

❑ *Radial alignment* is a measure of how well the head is centred over the track. This is illustrated in Figure 7.3. If the head is offset to one side or the other, it will not pick up the strongest signal from the magnetic dots on the disk, and so will be more prone to errors.

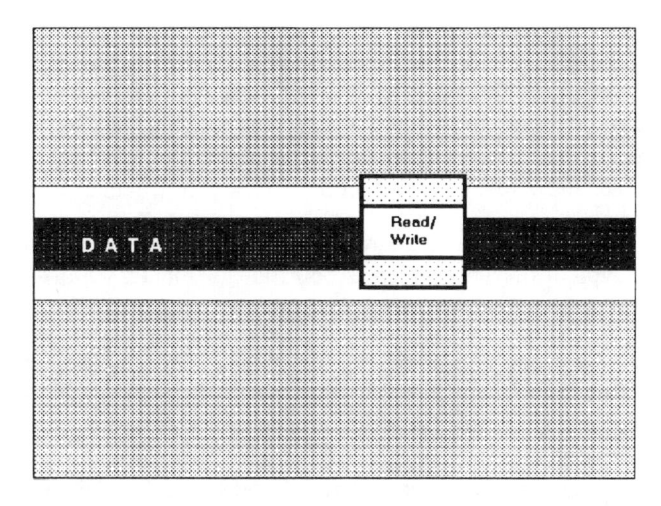

Figure 7.3: Radial misalignment of the head

❏ *Azimuth* is the angle made by the head with respect to the track itself, and is shown in Figure 7.4. The head should be exactly at a right angle to a radial line from the centre of the disk. Excessive deviation from this will increase the likelihood of errors occurring.

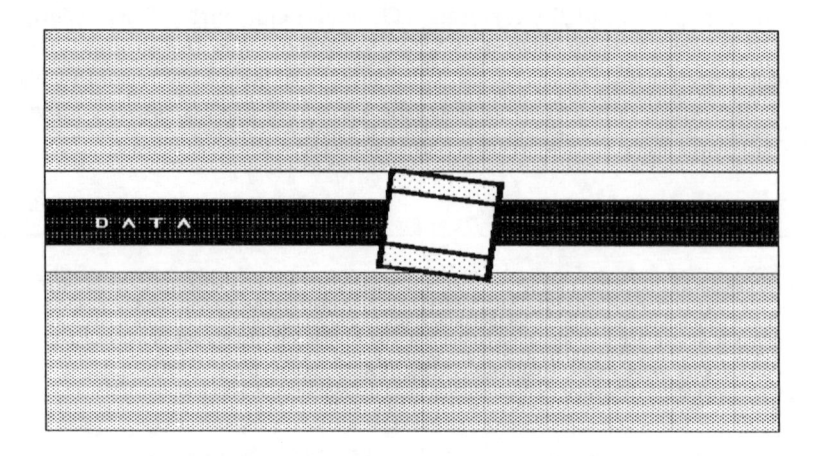

Figure 7.4: Azimuth misalignment of the head

❏ *Hysteresis* is a measure of how accurately the drive mechanism is able to position the head at a particular track when it is approached from either the outermost or the innermost tracks. If there is any wear in the head actuator mechanism the hysteresis will be excessive and the drive is likely to be unreliable.

❏ *Sensitivity* is a measure of over how wide an area the head will read data from a track. The wider the area over which it can read reliably, the less susceptible the drive will be to errors. *Hub centring* is an indication of how well the disk clamping mechanism holds the diskette centred on the hub so that it rotates in a perfect circle.

❏ The *spindle speed* must be accurate to within plus or minus 5 rpm of the nominal speed for the type of diskette, which is 360 rpm for the 1.2Mb diskettes, and 300 rpm for all others.

To check drive alignment, a special test diskette is needed, such as the Digital Diagnostic Diskette manufactured by Dysan. One DDD is required for each of the media types that you wish to test. In addition, a special software package able to read the DDD and display the results is needed, such as Interrogator by Dysan, or Test Drive by MicroSystems Development. Figure 7.5 shows the Test Drive main menu.

Diskette Drives

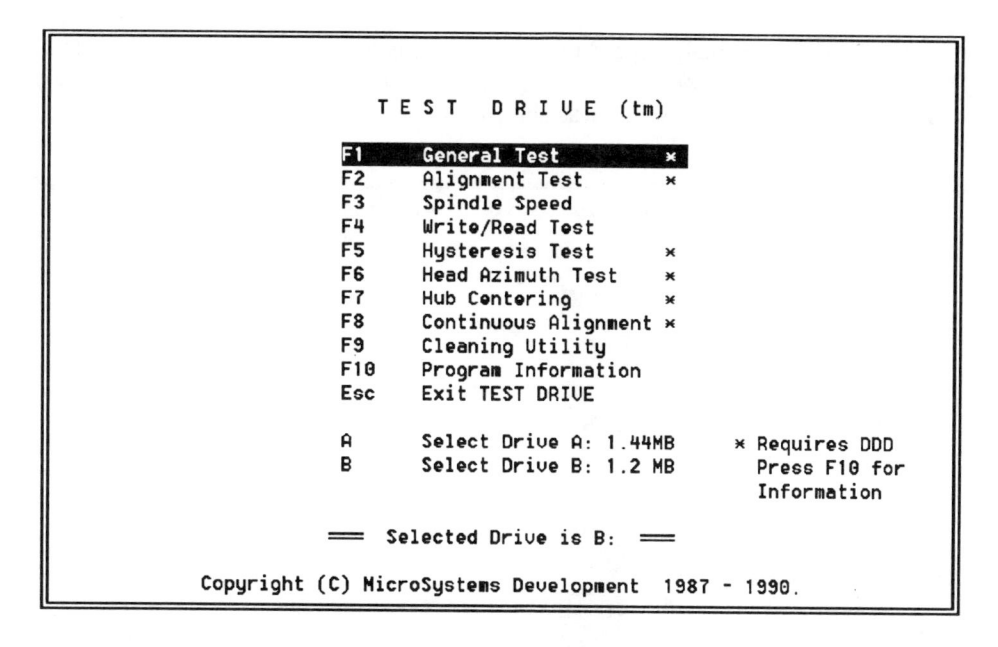

```
          T E S T   D R I V E  (tm)

          F1    General Test          *
          F2    Alignment Test        *
          F3    Spindle Speed
          F4    Write/Read Test
          F5    Hysteresis Test       *
          F6    Head Azimuth Test     *
          F7    Hub Centering         *
          F8    Continuous Alignment  *
          F9    Cleaning Utility
          F10   Program Information
          Esc   Exit TEST DRIVE

          A     Select Drive A: 1.44MB     * Requires DDD
          B     Select Drive B: 1.2 MB       Press F10 for
                                             Information

          ===  Selected Drive is B:  ===

    Copyright (C) MicroSystems Development  1987 - 1990.
```

Figure 7.5: Test Drive main menu

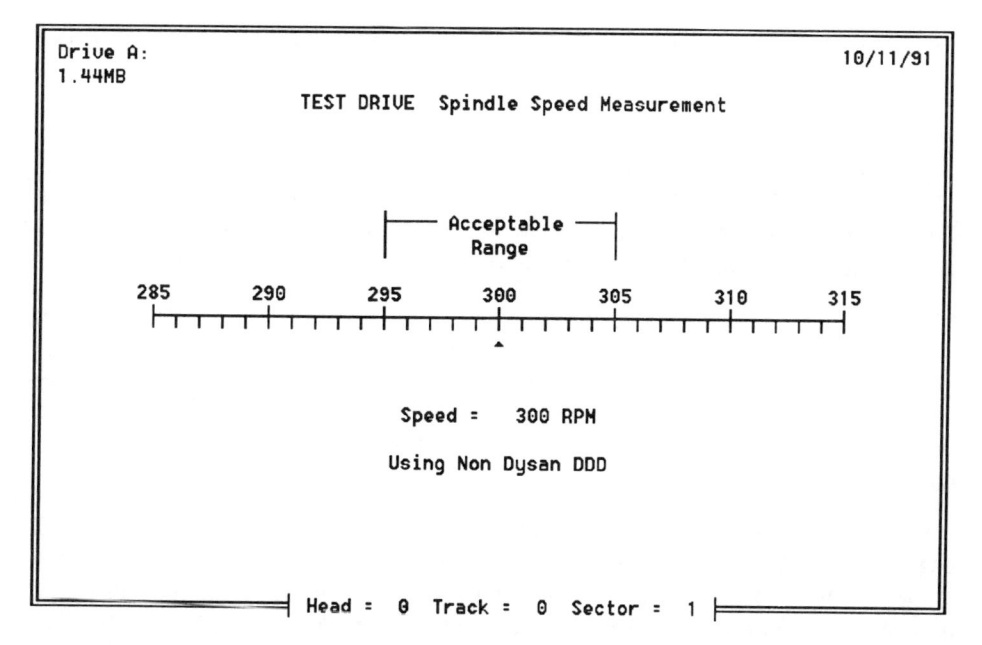

```
Drive A:                                              10/11/91
1.44MB
              TEST DRIVE   Spindle Speed Measurement


                         |— Acceptable —|
                         |    Range     |
       285      290      295     300     305      310      315
       |‒‒‒‒‒‒‒‒|‒‒‒‒‒‒‒‒|‒‒‒‒‒‒‒|‒‒‒‒‒‒‒|‒‒‒‒‒‒‒‒|‒‒‒‒‒‒‒‒|
                                  ▲

                      Speed =   300 RPM

                      Using Non Dysan DDD




                  | Head = 0  Track = 0  Sector = 1 |
```

Figure 7.6: Test Drive spindle speed measurement screen

Figure 7.6 shows the spindle speed measurement screen, and Figure 7.7 shows output from a read/write test carried out by Test Drive. A version of this program that works with 360Kb drives only is available as shareware.

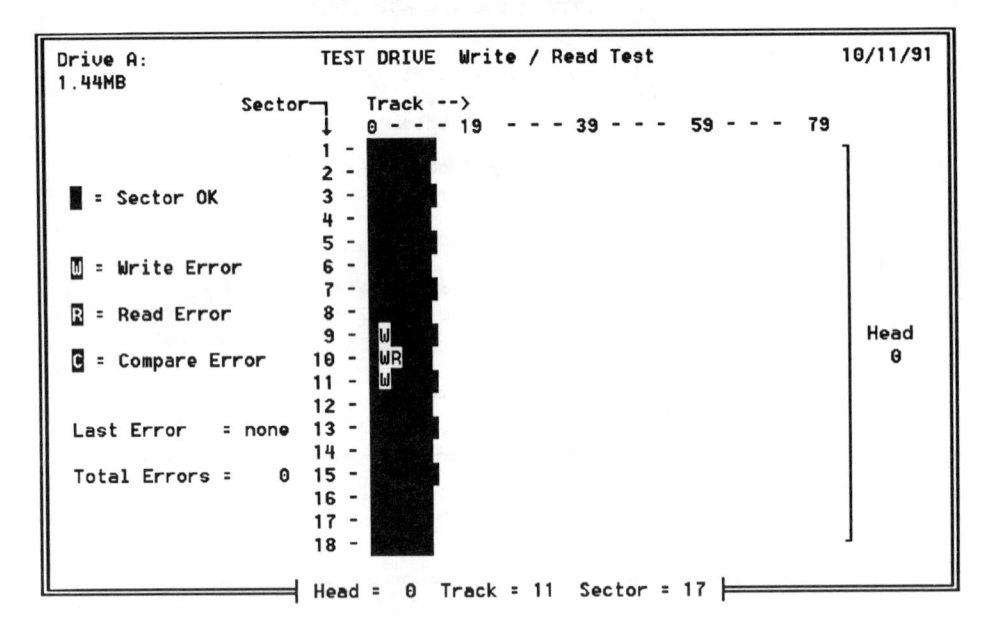

```
 ┌─────────────────────────────────────────────────────────────────────┐
 │ Drive A:              TEST DRIVE  Write / Read Test        10/11/91 │
 │ 1.44MB                                                              │
 │                 Sector┐  Track -->                                  │
 │                       ↓  0 - - - 19 - - - 39 - - - 59 - - - 79     │
 │                       1 -                                           │
 │                       2 -                                           │
 │     ■ = Sector OK     3 -                                           │
 │                       4 -                                           │
 │                       5 -                                           │
 │     W = Write Error   6 -                                           │
 │                       7 -                                           │
 │     R = Read Error    8 -                                           │
 │                       9 -   W                                  Head │
 │     C = Compare Error 10 -  WR                                  0   │
 │                       11 -  W                                       │
 │                       12 -                                          │
 │     Last Error = none 13 -                                          │
 │                       14 -                                          │
 │     Total Errors =  0 15 -                                          │
 │                       16 -                                          │
 │                       17 -                                          │
 │                       18 -                                          │
 │                  ┤ Head = 0   Track = 11   Sector = 17 ├            │
 └─────────────────────────────────────────────────────────────────────┘
```

Figure 7.7: Test Drive read/write test display

7.8 Servicing Drives

If diagnostics reveal that a drive is misaligned, you'll need to decide what to do about it. What you'll probably do is replace the drive with a new one.

Modern drives are mass-produced items. They cost a fraction of what they did 10 years ago. One way in which manufacturing costs have been reduced is to leave out alignment hardware. Drives are correctly adjusted when they leave the factory. If they go wrong, the intention is that you should replace them. Since new drives cost less than an hour of a service engineer's time, it isn't worth spending the time trying to repair them.

If you should be faced with a drive problem the simplest solution is to take the service engineer's approach. If a drive is malfunctioning, and cleaning does not cure the problem, replace it with a new one. This will save time and keep the user happy. If time is available, however, some drive alignment problems may be rectified. A hardware reference manual for the drive will probably be needed to identify the relevant adjustments.

Older drives, especially the full-height ones, have a variable resistor to adjust the spindle speed. Some of these drives have a set of stroboscopic markings on one of the pulley wheels. These should appear stationary when viewed in electric light if the drive is rotating at the correct speed. If two sets of markings are provided, then that with the marks farthest apart is for 50Hz power, while the other set is for 60Hz power used in the USA. If no markings are provided, the speed must be adjusted with the drive in the machine and Test Drive or another speed testing utility running.

Some drives also have an adjustment screw for head alignment. Test Drive has a continuous alignment option that can be run while adjustments to the head alignment are made. Only small adjustments are usually needed, so take care. It is easy to make things worse rather than better.

Drives do not usually provide any adjustment for head azimuth. If this is incorrect, either the drive was faulty when manufactured or it has been somehow pushed out of alignment. Azimuth cannot be checked for 3.5in. drives, as the DDD does not contain azimuth measurement tracks. Errors of hysteresis and hub centring are signs of wear in the drive, and would suggest that it should be replaced.

7.9 Drive Failure

If the system will not read from a drive at all the problem may be something other than dirt or misalignment. It may be difficult to run any diagnostics if the drive in question is the A: drive on a PC without a hard disk.

The first action should be to check that the data and power cables are attached to the drive, and the controller is correctly seated in its expansion bus socket. It is worth visually checking the data cable itself. I have seen cables in old machines where the insulation has been worn away by chafing against sharp edges inside the case, exposing the wire. This could short out a vital signal and cause a malfunction. With an old drive the spindle drive belt may have failed.

If the drive light comes on during the power-up tests, this will show that power is getting to the drive and the controller is functioning. If the system cannot be booted, it is a good idea to transfer the drive to another machine and install it as drive B:. This will enable cleaning and diagnostics to be carried out, and may also establish whether the fault is in the controller. On a two drive system the cable can be swapped over to make the second drive the A: drive, but remember to check the drive select setting on the logic board if a non-twisted cable is used, and to swap over the terminating resistor, if present. Also, on an AT, if the two drives are of different types, the CMOS set-up will need to be changed. Should neither of two drives present in a system work, the problem is almost certain to be in the controller.

7.10 Diskette Change-line Problems

AT class machines use drives that send a signal on pin 34 of the interface connector to show if the diskette has been changed. As already mentioned, there is an alternative use of this pin, and the choice is usually made by switch or jumper on the logic board.

When an AT reads from a diskette, it will read a copy of the file allocation table and the root directory into memory. It will only force a reread of this information if the system receives a signal that the diskette has been changed. If the drive installed supplies a *drive ready* signal, instead of *disk changed*, the AT BIOS will not be able to tell if the diskette has been changed. If a disk is inserted in the drive and read, and then a different one is inserted and a DIR command is run, the directory of the first diskette will be displayed. What is more disastrous is that, should a program open an output file on the second diskette, the system will actually think it is opening the file on the first diskette. It will write data to parts of the disk that would have been free on the first diskette but may contain data on the second. The second disk's directory and FAT will also be corrupted.

If this sort of problem is being experienced on an AT type system the probable cause is an incorrect diskette change-line signal. The jumper that enables this signal may be incorrectly set. Alternatively, the sensor inside the drive may be broken or stuck. This can be checked by examination. Finally, it may be that the drive was simply not designed to provide this signal.

If the drive does not provide a change-line signal, one solution is to open-circuit pin 34 of the interface. A jumper may be provided for this purpose, or it may be necessary to cut the PCB track leading to pin 34. An easier solution can be found if a version of MS-DOS which supports the DRIVPARM command is available. If CONFIG.SYS is amended to include a DRIVPARM line for the drive, without a /C switch, DOS will not expect the drive to provide a change-line signal. It will therefore reread the directory before every access. The line:

```
DRIVPARM=/d:1 /f:0
```

would be correct for a 360Kb diskette drive used as drive B:.

7.11 Problems Reading Diskettes Written by Other Machines

If a drive is unreliable when reading diskettes written by other machines, there are several possible explanations. The drive may be out of alignment, in which case it may be checked as described earlier. The problem may be confined to diskettes written by a particular machine which may have a misaligned drive. If the drive in question is a 5.25in. DS/DD drive, and the diskettes which are failing were written on high density drives, the problem is a common incompatibility between DS/DD diskettes produced by the two types of drive.

Low density 5.25in. drives are designed to read and write using a density of 48 tracks per inch. Each track is about 0.02in wide. High density drives are designed to read and write high density diskettes, using 96 tracks per inch, so the tracks they write are only half as wide. High density drives can write to low density disks. They simply leave more space between the tracks. However, the width of the tracks they write is still 0.01in, because it is governed by the physical construction of the head.

The problem is illustrated in Figure 7.8. If data is written to a low density disk using a low density drive, a full 0.02in width track is written. If a high density drive now writes to the disk, it's read/write head won't be wide enough to overwrite or erase the old data over the whole width of the track. When the updated disk is taken back and read on a double density drive, the wider head will pick up both the new data, and the remains of the old. It won't receive a clean signal, so read errors will occur.

a. High density drive head is unable to erase all the information written by the double density drive

b. Double density drive head picks up both the data written by the high density drive, and the remains of the original data; the result - errors.

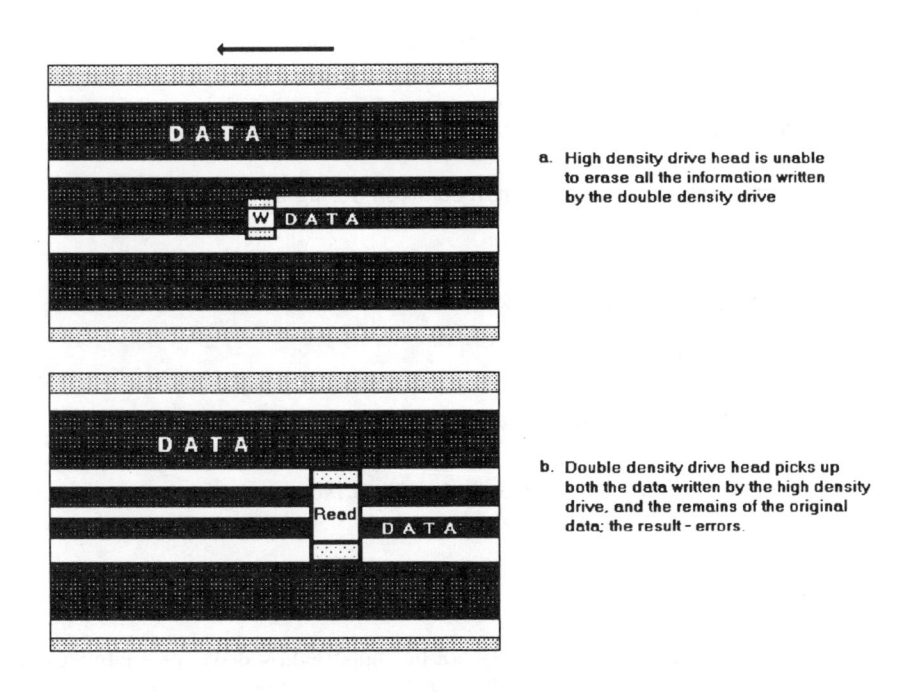

Figure 7.8: Writing to a low density disk with a high density drive

The solution is simple, and involves making up a transfer diskette that is used specifically for moving data *from* a high density drive *to* a low density one. Take a *brand new*, unformatted DS/DD diskette and format it to 360Kb on the high density drive. This diskette may be read on either type of drive, but it should only ever be written to by a high density drive. To make sure, you should label this disk to that effect. If you only write to the transfer diskette on a high density drive, 0.02in wide tracks will never be written to it, and the low density drive will always be able to read it.

7.12 Diskette Problems – Checklist

Read/write errors occurring:

❑ Diskette could be damaged.

❑ Diskette could be of poor quality or wrong density.

❑ Drive heads may be dirty.

❑ Drive may be misaligned; repair or replace.

System will not read from drive at all:

❑ Check data and power cables; does light come on during boot-up?

❑ Drive may be dirty.

❑ Possible drive logic failure; try another drive.

❑ Possible controller failure.

System displays directory of diskette which was previously in the drive:

❑ Diskette change-line may not be supported by drive, or jumper incorrectly set. Check drive; use DRIVPARM if available.

Diskettes are corrupted:

❑ If an AT, then diskette change-line may not be supported by drive, or a jumper may be incorrectly set. Check drive; use DRIVPARM if available.

❑ Drive controller or logic board fault.

Errors reading diskettes written on other PCs:

❑ If a double-density drive – diskettes may be written by a high density drive.

❑ Diskettes may be of poor quality.

❑ Drive may be misaligned.

7.13 Diskette Drive Installation

To install a diskette drive in a PC, carry out the following steps:

❑ Power off the system and remove the mains cable from the socket. Remove the system unit cover.

❑ If a blanking plate is fitted to the drive bay, remove it. You may need to remove the front panel, depending on the design of case.

❑ If the drive is to be fitted into an AT, check that the diskette change-line is enabled. If it is not supported by the drive, ensure that pin 34 of the interface is open circuited.

❑ Check that the media sensor of a high density 3.5in. drive is enabled, if a jumper is fitted for this purpose.

❑ If the drive is to be used as A:, observe the following:

  ➪ if the drive uses a removable terminating resistor, check that it is installed

  ➪ if the data cable has a twisted section between the two drive connectors, ensure that the drive select switch or jumper is set to the second position; if the cable is flat, set it to the first position

  ➪ slide the drive into the case and attach to the connector at the end of the data cable.

❑ If the drive is to be used as B:, observe the following:

  ➪ if the drive uses a removable terminating resistor, remove it

  ➪ ensure that the drive select switch or jumper is set to the second position

  ➪ slide the drive into the case and attach to the connector towards the middle of the data cable.

❑ Attach the power connector.

- ❏ Fit mounting screws, ensuring that drive is in the correct position.
- ❏ Refit the system unit cover, and power up the system.
- ❏ Update the CMOS configuration, on AT machines.
- ❏ Test the drive.

7.14 Diskette Drive Removal

To remove a drive from a PC, perform the following steps:

- ❏ Power off the system and remove the mains cable. Remove the system unit cover. Insert the card shipping insert into the drive or, failing that, use a discarded diskette.
- ❏ Remove the data and power cables from the drive.
- ❏ Remove the drive mounting screws. In some cases, it may be necessary to remove one or more expansion cards to get access to these screws. Take care to note the position of the cards and any associated cables if this is done.
- ❏ Slide the drive out of the mounting bay.

7.15 3.5inch Drives

IBM introduced 3.5in. drives into its PC range in April 1986. At the same time, PC DOS 3.2 was introduced, which provided support for such drives. 3.5in. drives have become the standard for IBM compatible PCs, so there is a frequent demand to install them in older machines. If you're going to attempt this, there are three potential pitfalls:

- ❏ Lack of operating system support (versions of DOS earlier than 3.2)
- ❏ Lack of BIOS support
- ❏ A diskette controller that is unable to support these drives.

Systems which can support 720Kb double density drives may not be able to support the high density versions. One reason, particularly on XTs, is that the controller can't operate at the higher data rate these drives require. However, you can buy alternative controllers that allow high density drives to be fitted to XTs. On such machines, BIOS support is also likely to be absent, so these controllers come with their own BIOS which replaces the diskette BIOS functions in the standard system ROM.

Some machines may support 3.5in. drives, but won't recognise one as such on boot-up. One thing you can try in this case is to use the DRIVPARM command in CONFIG.SYS to force the number of tracks and sectors to the correct value for the drive. For example:

```
DRIVPARM=/D:1 /F:7
```

would tell the system that the second drive is a 3.5in. 1.44Mb drive.

If this does not work, a ROM BIOS upgrade may be required. Many manufacturers can provide ROM upgrades for older machines. Alternatively, third-party BIOS upgrades are available for many better known machines.

Even if a PC supports high density 3.5in. diskettes, certain drives are incompatible with certain manufacturers' BIOSes. This shouldn't be a problem with new drives, but it's something to be aware of if you're thinking of buying a drive from a used or surplus stock dealer. Check that the drive is compatible with your system before purchasing.

One problem you'll probably experience when fitting a 3.5in. drive is that the drive connectors are incompatible. 5.25in. drives use an edge connector that fits directly on to the logic board. 3.5in. drives use a 34-way IDC connector that has two rows of pins. The mounting cradles normally used to fit a 3.5in. drive into a 5.25in. drive bay usually come with an appropriate adapter. If you don't have an adapter, one can be purchased at nominal cost from hardware suppliers such as Loutronics.

7.16 External Diskette Drives

Sometimes, you may wish to have more than two diskette drives. This can often be useful, particularly if you need to have a non-standard drive – for example an 8in drive – connected to a PC. Such drives must be fitted externally.

You can buy add-in controllers that support the use of more than two diskette drives. A software device driver will be provided with the controller card. You should install this in CONFIG.SYS along with DRIVER.SYS, which informs the system of the characteristics of the additional drives. If present, your first hard disk partition will always be C:, so the drive letters allocated to the third and subsequent diskette drives will follow on from the last fixed disk drive letter.

Summary

We began this chapter by looking at how diskettes are made and how data is stored on them. We saw that the different types of diskette – double density and high density – use a different type of magnetic media, and as a result, must only be formatted at the capacity for which they were made.

Next, we looked at drives, how they are made, and how they are configured and installed. IBM PCs use the standard Shugart interface, but there is a difference between the drives used in XTs and those for ATs. Problems can occur if XT drives are used in an AT.

We went on to look at some diskette drive faults. These are mostly caused by bad media, dirty read/write heads and misaligned drives. However, faulty drive electronics or controllers may also cause problems. The chapter concluded by describing the removal and installation of drives, and some of the problems that may be encountered fitting 3.5in. drives to an older machine.

8

Hard Disks

Few PCs these days don't have a hard disk, unless only used to access a network. It's hard to believe that when the IBM PC was introduced, no provision was made for a hard disk drive. But its power supply was inadequate, and no upgrade was offered. Nowadays, to use a PC without a hard disk would be unthinkable. Many software packages are too large to run from floppy, while the instant access to our programs and data that a hard disk provides is something we have come to take for granted.

Hard disks can store a phenomenal amount of information. The problem with taking them for granted is that, when they go wrong, it comes as something of a shock. It's often not until the data held on the disk becomes inaccessible that the user realises its true value, and the fact that the last back-up was made a fortnight ago! Dealing with a failed hard disk can be one of the most difficult support tasks you'll face. Often, the value of the unrecoverable data is greater than the cost of the disk itself. Replacement of the faulty unit is not the end of the problem as far as the user is concerned.

Hard disks are much more reliable than they used to be. At the same time, the amount of data many of them hold is greater and so, therefore, is the potential loss. Regular and frequent back-ups are the only salvation when a hard disk goes down, and doing them, or checking that they are done, is a vitally important function of PC support.

8.1 Hard Disk Basics

Hard disks operate on the same basic principles as diskettes, described in the previous chapter. However, some significant differences in the way they are constructed mean that they are faster, and can hold much more data. A hard disk is usually not one disk but several, mounted one above the other, as shown in Figures 8.1 and 8.2. Figure 8.3 shows the main components of a hard disk Each disk or *platter* can have a recording surface on each side, although the outermost two surfaces are not always used. A hard disk will therefore normally have more than two read/write heads.

Figure 8.1: A 3.5 inch hard disk (Seagate ST351A/X; 42 MB)

Figure 8.2: A large capacity 5.25 inch hard disk (Seagate ST4766NV; 676 MB)

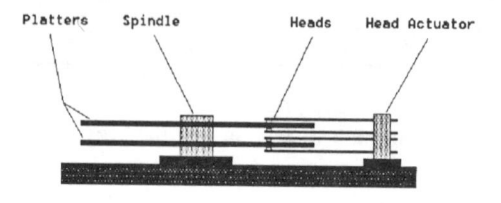

Figure 8.3: Hard disk construction

The disk surface is divided up into sectors and tracks, just like a diskette. However, with a hard disk, as well as tracks we also talk about *cylinders*. These can be visualised as the shape made by joining up all the same-numbered tracks one above the other on each platter of the disk. The storage capacity of a disk can be calculated by multiplying together the number of heads, the number of cylinders and the number of sectors per track, and the number of bytes per sector – 512. These characteristics vary widely between different models and different manufacturers. This is why fitting a new hard disk to a machine can be a bit more complicated than replacing a diskette drive.

The platters of a hard disk are rigid and made of aluminium. This is why it's called a *hard* disk. The platters are the same size as diskette recording media: 5.25in. or 3.5in., though 2in. drives are now becoming available. The disk rotates at high speed, usually 3,600 rpm. At this speed, the read/write heads do not touch the surface of the disk. Air pressure builds up under the heads and lifts them a few millionths of an inch off the surface. A dust or smoke particle that tried to pass through such a microscopic gap would cause the head to bounce over it and then plough into the rotating disk surface on the rebound. Consequently, the disks are contained in a hermetically sealed casing, and are assembled in a sterile, dust-free environment. It isn't possible to open the casing to try to repair a faulty disk, unless you have a special *clean room* in which this can be done.

8.2 Recording Media

Hard disks typically have several hundred tracks or cylinders, rather than the 40 or 80 of a diskette. It follows from this that the tracks are very much narrower, and the magnetic dots which represent the data are much closer together. This can only be achieved because of the controlled environment within the disk casing, and the use of much more sophisticated media and read/write heads. The earliest hard drives used a ferric oxide coating on the aluminium platters, just like a diskette drive. Because of the microscopic tolerances at which the head operates, this coating must be polished perfectly smooth. Oxide is still used in low-cost, low-capacity drives.

As recording densities get higher and higher, both to obtain greater storage capacities and to make smaller drives, manufacturers have had to develop a new type of recording medium. This is known as a *thin-film* medium. A cobalt alloy is used in place of ferric oxide. This is deposited on to the platter either by electro-plating or by a process known as *sputtering*. However it is achieved, the result is a very thin, smooth, hard magnetic coating that provides a much stronger signal to the read/write head, is more resistant to physical damage, and allows much greater storage capacities to be achieved.

8.3 Head Actuators

As in the diskette drive, the read/write heads have the job of recording magnetic dots on to the surface of the disk media. The heads are mounted on an actuator, which moves them from track to track (or cylinder to cylinder). They are spring loaded, and when the platters are stationary, they sit lightly on the media surface. The heads are aerodynamically shaped. Once the platters are spinning at full speed, the pressure of air moved around by the spinning disk builds up under them. This lifts them off the surface so that they fly a few millionths of an inch above it.

A hard disk should not be moved while it is running. Since the distance between the head and the disk itself is so tiny, it does not take a very great shock to cause the head to plough into the disk. This is called a *head crash* and can damage the recording surface, leading to permanent read/write errors or *bad sectors*.

The head actuators in many hard disks are stepper motors, such as are used in diskette drives. They are cheap and simple, but have several disadvantages. First, they are slow. The movement of the read/write heads from one cylinder to another is called a *seek*. There are two measurements commonly used to show the speed of a hard disk: the track-to-track *seek time* and the *access time*. The seek time is simply the time needed for the heads to move from one track to the next. The access time is the time taken for the heads to move an average distance, typically half the number of tracks on the disk. Both figures are quoted in milliseconds. Stepper motor actuators give a track-to-track seek of from 20ms to about 8ms, and an access time of between 75ms and 28ms.

Another problem with stepper motor actuators is *drive alignment drift*. The head positioning is mechanical, like the click positions of a rotary switch (though of course much finer). After a long period, the mechanism will wear, so that the alignment of the head with the track is not exact. When this happens, the data written to the disk will be out of line with the sector headers put there by the low-level format program (see Figure 8.4). Eventually, the heads will not read both the sector headers and the data reliably, and read/write errors will occur.

A second, related problem is one of thermal expansion. Hard disks get quite hot during operation and this causes the platters, the actuator mechanism, everything in fact, to expand. This means that the positioning of the head when the drive is cold will differ slightly from when it is hot. Thermal effects can exacerbate the problem of alignment drift. This explains why systems sometimes suffer from hard disk errors when cold, which disappear once they have warmed up, or vice versa.

To overcome the problems just described, better quality drives use *voice coil* actuators. The heads of these drives are driven by a moving armature inside an electromagnetic

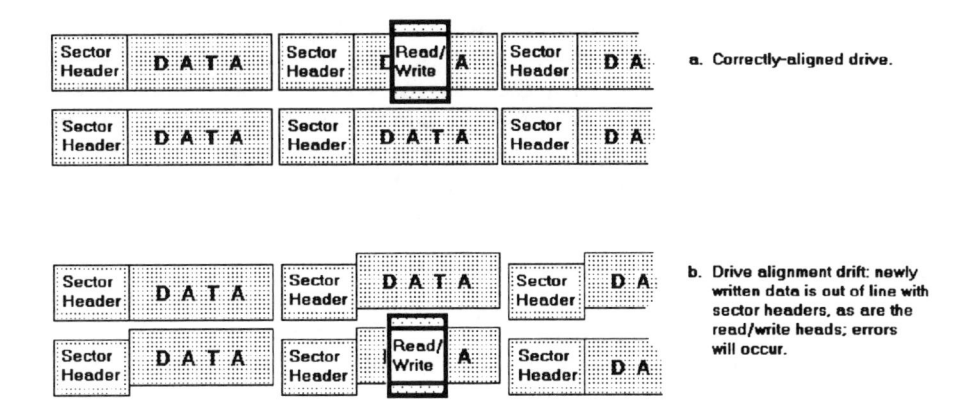

Figure 8.4: Drive alignment drift

coil. This is known as a voice coil because of its similarity to the coils used to drive loudspeakers. The head positioning is infinitely variable. One disk surface is used to hold special *servo tracks* placed there during manufacture. One head is dedicated to reading the servo tracks, and the control electronics use this to decide when the heads are positioned over the correct track, and can fine tune the positioning to get the strongest signal from the recorded data. This eliminates inaccuracy due to wear or expansion. Voice coil actuators are a lot faster than stepper motors, achieving typical track-to-track seeks of 8ms or less, and access times of from 28ms down to about 9ms. But they are also more expensive.

8.4 Head Parking

Before a hard disk is moved, it is important to ensure that the heads are *parked*. If the lightly-sprung heads are left resting against tracks that hold data, any shocks caused by movement will make them scratch against the recording surface. This will result in read/write errors. Parking is the process of moving the heads out of the way to a cylinder that isn't used to store data, so that any damage that might occur is unnoticed. This cylinder is known as the *landing zone*.

With stepper motor actuators, the head positioning is mechanical. When the power to the drive is turned off, the heads remain over the track they were last moved to. They will come to rest on that track once the spinning platters come to a halt. When the system is next switched on, the sudden application of power to the stepper motor can cause it to jerk the heads to one side. This could scratch the recording surface. To avoid the chance of damage, the heads should be parked. This usually involves running a special program that moves them to the landing zone before switching off.

A few Seagate stepper motor drives are self parking. These drives have a logic board containing some electronics that senses when the power is removed and then commands the stepper motor to move the heads to the landing zone using what power remains in the unit. Voice coil actuators are spring biased so that when power is removed from the voice coil, the heads move back to a safe, parked position. All voice coil drives are therefore inherently self-parking; there is no need to run any special park program.

The question of whether to park the heads of a hard disk whenever the system is switched off, whether it is going to be moved or not, is often the subject of debate. The heads are designed to land on the disk when the system is powered off, and the drive medium is intended to withstand this. Manufacturers of non self-parking drives only recommend that the heads are parked if the system or drive is to be physically moved. Nevertheless, friction between the head and the platter must inevitably result in wear of the recording surface. Parking the heads will ensure that they never come into contact with the area of the disk used to hold programs and data.

8.5 Recording Methods

Earlier in this chapter, and in the chapter on diskette drives, we spoke of data being stored on the surface of a disk platter or diskette as a pattern of magnetic dots. This is an easy way of visualising how data is stored, but it is not strictly correct. In fact, each dot is stored on the disk as a change in magnetic polarity or *flux*. When the disk is read, these flux changes induce an electrical pulse into the read head. The pulses are amplified by the drive logic board and then passed to the disk controller for processing.

The most obvious method of recording data would be to store it using one pulse for a 1 bit, and none for a zero. However, if the data contained many zeros – quite common in computer files – no pulses would be received for a long period, and it would be difficult to know how many zeros had actually been read. In theory, it would be possible to use a timing clock to count how many bits should have been received. In practice, though, this would fail because the speed of rotation of the disk may vary. This is particularly true of diskettes, where the drag of the disk inside its jacket can affect the spindle speed quite significantly.

Originally, diskettes used a modulation method known as *frequency modulation (FM)*, in which a 1 was recorded as two pulses XX and a 0 as X- (a pulse followed by a pause). In this method, there was never more than one pause between two pulses, so the speed of rotation was not critical. The hardware could easily recognise the difference between two consecutive pulses and a pulse followed by a pause, and hence decide what was a 1 and what was a 0. This method of data encoding is sometimes called 0,1 RLL. RLL stands for *run length limited*. What it means is that the length of a run of pauses is limited to between 0 and 1. Figure 8.5 (a) gives an example of data encoded using this scheme.

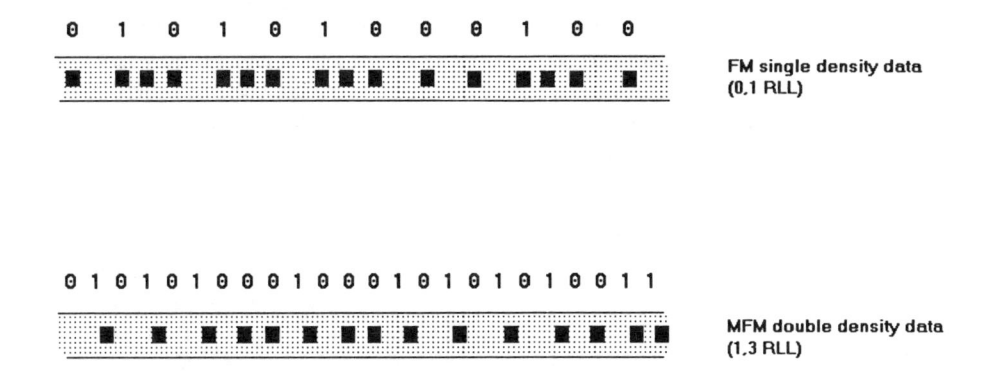

```
0  1  0  1  0  1  0  0  0  1  0  0
```
FM single density data
(0,1 RLL)

```
0 1 0 1 0 1 0 0 0 1 0 0 0 1 0 1 0 1 0 1 0 0 1 1
```
MFM double density data
(1,3 RLL)

Figure 8.5: Disk modulation methods

FM worked well, and was used for single-density diskettes. However manufacturers were looking for ways to get increased storage capacity. They found that if the pattern of flux changes was arranged so that there was always at least one pause between pulses, they could put twice as much data on to the same area of disk. This is illustrated in Figure 8.5 (b). A 1 is represented by a pause followed by a pulse, and a 0 is represented by either a pause or a pulse – the opposite of what preceded it – followed by a pause. Using this method, there will never be fewer than one, or more than three, pauses between pulses, so it is called 1,3 RLL.

Since there will always be at least one pause between pulses, it is possible to record the individual elements of the code closer together. This enables double the density of FM encoding to be achieved. This modulation method is called *modified frequency modulation* (MFM), and is used for double- and high-density diskettes, as well as older types of hard disk. MFM yields a density of 17 sectors per track in a hard disk. It is still used for low-capacity drives. The 20Mb Seagate ST-225, the world's biggest selling hard disk, is one example of an MFM hard disk.

With a standard PC hard disk, the disk controller performs the task of converting the sequences of pulses and pauses to bits and bytes. All the drive logic board does is move the heads, select the head to read from or write to, and convert the pattern of pulses read by the head into electrical signals for processing by the controller. When writing, it is the controller that tells the drive the pattern of flux changes to record on to the disk.

In their quest for still higher disk capacities, manufacturers devised a controller that used a code known as 2,7 RLL. This uses variable length patterns of pulses to represent groups of bits. 2,7 RLL achieves a 50% higher density by ensuring that there is always a minimum of two pauses between magnetic pulses on the disk surface. However, this code places more stringent demands on the drive, since it now has to be able to distinguish reliably between 2, 3, 4, 5, 6 or 7 *pauses* between recorded pulses. The controller must also be more complex because the variable length code makes error correction and detection more difficult. Drives designed to use 2,7 RLL encoding are known simply as RLL drives.

RLL controllers can be used with existing MFM drives, to squeeze an extra 50% of data capacity out of them – typically 25 or 26 sectors per track. However, errors are much more likely when the drive characteristics slowly alter through age, wear and other factors. When this happens, the controller will not be able to read back the encoded data correctly. True RLL drives are manufactured to closer tolerances than the MFM variants, and should therefore be more reliable. However, some unscrupulous companies in the competitive low-cost PC clone marketplace produced machines that used the cheaper MFM drives driven by RLL controllers. These systems were prone to hard disk errors, and are largely responsible for giving RLL a bad name.

Another reason early RLL drives tended to be unreliable was because the encoding and decoding of data was carried out by the disk controller and not the drive logic board. The encoded data travels between the controller and the drive on a lengthy ribbon cable that winds around other boards in the PC adding noise and distortion to the signal. Later types of hard disk controller perform the encoding and decoding on the drive logic board. This is known as an *integrated drive*. Integrated drives have the advantage that the controller can be matched to the drive characteristics, and eliminate the noise and distortion problem.

8.6 Hard Disk Interfaces

The interface of a hard disk describes the set of control signals expected at the connector on the drive logic board. For the PC, IBM chose to use an industry standard interface developed by Seagate Technology and known as the ST-506 or ST-412 after the two Seagate drives that originally used it. The ST-506 interface uses two cables between the controller and the drive, a control cable and a data cable. The connections are listed in Table 8.1.

Table 8.1: ST-506 interface pin assignments

PIN	SIGNAL NAME	I/O
Control Cable		
odd nos	Ground	
2	Head Select 3	O
4	Head Select 2	O
6	Write Gate	O
8	Seek Complete	I
10	Track 0	I
12	Write Fault	I
14	Head Select 0	O
16	Not used	
18	Head Select 1	O
20	Index	I
22	Drive Ready	I
24	Step pulse	O
26	Drive Select 0	O
28	Drive Select 1	O
30	Not used	
32	Not used	
34	Direction (of head movement)	O
Data Cable		
1,3,5	Not used	
2,4,6	Ground	
7,8,9,10	Not used	
11,12	Ground	
13	Write MFM Data +	O
14	Write MFM Data −	O
15,16	Ground	
17	Read MFM Data +	I
18	Read MFM Data −	I
19,20	Ground	

It is very basic; most of the work is done by the controller. For example, a signal on one pin of the interface specifies that the heads should be moved by one track, another specifies the direction — in or out. The data cables simply convey the patterns of pulses to be written to or read from the disk. Conversion to and from bits and bytes using the MFM or RLL encoding methods, and the handling of sector headers and other formatting information present on the disk, is all done by the controller.

The ST-506 interface suffers from one major limitation: speed. Using MFM encoding the maximum speed at which it can transfer data to the controller is 5Mbit/s, or 7.5Mbit/s if 2,7 RLL is used. This is the number of bits which pass under a read/write head in one second. For a long time, this was not a limitation. The first disk controllers couldn't process the data at that speed. Nor was the IBM XT bus fast enough to handle it. However, with the arrival of the AT, with its 16-bit bus, and faster controllers, the interface became the factor limiting data transfer rate. Also, other aspects of the design restrict the maximum capacity of an ST-506 drive to 127.5Mb, or about 190Mb if RLL is used.

The ESDI standard is an improved version of ST-506. ESDI stands for *Enhanced Small Device Interface* and was originally developed by Maxtor Corporation as a standard interface for hard disks and optical disk drives. It uses the same control and data cables as the ST-506 interface. However, the drive logic does much more of the work. RLL encoding and the separation of data from formatting information is carried out by the drive itself. Only data is passed to the disk controller.

A feature of ESDI is that drives can pass identifying information to the controller. This can then adopt the appropriate configuration automatically, without the need for jumper settings to be changed. The controller makes disk accesses by sending to the drive control words containing the absolute address of the data to be read or written. This means that there is only a very small control overhead, which makes these drives very fast.

Most ESDI drives are formatted at 34 or 35 sectors per track. This gives a transfer speed of 10Mbits/s – double that of an ST-506 MFM drive. However, greater densities and higher transfer rates are possible. Large capacity drives can be accommodated, with a maximum of over one gigabyte.

The SCSI or *Small Computer Systems Interface* – usually pronounced *scuzzy* – is a general purpose interface used for attaching various types of device to a computer system. SCSI is an eight-bit parallel bus that can support up to eight devices. Each device has its own controller, which is sent instructions over the bus. The SCSI interface card, which sits in the PC expansion bus, is known as a *host adapter*. It controls the SCSI bus, sending commands and data to the devices, and receiving acknowledgements and data from them.

SCSI is a command protocol rather than a drive interface. To read a block of data, the host adapter sends a command out on the bus as a stream of bytes. The command is decoded and executed by the destination device, which then sends the data. Theoretically, this offers device independence. In practice, though, this is not always achieved because of differences in SCSI implementations between different manufacturers.

Concepts like the number of cylinders and heads in a drive are not important with SCSI, as these characteristics are hidden from the user software. However a PC, which provides BIOS functions to allow programmers to access disk drives at this level, must have special driver software loaded to emulate the BIOS functions and interface with the SCSI host adapter. Incompatibilities can arise with some PC software packages. The likelihood of avoiding such problems depends largely on the quality of the drivers and how transparent they are to the software.

SCSI is capable of high transfer rates – typically 12Mbit/s, but up to 32Mbit/s using *synchronous SCSI*, a variant of the protocol in which the receiver does not have to acknowledge each byte of data before the next one is sent. However, the time needed to translate SCSI commands adds a fixed delay of a few milliseconds to every data transfer. SCSI is also relatively expensive to implement. This means that it is normally only used for fast, high-capacity devices which would be expected to bear a high price tag. Faster SCSI support chips, and developments like SCSI II, which has a 32-bit wide data bus, will ensure that the standard is able to keep up with the latest developments in high-speed storage devices.

The IDE interface is a fairly recent development. It is rapidly taking over from the traditional ST-506 controller, particularly in low- and medium-cost machines. IDE stands for *Integrated Drive Electronics*, and means just that – a hard disk and controller integrated into a single unit. An IDE drive controller may be an ST-506/RLL or ESDI type. It frequently contains a small disk cache, which gives it excellent performance. The controller is connected to the system bus using a single flat ribbon cable. This plugs into a 40-pin connector either on the motherboard or a separate adapter card. The adapter card is simply a buffered interface to the PC system bus.

8.7 Hard Disk Controllers

The hard disk controller is a hardware interface that converts instructions from the software running on the machine to the electrical signals needed to control the hard disk. For example, to read the contents of a particular sector on the disk into memory, DOS will call the system BIOS. This will output parameters to the controller I/O ports telling it the drive number, head, cylinder and sector to read. An ST-506 controller must step the drive head one track at a time until it reaches the right position, wait for the required sector to come under the head, read the pulses representing the encoded information and convert them into 512 bytes of data, perform an error check and if correct, write the data into the user program's buffer.

Different hard disk controllers are used in XT and AT class systems. XTs do not have

BIOS support for a hard disk built into the system ROM, so XT controllers contain a ROM extension usually located at address C8000 to C9FFF (hex) in the memory map. Since XT-class systems have only an 8-bit bus, the XT controller has only an 8-bit expansion connector.

XT controllers normally use I/O port addresses 320 – 323 (hex) for the control registers, and IRQ5 as the request line for interrupt processing. Data is transferred between system memory and the controller buffer using DMA channel 3. If two controllers are to reside in the same system, a jumper allows the second one to be set up to use different addresses – typically CA000 for the ROM, 324 – 327 for the I/O ports, and IRQ2. XT controllers are usually ST-506 MFM or RLL types, or IDE versions of them. There is no advantage in using ESDI or SCSI drives in an XT, because the speed of the bus, not the drive, is the limiting factor in any data transfer.

AT hard disk controllers are 16-bit cards. ST-506 controllers, such as those used in the IBM AT and many compatibles, don't have an on-board ROM, because the BIOS routines to support the use of a hard disk are built into the system. AT controllers use I/O port addresses 1F0 – 1F7 for the control registers, and IRQ14 for interrupt servicing. Programmed I/O through the data port 1F0 is used to transfer data between system memory and the controller, since on an AT this is faster than using DMA.

AT controllers for ESDI hard disks are usually compatible with standard ST-506 controllers. However, they may contain their own BIOS ROM. The reason is that, as mentioned earlier, ESDI drives are commonly formatted to 34 or more sectors per track, and it is rare for the standard BIOS to support this. On ESDI controllers such as the Western Digital WD1007V, an internal ROM may be enabled using a jumper on the board. This then replaces the hard disk functions provided by the standard system ROM, so that the characteristics of the ESDI drive can be supported.

ESDI controllers may contain such features as look-ahead cacheing. This gives improved performance, The controller loads the sectors following the one just read into a RAM cache. Since many disk reads are from adjacent sectors (particularly if the disk has recently been de-fragmented using a utility such as Norton's Speed Disk) this will result in the next read being from RAM rather than from disk, giving a near-instantaneous access time.

With SCSI drives the controller is in the hard disk itself. The SCSI host adapter is a general-purpose interface. In hardware terms, it looks nothing like a conventional hard disk controller. IBM never offered a SCSI adapter for any of the PCs, so there are no standards for the I/O port addresses, interrupts or DMA channels used. A SCSI adapter must be set up to use resources that are not required by any other card in the system. Every manufacturer's SCSI card is different, and must be used with the special software drivers supplied with it.

Because an SCSI interface is not a standard device, it is only suitable for use under operating systems for which drivers are provided. DOS is not usually a problem. Installing a driver is usually just a matter of including a DEVICE= statement in CONFIG.SYS. If a different operating system is to be used – such as Unix, Concurrent DOS or NetWare – then it is essential to check that a driver is available, and that it has been tested with the specific version of the software you intend to use.

SCSI can work well in PCs, but problems are not uncommon, and can be very frustrating to solve. It is worth ensuring that the supplier of the equipment has good technical support and can provide help if difficulties are experienced getting the system up and running.

8.8 Drive Types

Under DOS, files are held as groups of *clusters*. Each cluster is made up of one or more 512-byte sectors on the disk. The directory entry for a file holds the cluster number of the first cluster used by the file. The File Allocation Table (FAT) is used to link together all the clusters that make up individual files.

To read from (or write to) a file, DOS must convert from the cluster number to the cylinder, head and sector number, then issue a BIOS function call with this information as its parameters to get the drive to access the right part of the disk. To do this, DOS needs to know the number of sectors per track and the number of heads. It also needs to know the total number of cylinders, since this determines the total number of clusters that the disk can hold. This information is stored in the *boot sector*, which is the first physical sector on the disk.

Table 8.2: Hard disk type table (IBM AT)

TYPE	CYLINDERS	HEADS	SECTORS PER TRK	WRITE PRECOMP	LANDING ZONE
1	306	4	17	128	305
2	615	4	17	300	615
3	615	6	17	300	615
4	940	8	17	512	940
5	940	6	17	512	940
6	615	4	17	-	615
7	462	8	17	256	511
8	733	5	17	-	733
9	900	15	17	-	901
10	820	3	17	-	820
11	855	5	17	-	855
12	855	7	17	-	855
13	306	8	17	128	319

14	733	7	17	-	733
15	reserved				

Additionally, information about the drive is held in a *drive table*, which is part of the system BIOS, and is accessed using the *drive type number*. The drive table for an IBM AT is shown in Table 8.2. In many compatibles, the range of drive types extends up to 46, but the actual values, particularly for the numbers above 14, vary between different manufacturers. Many machines have a user-definable drive type. This allows the user to enter the drive characteristics using the SETUP utility. They are then stored in the battery-backed CMOS RAM.

When the original PCs were designed, the number of types of hard disk that could be installed was limited. The controller fitted to the original PC XT had four different drive types available. These were selectable using switches on the controller card. The IBM AT offered a choice of 14 drive types. However, the range of drives available nowadays is enormous! Appendix 4 lists the characteristics of popular drives from a number of manufacturers, but is not exhaustive.

At some time you may want to fit a drive that isn't supported by the system's BIOS. It may be that you want to fit an RLL drive with 26 or 27 sectors per track into an older machine that only provides for MFM drives. Or, you may be fitting an ESDI drive into almost any system. There are several possible solutions to this problem. The simplest is to pick a drive type that nearly corresponds to the characteristics of the drive you wish to install. No parameter of the type picked should exceed the actual value pertaining to the drive. The number of sectors per track and the number of heads should preferably be exactly right. The number of cylinders should be as near as you can get to the actual number without exceeding it. Only the number of sectors, heads and cylinders specified for the chosen drive type will actually be used. This means that some capacity of the drive will be wasted.

As more and more makes and models of hard disk are produced, the problem of finding a drive table entry that exactly matches a drive's characteristics is increased. If an AT has a user-definable drive type, this should be used whenever possible. XTs, of course, don't have CMOS RAM in which to store the drive parameters, and so cannot offer this option. Some XTs overcome the problem by using what are known as *autoconfigure controllers*. When the disk is low-level formatted, the format utility asks for the drive parameters, and writes them to a protected area of the disk. On boot-up, the controller reads the parameters back from the disk. This means that the controller can support any disk drive of the right type, irrespective of size.

Another solution has been developed by a company called Ontrack Computer Systems, who produce a package called Disk Manager. This consists of formatting and diagnostic utilities, plus a device driver DMDRVR.BIN. This allows drives with non-standard (unsupported by the BIOS drive table) numbers of cylinders, heads and sectors per track to be used. This package is bundled with many third-party add-in hard disk drives.

The principal object of Disk Manager is to allow drives of greater than 32Mb capacity to be fully utilised under DOS. This was once necessary, since versions earlier than DOS 3.3 could not support the partitioning of large hard disks into smaller logical drives. Disk Manager enables DOS to use drives larger than 32Mb by fooling it into thinking that the sectors are larger than 512 bytes.

Disk Manager overcomes the problem of drives that don't match the system drive table parameters, by using its own set of parameters, stored on the disk. The initial DOS partition (C:) must have the same number of sectors per track as the entry in the drive table; if the drive actually has more then some space will be wasted, but this can be minimised by keeping the C: partition small. The partitions accessed through Disk Manager will use the full capacity of the drive.

If the drive being installed is an RLL or ESDI drive, it's quite likely that there will be no options in the drive table with the requisite number of sectors per track. Many drive controllers now offer an alternative solution: *sector translation*. What this does is allow a drive with 26, 34 or however many sectors per track to be addressed as one with 17 sectors per track but more heads and/or cylinders. The controller pretends to have 17 sectors per track, and converts the head, cylinder and sector numbers used to the correct physical values for the drive. Sector translation is usually selectable using a jumper on the controller board.

ESDI drive controllers may use an on-board BIOS ROM to replace the system BIOS routines and support the correct physical parameters for the drive. Again, the ROM, if used, is generally selected using a jumper on the controller.

With the high capacity drives now becoming available, we run into another problem. The Int 13h BIOS interface only allows a maximum of 16 heads, 1,023 cylinders and 63 sectors per track. Many drives have fewer heads and sectors per track, but more than 1,023 cylinders. The ESDI controller ROM can provide translation schemes to maximise the capacity accessible by the BIOS by emulating a drive with 16 heads and 63 sectors per track. Despite this, the maximum size of disk that can be addressed is still 512Mb.

8.9 Cylinder Wraparound

Because the PC BIOS can only handle cylinder numbers up to a maximum of 1,023, large hard disks can cause a problem known as *cylinder wraparound*. The symptom of this is that the boot sector, system tracks and root directory of a disk become corrupted once the disk starts to fill. Since the boot sector and partition table are destroyed, the drive appears completely unreadable. In this situation, most people would suspect a hardware fault, and if the last backup was not very recent, panic ensues! In fact, the problem is because the BIOS only allows 10 bits — which can represent numbers from 0 to 1023 — for the cylinder number. If the system attempts to access higher cylinder numbers, they are simply truncated to modulo 1024.

Some RLL hard disk controllers, such as the WD1002-27X, allow a 26 sectors per track RLL drive to be used in a system that only supports 17 sectors per track standard drives, by using sector translation which simply increases the number of cylinders. The number of cylinders needed to access a drive as 17 SPT using this controller can be obtained using the formula:

cylinders = (actual no. of cylinders) x 26 / 17

To keep the cylinder numbers below 1024, the actual number on the drive must not exceed 682. Effectively, the size of disk that can be used with this controller is limited to about 32Mb for a typical four-head drive. Larger drives should be used in non-translated mode, or with controllers that perform sector translation by increasing the number of heads rather than cylinders.

8.10 Hard Disk Cards

Hard disk cards, often known as *hardcards* after the Plus 4 Hardcard (a 10Mb device that was the first on the market), are simply a hard disk and controller board mounted on a single metal chassis and designed to plug straight into a PC expansion slot. Hardcards are a popular way of adding hard disk storage to a system because they are simple to fit. They avoid the difficulty of having to mount the disk drive, attach the cables and so on.

If a hardcard is fitted to a PC with no existing hard disk, no difficulty should be experienced, unless the machine contains an unusual add-in card such as a network card or tape streamer that uses the IRQ line needed by the hard disk. If the machine already has one conventional hard disk, the thing to bear in mind is that you are not only adding a hard disk to the system, *but also another hard disk controller*. This means that you may need to configure the hardcard, probably using jumpers, to use a different location for its BIOS ROM (if an XT card), different I/O addresses and an alternative IRQ line, to avoid conflicts with the existing controller.

If you are adding a hardcard to an AT with an existing hard disk, you don't need to enter the details of the second drive into the CMOS RAM. The CMOS disk drive information relates purely to devices serviced by the system's own BIOS ROM. If the hardcard details are entered the system will spend a long time searching for the second drive before reporting an error.

In all respects, hardcards are no different from conventional hard disks. In fact, many cheaper cards are simply a standard 3.5in IDE drive with a half length bus interface card mounted in a metal frame. Higher capacity units contain an intelligent SCSI interface card giving high performance, and providing a SCSI bus connector to which external devices could be attached. If the hardcard is an addition to a system with an existing hard disk, you must take care that the power supply is capable of running two drives. The current drawn by two drives, especially at switch-on, can be quite high. Chapter 3 contains more information about calculating power supply loadings.

8.11 Low-level Formatting

When a new hard disk is manufactured, the magnetic recording surfaces are completely blank. Before any kind of data can be written to a hard disk, it must be low-level formatted. This is a process that divides up the circular tracks on each platter into 17, 26 or however many 512-byte sectors. The start of each sector is marked with an *address mark* – a unique pattern of magnetic dots that will never appear in normal data – followed by a *sector ID header* containing the cylinder, head and sector number that uniquely identify the sector. When the controller receives a command to read from or write to a specific sector, it uses the cylinder number in the sector ID header to verify that the heads are positioned over the correct track. It uses the head number to check that faulty cabling is not causing the wrong head to be selected, and the sector number to find when the required sector has rotated beneath the head.

Some manufacturers do not supply a low-level format program as standard with the machine. The hard disk is supplied already formatted, and it is considered a service engineer's job if another low-level format is required. There is some sense in this, as low-level formatting should rarely be needed for good quality drives. Unnecessary low-level formatting is a waste of time, and can sometimes do more harm than good.

Theoretically, it should never be necessary to low-level format a disk more than once. However, in practice it is often useful to be able to do so. Earlier in the chapter we noted that the head positioning accuracy of drives that have stepper motor actuators deteriorates with age. This can lead to the situation where a drive fails to boot up or is prone to read/write errors when cold, but is fine once warmed up, or vice versa. A low-level format will write new sector headers to the disk at the position currently favoured by the head actuator mechanism. This will often cure the problem. Another reason for low-level formatting a disk would be if the sector headers had become corrupted, perhaps due to a hardware fault, or if a controller had been replaced by a different model that did not recognise the sector headers written by the original.

To carry out a low-level format you'll need to know how to invoke the format utility, either from the BIOS ROM, the diagnostics disk or a separate program such as Disk Manager, supplied by the manufacturer. You'll require some information about the disk drive, such as the number of sectors per track, the number of heads, the number of cylinders, the write precompensation value, the sector interleave factor and the sector skew. You will also need to know the location of any bad sectors on the disk. If you don't know this information, you can't successfully low-level format the disk.

Appendix 4 contains a list of the characteristics of many drives from the more well-known manufacturers. However, it is not exhaustive. If the data for your drive is not available you'll have to contact the manufacturer for information. Always use the physical number of cylinders, heads and sectors per track when formatting a disk, not the values presented by any translation mechanism which may be provided.

A label containing the location of any defects on the disk, by head and cylinder number, is affixed to the drive casing. The defect information must be entered after the low-level format has been completed. This marks the bad tracks so that they aren't used by the system. If this isn't done, the system will use the defective tracks, and they will cause problems with read/write errors once data has been written to them. The surface testing performed by most low-level format routines isn't rigorous enough to ensure that defects on the disk are automatically detected and marked as not to be used. More information about defects is given later in this chapter.

The way a low-level format is initiated depends on the type of controller. With standard XT controllers, a low-level format program is built into the controller ROM. The program is invoked by calling it from within the DOS DEBUG utility. The address of the format routine may vary between controllers from different manufacturers and is relative to the segment address of the ROM: C800 for most XT controllers, CA00 or CC00 if it is the second controller in the machine. You'll need to refer to the technical reference manual for the machine, or the installation guide for the controller, to find the correct address to use.

Western Digital controllers use offset 5 for their low-level format routine. If the controller is the first or only controller in the machine, the program would be invoked by typing:

```
DEBUG
```

and then, at the DEBUG prompt:

```
G=C800:5
```

and then answering the questions that are presented.

Some controllers, such as the Xebec controllers used in the early Amstrad PC1512 machines, used offset 6. Others may use something completely different, so it is important to have the technical documentation for the controller to hand when attempting to low-level format a disk.

On ATs, the problem is simpler, as the disk is formatted using a separate program that isn't part of the ROM BIOS. Usually, it comes with the diagnostic or SETUP utility

Hard Disks

provided with the system. Another possibility, if available, is to use the Ontrack Disk Manager utility, which has an option to perform a low-level format of a disk. Disk Manager will do this completely automatically if the drive is a standard type.

Low-level formatting is a hardware-specific procedure, and should always be carried out using the correct utility supplied by the manufacturer. One exception to this is hard disks that are to be used in file servers for the Novell NetWare network operating system. NetWare version 2.1 and later use a more sophisticated system of dealing with defects. File server disks are usually formatted using a utility called COMPSURF, which performs exhaustive surface testing to ensure that sectors of dubious reliability are not used. However, ESDI and SCSI drives store information about the drive characteristics and defective tracks on a reserved part of the disk. COMPSURF will overwrite this information, making the disk unusable, unless you answer *NO* to the question *Format the disk?* and then *YES* when asked if you wish to maintain the defect map.

8.12 Interleave

One parameter that can have a dramatic effect on the performance of a hard disk is the *interleave factor*. As we've seen, the hard disk controller has the job of transferring data between a buffer in the system memory and a sector on the hard disk. There are quite a few steps involved, particularly for an ST-506 controller, since ST-506 hard disks have very little intelligence, and the controller does most of the work. For example, during a read transfer, the controller has to verify that the correct sector is

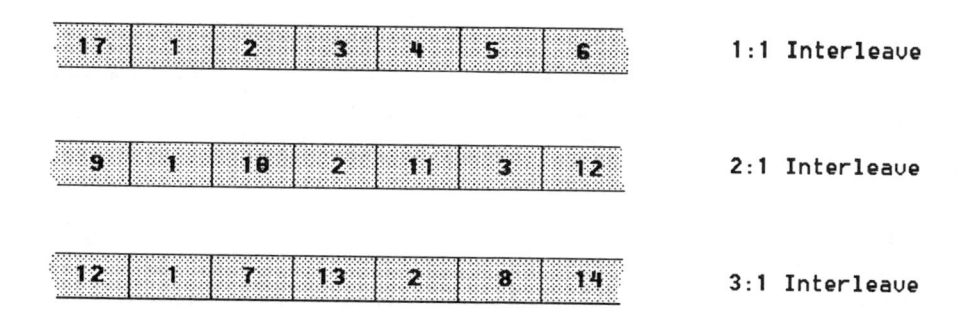

Figure 8.6: Sector interleaving

being read, receive the stream of pulses picked up by the read/write head, convert them to data bits according to the encoding method in use, check that the block of data has been received correctly using the error correction algorithm, and then transfer the data into system memory.

This process takes a certain time to complete. On some older hard disk controllers this meant that, once one sector had been read, several others would pass under the read/write head before the controller was ready to read the next one. Since the system software normally reads clusters of adjacent sectors, the controller would have to wait for the disk to complete a revolution before the next sector required was under the head again and available for reading. This significantly reduced the hard disk performance.

To overcome this problem, the disk sectors are interleaved. Sectors aren't numbered 1, 2, 3 and so on, consecutively around the disk. Instead, they may be arranged in the order 1, 4, 7, 2, 5, 8 etc. This is illustrated in Figure 8.6. By interleaving the sectors, you can arrange for the next logical sector to be just about to pass under the read/write head as the controller completes processing of the previous one. The interleave is set when the disk is low-level formatted. It is this process – not the DOS FORMAT – that puts the sector numbers into the sector headers on the disk.

The correct interleave to use depends on the controller in use, and the processor and bus speed of the PC in which it is installed. The controllers in an IBM XT used an interleave of 6, while an IBM AT used 3. In fact, these figures are a result of IBM being conservative. Values of 5 and 2 respectively will usually give better performance. On Amstrad PC1512 and PC1640 XT compatibles, which have a slower-than-standard bus, the interleave may need to be as high as 11. The latest AT type hard disk controllers are all able to support an interleave factor of 1 – i.e., no interleave – so on modern machines there is usually no need to worry about it.

8.13 Skew

Another factor influencing hard disk performance that is related to the interleave is *skew*. The effect of skew is to offset identically-numbered sectors on adjacent tracks by a fixed number, as shown in Figure 8.7.

Although the size of a sector is fixed at 512 bytes, DOS uses the cluster as a unit of storage. The cluster size varies according to the size of the disk partition and the version of DOS, but it is typically 4, 8 or 16 sectors in size. Therefore, though individual clusters making up a file may be scattered all over the disk, many disk reads made by the system will be for consecutive sectors.

If the interleave factor is correct the hard disk will be able to read data from consecutively-numbered logical sectors as fast as it is able. However, because the number of sectors per track is typically 17, 26 or 34, not a multiple of the cluster size, some clusters will span two tracks. For those clusters, a head movement from one track to the next will be needed when it is read. A head movement takes a few milliseconds – the seek time, described earlier – and in that time, the disk will have moved round by part of a revolution. The skew factor means that the first sector of each track and the last sector of the previous track are offset by that number of sectors. This ensures that once the last sector of a track has been read, there is time for the head to move in one track, before the first sector of the next track comes round for reading.

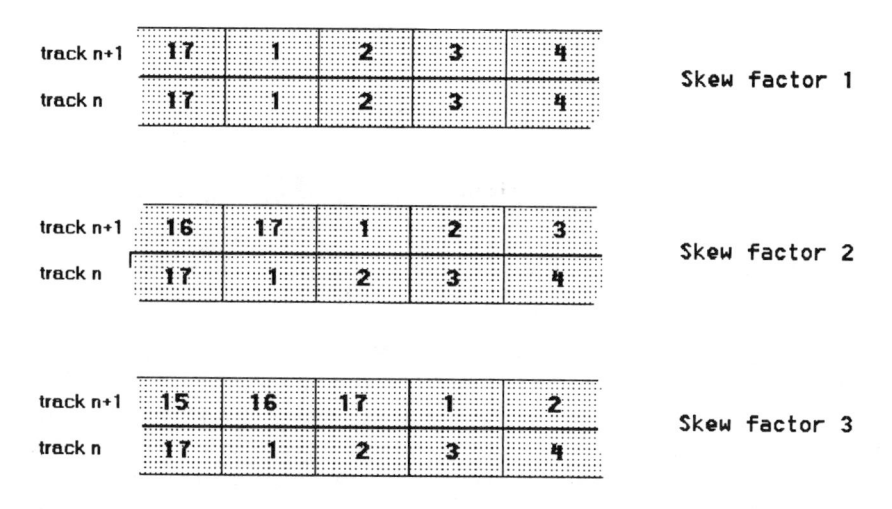

| track n+1 | 17 | 1 | 2 | 3 | 4 | Skew factor 1 |
| track n | 17 | 1 | 2 | 3 | 4 | |

| track n+1 | 16 | 17 | 1 | 2 | 3 | Skew factor 2 |
| track n | 17 | 1 | 2 | 3 | 4 | |

| track n+1 | 15 | 16 | 17 | 1 | 2 | Skew factor 3 |
| track n | 17 | 1 | 2 | 3 | 4 | |

Figure 8.7: Sector skew

8.14 Disk Optimisation

There are several software utilities that will help you decide the optimum interleave factor for a particular system. One of the best-known is a little public-domain utility called Spintest. This program determines how many revolutions of the disk are required to read an entire track. The smaller the number, the faster the response. A disk formatted with an interleave of 1, used with a controller able to support that interleave factor, will take just one revolution. Similarly, a disk with an interleave of 3, used with a controller able to support an interleave of 3 or better, will take three revolutions. A disk that is interleaved more tightly than the controller can handle will usually take as many revolutions to read a complete track as there are sectors in the track. It will only be able to read one sector per revolution. Such a disk will be very slow. Typically, it will be able to transfer data at no more than about 30Kb per second.

If you suspect that a disk is wrongly interleaved, one way to correct the problem is to low-level format the disk with a new interleave, DOS FORMAT it, then rerun Spintest and see if there is an improvement. You may have to repeat this procedure several times to find the optimum value. This is a sure method of achieving the correct result, but it takes a long time.

Alternatively, you can use a program that will do this for you automatically. It will check for the correct value by formatting the engineering cylinder – this is one of the innermost cylinders of the disk that is out-of-bounds to DOS – using different interleave factors, and then test the data transfer rate. The interleave that results in the best transfer rate is the one to use.

One program that is readily available in the public domain is T-LEAVES.COM. However, if you use it, you should be careful, and take a backup first. Utilities like T-LEAVES are quite safe to use on the older type MFM hard disks for which they were designed. But with the later types of disk there is no guarantee that they will work correctly. It is inadvisable to run any utility that formats any part of the hard disk without first taking a complete backup of the data.

This warning applies even more strongly to the next category of disk optimisation programs, which are designed to reinterleave a hard disk to the optimum value without destroying the data stored on the disk. One such program, which is widely available from public domain software sources, is IAU. Use this program at your own risk! I have seen many cries of anguish on computer bulletin boards from people who have used it and trashed their hard disks. Your data is safe *only as long as nothing goes wrong*. Play safe, take a back-up.

There are, of course, commercial programs that will reinterleave a hard disk, including SpinRite from Gibson Research, PC Probe from Landmark Research and Calibrate, which is part of the Norton Utilities. Commercial programs are much safer to use. The manufacturers expect to sell hundreds of thousands of copies. They don't want to get sued for destroying somebody's vital data, so they have to ensure that the programs will run safely on every conceivable configuration of PC. Even so, something can still go wrong at a crucial moment during the reinterleave, such as a power cut, and your disk would still be corrupted. Not taking a backup is like playing Russian roulette with your data.

Norton's Calibrate is a useful utility that can provide much information about the performance of a hard disk, as illustrated in Figure 8.8. For standard MFM and RLL disks it can produce a bar chart showing the results of different interleave factors. As befits a program that is expected to be widely used, Calibrate is very cautious. It performs several tests on the hard disk controller to ensure that it is a standard type before it tries to do anything else. If it doesn't recognise the controller it will leave well alone. Most of the new types of hard disk can't be low-level formatted except by the manufacturer's special software. Increasingly, you'll find that Calibrate will report that it can't do anything.

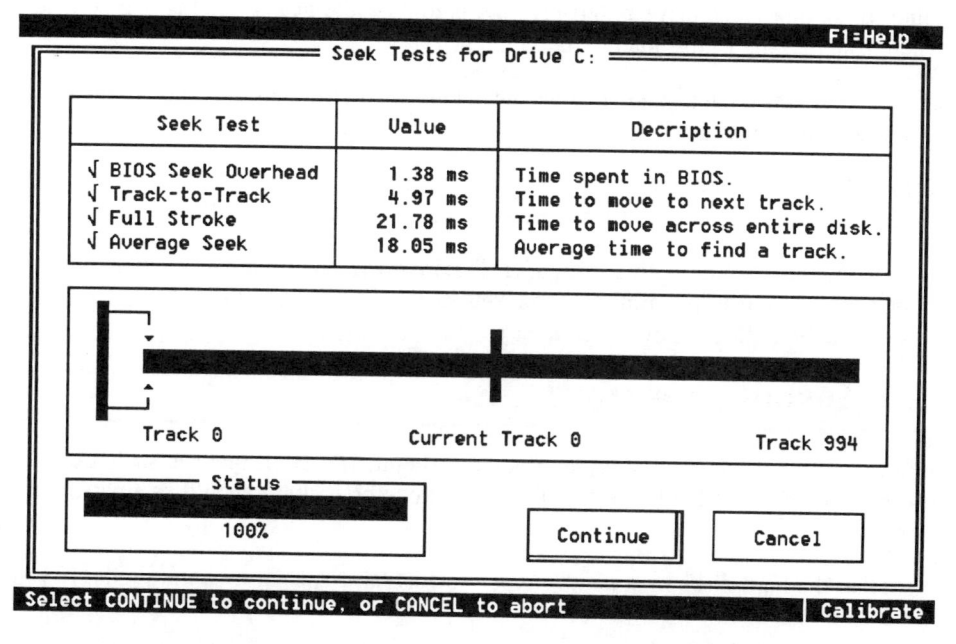

```
                                                              F1=Help
═══════════════ Seek Tests for Drive C: ═══════════════

  Seek Test            Value              Decription

√ BIOS Seek Overhead   1.38 ms   Time spent in BIOS.
√ Track-to-Track       4.97 ms   Time to move to next track.
√ Full Stroke         21.78 ms   Time to move across entire disk.
√ Average Seek        18.05 ms   Average time to find a track.


      Track 0          Current Track 0              Track 994
           Status
           100%                  Continue            Cancel

 Select CONTINUE to continue, or CANCEL to abort       Calibrate
```

Figure 8.8: Norton Calibrate test output

Once you've formatted a hard disk to the correct interleave, it should never need changing. However, there's another form of optimisation that is worth carrying out at regular intervals: *defragmenting*. One of the utilities most frequently used to do this is Norton's Speed Disk.

Defragmenting is the process of collecting together the clusters that make up individual files, so that they occupy adjacent sectors and tracks on the disk. DOS's file allocation strategy is not very sophisticated. When data is written to disk, DOS just picks the next free cluster. So the clusters that make up a file can be scattered all over the disk. This means that a lot of head movement is needed every time the file is subsequently used. Accessing the file is much faster when it occupies a contiguous area of the disk. This is especially true with modern disk controllers, which contain a disk cache employing *read-ahead*. These controllers automatically read the sectors following the one just asked for, on the basis that they are likely to be the ones wanted next. If files are contiguous, this will probably be true. The read will then be virtually instantaneous, since the data will be read from cache memory, and not from the disk itself.

8.15 Removing a Hard Disk

Removing a hard disk from a machine is simpler than installing a new one. The first thing to do, unless the drive is self-parking, is to park the heads. This is one occasion when head parking is absolutely vital.

- ❏ Power off the system and remove the mains cable from the socket. Remove the system unit cover.

- ❏ Remove the data and power cable connections from the drive, noting the orientation of the red-striped edge of the cable for the benefit of later reinstallation.

- ❏ Remove the drive mounting screws. (If the drive is mounted in an AT using rails, it may be secured using miniature brackets at the front of the drive bay.) Carefully slide the hard disk out of the drive bay.

8.16 Installing a Hard Disk

Fitting a new hard disk into a system is not difficult. However, there is such a choice of types and sizes of hard disk that the instructions given here should be treated only as a guide.

Note that the hard disks in some AT type systems have special mounting rails. If you

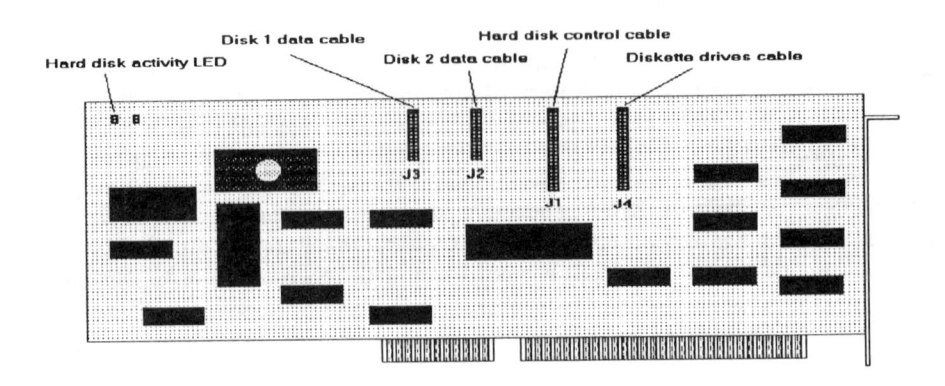

Figure 8.9: A typical disk controller card

purchase a drive from the original manufacturer then it should be fitted with these rails. If you buy a drive from another supplier, you'll probably receive just a bare drive with no rails. In this case, you'll have to fit the drive into the chassis using screws (if there are corresponding holes in the drive bay), or obtain a set of rails from the PC manufacturer.

Drives intended for fitting in an XT compatible system usually have a front bezel with an LED drive activity light. AT drives should be bare, and are usually hidden behind the front panel of the system unit. It isn't advisable to try to remove the bezel from a drive to enable it to be fitted into a machine that doesn't require one, so when ordering it, remember to specify if a bezel is needed. You'll also need a mounting frame if you're fitting a 3.5in drive into a 5.25in drive bay.

First, collect together all the parts you need. If you're fitting a hard disk to a system that doesn't already have one, you'll need a controller card. A typical hard disk controller is shown in Figure 8.9. IDE disks need an IDE adapter card, unless the appropriate 40-pin connector is provided on the motherboard. You'll also need cables. ST-506 and ESDI drives have one 34-way control cable that can control up to two drives. A separate 20-way data cable is also required for each drive. IDE and SCSI drives use just a single cable. Finally, check that you have a power supply connector for the drive.

The control cables for ST-506 and ESDI drives may be either flat or twisted, like diskette drive cables. However, although both hard and floppy drives use 34-way cables, the two types aren't interchangeable. The twisted part of the hard disk cable is further from the pin 1 position (striped edge of the cable) and affects only five wires.

Power off the system and remove the mains cable from the socket. Remove the system unit cover. Remove the drive bay's blanking plate if you're fitting a drive that has a bezel. You may have to remove the entire front panel of the system unit to gain unrestricted access to the drive bay.

Check the settings of any jumpers on the drive, to ensure that, for example, translation mode is enabled if you expect it to be. An ST-506 drive normally has a terminating resistor fitted, which should be removed if it is going to be used as a second drive. The position of the drive select jumper or switch should be checked. For a second hard disk, it should be set to Drive Select 2. For the first hard disk, Drive Select 2 should be used for a twisted cable; for a flat cable use Drive Select 1. (In some systems the jumpers are numbered starting at zero; use positions numbered one less than the values given above in that case.) With IDE drives, the first should be configured as Master, and the second as Slave.

Make a note of the contents of the defect list. This is usually printed on a label affixed to the outside of the drive. Keep the list for future reference. It won't be so accessible once the drive has been installed inside the machine! Also note the location of pin 1 on the connectors on the drive logic board. This is also hard to see once the drive is installed.

Fit the mounting rails to the sides of the drive, if appropriate, then slide the drive into the bay. Fit the cables. The first drive (C:) should be attached at the end of each cable, and the second will use the intermediate connector. The cables must be fitted so that the striped edge of the ribbon cable goes to the side of the connector that has pin 1; this is usually marked with a 1 on the circuit board. IBM cables have a keyed connector so that the cable can't be fitted the wrong way round, but many other manufacturers don't provide this.

Fit the power supply cable. Check that the drive is correctly positioned with respect to the front of the case, then fit and tighten the mounting screws. Ensure that the mounting screws don't foul the casing of the hard disk itself, as this would defeat the effect of the rubber shock mountings. Drives fitted with rails may be secured using miniature brackets at the front of the drive bay. Refit the system unit cover.

Power up the system. You'll need to boot from diskette if you've fitted a new C: drive, and it isn't formatted. Update the CMOS configuration on AT machines, if appropriate. Low-level format the new drive, if necessary. Partition the drive, using FDISK, then DOS FORMAT it, using the /S switch if it is to be used as a boot drive.

8.17 Preparing a Hard Disk

If you've installed a new hard disk in a system as drive C:, what will happen if you try to boot from it is that there will be a long delay – perhaps of a couple of minutes – and then the system will display a 1790 or 1791 POST ERROR or some other disk error message. This is quite normal when installing an uninitialised disk. Once the disk has been prepared for use the error will disappear.

A *standard* PC hard disk – this includes most ST-506 MFM and RLL drives – will first need low-level formatting. The exact procedure will depend on the type of controller in use. Typically, it will involve running a routine from the controller's ROM BIOS using DEBUG, or using a utility provided by the system or drive manufacturer. Low-level formatting was described in some detail earlier in the chapter.

Next, the drive must be partitioned. This is usually done using the FDISK utility supplied with DOS. If your hard disk is larger than 32Mb you should make sure you are using DOS 3.3 or above. Earlier versions won't allow more than one DOS partition on a disk, and no partition can exceed 32Mb, so you will be restricted to using just 32Mb of each hard disk for DOS. The third-party package Disk Manager, mentioned earlier, was developed to overcome this restriction. DOS 3.3 allows an extended partition to be created following on from the primary DOS partition. This can be subdivided into logical DOS drives, each of up to 32Mb. Version 4.0 and up remove the restriction that a DOS partition may not exceed 32Mb.

FDISK is menu-driven. An option is chosen by entering the number displayed against it on the menu. First, select the option to create a DOS partition. Next, you must create a primary DOS partition. When this is selected, FDISK will ask if you want to use the maximum size for the DOS partition, and make it active (i.e., bootable). Usually, you answer Yes to this question. You can make the primary partition smaller by answering No, and then entering the size of the partition in cylinders. You might do this if you are using an RLL or ESDI disk on a system that only supports 17 sectors per track, and are using Disk Manager to provide support for the 26 or 34 sectors per track used by the disk. Disk Manager cannot do anything for the primary DOS partition, so only 17 sectors of each track will be used in this partition. In this situation it is best thing to minimize the wasted space by making the primary partition as small as possible, and accessing the rest of the disk using Disk Manager.

After the primary partition has been defined, FDISK will ask for a DOS diskette to be inserted in drive A:, and then reboot the system. Once this has happened, you should format the primary hard disk partition, using the command:

```
FORMAT C: /S/V
```

This formats the drive, installs the operating system, and prompts for a volume name. You will then be able to boot up the system from the hard drive. Under DR-DOS, FDISK formats the hard drive as well as partitioning it, so this step isn't required.

If the primary partition doesn't take up the whole of the hard disk, and if DOS 3.3 or later is used, FDISK may be run again to partition the rest of the disk for DOS. Again, you must select the option to create a DOS partition, followed by the option to create an extended DOS partition. FDISK will display the total disk space available, in cylinders, followed by the space available for a partition. The partition size – usually the total remaining space – should be entered. Then press Esc to return to the menu.

Now you must create one or more logical drives within the extended DOS partition. Each logical drive will have a drive letter, beginning at D: (assuming this is the first or only hard disk) since the primary partition will be C:. Again, FDISK will show the total space and the maximum space available in cylinders, and will ask for the size of the logical drive to be entered. You can define any number of logical drives. FDISK will continue to prompt for logical disk information until all the extended partition has been assigned to logical drives.

From the FDISK menu you can return to DOS. Each logical drive must then be formatted, using the command:

```
FORMAT D:
FORMAT E:  .. etc ..
```

The way a hard disk is partitioned can affect the disk performance and the efficiency of space utilisation. This is discussed in more detail in Chapter 15.

8.18 Dealing with Bad Sectors

Hard disks have improved greatly in reliability over the years. The occasional unit may suddenly stop working due to electrical or mechanical failure, but such problems are thankfully rare. However, it's quite common for a few sectors to develop faults and become unreadable over a period. This can cause some anguish if the sector is part of an important file. However, it's possible to deal with these problems, and prevent or at least minimise the chances of a bad sector causing loss of data.

All hard disks have bad sectors. The manufacturing process is not perfect, and the magnetic tracks of data on the disk are very fine. A tiny flaw on the surface of the disk can cause read/write errors to occur when that part of the disk is used. So even a new hard disk is likely to have some bad sectors. When the PC was first introduced, IBM allowed up to 5 per cent of a disk's capacity to be bad before it was rejected by quality control; that's 1Mb of a 20Mb disk. However, a disk would be very poor to have that proportion of bad sectors. A more typical figure would be one per cent.

A more serious problem is if there are bad sectors in cylinder zero. At boot-up, the system reads the very first sector of a disk – cylinder 0, head 0, sector 1 – to load the bootstrap code and partition table. The ROM boot-up procedure has insufficient intelligence to cope with this sector being bad. If it is bad, the disk is effectively useless, and will have to be replaced.

Some newer types of hard disk are designed to appear free of defects. These disks have more sectors per track than they admit to. When a bad sector is found by the manufacturer's low-level format procedure, one of the *alternate* sectors is transparently mapped in its place by the drive electronics. This enables a defect-free drive to be presented to the system. However, bad sectors may still develop during normal use.

One problem with the older, cheaper drives is that, after a year or so, they start to have difficulty reading and writing to certain parts of the disk. These problems are caused partly by wear in the head actuator mechanism, and partly by thermal expansion and contraction. Often, the problems are worst when the system is cold, and clear up once it has warmed up, or vice versa. Often, the system won't boot, because the boot tracks are at the outermost part of the disk, where the effects of expansion and contraction are most noticeable.

A quick and often successful fix for the booting problem is to reload the operating system files using the SYS command:

```
SYS C:
```

This causes the boot sectors and the two hidden system files to be rewritten to the disk. While this may provide a temporary solution, it will rarely work for long, because the sector headers, put there by the low-level format program, aren't rewritten, and may still be difficult to read.

The only long-term solution to intermittent read/write errors is to low-level format the disk. Before you can do this, you must pick a time when the number of errors is least, and back up all the data. Then low-level format, repartition and DOS format the disk, and restore the data. When this needs to be done so often that it becomes a chore, replace the drive!

All types of hard disk can develop bad sectors. To keep an eye on the situation, there are many utilities that can be run on a periodic basis. Examples include Check It, Disk Technician Advanced, SpinRite, Disk Doctor or Calibrate from the Norton Utilities, and the shareware HDTEST by P R Fletcher. Any of these programs will test every sector on the drive with a variety of bit patterns, check for errors, and mark any newly-discovered bad sectors as not to be used. Some utilities can be set to perform tests having varying degrees of rigour. Calibrate offers the choice of zero, five, 40 or 80 different tests on each sector. The last will take several hours to run on a typical disk.

All the above programs will test a disk without destroying the data held on it. For each track, the data is read into memory, the pattern testing is carried out, and then the data is written back to disk. If an error is found, the data is written to an unused part of the disk, and the FAT updated accordingly. However, a power failure occurring while pattern testing was going on could cause files to be corrupted, and so a back-up is advisable.

Programs like Disk Technician Advanced and Disk Doctor can be run on a daily, weekly or monthly basis to detect emerging disk problems. However, I'd suggest that anyone who runs this type of utility on a daily or weekly basis is worrying unnecessarily about the chances of a hard disk error developing. These utilities are best treated as tools to be used to resolve hard disk problems when they occur. It would certainly be worthwhile to run a thorough disk test as part of a preventive maintenance check. However, the time taken for the test to run to completion would probably put a machine out of action for the entire day.

8.19 File Recovery

The power of present day PCs and the size of their hard disks make them ideal platforms for large applications. Data files build up over time, becoming increasingly valuable and representing years of work. Yet they can be wiped out with a single command. Frequent backups are the best possible safeguard against this sort of occurrence. However, in the real world people don't have them, or they think they have, but then they won't restore. When this happens, we have to resort to other methods of file recovery. Lost files can occur with floppies, too, but it is hard disks where the potential loss is most serious.

The simplest data recovery problem is the accidentally erased file. Often, the file was only created that day, and isn't on any back-up. The user can often recreate the file from scratch. However, it's annoying and frustrating to have to do so, when the sectors containing the lost data are still on the disk.

The important thing to observe when a file has been accidentally deleted is not to create any new files or cause any more data to be written to disk. When a file is deleted, all DOS does is to change the first byte of the filename to an ASCII E5 (hex) to show that it has been deleted, and mark the FAT entries for clusters that were used by the file to show that they are available for use again. So all the information needed to recover the file, the clusters used, its size, the date and time it was created, everything except the first character of the filename, is still there on the disk.

However, as soon as another file is created, the newly-freed clusters are prime candidates for reuse. Once they've been overwritten with new data, any hope of recovering the lost file is gone. Obviously, the longer the time that elapses before it is realised that a file has been deleted, the slimmer the chances of recovering it. So as soon as the accidental erasure has been discovered, the PC should be left exactly as it is until the recovery procedure can be attempted.

Some undelete utilities are available in the public domain, such as UNDEL.COM. Most of these were written in the days before DOS 3.3 and extended partitions. They are rarely able to recover large files, don't work on partitions larger than 32Mb, or under DOS 4.0 or later. Frequently, they are no use at all.

Given the time that can be saved if an accidentally deleted file can be quickly recovered, the cost of a decent file recovery tool isn't hard to justify. UNERASE – one of the Norton Utilities – is a superb, easy-to-use menu-driven tool for recovering deleted files. It will display all the deleted files in a directory, together with the chance of recovery of each one, and then attempt an automatic recovery of the files selected. If you're not sure if a file is really the one you want, it'll let you view the file before unerasing it. You can search the entire disk for the name of a deleted file, in case you can't remember the directory it was in. Finally, as a last resort when some of the clusters of a file have already been reused, the bits that are left can be pieced together manually, cluster by cluster.

Bad sectors can cause file recovery problems. If a user experiences the dreaded *Disk Read Failure* while reading a vital file, and an up-to-date back-up isn't available, the support technician is expected to work miracles. The DOS RECOVER utility – syntax: RECOVER filename – simply copies as much of the file as it can read into a file named FILE0001.REC in the root directory. Since with most types of file, such as databases, spreadsheets or executables, anything less than the whole thing is useless, this isn't much help.

The best solution to this problem is to back up as much of the disk as you can, then run a non-destructive low-level format program such as HDTEST or SpinRite. These programs try harder than DOS to recover hard-to-read data from bad sectors, and will relocate the data to a good part of the disk. If you're lucky, no data will be lost.

A more difficult recovery task is presented by the accidental format. There's a lot that can be done when a PC is first set up to prevent this from ever happening. Deleting FORMAT.COM from the hard disk is one solution. If the user needs to be able to format diskettes, then you can rename it XYZXYZ.COM (or something else that's unlikely to be typed in accidentally) and run it using a batch file called FORMAT.BAT, which accepts only the parameters A: or B:. Such a batch file is given in Listing 8.1. DRDOS's FORMAT utility won't format hard disks at all; this is carried out using FDISK. Safe Format – another Norton Utility – won't reformat a disk that it thinks has already been formatted, instead it simply marks all the files or directories as deleted.

```
@ECHO OFF
IF "%1"=="A:" GOTO OK
IF "%1"=="a:" GOTO OK
IF "%1"=="B:" GOTO OK
IF "%1"=="b:" GOTO OK
IF "%1"=="?" GOTO HELP
ECHO *** INVALID FORMAT COMMAND ***
ECHO Only drives A: and B: may be formatted.
ECHO FORMAT ? gives help.
GOTO END
:OK
XYZXYZ %1 %2 %3 %4 %5 %6
GOTO END
:HELP
ECHO Help for FORMAT command.
ECHO ========================
ECHO Parameters:
ECHO       A: or B:   - Drive to be formatted
ECHO       /S         - Format as a system disk
...
...
:END
```

Listing 8.1: FORMAT.BAT – A safe format command

MS-DOS version 5 has a utility called MIRROR. This will save disk storage and partition information to a special file, to aid recovery of an accidentally formatted disk. It can also optionally record information about deleted files, to allow them to be more easily recovered. (There's a similar facility in DRDOS version 6.) MIRROR's effectiveness depends on the information it has stored being up-to-date, so it should be run at start-up in AUTOEXEC.BAT. DOS 5 comes with its own UNDELETE and UNFORMAT commands. If you haven't used MIRROR, they'll still attempt to rescue the file or disk, but you may not be quite so successful.

If you have to recover a hard disk that wasn't using MS-DOS version 5, you'll have to use commercial tools. The Norton Utilities has an UNFORMAT command that will recover as much as possible from disks that have been formatted. A newly-formatted disk contains just a root directory. This may either be completely empty, or will contain the two hidden DOS system files and COMMAND.COM if the disk was formatted with the /S option. The standard DOS format doesn't overwrite the data part of a hard disk, so the subdirectories and the files they contain aren't destroyed. Only the contents of the root directory, including the names and locations of the subdirectories it contained, are lost. Everything else is still there, though invisible to DOS.

UNFORMAT scans the disk, looking for clusters that it recognises as directories. When it finds one, it updates the FAT to show that all the clusters used by files in the newly-discovered directory are in use, and creates an entry in the root directory for it. Because it has no way of telling what the correct name for the recovered directories should be, UNFORMAT names them DIR0001, DIR0002 and so on. When it has finished, you'll have to find out the name of each of the recovered directories by seeing what they contain, and then manually rename them. Any files in the root directory will be lost, and you'll have to recreate them or restore them from a backup.

Sometimes a hard disk becomes unreadable for no apparent reason. On ATs, this is often because the CMOS setup data, containing the drive type number, has been lost. If the drive type number is anything other than the correct value the hard disk is likely to be unreadable as far as the system is concerned. The solution in this case is to run SETUP and enter the correct drive type.

However, sometimes the problem lies on the hard disk itself. That very first sector, containing the partition table, is the key to making sense of the rest of the disk. If that becomes corrupted, the disk will be unrecognisable. This could happen as a result of a program error, a hardware fault, an electrical glitch or a virus. Another possible cause of corruption is cylinder wraparound, which was described earlier in the chapter.

Should the problem be simply a corruption of the DOS file system, Norton Disk Doctor will usually provide a cure. If the disk is unrecognisable to DOS then first you'll have to repartition it using FDISK. If the partitions are set up exactly the same size as they were originally, the disk may immediately become usable with all files intact. However, if the corruption is more extensive, you may have to format it first, using something like Norton's Safe Format. You can then use UNFORMAT to recover the subdirectories and files, as described above.

8.20 Hard Disk Problems

The hard disk sub-system is one of the most complex parts of an IBM compatible PC. There are so many different types of hard disk and controller that it's difficult to provide comprehensive guidance on the sort of problems you may encounter. Some common faults and their possible solutions are outlined below.

Long delay followed by 1790, 1791 or other disk error:

- Disk drive not formatted.
- CMOS drive type incorrect or lost (AT).
- Check cabling and controller seated; check power to drive.
- Incorrect drive installation (e.g., drive select jumper setting, terminating resistor location).

1701, 1702, 1704, 1782 POST error:

- Check cabling and controller seated; check power to drive.
- Possible controller fault; try an identical substitute controller.

System will not boot, 1780 or other disk boot error:

- CMOS drive type incorrect or lost.
- Boot tracks corrupted (possible software or hardware fault, or sector wraparound). Reinstall boot tracks using SYS. If necessary, repartition with FDISK and reformat first.

System intermittently will not boot, has read/write errors:

- Likely creeping disk errors due to wear and thermal expansion and contraction. Repartition with FDISK and reinstall operating system using SYS for a temporary fix. Use HDTEST, SpinRite, Norton Calibrate etc., or carry out a complete reinitialisation starting with a low-level format for a long-term solution.
- Drive badly worn or damaged; replace.

Read/write errors affecting files:

- Run HDTEST, SpinRite, Norton Calibrate etc., or carry out a complete reinitialisation starting with a low-level format.

Disk performance is slow:

- BUFFERS set too low in CONFIG.SYS.
- Interleave may be incorrect; check and correct with SpinRite or Calibrate, or use SpinTest and low-level format.

- Files may be fragmented.
- Possible disk controller fault.

Disk files or directories corrupted:

- Disk buffers in memory may have been corrupted. Try rebooting before doing anything else.
- Cross-linked files and other file system errors. Repair using CHKDSK, and run it regularly thereafter.
- SHARE not loaded with partitions larger than 32Mb.
- Possible software or hardware fault, or sector wraparound error.

Summary

This chapter began by looking at how hard disks are constructed. We saw how the different types of recording media and head actuator mechanism result in big differences in performance and reliability of drives. We looked at recording methods, and showed how RLL encoding is used to increase the storage capacity of drives by 50% compared to MFM.

We went on to examine the various types of hard disk interface and controller available. IDE drives are becoming popular. Both IDE and ESDI controllers retain software compatibility with the standard ST-506 controllers used in the earliest PCs. SCSI is really a different type of interface, which happens to support hard disks as well as other devices. The extent of its compatibility depends very much on the software drivers provided.

Next we looked at drive types – the tables of parameters that define to the system the hardware characteristics of each drive. Special driver software or translating controllers are used to overcome the problem of using drives that are not supported by the drive table in a particular PC.

We went on to describe how a low-level format is carried out, and looked at the related topics of the interleave and skew factor, which are important in obtaining maximum disk performance. We discussed programs that can dynamically optimise the interleave without destroying the data held on the disk. However, it is still a good idea to take a back up beforehand. Defragmenting will ensure that the maximum disk performance is always obtained.

We outlined the procedures for removing and installing hard disks and preparing them for use. We also looked at how to deal with bad sectors, which most hard disks will develop over a time. The recovery of deleted or damaged files and accidentally formatted disks was described. The chapter concluded with a summary of some common hard disk problems and their possible solutions.

9

Serial Ports

The serial port is the most versatile input/output port on a PC. You can use it to interface to printers, plotters, modems, mice, other computers, laboratory instruments and measuring devices, data capture devices such as bar code readers, in fact just about anything you care to think of that can receive commands or generate data in digitised form.

A serial port is a standard fitting on all modern PCs. In many designs, the circuitry is actually built on to the motherboard. However on IBM's original models, it was an option available as a plug-in card at extra cost.

Getting serial devices to work can be a real headache. There are so many different serial port settings and permutations of cable wiring, and many manuals aren't at all specific about the configuration to use. It's easy to waste a lot of time on trial and error.

This chapter looks at the important fundamentals of PC serial communications in some detail. This will help provide the background for understanding the problems that can arise. A fault finding guide to the most common serial interfacing problems is also included.

9.1 Serial Port Basics

Though *serial port* is the most commonly used name, some people refer to this device as an *RS-232C port* or *communications port*. IBM calls it an Asynchronous Communications Adapter. A short explanation of these terms may be useful. A serial port has a single connection for data in, and one for data out. The smallest unit of data that is input or output by a PC is a byte. One byte is eight binary digits or bits. Each bit can be transmitted as an electrical signal, which may be positive or negative, on or off, 1 or 0. By contrast, a parallel interface has eight data lines, so that each bit in a byte can be transmitted simultaneously, in parallel. Since the serial interface has only a single data line in each direction, the bits in a byte must go out (or come in) one after the other, serially. Hence the common name serial port.

To ease the task of connecting equipment produced by different manufacturers, the Electrical Industry Association (EIA) developed a standard for an interface, which they called RS-232C. This defines the purpose and voltage levels of the various signals used by the interface, and the pin connections to be used for them on standard plugs and sockets. For example, there must be data in and data out pins, an earth or ground wire, signals to show that the device is switched on, and that it is ready to send or receive data. In talking about serial communication, devices are classified into two types: Data Terminal Equipment (DTE) and Data Communications Equipment (DCE). A PC is a DTE, while a modem is a DCE.

Table 9.1: RS-232C connector pin assignments

PIN (25D)	(9D)	SIGNAL NAME		FROM DCE	TO DCE
1		Protective Ground	(GND)		
2	3	Transmitted Data	(TD)		x
3	2	Received Data	(RD)	x	
4	7	Request to Send	(RTS)		x
5	8	Clear to Send	(CTS)	x	
6	6	Data Set Ready	(DSR)	x	
7	5	Signal Ground	(SG)	x	x
8	1	Rcvd Line Signal Detect	(DCD)	x	
9		Not used			
10		Not used			
11		Select Standby			x
12		Not used			
13		Not used			
14		Not used			
15		Transmit Signal Element Timing		x	
16		Not used			
17		Receiver Signal Element Timing		x	
18		Test			x
19		Not used			
20	4	Data Terminal Ready	(DTR)		x
21		Not used			
22	9	Ring Indicator	(RI)	x	
23		Speed Select			x
24		Not used			
25		Not used			

RS-232C is the most common standard for serial interfacing with microcomputers. The pin designations used by a PC serial port are shown in Table 9.1. There is another, later standard that is sometimes encountered, particularly in industrial or laboratory equipment. This is the RS-422A interface. This isn't commonly used with PCs, and we won't be looking at RS-422A interfacing in this chapter.

A serial port on an IBM PC doesn't conform exactly to the RS-232C standard. However, all the important signals are present. The Transmitted Data (TD) and Received Data (RD) pins are used to carry data between two serial devices. The RTS, CTS, DSR and DTR pins are used to control the process of communication, as we shall see later. For example, terminals should not transmit until Clear to Send is received from the other device. The Received Line Signal Detector, often known as Data Carrier Detect (DCD) is used by a modem to tell the PC when it has received a signal of adequate strength over the telephone line. Ring Indicator (RI) is used to signal to the PC that the phone is ringing.

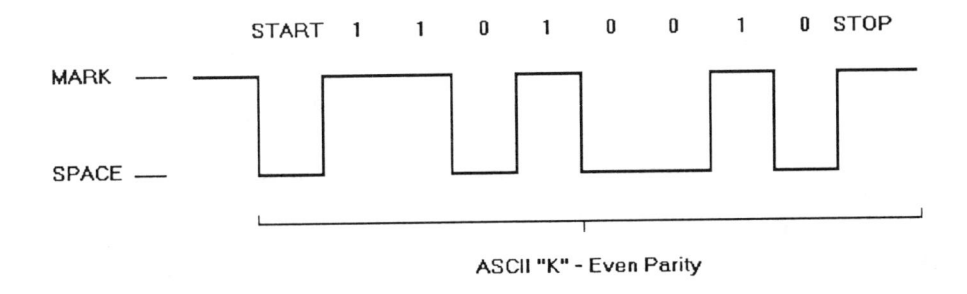

9.2 Synchronous and Asynchronous Communication

There are two basic types of serial communication: synchronous and asynchronous. Asynchronous communication transmits and receives data character by character. It derives from the early days of teleprinters when the electrical signal for each character was generated and decoded mechanically. When a key was pressed, an armature would rotate over a set of contacts. This would generate a couple of start bits, to signal to the receiver that a character was on its way. Then the bit pattern for the character would be generated, followed by a couple of stop bits to mark the end. This is illustrated in Figure 9.1. Modern asynchronous communications using solid-state devices at much higher data rates still use the same system of start, data and stop bits, though the number of start and stop bits is generally reduced to 1.

Figure 9.1: Asynchronous communication

In synchronous communications, data is transmitted in blocks of characters as shown in Figure 9.2. There are no time-wasting start and stop bits between characters in a block, so this mode of communication is more efficient. A couple of synchronisation characters are sent at the beginning of each block, and there are usually other characters that denote the start and finish of the data, and provide error checking. The precise format of the blocks – their length, the characters used to delimit the data and so on – is known as the *communications protocol*.

Synchronous communication is usually used between terminals and mainframe computers. Each mainframe manufacturer generally uses its own proprietary communications protocol. PCs can communicate synchronously only if they are fitted with a special synchronous communications adapter card. This is generally used with a piece of software called a terminal emulation program. This interfaces with the card and allows the PC to behave as if it were a mainframe terminal. Synchronous communications adapters differ greatly between manufacturers, so it isn't possible to give specific configuration or troubleshooting information about them.

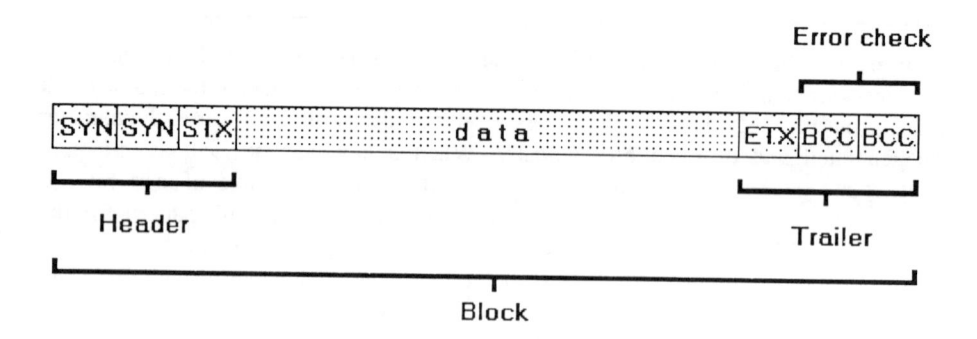

Figure 9.2: Synchronous transmission

The speed of a serial port is measured in bits per second, the unit for which is the *Baud*. (Actually, a Baud is the number of times the data signal changes state, but for a serial port that's the same thing as bits per second.) Since on an IBM PC or compatible the number of data, stop, start and parity bits must always add up to 10, the speed in characters or bytes per second can be obtained by dividing the baud rate by 10. IBM specify that their Asynchronous Communications Adapter can operate at speeds of up to 9600 baud. On the PS/2 range speeds of up to 19200 baud are supported. In fact, most clones will operate satisfactorily at 38400 baud. Many will work at 115,200 baud, the maximum possible, when using software such as LapLink to transfer files between machines.

9.3 Serial Port Hardware

The way a serial port is fitted varies from machine to machine. If it's a modern PC, the circuitry may be built into the motherboard. If it's an IBM system or older clone, it may be an expansion card with a single socket on it. Alternatively, it may be part of a multi-function expansion card containing one or more parallel and serial ports, and possibly combined with a game port (for a joystick) or a disk controller as well.

If the machine is an IBM XT or an 8086/8088-based clone, the serial connector will normally be a 25-way male D-type socket. If it's an IBM AT or an AT-class clone it will be a 9-way male D-type socket. However, there's no reason why a 9-way socket can't be used on an XT or vice versa. Some manufacturers of modern, small footprint XT compatibles use a 9-pin socket for the serial port to save space, and some early AT clones did have 25-pin sockets. Most manufacturers, though, use the same types of connector as IBM did for the two classes of system. Figure 9.3 shows the pin configuration of the two types of socket.

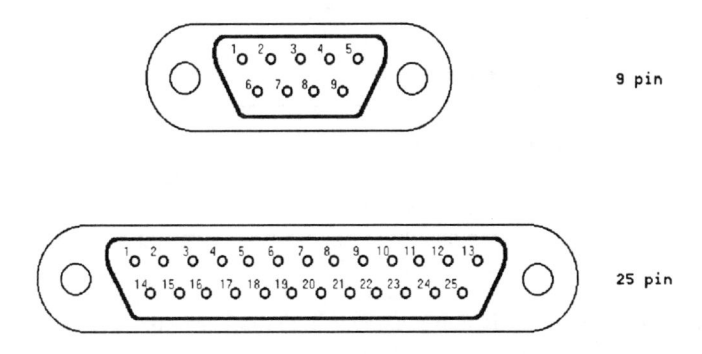

Figure 9.3: Serial port sockets – pin diagram

The hardware standard for the IBM PC Asynchronous Communications Adapter is based around the Intel 8250 Universal Asynchronous Receiver-Transmitter (UART) chip. Later PCs may use different chips that are compatible with the 8250, such as the 8250A or B, or the 16450. Or they may use LSI chips that emulate the 8250 functions. Serial adapters that don't are unable to run standard PC communications software.

A single serial port looks in hardware terms like a set of eight I/O ports. The first of these allows data bytes to be read from or written to the serial port. The others are used to initialise the port for the required baud rate, parity and number of start and stop bits, and to set or test the status of the various RS-232C control lines. The IBM PC design allows for a maximum of four serial ports to be fitted to a PC. These are accessed through DOS as COM1 to COM4. The I/O port addresses are as follows:

COM1: 03F8h – 03FFh

COM2: 02F8h – 02FFh

COM3: 03E8h – 03EFh

COM4: 02E8h – 02EFh

In addition, there are two IRQ lines that can be used by a serial adapter: IRQ4, which is used by COM1 or COM3, and IRQ3, which is used by COM2 or COM4.

The 8259A interrupt controller can be programmed to ignore specific interrupts. This is done during the system boot-up procedure. The routines included in the BIOS for using the PC serial ports don't use hardware interrupts, and DOS simply uses the BIOS functions. This is why it's not as silly as it seems to have four serial ports, yet only two interrupt lines for them. However, there are disadvantages if you use serial ports without using interrupts, particularly for data input.

9.4 Driving Serial Ports

There are two main methods of handling serial communications: polling, or using interrupts. Using the polled method for input, a program looks to see if a byte has been received. If not, it can go and do something else, then come back a few moments later to do another check. As soon as a byte has been received, it is read from the port and processed.

The problem with polled input is that whatever the computer does between each check must never take longer than the interval between receiving two consecutive bytes. If it does – and even at 1200 baud many activities can take too long, like writing a block of data to disk or scrolling the contents of the screen – a character is lost, because it is overwritten by the next one before it can be read by the program. Polled output doesn't suffer the risk of losing data. However, since the computer may be doing something else when the port is ready to send the next byte, the maximum data throughput won't be achieved.

To use interrupt driven communications on a PC, the software must provide its own interrupt service routines. For input, the 8250 will generate an interrupt as soon as a new byte of data has been received. Whatever the computer is currently doing, the interrupt will cause the ISR to be executed. The ISR will read the byte into a data buffer, and set an indicator or increment a counter to show that data is in the buffer waiting to be processed. The main program tests the indicator or counter, rather than checking the serial port input register directly. Consequently, as long as the buffer is big enough, it doesn't matter how long a process carried out by the main program takes. Data can build up in the buffer, and can be read from it when the program is ready to process it.

Polled serial I/O, such as is provided by DOS and the BIOS, is usually only satisfactory at low data speeds – up to 300 baud – or for one-way data transfers such as printing. For two-way communication, or data input, software which implements interrupt processing must be used. Because only two interrupt lines are reserved for use by serial adapters, it isn't possible to have interrupt processing on more than two serial ports at the same time. For applications in which several serial data inputs are needed – bulletin board software or data capture applications, for example – special serial I/O boards requiring special software drivers will be needed.

At high communication speeds – 9600 baud and above – it's possible for characters to be lost even when interrupt driven software is used. Usually this occurs if the PC is operating in a multi-tasking environment such as Microsoft Windows or Desqview, or if a disk cache using extended memory is in use. This type of software is, from a programming point of view, very complex. The problem is that, if an interrupt occurred during certain processes, vital information would be lost. Consequently, the software uses a special machine instruction to disable all interrupts while these critical activities take place. The serial port generates an interrupt for every character that is received, which at 9600 baud is 1200 interrupts per second. As a result, the chances of a character being lost – because interrupts were disabled for too long and the next incoming character overwrote the first – is quite high.

There are solutions to this problem. They include disabling the disk cache, and only running high speed communications software in the foreground of Windows or Desqview. It's also possible to fit a 16550 UART chip in place of the 16450 used on the serial card of the IBM AT. The 16550 is compatible with the earlier chip. However, it has an internal buffer of its own, so a character isn't lost if it isn't read before the next one is received. Software that recognises the 16550 is needed to take full advantage of the chip.

9.5 Handshaking

If one device is sending data to another, and the receiving device is for one reason or another temporarily unable to process any more data, then unless it is able to tell the sending device to stop sending, data will be lost. The mechanism by which this is accomplished is known as *flow control* or *handshaking*.

There are two methods of flow control, software handshaking and hardware handshaking. Each is most appropriate in certain circumstances, and has an influence on the cabling configuration used.

9.6 Software Handshaking

Software handshaking uses only the transmit and receive data lines. It is commonly known as *XON/XOFF protocol*. When the receiving device wishes to halt the incoming flow of data, it sends an XOFF (ASCII 13h – Ctrl/S) character to the sending device. The sender stops sending and waits until an XON (ASCII 11h – Ctrl/Q) character is sent.

Software handshaking is commonly used when two computers, or a terminal and a computer, are connected. Very often the connection is made over a telephone line, using a pair of modems. A telephone line can normally only support two data channels, one in either direction. It doesn't support the signal lines present in the RS-232C interface which are used to control the flow of data. Therefore, if flow control is needed, a software method must be used. Note that some programs have an option to allow different characters to be used for XON and XOFF. This must be enabled or disabled at both ends of the link if required.

If a communications program locks up unexpectedly, or continues to receive but won't send, it may be that XON/XOFF is enabled when it ought not to be. Where the communications link is over a telephone line and non error-correcting modems are being used, line noise could randomly generate an XOFF character. When data is being transferred which includes non-printing ASCII characters – this includes binary data such as .COM or .EXE, database or spreadsheet files – an XOFF may quite legitimately appear in the data. If XON/XOFF is enabled then the software will interpret any XOFF character received as a command to stop sending.

9.7 Hardware Handshaking

Hardware handshaking is generally used when two devices are connected using cables. A typical example of this is where a PC is connected to a serial printer. Most printers can receive data from a PC faster than they can print it. Although printers usually have a data buffer, this quickly fills up. When this happens, the printer must tell the PC not to send any more data until it has printed another line and freed up some space in the buffer. If the cable wiring is incorrect, so that the handshake signal doesn't get to the PC, or if the software isn't set up to take any notice of it, the PC will continue to send characters to the printer. Text will be lost. This is one of the most common problems.

DOS won't send to or receive from a serial device unless the Data Set Ready (DSR) signal is high. This tells it that a remote device is present and on-line. DSR should normally be connected to Data Terminal Ready (DTR) on the remote printer or terminal. The handshaking input signal on the PC is Clear To Send (CTS). This must also be high, indicating that the remote device is ready to receive, before DOS will send any data. The handshaking output on the remote terminal or printer is usually Request To Send (RTS).

If I sound a little imprecise here, it's unfortunate but necessary. The problem is that the RS-232C standard wasn't designed with flow control between computers and printers in mind, so printer manufacturers have had the flexibility to devise their own flow control methods. Consequently, printers don't all implement the control signals in the same way. Often, though, you'll find that they use DTR as a handshaking signal. A cable which links DSR and CTS together at the PC end, and joins them to the printer's DTR output, will work correctly in most cases.

Some serial printer interfaces have an option to implement software XON/XOFF handshaking. This is primarily intended for use in the situation where computer and printer are connected via a telephone line, using modems.

Modern high speed modems must have handshaking enabled on the link between the PC and the modem. High speed modems employ data compression and error correction to increase the throughput of data. For example, a text file may compress to half its actual number of characters, so a 2400bps modem must be fed with data at 4800bps or more in order for maximum performance to be achieved.

Modems that use data compression contain buffers, so that they aren't kept waiting while data is transferred between them and a PC. The communications software should be set up to use a higher data rate than that used over the phone line. This helps to ensure that the modem's buffer is always kept full when sending, and empty when receiving. When the buffer becomes full, the PC must stop sending. As with the printer, handshaking is needed to tell the communications software when the modem's buffer is ready to accept more data. XON/XOFF should not be used if you are going to be performing binary file transfers, or using terminal emulation, since XOFF characters may legitimately appear in the received data, and will be interpreted as a command to stop sending. Hardware handshaking should be used instead.

9.8 Diagnosing Problems

Electronically, the serial port is a simple device. On a PC of recent design, the functionality of the 8250 IC and its support circuitry may be integrated on to a single LSI chip. If the port isn't working at all, then component failure is a possibility, but it's more likely that there is a fault in the cable or a handshaking problem, or that the port has been disabled or set up as a different port number to the one intended.

If there is some form of output from the serial port: for example, garbage appears on the printer, or the modem's TXD light flashes when characters are typed from within a terminal program, it's probable that the parameter settings (baud rate, number of stop bits, word length and parity) on the PC don't match those on the external device. Rectifying this shouldn't be difficult.

If the problem seems to be more obscure, diagnostic software such as Check It can be of assistance. First, it's a good idea to check that the existence of the port is recognised. If you don't have any diagnostics then the short BASIC program in Listing 9.1 will show how many serial ports the system thinks it has, and which ones they are. This program also gives the base address that the BIOS and DOS serial port functions use to access each port. If the base address doesn't correspond with the way the port was set up using the jumpers on the board, or if the PC software or the external device is using different parameter settings, then this will explain the problem.

```
3100 REM ====     LISTING 9.1      ====
3105t REM ==== CHECK SERIAL PORTS ====
3120 DEF SEG=&H0: E1%=PEEK(&H411)
3130 N%=INT(E1%/2)-INT(E1%/16)*8
3140 PRINT "Number of serial ports installed is:",N%: PRINT
3150 FOR I%=0 TO 3
3152 PRINT "COM";I%+1;": ";
3153 J%=(PEEK(&H400+I%+I%+1))*256+PEEK(&H400+I%+I%)
3154 IF J%=0 THEN PRINT "not installed": GOTO 3188
3156 PRINT "installed - base address ";HEX$(J%);"h ";
3158 LC%=INP(J%+3)
3160 IF INT(LC%/128)-INT(LC%/256)*2 = 0 THEN LC%=LC%+128
3162 OUT J%+3, LC%
3164 B=INP(J%)+INP(J%+1)*256
3166 OUT J%+3, LC%-128
3168 PRINT INT(115200!/B);"baud, ";
3170 PRINT LC%-INT(LC%/8)*8+5;"- ";
3172 N%=INT(LC%/8)-INT(LC%/64)*8
3174 IF N%=1 THEN PRINT "O -"; :GOTO 3184
3176 IF N%=3 THEN PRINT "E -"; :GOTO 3184
3178 IF N%=5 THEN PRINT "S -"; :GOTO 3184
3180 IF N%=7 THEN PRINT "M -"; :GOTO 3184
3182 PRINT "N -";
3184 PRINT INT(LC%/4)-INT(LC%/8)*2+1
3188 NEXT I%
```

If the serial port is recognised by the system, the next step is to test its functionality. To do this, a loop-back plug will be required. This is a standard 9-way or 25-way plug, internally wired so that TXD is connected to RXD, RTS is connected to CTS and DSR is connected to DTR, as shown in Figure 9.4. Check It or the system diagnostics disk can be used to test the serial port; alternatively the BASIC program in Listing 9.2 may be used.

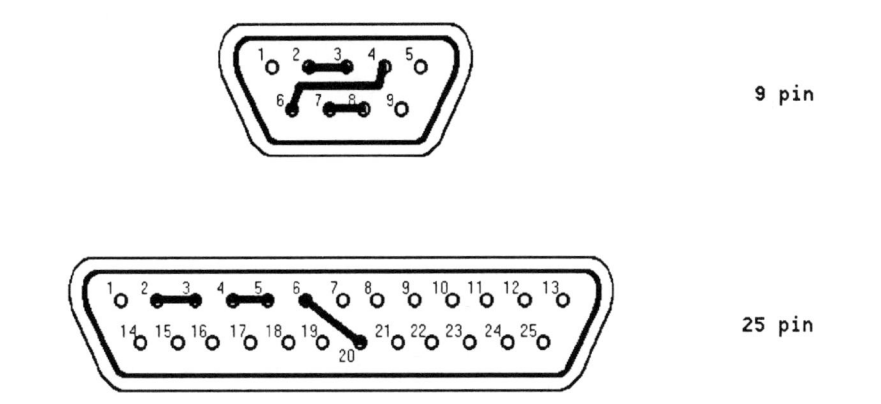

Figure 9.4: A loop-back plug for serial port testing

```
3200 REM ====    LISTING 9.2    ====
3205 REM ==== TEST SERIAL PORTS ====
3210 PRINT: PRINT
3220 INPUT "Test serial ports (Y/N)? ",A$
3225 IF A$<>"Y" AND A$<>"y" THEN 3900
3300 PRINT: PRINT "Test plug should be fitted": PRINT
3310 INPUT "Enter port to test: 0) Quit 1) COM1 2) COM2 3) COM3 4) COM4
";N%
3315 IF N%<0 OR N%>4 THEN 3310
3320 IF N%=0 THEN 3900
3330 DEF SEG=&H0: J%=(PEEK(&H400+N%+N%-1))*256+PEEK(&H400+N%+N%-2)
3332 IF J%=0 THEN PRINT: PRINT "Port";N%;" not installed": GOTO 3900
3400 REM ==== TEST TRANSMIT/RECEIVE ====
3410 PRINT: PRINT "Testing transmit/receive - ";
3415 E%=0
3420 FOR I%=32 TO 96
3422 OUT J%,I%
3423 K%=0
3424 WHILE K%<64
3426 L%=INP(J%+5): IF L%-INT(L%/2)*2 = 1 THEN K%=999
3428 K%=K%+1
3430 WEND
3436 IF INP(J%)<>I% THEN E%=E%+1
3438 NEXT I%
3440 IF E%>=64 THEN PRINT "Failed": GOTO 3500
3445 PRINT E%;"errors"
3500 REM ==== TEST INTERRUPT PROCESSING ====
3505 PRINT: PRINT "Testing interrupt - ";
3508 ON ERROR GOTO 3544
3510 IF N%=1 THEN OPEN "COM1:9600,N,8,1" AS #1
3515 IF N%=2 THEN OPEN "COM2:9600,N,8,1" AS #1
```

```
3520 T$="0123456789ABCDEFGHIJKLMNOPQRSTUVWXYZ": U$=""
3522 ON COM(N%) GOSUB 3580
3524 COM(N%) ON
3526 FOR K%=1 TO 1024: NEXT K%
3528 U$=""
3530 PRINT #1,T$;
3535 FOR K%=1 TO 1024: NEXT K%
3540 IF U$=T$ THEN PRINT "OK": GOTO 3590
3542 PRINT "Failed": GOTO 3590
3544 PRINT "Failed": GOTO 3600
3580 L%=LOC(1): IF L%=0 THEN RETURN
3582 U$=U$+INPUT$(L%,#1)
3586 RETURN
3590 COM(N%) OFF: ON ERROR GOTO 0
3600 REM ==== TEST RTS/CTS ====
3610 PRINT: PRINT "Testing RTS/CTS - ";
3615 E%=0
3620 FOR I%=1 TO 16
3630 OUT J%+4,2
3632 FOR K%=1 TO 256: NEXT K%
3634 L%=INT(INP(J%+6)/16)
3636 IF L%-INT(L%/2)*2 <> 1 THEN E%=1
3640 OUT J%+4,0
3642 FOR K%=1 TO 256: NEXT K%
3644 L%=INT(INP(J%+6)/16)
3646 IF L%-INT(L%/2)*2 <> 0 THEN E%=1
3648 NEXT I%
3650 IF E%=0 THEN PRINT "OK": GOTO 3700
3655 PRINT "Failed"
3700 REM ==== TEST DTR/DSR ====
3710 PRINT: PRINT "Testing DTR/DSR - ";
3715 E%=0
3720 FOR I%=1 TO 16
3730 OUT J%+4,1
3732 FOR K%=1 TO 256: NEXT K%
3734 L%=INT(INP(J%+6)/32)
3736 IF L%-INT(L%/2)*2 <> 1 THEN E%=1
3740 OUT J%+4,0
3742 FOR K%=1 TO 256: NEXT K%
3744 L%=INT(INP(J%+6)/32)
3746 IF L%-INT(L%/2)*2 <> 0 THEN E%=1
3748 NEXT I%
3750 IF E%=0 THEN PRINT "OK": GOTO 3900
3755 PRINT "Failed"
3900 END
```

9.9 Break out Box

A break out box is a useful tool for trouble-shooting serial interfaces. It's a small box, as illustrated in Figure 9.5, fitted between the two serial devices that you want to test.

It has sockets for the cable connections, LEDs to show the status of the various RS-232C signals, switches that are used to open-circuit the connection between two pins, and jumper wires which are used to link any desired input and output pins together.

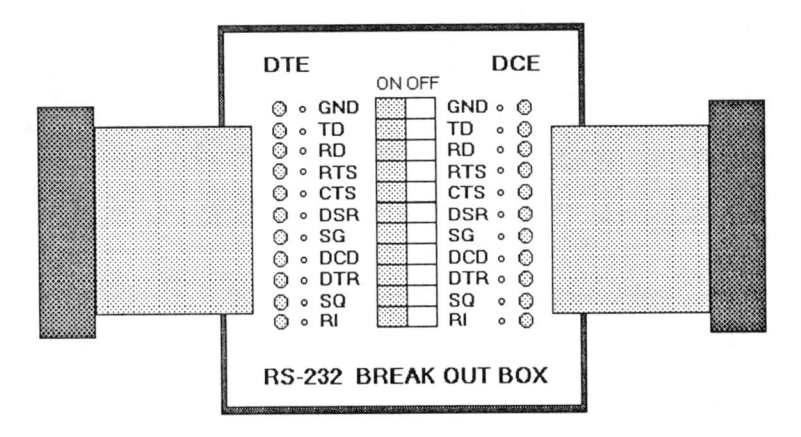

Figure 9.5: A break-out box

When all the switches are closed the break-out box, when used with flat ribbon cable, will give a straight connection from one device to another. Pin 1 at one end will go to pin 1 at the other, pin 2 will go to pin 2 and so on. This configuration is rarely useful. Normally, the output from one end of the cable goes to a different pin at the other end. To do this, the straight through connection is open-circuited using the switches, and one of the jumper wires is used to make the appropriate connection.

For example, a printer cable requires TXD at the PC to go to RXD at the printer, and vice versa. To achieve this, open the switches at positions 2 and 3 (the TXD and RXD interface pins). Then use two jumper wires to cross-link them, as shown in Figure 9.6. The printer DTR should be raised – shown by the LED being on – when the printer is ready. That signal should be linked across to DSR and CTS at the PC end of the connection.

In more difficult cases, the break out box allows different wiring configurations to be tried experimentally until success is achieved. Then a proper cable can be made up to the right wiring configuration.

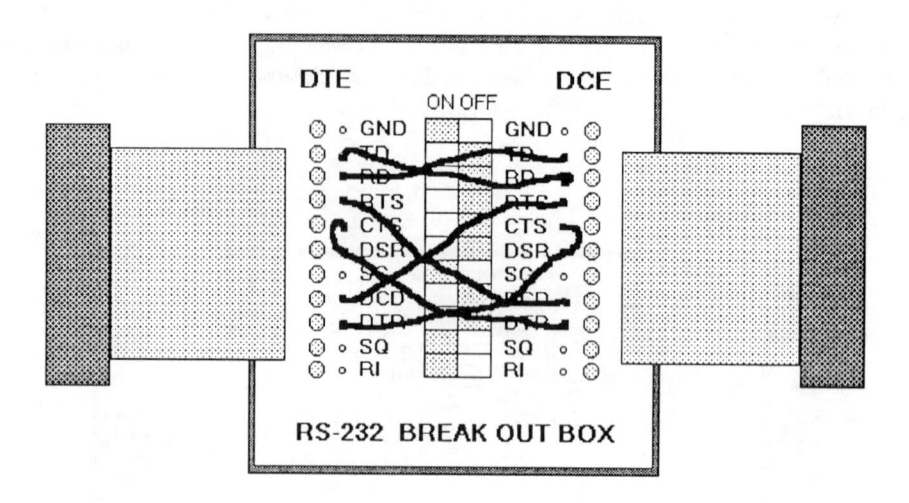

Figure 9.6: Making a cross-connection

9.10 Serial Port Problems

Serial port problems, and their likely solutions, are summarised below:

No activity from external device:

❏ Check power, and perform self-test if possible.

❏ Check cable is plugged in to the correct sockets.

❏ Check cable wiring for correctness and continuity. Check handshaking (DTR/CTS connections). Swap with another cable if possible.

❏ Check software settings (speed, word length, parity etc.) match hardware settings.

❏ Check serial port using loop-back plug and diagnostic software.

External device outputs rubbish:

❏ Check software settings (speed, word length, parity etc.) match hardware settings.

❏ Check device for malfunction. Perform self-test if possible.

Large blocks of data are being lost:

❏ One device is transmitting data when the other isn't ready. Check handshaking (XON/XOFF or RTS(DTR)/CTS) is enabled and cable is correctly wired.

Random characters are being lost:

❏ Use interrupt-driven software.

❏ Remove background processing tasks from the PC.

❏ Use a serial card with a 16550 UART chip (if supported by your software).

❏ Use a lower communication speed.

Certain characters are consistently incorrect:

❏ Check word length/parity settings,

Characters are randomly corrupted:

❏ Check connection between cable plug and socket is good.

❏ Noise pickup on data cable – try rerouting it or use screened cable.

Everything operates normally for a while, then hangs:

❏ Check software handshaking isn't enabled when it shouldn't have been.

❏ Check hardware for malfunction. Perform self-test if possible.

❏ Possible software conflict. Remove TSRs and background processes and try again.

Device time-out errors occur:

❏ Increase time-out period in software. Use P parameter to MODE command, if I/O is via DOS.

Summary

The PC serial port itself is a relatively simple piece of hardware. However, to use it successfully requires a certain level of understanding about serial communications.

Most of the problems with serial interfacing come about because there are so many parameters that must be correct for things to work. The data speed and format of the PC serial port must match those used by the external device. Handshaking is usually necessary to prevent the sender from overwhelming the receiver with more data than it can process. Again, the right form of handshaking must be selected at both ends of the link, and the interface cable used must be wired correctly. Finally, the type of software driver used – polled or interrupt-driven – will affect the reliability and maximum speeds obtainable.

If a pair of serial devices aren't communicating correctly then a break out box can be used to investigate the problem.

10

Modems and Other Serial Devices

Many of the peripherals you can use with a personal computer can be linked to it using the serial interface. They include printers, plotters, mice and modems.

Modems are becoming more popular as they reduce in cost. A modem can give you access to a wealth of useful information. It will also enable you to download public domain and shareware software from electronic bulletin board systems. However, communications is a notoriously hard subject to understand, and this puts many people off.

In this chapter, we'll look at several sorts of serial device. You'll see how to interface them to a PC and what regular maintenance is required. We'll look at the subject of modems and communications in some detail, and explain some commonly encountered jargon.

10.1 Printers

Probably the most common use of the serial port is to drive a serial printer. Some of the problems you may encounter when interfacing one to a PC were described in the previous chapter. The main trouble is usually the cable. It must be correctly wired, to support the type of hardware handshaking used by the printer. This can vary from machine to machine. If the printer manual provides a wiring diagram for the data cable, then use that configuration of cable. If not, you'll find that a cable wired as shown in Figure 10.1 will work correctly for most printers.

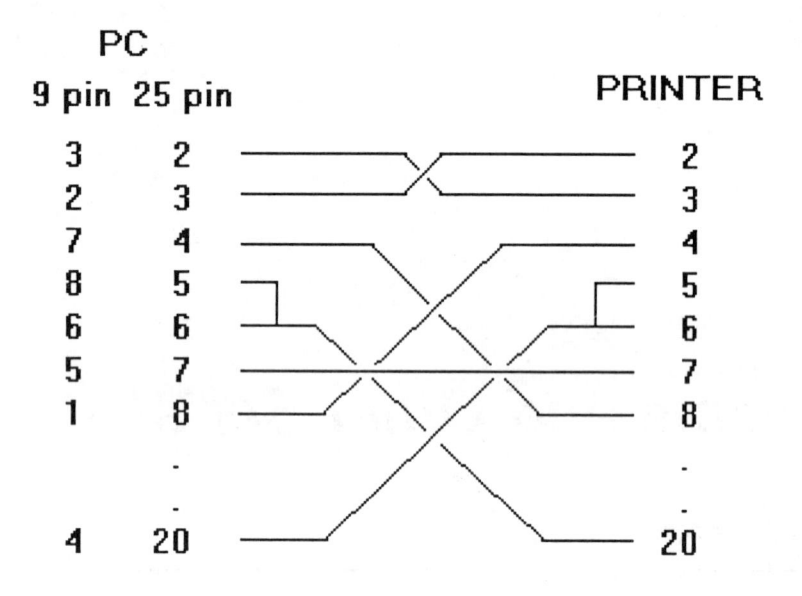

```
        PC
    9 pin  25 pin                            PRINTER
      3      2    ─────────┐   ┌───────────    2
      2      3    ─────────┘   └───────────    3
      7      4    ─────────┐   ┌───────────    4
      8      5    ─────┐   │ ╲ │   ┌───────    5
      6      6    ─────┘   │  ╳│   └───────    6
      5      7    ─────────┤ ╱ ├───────────    7
      1      8    ─────────┘   └───────────    8
             -                                 -
      4     20    ─────────────────────────   20
```

Figure 10.1: Serial printer cable wiring

A variety of mechanical problems can affect a printer. Preventive maintenance should be carried out from time to time. Most printers are parallel devices, so we'll look at printers, and the maintenance of them, in more detail in the chapter on the parallel port.

10.2 Plotters

Plotters are useful for producing good quality line graphics. They are available in a range of sizes, from the most common A4 flat bed plotter up to giant machines that can produce full size maps and plans. Large plotters may be driven using a high speed Ethernet connection, but the smaller ones generally use an RS-232 interface.

A plotter draws lines on paper using pens. Coloured output can be produced by getting the plotter to select different coloured pens from a carousel. The pen holder is mounted on a metal arm. The arm allows the pen to be raised from and lowered on to the paper, and moved from left to right across it, under software control. The paper is gripped between small rubber wheels, and moved up and down beneath the pen. Using a combination of these movements, pictures and graphs can be drawn.

A plotter is a line drawing or raster device. It can't easily produce solid blocks of colour, except by laboriously filling in an area with the pen, which is a lengthy process. Using different types of ink, a plotter can draw on to both paper and acetate transparencies.

Most plotters are controlled using a command language called Hewlett Packard Graphics Language (HPGL). Originally developed by Hewlett Packard this has become a *de facto* standard for hard copy graphical output devices.

There are too many mechanical differences between makes and models of plotter for any general guidance on maintenance to be given. Few receive anything like the amount of use that the average printer gets, however, so fortunately the incidence of mechanical failure is small.

Plotters suffer from much the same interfacing problems as serial printers. However, they are more prone to device time-out failures. Many plotter operations are quite lengthy to perform. For example, selecting a new pen can take several seconds. Also, some HPGL commands are quite complex and, again, time-consuming to carry out. To stop the PC from sending commands to the plotter while it is busy, and its buffer is full, handshaking must be used. Time-outs will happen if the plotter is busy for too long a period. If this is a problem, you may need to use the P parameter to the DOS MODE command to disable time-out.

10.3 Mice

The first mouse for IBM PCs was introduced in 1982 by Mouse Systems. Today it's estimated that one in four PC users have one. As Microsoft Windows increases in popularity, many more PCs will sport a mouse alongside the keyboard.

A mouse is really quite simple. There isn't much to go wrong with it, but like any computer peripheral, it can benefit from a little preventive maintenance. Simply through use, a mouse will pick up dust and dirt from the desk-top. In time, this will affect operation, making it erratic and unreliable.

There are two basic types of mouse: the serial mouse and the bus mouse. A bus mouse can be recognised by its special connector, which looks like a miniature audio DIN plug. It uses a special interface card that plugs directly into the PC expansion bus. The advantage of this is that it leaves the serial port free for other things. The interface card supplies power to the mouse, and processes the signals from it. Periodically, it generates interrupts to pass mouse movement and button press information to the mouse driver. Many PCs today have a bus mouse interface built on to the motherboard. Both Microsoft and Mouse Systems make bus mice.

As the name implies, a serial mouse interfaces to the PC via the serial port. It can be recognised by the presence of a standard 9- or 25-pin plug at the end of its cable. The serial mouse controller within the mouse body draws its power from the RTS line of the RS-232C port. The controller processes the electrical signals from the mouse mechanism and converts them to packets of data, which are transmitted to the serial port. Serial mice are available from several sources including Microsoft and Logitech, and a range of cheap but effective mice are made in the Far East.

A mouse requires a special driver to be installed before it can be used with software applications. The mouse driver is an interrupt driven communications program. It processes the data packets and provides an interface to applications that allows them to get information about mouse movements and button presses. The mouse driver is usually installed in CONFIG.SYS, using a line like:

```
DEVICE=MOUSE.SYS
```

Some mouse drivers are .EXE or .COM programs, and can be run from the command line when needed. Microsoft Windows 3 doesn't require a mouse driver. It has one built-in. An external driver is only needed if you want to use the mouse from within non-Windows applications.

10.4 Mouse Operation

The way a mouse works is shown in Figure 10.2. A small rubber ball protrudes through the base of the device, and rotates as the mouse is moved around the desk-top. This rotation is transmitted to two metal rollers, positioned at right-angles to one another. The rubber ball is kept in contact with the metal rollers by means of a third, spring loaded roller. The amount and direction of rotation transmitted to each metal roller varies, depending upon the direction of movement of the mouse.

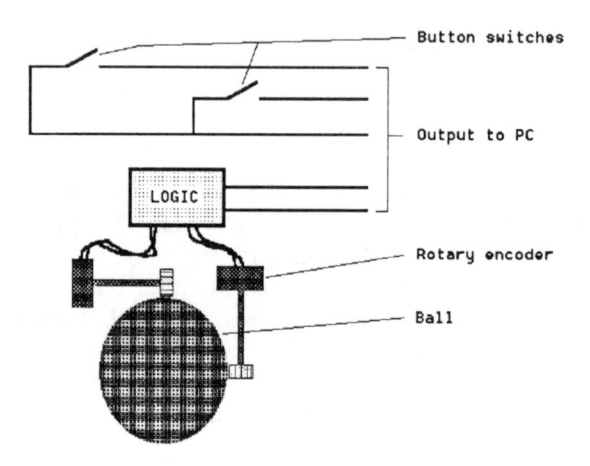

Figure 10.2: The mouse – principles of operation

Each roller drives a rotary encoder. This is a small wheel containing perforations. Light from a light-emitting diode (LED) shines through the perforations, and is interrupted as the wheel rotates. The interrupted light beam is detected by a photodetector, which generates electrical pulses. These are interpreted by the mouse controller to determine the amount of movement in each of the x and y axes. This information is transmitted to the PC via the interface cable, for processing by the mouse driver.

The mouse buttons operate simple switches. The switches control a voltage which is brought out to pins on the mouse connector, where they can also be detected by the software.

10.5 Cleaning a Mouse

Dust and dirt picked up by the rubber ball will reduce the amount of grip between it, the desk-top and the metal rollers, and mouse movements will not be tracked accurately. The mouse should be cleaned regularly, as follows:

- ❑ Remove the ball from the ball housing. This is usually accomplished after first removing a plastic locking ring by turning it in the direction shown.

- ❑ Clean the ball by washing it in warm water, using a little soap or detergent if necessary, then dry it using a lint-free cloth.

- ❑ Blow into the interior of the ball housing to remove excess dust, then wipe clean with the lint-free cloth. If necessary, the rollers may be cleaned using a cotton wool bud.

- ❑ Replace the ball in the housing, and test the mouse.

After a long period of use, a mouse may work poorly even after maintenance. The metal rollers must move freely or they won't respond to the slightest movement of the ball. Also, the action of the buttons may become unreliable after extensive or heavy-handed use. Repair, involving the replacement of individual parts, isn't economic for a device costing as little as a mouse. If careful cleaning and reassembly doesn't restore satisfactory operation, the only practical solution is complete replacement.

Some serial mice may not work correctly with laptop PCs. Many laptops don't supply +12V to the RTS output of the serial interface when running from their internal batteries. As a result, the mouse doesn't receive sufficient power to operate. Plugging in the mains adapter, which provides a +12V output, will cure the problem.

10.6 Mouse Problems

Apart from erratic operation, which can usually be remedied by cleaning, difficulties with mice are usually software problems. Some possible problems and solutions are outlined below:

Erratic pointer movement, large mouse movements needed for small pointer movements on screen:

❏ Clean moving parts.

❏ Roller movement sticky – replace mouse.

Mouse button operation intermittent:

❏ Micro-switches worn or broken – replace mouse.

No mouse pointer appearing:

❏ Mouse driver not installed.

❏ Mouse not connected, or connected to wrong port.

❏ Application software not configured to use mouse.

Mouse pointer appears, but no movement:

❏ Wrong type of mouse driver installed.

❏ Mouse not connected, or connected to wrong port.

❏ Software error – try rebooting machine.

10.7 Modems

A modem is a device used to connect two computers, or a computer and another serial device, using a telephone line.

Computer data is digital. The bits and bytes are represented by electrical signals, which may either be on or off. A telephone line is designed for carrying speech, which is an analogue (infinitely variable) signal. A modem converts digital data to an analogue signal, which enables it to be sent over a telephone line. It does this by transmitting an audio tone, and then modulating it (varying it) in direct relation to the pattern of bits to be sent. At the far end, the remote modem demodulates the tone to recover the digital information. The name modem is short for *modulator/demodulator*.

Early modems could only handle data at very low speeds, perhaps 10 characters per second. If you had a telephone connected to the line, you could listen to their output, and hear the tone warbling in time with the data. Modern modems use very sophisticated methods of modulation and multiple tone frequencies to achieve much higher data speeds. They also employ data compression to achieve still greater throughput. Speeds of 1,800 characters per second over standard telephone lines are not uncommon these days. The electronics inside such modems is complex, and requires specialised test equipment to set up and repair.

Apart from the modulator and demodulator circuitry, a modem has a relay to perform the equivalent of lifting the telephone receiver and hanging up the line after use. Other circuits give it the facility to dial the number of the remote computer – this is known as *autodialling*. Most modems can also respond to incoming calls; this is called *auto-answer*. Many have a battery-backed memory. This is used to store various operational settings, and even the telephone numbers of remote computers, so that they don't need to be entered each time.

A typical modem can operate in a variety of modes and at several different data speeds. To control it – put it into the correct mode, instruct it to dial a number and so on – a command language is used. The one most commonly used is the Hayes command set, named after the manufacturer Hayes Microcomputer Products who invented it. It's sometimes called the AT language, because every command begins with the characters AT.

The AT language has become a *de facto* standard for modem control, and the commands for the most basic functions, such as dialling a number or hanging up the line, are the same for all modems. Some of these commands are given in Table 10.1. However, modems are becoming increasingly complex and sophisticated, and need far more commands than were used by the original Hayes models. Each manufacturer has tended to choose his own AT commands for the extra functions. So, just because a command works on one modem, you shouldn't assume that it will give the same result on another.

Setting up a modem can be a complicated business, and requires an understanding of communications terminology. How a modem is set up depends very much on the individual device. A basic model such as a 2400 baud non error-correcting modem may simply be initialised to the factory default settings, then told to dial a number. Others, with a choice of speeds, error correction and data compression methods, may need special setting-up to suit both the terminal software and the remote system, before they can be used. There is no avoiding the need to study the modem's manual, and that of the communications software, to get things working.

Table 10.1

Command	Description
ATZ or ATZO	Reset modem
ATDPnnnn	Dial number, using pulse dialling
ATDTnnnn	Dial number, using tone dialling
ATMn	n=0: Speaker always OFF n=1: Speaker On until carrier detacted n=2: Speaker On all the time
ATLn	n=0: Speaker volume low n=3: Speaker volume high
ATQn	n=0: Show result codes n=1: Do not show result codes
ATVn	n=0: Use short result codes n=1 or more: Use extended result codes modem specific
ATBn	n=0: Use CCITT V.22 mode n=1: Use Bell 103 and 212A mode
ATPn	n=0: Do not echo command characters to terminal n=1: Do echo command characters to terminal
ATHn	n=0: Hang up line n=1: Listen to line (life receiver)
ATIn	Obtain data about modem

10.8 External Modems

There are two types of modem commonly used with PCs – internal and external. An external modem is a small box, with its own power supply, and usually some push buttons and indicator lamps on the front panel. The modem is connected to the PC serial port using a serial data cable wired as shown in Figure 10.3 overleaf.

The layout of the buttons and indicators on the front panel will vary to some extent between modems, but their basic functions are all much the same. There's usually an indicator lamp to show that power is connected. One labelled TXD or TD shows when data is being transmitted; another marked RXD or RD shows when it is being received. A lamp marked DTR should be illuminated when the communications software on the PC is active. One marked DCD (Data Carrier Detect) will come on only when the carrier (audio tones) from a remote modem is being received over the telephone line – in other words, when a call is in progress. Some modems have an indicator marked RI (Ring Indicator), which flashes when the line is ringing. This can be a useful monitor if the modem is being used so that people can dial in to the computer.

```
         PC
   9 pin   25 pin                              MODEM

     3        2    ─────────────────────────    2
     2        3    ─────────────────────────    3
     7        4    ─────────────────────────    4
     8        5    ─────────────────────────    5
     6        6    ─────────────────────────    6
     5        7    ─────────────────────────    7
     4       20    ─────────────────────────   20
```

Figure 10.3: Modem cable wiring

If the modem has buttons on the front panel, there is usually one marked DATA. This is used to switch the line to the modem, instead of the attached telephone. Older modems didn't have the facility to autodial. They always had a DATA button, since it was necessary to use the telephone to dial the number. The button was pressed after the connection was made, as soon as the tone from the remote modem was heard.

All new modems can autodial, but the DATA button can still be useful. Some types of system, such as minicomputers or mainframes, use communications software that doesn't support the use of the Hayes command language. For the same reason, a modem also has a button that is used to put it into *originate* (where it dials out) or *answer* mode.

Two buttons which may be present are used for testing. One, which is sometimes marked DL, puts the modem into digital loop-back mode. In this state, any data received at the RS-232C input is immediately reflected back to the sender. Another button, marked AL, sets up an analogue loop-back. Here, the modulated output from the modem's transmitter is directed back into its receiver. Some modems can also be configured for a remote digital or analogue loop-back. In this mode, data received from a remote modem over the telephone line is sent straight back to it. The purpose of these modes is to test the correct operation of the modem and the communications link. They are normally used with a test program, which sends out continuous streams of data and checks what comes back for errors.

10.9 Internal Modems

The second type of modem that may be used with a PC is the internal or card modem. This is an expansion card, which can be fitted inside the PC. It draws its power from the PC bus. The telephone cable plugs into a socket mounted on the back plate of the modem card.

The card modem combines the function of a PC serial port and a Hayes compatible modem on a single circuit board. It has the advantage that it saves desk space compared with an external modem, and cabling problems are avoided. However, until recently, card modems were limited to the lower performance end of the market – 1200 or 2400 baud – because the complex electronics needed by higher performance models took up too much space to fit on an expansion card.

An internal modem must be entirely controlled by software – using the Hayes command language – since there are no external buttons or indicators. To help the user know what is going on, the modem has a loudspeaker. This acts as a telephone earpiece, so that you can hear the dialling tone, the number being dialled, and the sound of the answering modem. This is very useful for trouble-shooting if a modem has difficulty making a connection. The loudspeaker can be controlled using a Hayes command, and is usually set to switch off once a connection has been successfully established.

Using an internal modem will not always release a serial port for other uses. The modem looks just like a standard serial port to any PC software. Jumpers on the board can be used to configure it to COM1 or COM2, and possibly COM 3 or 4. However, if there is an existing serial port set up for one of these designations, it must be removed or disabled. If the modem and the software that will drive it support COM3 and 4, this will often allow two existing serial ports to be retained. However, you'll remember that there are only two interrupt request lines available for use by serial ports, and you must ensure that these aren't already being used. COM3 usually uses the same interrupt as COM1, and COM4 the same as COM2. Therefore, if the modem is configured as COM3, COM1 can't have an interrupt driven software driver – such as a mouse driver – associated with it. Typically it could only be used for printing through the standard facilities provided by DOS.

10.10 Communications Terminology

A modem can provide access to a wealth of information and on-line services. These can be of great benefit to both technical and non-technical PC users. Unfortunately, communications (often shortened to comms) is a subject that has some particularly arcane terminology. This often causes confusion, even among technical people who are not comms specialists. To the end user, the jargon simply perpetuates the mystique of communications as a black art. Some of the terms which will be encountered are explained here.

In comms jargon, a terminal or PC is often referred to as a DTE. This stands for *Data Terminal Equipment*. This term originates in the days when a terminal might have been a teleprinter, a paper tape punch, a dumb terminal or a microcomputer. A modem is called a DCE, or *Data Communications Equipment*. Some data cables may have DTE and DCE marked on the plugs, and the serial interfaces on some printers have the option to be set up as either a DTE or a DCE.

If both ends of a communications link can send information to each other at the same time, then the link is said to be *full duplex*. This is the most common type of connection. If only one end can send at a time (rather like a CB radio channel) the link is *half duplex*.

When communicating over the public switched telephone network (PSTN) the remote computer to which you are connected is termed the *host*. In order for a link to be established, both the local and the remote modem must be set to use the same communications standards. The most important parameter of a communications link to a user is the speed. Over a telephone line, however, there are many other important factors: the tone frequencies and method of modulation used, for example. These parameters are defined by international standards.

In most parts of the world, the standards used are those developed by the CCITT. This is an international organisation, based in Geneva. CCITT standards have designations beginning with the letter V. V.21 is a standard for 300bps communication, and is seldom used today. V.23 is a standard in which one end transmits at 1200bps and the other at 75bps. This was popular for Viewdata type systems, where most of the data travels from the host to the terminal, and only a few key-presses need to be sent the other way. V.23 is mostly used in Europe, so only European-made modems or communications packages support it. As faster modems come down in cost, both of these slower standards are dying out.

V.22 is a standard for 1200bps communication. In America, the corresponding standard is Bell 212A. This uses different tone frequencies, and is therefore incompatible with V.22. Most modems can be switched between one or other of these two standards, using the ATB Hayes command. ATB1 selects Bell 212A mode, and ATB0 selects V.22.

For 2400bps communication, the standard used is V.22bis. This is used throughout the world, as the Bell standard for 2400bps data was never accepted. Most of the low-cost modems available today implement V.22 and V.22bis. The former is quite reliable over all telephone lines, while the latter is more susceptible to line noise, and is usually used with some form of error correction.

In 1984 the V.32 standard was introduced. This used advanced technology to achieve 9600bps transmission over ordinary telephone lines. Modems capable of operating using this standard have only been available since 1986. They are complex, and therefore expensive. Because the V.32 modem is pushing the capabilities of the telephone line to the limit to achieve its high throughput, the signal is much more prone to interference by noise. Complex encoding and error detection techniques are used to counteract this. Sophisticated technology has enabled the size of the circuit boards of a V.32 modem to be reduced, and card modems started to become available during 1990.

10.11 Error Correction and Data Compression

Increasing data speeds have brought about an increased susceptibility to error. Most high-speed modems offer error correction, so that the user or application program receives only clean data, and not the irritating garbage characters that appear as a result of noise on the line.

Data compression is also becoming commonplace. Most data that is transmitted is plain text. This frequently contains repeated characters. For example, quantities of spaces are often used to ensure that reports are nicely formatted. Many computer data files contain large areas filled with zeros. An encoding method is used which exploits these and other characteristics to enable the data to be transmitted using fewer bytes. The receiving modem expands the data back to the original size. The result is a substantial increase in throughput.

The most common error correction and data compression method in current use is the *Microcom Networking Protocol* (MNP). This has become a standard, at least at the lower end of the modem market. The protocol has a number of levels, each of which builds upon the levels below to achieve further improvements in performance.

Level 2 is the lowest level of MNP encountered and offers basic error correction only. In simple terms, data is transmitted in blocks, with a checksum included. If the receiving end detects an error, it asks for the block to be sent again. Level 4 offers improved error correction, by varying the size of the individual blocks of data according to the quality of the line and the incidence of errors. This enables improved efficiency to be achieved. Large blocks minimise the overheads and result in the highest throughput over a good line. When the line is noisy, small blocks are used, since the smaller the block, the greater the chance of it being received in its entirety without error. MNP level 5 includes data compression. It can achieve up to double the throughput of the line, so that a 2400bps link can give up to 4800bps effective speed.

Higher levels of MNP up to level 10 have been introduced. These enable a modem to vary the communication speed to suit prevailing line conditions, and to change the method of data compression used to that which gives the best results for the type of data being transmitted. These proprietary protocols are predominantly found in modems manufactured by Microcom.

Belatedly, the CCITT introduced their own standards for error correction and data compression. V.42 is the standard for error correction, and V.42bis is for data compression. The compression technique used by V.42bis is more sophisticated than MNP level 5, and compression ratios of up to 4 to 1 can be achieved. This equates to an effective rate of 38400bps over a 9600bps line.

10.12 Making a Connection

Though high-speed modems are a great time and money saver, they can be a lot of trouble to set up. With old, single speed modems, there wasn't much that could go wrong. Either they heard each other or they didn't. With fast modems, however, you have a choice of speeds that you can use. Fast modems use a system called *fallback*, which means that, if they fail to talk to each other at their highest speed, they try a lower one. They repeat this, until they hit on a common speed. Having established a connection, the modems will then *negotiate* the error correction and data compression protocols to use. All this can take a few seconds.

Sometimes, a bit of line noise at the wrong moment will prevent one modem from recognising the other. This causes them to go into fallback mode. Frequently, they get down to 1200 baud before managing to get *in sync*, or they may fail to make a connection at all. Even if they make a connection, line noise may result in failure to establish an error corrected link. This can be very irritating.

If you know for sure what speed the remote modem will be using when it answers the phone, you can avoid this problem by setting up your modem to only make a connection at this speed. Similarly, you can tell it to drop the line if it fails to establish an error corrected link. The commands to do this vary from modem to modem.

With some systems, particularly amateur bulletin boards, you may get a different modem every time you dial in. Consequently, you may not know what speed or protocol to use. In this situation, you have no alternative but to use fallback mode. If you do, you need to make sure that the modem won't reset the speed of the modem-to-PC connection to the same speed as the modem-to-modem link, when the connection is made. This is an option that's usually available, but most comms software can't handle it. Use the highest speed between your modem and your PC that you can, and tell the modem to stick at that speed, no matter at what speed it finally connects to the remote system.

10.13 Modem Problems

With so many variables to consider, solving communications problems can be a difficult business. Faults generally fall into three main areas:

❑ Interfacing the modem to the PC

❑ Getting the right communications settings

❑ Line problems.

Often there is little you can do about the latter, other than using a lower speed if reliability is consistently bad.

Interfacing a PC to a modem is mostly a question of using the right cable and method of handshaking, and ensuring that both the modem and the communications software are set up for the same speed, word length and so on. Sometimes, it can be a problem ensuring that the modem receives the Hayes commands (or others, if appropriate) that the comms software sends to it. Some modems don't seem able to accept commands at the speed at which software can send them (as distinct from the speed at which they might be manually typed in). However, you may not realise what's going on, because most communications packages insist on hiding the commands that are sent to the modem, and the replies it sends back.

Listing 10.1 is a terminal program written in BASIC, which can be used to test modems. The program is restricted to the serial ports COM1 and COM2 since only these two are supported by BASIC. Using the program you can send commands directly to the modem, and observe the results. You could use it to log on to a remote computer if required, though no data capture or file transfer facilities are provided. If Control/Q is pressed, the program sends a *quick brown fox* message. If you put the remote modem into a loop back mode you could use this to test the overall circuit. Type Control/Z to exit the program.

```
4000 REM ====    LISTING 10.1    ====
4005 REM ==== TERMINAL PROGRAM ====
4020 S$="": GOSUB 4800: REM Set serial parameters
4025 IF S$="" THEN 4599
4040 OPEN S$ AS #1
4050 ON COM(N%) GOSUB 4600
4060 COM(N%) ON
4070 CLS: PRINT "Type CTRL/Q for 'quick brown fox', CTRL/Z to quit"
4080 LOCATE ,,1
4100 REM ==== MAIN PROGRAM ====
4120 K$=INKEY$: IF K$="" THEN 4120
4130 K%=ASC(K$)
4140 IF K%=26 THEN 4200
4150 IF K%=17 THEN PRINT #1,"The quick brown fox jumps over the lazy dog": GOTO 4120
4160 PRINT #1,K$;
4170 GOTO 4120
4200 PRINT: INPUT "Exit Terminal (Y/N) ";K$
4220 IF K$="Y" OR K$="y" THEN 4240
4230 GOTO 4120
4240 COM(N%) OFF
4599 END
4600 L%=LOC(1): IF L%=0 THEN RETURN
4610 PRINT INPUT$(L%,#1);
4620 RETURN
4800 REM ==== SET SERIAL PARAMETERS ====
4810 CLS
4820 INPUT "Choose serial port: 0) Quit  1) COM1  2) COM2 ";N%
4821 IF N%>2 THEN 4820
4822 IF N%=0 THEN RETURN
4823 IF N%=1 THEN S$="COM1:"
4824 IF N%=2 THEN S$="COM2:"
4830 INPUT "Choose speed: 1) 300 2) 1200 3) 2400 4) 4800 5) 9600 ";I%
4831 IF I%<1 OR I%>5 THEN 4830
4832 IF I%=1 THEN S$=S$+"300,"
4833 IF I%=2 THEN S$=S$+"1200,"
4834 IF I%=3 THEN S$=S$+"2400,"
4835 IF I%=4 THEN S$=S$+"4800,"
4836 IF I%=5 THEN S$=S$+"9600,"
4840 INPUT "Choose data format: 1) 8-N-1 2) 7-E-1 3) 7-O-1 ";I%
4841 IF I%<1 OR I%>3 THEN 4840
4842 IF I%=1 THEN S$=S$+"N,8,1"
4843 IF I%=2 THEN S$=S$+"E,7,1"
4844 IF I%=3 THEN S$=S$+"O,7,1"
4850 RETURN
```

Some communications problems, and some pointers to possible solutions, are summarised overleaf. For more information about general interfacing problems, see the previous chapter.

Unable to send commands to modem:

❑ Modem not powered up: check cable, switch, fuse.

❑ Faulty data cable.

❑ Cable attached to incorrect serial port.

❑ Internal modem configured as incorrect serial port.

❑ PC contains two devices configured as the same port.

❑ Communications software using wrong port/speed/format.

❑ Modem command echo off: try ATQ0E1.

Modem does not dial number:

❑ Modem not receiving dial command. Try entering command manually.

❑ Wrong dialling method selected (tone/pulse).

❑ Incorrect dial command specified in comms software configuration.

❑ Dial suffix in comms software not terminated with Enter.

❑ Faulty telephone cable.

❑ Too many devices (phones/modems/faxes) on line.

Modem responds to typed commands, but not to automatic commands sent by communications software:

❑ Check commands sent by software are valid.

❑ Check type of result code expected by software.

❑ Commands are sent too fast. Check software configuration.

❑ Insufficient delay between commands. Check software configuration.

Modem dials number, but will not connect:

❑ Remote modem is using different speed or mode.

❑ Incorrect modem configuration.

Modem makes connection, but only garbage is displayed:

❑ PC to modem link using incorrect speed/word length/parity.

❑ Modem is autobauding (changing DTE-DCE link speed to same as connect speed) and software cannot handle this.

❑ Faulty modem (either end).

❑ Poor line quality.

Modem makes connection, but a lot of garbage is displayed:

❏ Bad line. Reduce speed or use error correction.

❏ Too many devices (phones/modems/faxes) on line.

❏ Faulty modem.

Communication works for a while, then program hangs:

❏ XON/XOFF enabled when it should not be.

❏ Two devices using same hardware IRQ line.

❏ Software problem: remove multitasking programs and TSRs.

❏ Communications software bug.

File transfers fail:

❏ Bad line.

❏ Wrong protocol (or CRC/checksum) selected.

❏ PC to modem handshaking not working: check cable, modem and software configuration.

❏ Characters are being lost. Remove multitasking programs and TSRs.

❏ Disk full (for downloads).

Displayed data contains unexpected strings beginning with a [:

❏ Wrong terminal emulation mode selected.

Line drops during communications session:

❏ Bad line.

❏ Interference from telephone extension.

❏ Interruption from switchboard or call-waiting tone.

10.14 Null Modems

A pair of modems is only needed if the computers that are to be connected are so far apart that the only possible link between them is a telephone line. If they are in the same building, and separated by metres rather than kilometres, you can make a direct connection using wire.

If two computers are connected without a modem, the connecting cable should ensure that the various RS-232C signals are changed over, as they would be if modems were used. The TXD output from one computer must become the RXD input of the other, and similarly DSR must go to DTR. If ordinary PC-to-modem cables are used, then a device is needed to effect this change-over. The device is called a null modem. A wiring diagram for a null modem is shown in Figure 10.4.

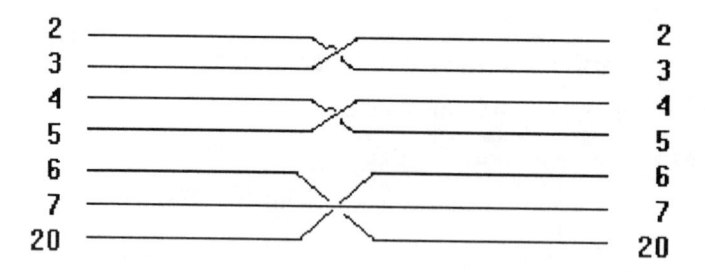

```
2  ────────────╳────────────  2
3  ────────────╱╲────────────  3
4  ────────────╳────────────  4
5  ────────────╱╲────────────  5
6  ────────────╲────────────  6
7  ────────────╳────────────  7
20 ────────────╱────────────  20
```

Figure 10.4: Null modem cable wiring

You can wire up a cable so that the signals are changed over in the same way as if a null modem was used with standard cables. This is called a null modem cable.

Summary

Many peripherals can be attached to a PC using a serial port. In this chapter we looked at several common devices. We will look at printers along with parallel ports in the next chapter.

Plotters are useful where there is a need for good quality drawings to be produced. There are many types and models, so it's difficult to give general guidance on how to deal with mechanical problems. Plotters interface with a PC in the same way as printers. However, they are more prone to timing out, as some operations take a long time.

Mice are popular additions to a PC. There are two types of mouse: serial and bus. Interfacing is straightforward, as an integral cable and plug are supplied. Mice need regular cleaning if they are to work well. A procedure for cleaning was described. A mouse normally requires a mouse driver to be installed and properly configured before it can be used with software applications. The exception to this is Windows 3, which has its own mouse driver built-in.

Modems can be difficult to get working. There are many different communications standards in current use. A good grasp of communications practice and terminology is needed to set up a modem and overcome any problems that may occur. The chapter included an overview of communications terminology and current standards. A simple terminal program was described, for use when testing modems. A fault-finding check list was given, to help resolve problems.

11

Parallel Ports and Printers

A printer is an essential PC accessory. The arrival of the paperless office is something that has been heralded for years. In the real world, though, hard copy is still the most convenient way of sending and storing letters, memos, reports and so on. So it's impossible to make full use of a PC unless a printer is available.

From a support point of view, printers are more complicated to maintain and repair than PCs. For one thing, there are mechanical aspects to the job, so engineering skills are likely to be needed. Another problem is that there is little standardisation in the design of printers. To carry out many repairs, specialised training, or at least a workshop manual, will be needed. It is also harder to obtain replacement parts for printers than it is to get PC boards and disk drives.

In a book such as this it clearly isn't possible to give machine-specific instructions for repairing all the different models of printer. There are simply far too many of them. Many problems, though, are configuration faults, or can be rectified by simple cleaning and adjustment. This is the level of troubleshooting that we will aim to describe in this chapter.

11.1 The Parallel Port

Most PC printers use the parallel or Centronics interface. On a PC, this is a 25-way female D-type socket. Printers use a 36-way female Amphenol socket. The pin-outs of these connectors are shown in Figure 11.1. The parallel interface was first used by the printer manufacturer Centronics, in the late 1970s. It became popular in home computers and low cost printers because it is simple and cheap to implement.

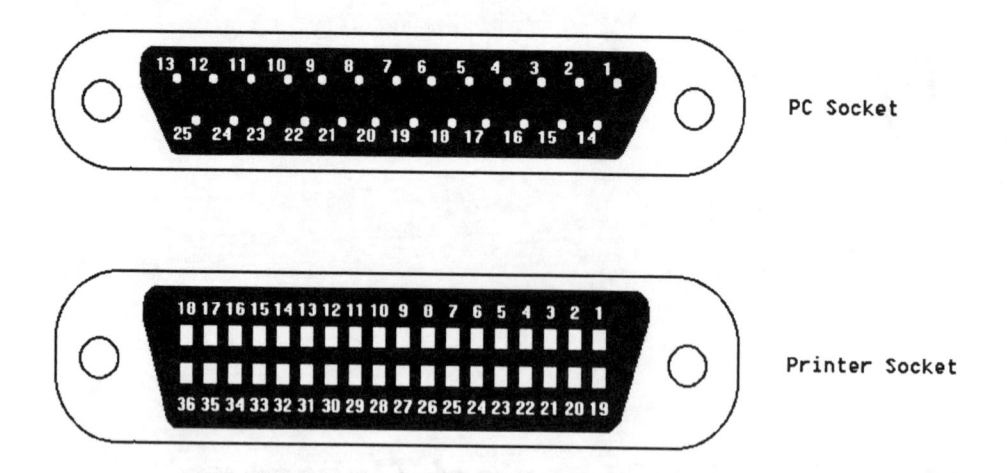

Figure 11.1: Parallel connectors – pin diagrams

The parallel interface is so called because all eight bits of each byte of data are sent to the printer simultaneously, in parallel. Table 11.1 shows the pin assignments. There are eight data lines – DATA 0 to DATA 7 – one for each bit. There is also a signal line called STROBE. This is used to tell the printer when there is a character to be read. When the signal goes low, the printer reads the values on the eight data lines as a byte. After it has done this, the printer uses the ACKNLG signal to tell the computer it is ready to accept another byte of data. Other signals are used by the printer to tell the PC if it is on-line or busy, if an error condition has occurred, or if the paper is exhausted.

The parallel interface can achieve much higher data rates than the serial port. This is because data bits are transmitted in parallel, so there is no overhead of stop, start and parity bits. However, it is essentially intended to be a one way device – from the computer to the printer.

The parallel port circuitry is quite simple. In the original IBM PCs and many older clones a parallel port was included as part of the display adapter. It was implemented using discrete electronics. Since a printer is considered essential equipment by almost all PC users, most manufacturers now build a parallel interface onto the motherboard.

The IBM PC architecture supports up to three parallel ports. Under DOS these are referred to as LPT1, LPT2 and LPT3. The I/O port addresses used are: 03BCh – 03BEh, 0378h – 037Ah, and 0278h – 027Ah. The addresses 03BCh – 03BEh are normally used by a parallel port that is part of a display adapter. If it isn't present, 0378h – 037Ah is used for LPT1.

There are three I/O ports for each parallel port. The first in the group of three is the data port. When a byte of data is written to it, it is stored in a logic device called a *latch*. The second I/O port is then read by the BIOS software. This port gives the condition of the various status lines. If a bit is set, indicating that the printer is ready to accept a character, a value is written to the third I/O port which causes the STROBE signal on the interface to go low. This tells the printer to read the character.

On an XT-compatible machine, IRQ7 is reserved for use by the printer adapter. ATs may use IRQ5 for LPT2 or 3. The printer adapter is supposed to generate an interrupt when the printer is ready to receive a character. This would enable software to drive a printer in the background without having to poll the status port continually to see if it is ready. However, not all printer adapters reliably generate this interrupt. Consequently, most software, including DOS, ignores it.

Unlike the serial port, software applications don't usually drive the parallel printer adapter directly. The PC ROM BIOS provides functions that can be used to write data to the parallel port and test its status. These (or the higher-level functions provided by DOS) are used almost exclusively.

The exceptions are programs that use the parallel port in a non-standard way, for example, as an *input* port. They do this because the serial port can't operate faster than 115,200 baud, or 11K characters per second. Programmers who were looking to provide a faster means of interfacing external devices to a PC hit upon using the parallel port. Data can be transmitted from the PC to the device using the normal eight parallel data lines. Data may be input from the device to the PC using the status lines. However, the data lines in many PC parallel interfaces are designed to be bidirectional, and software can detect and make use of this feature if it is available. Surprisingly, because of the simplicity of the electronics, very high speeds can be achieved.

Many packages use the parallel port as a two-way interface. These include LapLink, a program that connects two PCs using a special cable to allow files to be rapidly transferred between them. You can also buy portable tape streamers that hook up to the parallel port, and enable back-ups on to tape to be made. Another recent device is the pocket network adapter. This is mainly intended for use with small lap-top PCs that have no internal expansion bus. It's a small box that plugs in to the parallel port and, when special software drivers are loaded, allows the PC to access a network.

11.2 Types of Printer

There is a huge choice of printers that you can buy. The cheapest are dot-matrix and range in price up to £1,000 ($1500 US), or even more for particularly fast or heavy-duty models. Those at the bottom of the range produce a rather basic quality of print in draft mode. However, even the cheapest models now offer near letter quality printing, though at a low speed. The popularity of home micros is largely responsible for the development of very low-cost printers. These are really only suitable for occasional use, not the constant daily hammering they would receive in an office environment.

Next in terms of cost are ink-jet printers. Currently, these start at £400 ($600 US). A fairly recent development, they offer a much higher quality output than dot-matrix printers, though at the expense of higher running costs. They are also much quieter in operation. The success of ink-jets has largely caused the demise of the daisywheel printer, which was popular throughout most of the 1980s. Daisywheels are based on electric typewriter technology, and therefore provide true letter quality.

The printer of the 1990s is the laser. Silent in operation, lasers can produce very high quality output. They are also true letter quality printers. Over the last few years, both the size and cost of laser printers has been coming down. The cheapest available now cost about £600 ($1000 US). It's likely that they will replace ink-jets for quality printing, except at the bottom end of the market. PC laser printers are exclusively page printers. So if you have a need to output on continuous stationery, an ink-jet or dot-matrix printer is still the best choice. However, it's possible that laser printers for continuous stationery could be developed. The earliest laser printers – in the early 80s – were high speed printers for mainframes, using fan-fold paper and costing around a quarter of a million pounds each!

11.3 Dot-matrix Printers

Dot-matrix printers are the most popular type of printer for use with micros. They use a print head which is pulled horizontally across the paper from left to right and back again using a rubber belt and an electric motor. Each character is generated from an array or matrix of dots. The print head consists of a number of tiny pins, which are operated electromagnetically. As the head moves across the paper, the pins move rapidly in and out, under the control of the printer's electronics. Characters are formed when the pins strike the ribbon, leaving dots of ink on the paper.

The ultimate resolution of a dot-matrix, and hence the quality of printing, is determined by the number of pins in the print head. The earliest printers, and all the cheap ones, use a 9-pin print head. Those offering near letter quality use a 24-pin head giving more than double the resolution. However, printer control electronics is becoming increasingly sophisticated, so that even 9-pin printers can produce near letter quality output. This is achieved by making multiple passes of the print head, repositioning the paper fractionally between each pass, to give 18-pin resolution or better.

Because dot-matrix printers are impact printers, they can be used with multi-part stationery. Most printers have a lever that adjusts the distance of the print head from the roller or platen, so that different thicknesses of stationery can be accommodated. Another lever controls the pinch rollers which are necessary when single sheet, non sprocket-fed paper is being used.

Price is obviously a major factor contributing to the popularity of dot-matrix printers, but low running costs are also important. They will happily print onto almost any type of standard paper, either sprocket fed or single sheets. Many offer the option of an automatic sheet feeder for standard office stationery. The major consumable item is the ribbon, and these are cheap and long-lasting. Even the print head is cheap and easy to replace once that wears out. So the dot-matrix is the ideal printer in many situations, especially where cost is an important consideration.

Although dot-matrix printers are mechanical devices, there isn't a lot to go wrong. One or more of the print head pins may stick, resulting in only partly-formed characters. Fragments of paper or adhesive labels may become stuck in the paper feed path, interfering with the free movement of the paper. Constant use can eventually result in breakage of the paper feed or print head positioning levers, or the tractor feed sprockets. Only close examination will reveal whether replacement of these items a DIY repair job.

11.4 Ink jet Printers

Most ink jets resemble dot-matrix printers in that the paper is fed round a typewriter-like roller and printing is done by a print head that is pulled back and forth across the page. However, instead of dots being made by pins hitting a ribbon on to the paper, they are produced by squirting ink through an array of tiny nozzles. The resolution, and hence print quality, is dependent upon the number of nozzles, and this can be very high. Since there is no impact noise from pins hitting the paper, ink-jets are quiet. The noise they make is mainly confined to the muted whirr of the electric motor driving the print head back and forth.

A variant of the ink-jet is the bubble-jet printer. Here, the ink nozzles in the print head contain tiny semiconductor heating elements. These heat the ink, forming bubbles, which are squirted on to the page. The heating elements are microscopic in size. This enables many more nozzles to be used than in a conventional ink-jet, thereby increasing the resolution. One example of a bubble-jet printer is the Hewlett Packard DeskJet. This can produce output comparable in quality to that of a laser printer.

A disadvantage of ink-jet printers is that running costs are higher. Ink cartridges are more expensive than ribbons, and don't generally last as long. The ink used by some printers is slow to dry unless absorbent paper is used, and can therefore be prone to smudging. However, fast-drying inks are under development and rapidly coming into use.

Ink-jet printers can suffer from the same sort of problems as dot-matrix printers, since in many respects the mechanical design is the same. However, the ink-jet print head contains no moving parts, unlike its dot-matrix counterpart, and so is usually more reliable.

11.5 Laser Printers

Laser printers have become increasingly popular where high print quality is required. This is largely due to decreasing cost, which has now reached a similar level to that of a good quality dot-matrix or ink-jet printer.

They use similar technology to an office photocopier. A laser beam scans a bit-mapped image of the page on to an electrostatic drum, in a process known as *exposure*. Toner is attracted to the charged areas of the drum, in a process called *development*. The toner is then transferred electrostatically to the paper, and fused on using hot pressure rollers.

Lasers are more complex than other types of printer, and consequently the cost of manufacture is much higher. Most manufacturers don't make their own printer mechanisms or *print engines*, but use one of the standard engines made by companies like Canon, Ricoh or Hitachi. This is why so many laser printers from different manufacturers look the same. Mechanically they *are* the same. Only the firmware is different.

There are basically two types of laser printer engine. These are called write-white and write-black. In a write-white engine, the laser writes a negative image to the drum, and toner is attracted to the areas untouched by the laser beam. In the write-black engine, it is the image produced by the laser light to which toner is applied. The Canon engine used in the Hewlett Packard LaserJet printers, as well as those by Brother, Star and others, is a write-white engine.

Low cost laser printers have been brought about through the development of simpler and cheaper systems for building up the image of a page on the drum. These printers use light-emitting diodes (LEDs) or liquid crystal shutters (LCS). In an LED printer, light from a row of light-emitting diodes is used to build up the bit-mapped image. LCS printers project fluorescent light through a liquid crystal display, which is selectively turned on and off to allow the light through only where required. In other respects, these printers resemble true laser printers and are generally thought of as such.

Because laser printers are so complex, anything more than routine preventive maintenance really requires the attention of a specialist engineer. The paper feed path is tortuous. After a long period of use, the pinch rollers can get out of adjustment so that the paper slips, and misfeeds become more frequent. The electronics is equally complicated. A printer may contain one or two microprocessors, operating system firmware in ROM, and often several megabytes of memory. If a fault should occur, tracing it will require special test equipment and diagnostic software. So for laser printers, a manufacturer's support contract could well be worthwhile.

Preventive maintenance tasks will vary depending on the print engine used. The printer's Operations Manual should be consulted for details. For the Canon engined printers, maintenance is confined to replacement of the toner cartridge, and cleaning the two corona wires.

11.6 Daisywheel Printers

Daisywheels are impact printers, as anyone who has stood within earshot of one will be aware. The daisywheel is a small plastic wheel holding a number of spokes, at the end of each of which is the raised negative image of a character. As the print head moves across the paper, the daisywheel revolves. A solenoid-driven hammer hits it at the appropriate moment. This causes the spoke containing the desired character to be pressed against the ribbon, printing it on to the paper.

A daisywheel printer gives true letter quality. Indeed, typewriters using this method of printing are made by several manufacturers. Daisywheels can use carbon-film ribbons, which give a crisper print quality than fabric ribbons. However, they are slow, noisy, and incapable of printing graphics, or different fonts except by changing the daisywheel.

The reducing cost of laser printers, which are much quieter, capable of better quality, and offer more flexibility, has almost killed off the daisywheel. At the bottom end of the market, the ink-jet has also taken market share from it. About its only advantage is the ability to use multi-part stationery or produce carbon copies. The demand for daisywheel printers has diminished to such an extent that many companies no longer produce them.

The technology of daisywheel printers is tried and tested and therefore reliable. The paper feed mechanism is similar to that of a dot-matrix and suffers from the same problems. Maintenance is limited to replacing the ribbon periodically, and cleaning or replacing the daisywheel as it becomes worn.

11.7 Thermal Transfer Printers

Thermal transfer printers are relatively uncommon. Mostly they are high quality colour printers, expensive to buy and expensive to run, and only used for certain specialised graphical applications. However, this technology is also used in many low-cost ultra-compact portable printer designs.

Thermal colour printers work by using small semiconductor heating elements which melt ink from a special ribbon on to the page. Often, special paper is required as well. Characters or graphics are built up from patterns of dots in the same way as with ink-jet or dot-matrix printers. The cost of the special ribbons and special paper is high, so thermal printers aren't really economic for general purpose use.

Some portable thermal printers don't use a ribbon at all. Instead, they use a special heat-sensitive paper. The dots that make up the characters are formed when the tiny elements in the print head heat up, turning the heat-sensitive coating black. The mechanics of this type of printer are simple, and the power requirements low, making them ideal for battery operation. Again, the special paper is expensive, but this may be an acceptable price to pay for the benefits of portability.

11.8 Preventive Maintenance

Printers, like all other equipment, benefit from a little care and attention now and again. Preventive maintenance can either be carried out regularly, as recommended for PCs, or it can be done whenever consumables such as ribbons or toner cartridges need to be replaced. The last is the better solution, since it can be messy to remove ribbons, ink cartridges and so on before they are used, and it's difficult to service the printer with them in place.

With most printers, performing a full PM every time the ribbon needs changing would be excessive. It would perhaps be more practical to do it every fourth ribbon change. The difficulty is in keeping a record so that you know when a particular device is due for some attention. It's a good idea to affix a sticker to each printer on which you can record the date of each consumable replacement. This will enable you to see when a service is needed. It's also a simple method of measuring how much use a particular machine gets. If a printer needs a new ribbon every few days, it's probably in almost constant use, and you should expect it to wear out more rapidly than average.

To carry out preventive maintenance, first switch off the printer, remove the mains plug from the wall socket, and remove the cover. For laser printers you should follow the procedure laid down in the manual for cleaning and replacement of toner cartridges. Different print engines have differing maintenance requirements. For HP LaserJets using the Canon engine, the corona wire should be carefully cleaned to remove any deposits of toner. It should be replaced every three or four changes of toner cartridge. It's a good idea, while the printer is open, to inspect the mechanism and carefully wipe away any dirt, toner or paper dust that may have built up inside.

For dot-matrix or ink-jet printers, remove the ribbon or ink cartridge. Note how the ribbon feeds past the print head. Carefully wipe away any paper dust that may have fallen into the mechanism. Check that there are no fragments of paper or adhesive labels obstructing the paper path. A piece of thin card is often useful in removing obstructions. Check that paper – both sprocket-fed and single sheets, if applicable – feeds through easily.

The dot-matrix or daisywheel print head can be cleaned using a special cleaning kit, such as that produced by Perfect Data. This consists of a cleaning sheet, which is fed through the printer as if it were paper, and cleaning solution. Moisten the cleaning sheet with the solution. Then get the printer to print on to it (without the ribbon), by performing a test print. The solution will dissolve away any dried up ink deposits, which are then absorbed by the cleaning sheet. An alternative method of cleaning the print head uses a special cleaning cartridge fitted in place of the ribbon.

You should also clean the platen of the printer, to remove any ink that may have been transferred to it if printing has run off the paper. Again, Perfect Data make a special cleaning kit with moulded brushes. This is probably useful for badly inked-up platens, but usually the solvent-impregnated pads used for cleaning the exteriors of equipment can be used successfully.

If any of the moving parts of the printer aren't moving freely, it may be beneficial to apply a small amount of light machine oil to the affected parts. Consult the printer manual before trying this. Most printers use bearings which are designed not to need lubrication. However, if dirt and paper dust has caused things to seize up, a little lubrication will probably help. If oil is applied, take care to use only the minimum amount necessary.

Once you've finished cleaning and servicing the printer, a new ribbon or ink cartridge can be installed. Test the printer, to check that the print quality is satisfactory. Most impact printers have an adjuster that controls the distance between the print head and the platen. To minimise wear, this should be set to the maximum spacing that will give good print quality. Finally, clean the printer covers using a soft cloth and a mild detergent solution, and replace them in position.

The steps described above are summarised in the following check-list (taking as an example a dot-matrix printer):

- ❑ Switch off printer; remove covers and ribbon
- ❑ Clean out dust from mechanism
- ❑ Check and clean paper feed path and platen
- ❑ Clean or replace print head
- ❑ Replace ribbon if worn
- ❑ Test for satisfactory print quality
- ❑ Clean and replace covers.

11.9 Parallel Printer Problems

When setting up any printer to work with a PC, there are two areas that require attention: the interface between the PC and the printer, including the cable, and the software configuration or printer setup. Often, the printer is simply hooked up to the PC, and if it appears to work, no more is done to it. Later, problems may be found, such as graphics characters not printing properly, the pound sign not printing, or sections of text being omitted when long documents are printed.

When IBM designed the PC they decided that the standard printer port would use the Centronics parallel interface. Whoever made that design decision deserves thanks from everyone, because it eliminates the need to wrestle with serial interfacing – the bane of the PC support person's life – for most PC installations. The parallel port is a straightforward plug and play interface. There are no options to set for speed, word length, parity or any of the other variables that can make setting up serial devices such a nightmare.

The wiring diagram for an IBM PC to parallel printer cable is shown in Figure 11.2. The correct wiring of this cable is the only *configuration* the parallel interface needs. As we have seen, the parallel interface has a separate STROBE signal for timing, which is why the speed doesn't have to be set either in software or hardware. Handshaking, in the form of the BUSY line, is also built in.

If the data cable isn't specifically an IBM PC parallel cable then it's possible that some error signals are not correctly fed back from the printer to the PC. The equipment may work satisfactorily most of the time, but if the printer is de-selected or the paper runs out, the PC may be unaware of it, and will continue to send data. If this happens, the data will be lost.

One problem that can occasionally rear its head is that of time-outs. Some operations on certain printers take a long time, for example, form feeds on a particularly slow printer. If the machine keeps its BUSY signal raised for too long, DOS will report the device as having timed out. The time out period is set during initialisation by the ROM BIOS and isn't alterable through DOS, although the MODE command can be used to tell the system to ignore it. A few applications programs provide a means to change the time-out period, however.

Parallel interfaces can be damaged by static, or even by plugging in cables while the PC and the printer are switched on. The ICs used in the parallel port aren't as rugged as those used in the serial interface. They are designed to work with smaller voltages and currents, so their resistance to abuse is lower. Most PCs provide buffering devices between the interface circuitry and the connector, so that they are less prone to damage. Other types of microcomputer, printers, and a few PC clones, may not. If a printer consistently prints incorrect characters then one or more of the data lines on the parallel interface may be faulty.

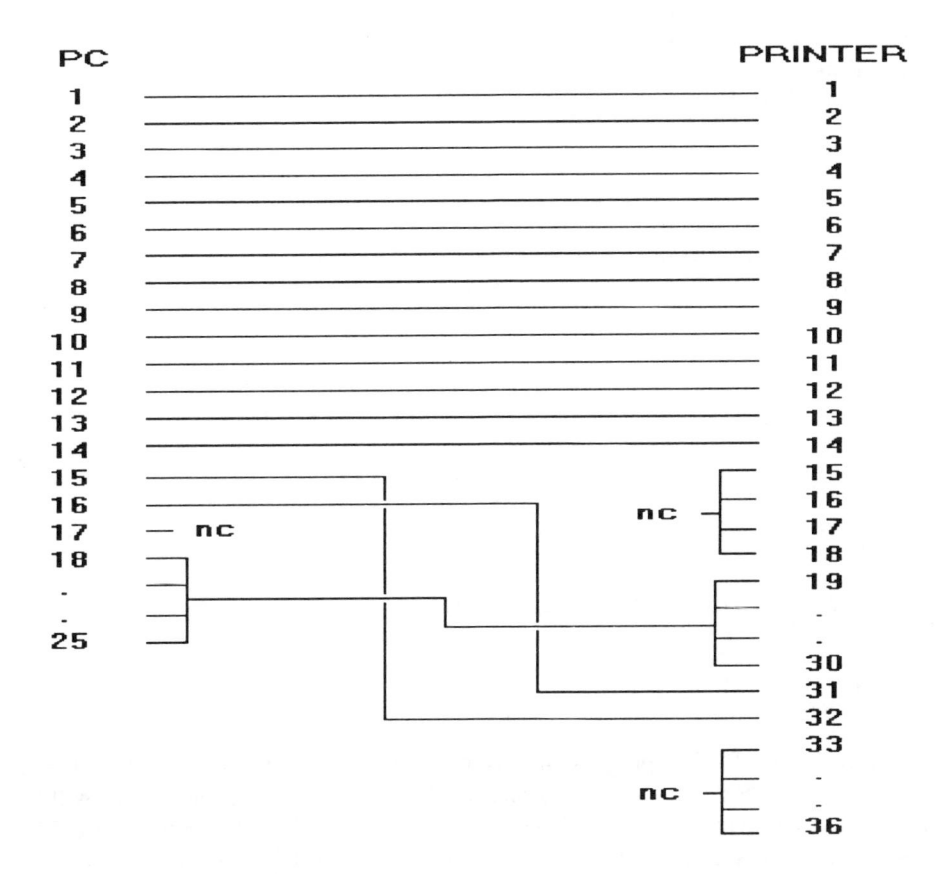

```
PC                                              PRINTER
1  ─────────────────────────────────────────────  1
2  ─────────────────────────────────────────────  2
3  ─────────────────────────────────────────────  3
4  ─────────────────────────────────────────────  4
5  ─────────────────────────────────────────────  5
6  ─────────────────────────────────────────────  6
7  ─────────────────────────────────────────────  7
8  ─────────────────────────────────────────────  8
9  ─────────────────────────────────────────────  9
10 ───────────────────────────────────────────── 10
11 ───────────────────────────────────────────── 11
12 ───────────────────────────────────────────── 12
13 ───────────────────────────────────────────── 13
14 ───────────────────────────────────────────── 14
15 ──────────────┐                      ┌─────── 15
16              │              nc ─┤    ├─────── 16
17 ── nc        │                   └── 17
18 ─┐           │                      ┌─────── 18
    │           │                      ├─────── 19
.   │           │                      ─
.   │           │
25 ─┘           │                      ┌─────── 30
                │                      ├─────── 31
                └──────────────────────┤─────── 32
                                       └─────── 33
                                                 ─
                                  nc ─┤
                                       └─────── 36
```

Figure 11.2: Parallel printer cable wiring

A similar effect — consistent substitution of one character for another — can also be caused by a faulty cable. Either one of the data lines is not connected, or there could be a short between two of them. In this case, you should check the cable with a multimeter, or try substituting a new one, to see if the problem goes away.

If you have a diagnostic program such as Check It, you can use this to test the PC to printer interface. The program sends several patterns to the printer. These test the quality of printing, the correct operation of carriage return, line feed and backspace, and that the first seven data lines are operating.

```
5100 REM ====        LISTING 11.1       ====
5105r REM ==== PARALLEL PRINTER TESTS ====
5110 CLS
5120 INPUT "Enter port to test: 1) LPT1  2) LPT2  3) LPT3 ";D%
5130 IF (D%<1) OR (D%>3) THEN 5120
5140 IF D% = 1 THEN D$ = "LPT1:"
5142 IF D% = 2 THEN D$ = "LPT2:"
5144 IF D% = 3 THEN D$ = "LPT3:"
5148 OPEN D$ AS #1
5150 GOSUB 5800
5152 PRINT "Test completed."
5154 END
5800 REM ==== OUTPUT TEST LOOP ====
5802 ON ERROR GOTO 5850
5805 INPUT "Enter number of test lines to print ";N%
5810 PRINT : PRINT "Press any key to terminate test"
5820 I% = 0
5822 WHILE (I% < N%) AND (INKEY$ = "")
5824 PRINT#1,I%,"The quick brown fox jumps over the lazy dogs back. ";
5825 PRINT#1,"8 bit test: wê"
5828 I%=I%+1
5829 WEND
5830 GOTO 5880
5850 REM ==== ERROR MESSAGES FOR PRINTER TESTS ====
5852 PRINT "Error: ";
5854 IF ERR=24 THEN PRINT "Device Timeout."
5856 IF ERR=25 THEN PRINT "Device Fault."
5858 IF ERR=27 THEN PRINT "Out of Paper."
5860 IF ERR=68 THEN PRINT "Device Unavailable."
5862 PRINT "Test Terminated."
5880 ON ERROR GOTO 0
5885 RETURN
```

Alternatively, the BASIC program in Listing 11.1 can be used. This program will repeatedly send a test pattern to the printer. Each line is numbered. The pattern will be sent a pre-determined number of times, depending upon what you want to test. The program uses the standard error trapping facilities of BASIC to report on any error conditions that may occur.

To test if the paper out signal is being detected by the PC, set the program to output 100 lines, and put a single sheet of paper in the printer. To test the operation of the *printer ready* signals, run the program with the printer turned off or off-line. To check that handshaking is operating correctly, set the program to run for several hundred lines. This will ensure that it fills the printer buffer, and has to wait for buffer space to become available before more data can be sent. Examine the resulting printout to see that no characters are missing, and that there are no gaps in the numbered sequence.

You can also use the test pattern to check that the eight data lines of the parallel interface and data cable are all working. If the *quick brown fox* message is slightly garbled, then it's likely that one data bit is either permanently off or permanently on. This could be caused by either a broken wire, a short in the cable, or a fault in the interface (at the PC or the printer). By looking at which characters in the message are incorrect, and comparing the ASCII codes for the correct character and the one that was actually printed, you can work out which data lines are affected by the fault.

11.10 Serial Printer Problems

When connecting a serial printer to a PC there are many variables to consider, such as: baud rate (speed), data format (word length, stop bits), parity and handshaking (cable wiring). The significance of these was described in Chapter 9. All of them must be correct, for a serial printer to work.

Since serial printers are more of a headache to get working, and as PCs come with a parallel port, why use them at all? The Centronics parallel interface came into use at the end of the 1970s, at the time the first microcomputers were beginning to appear. Before that, all printers used serial connections or some form of proprietary interface. When the IBM PC was launched, most of the printers available were serial-only devices. Indeed, the earliest PCs had neither a serial nor a parallel port fitted as standard, so that the user could choose which one he required.

Although the parallel interface rapidly became the standard for printers, it can't be used if the printer is sited some distance away from the PC. It's a high speed interface, with many signal wires closely spaced in either a conventional multi-core or a flat ribbon cable. The probability of noise pick-up, or of mutual interference between the signal wires in the cable, mean that reliable operation cannot be guaranteed with cable lengths greater than about five metres. Serial interfaces, on the other hand, operate using higher currents and at lower speeds, and are therefore less susceptible to noise or signal degradation. You can use them, without special signal boosters, over distances of 50m or more. If a printer is remote from the user – as often happens when a group of PCs share a printer using a data switch – then a serial interface should be used.

The minimum basic interface between two serial devices is a cable linking the transmit data output on one device with the receive data input on the other, and providing a signal ground or earth path. However, for communication with a printer, something more sophisticated is required. Generally, a PC can transmit data to a printer faster than it can output it. Most printers these days have a buffer of perhaps 4k bytes or more, but if a long document is being printed, this will fill up. When this happens, the printer has to tell the PC to stop sending until the buffer has got some space in it. It does this by lowering the handshake signal – usually DTR – whenever the buffer is full. The applications software running on the PC should not send any data to the printer unless the handshake line indicates that the printer is ready to accept it.

If a serial printer works (i.e., will self-test) but won't print any data sent by the PC, quite probably the reason is incorrect handshaking. The trouble is that the RS-232C serial interface wasn't designed for linking computers to printers, and the various control signals it provides weren't intended to be used for flow control. Consequently, their use for this purpose isn't defined in the RS-232C standard. Printer and computer manufacturers have implemented flow control using these signals in different ways. The result is confusion; there is no standard configuration of serial cable that is always guaranteed to work. Serial interfacing and handshaking were described in more detail in Chapter 9.

11.11 Printer Configuration Problems

Often, if a printer isn't printing documents correctly, it's because the configuration or setup is wrong. There are two common reasons for this: using the wrong control code emulation or the wrong character set.

Control code emulation concerns the codes that are used to get the printer to use different print styles and fonts, print graphical images and so on. Almost every manufacturer has its own set of control codes. However, there are three which are used most often, since almost all printers have an option to emulate at least one of them. Most dot-matrix printers, and others which use continuous stationery, emulate Epson or IBM Proprinter control codes. Since most software can drive either an Epson or an IBM Proprinter, the printer can be used by setting it to emulate one of these.

Many laser printers also provide Epson or Proprinter emulation. However, lasers support a range of facilities that aren't available on dot-matrix printers, and control codes to access them aren't provided in these two modes. Laser printers usually support Printer Control Language (PCL), which was developed by Hewlett Packard. This is really a complex set of control codes rather than a language as such. It's an evolving standard. Each new HP printer adds new features and hence new commands, and other manufacturers follow on.

The most sophisticated laser printers use PostScript. This really is a programming language, which is executed by the controller inside the printer. It provides a wide range of facilities, including support for 35 scaleable fonts. To obtain output from a PostScript printer, the device must be sent a PostScript *program* to generate the output. Anything sent to the printer which isn't a valid PostScript command is ignored. Consequently, PostScript printers can only be used by software that has a PostScript driver. Plain text files, such as output from DOS, cannot be printed.

If a software package isn't using the appropriate driver for the printer, the output is likely to be incorrect. In some cases, plain text may be printed correctly, and it may only be where some form of print enhancement is selected that the output is wrong. However, if graphics is printed using the wrong driver then complete gibberish is usually the result.

Selecting the right character set is another source of confusion. The IBM PC has its own character set. This is more or less standard ASCII for the first 128 characters 0h – 7Fh, but the upper 128 contain a mixture of foreign language and line drawing characters, Greek and mathematical symbols, including a pound sign at character position 9Ch. Most printers support this character set, which is sometimes referred to as PC-8. Many also – and some only – support the International Standards Organisation (ISO) character set. This contains italics in the upper 128 characters. There are several variants of the ISO set, for different nationalities. These substitute different national characters for the less commonly used ones in the standard set. For the UK, the pound sign replaces the hash symbol at character position 23h.

11.12 The Pound Sign Problem

Since there are two possible character values that can be used for the pound sign, getting it to print can be a headache. Some printers will offer the IBM character set in IBM Proprinter mode, and the ISO set if switched to emulate Epson. Others allow the emulation and character set to be selected independently. Many older printers only support the ISO character set, so many software packages use character 23h for the pound sign. This means that you are forced to use the UK ISO character set, even if the IBM set is an option, and consequently, IBM line graphics can't be printed.

The real difficulty comes when two or more packages are used, each of which requires a different character set to be selected. Depending on the hardware and software involved, there may not always be a solution to this.

For the pound sign problem alone, one solution is a set of utilities called THEPOUND from S & S International. This includes a TSR program that can be loaded to reside permanently in memory, monitor all output to the printer, and substitute the correct code whenever a pound sign is seen. The utility may have an adverse effect if it is present when graphics are being printed.

11.13 Other Problems

Another common problem is double spacing. On the IBM PC, the convention is to terminate each line of text with two characters: carriage return (CR) and line feed (LF). On a dot matrix printer, CR causes the print head to return to the beginning of the line it has just printed. LF causes the paper to move up one line. Some older computers terminated each line with just a single CR or LF character, and the printer had to perform both a carriage return and a line feed when this was received. Most printers can be set up to do either of these things. If single spaced output is being printed double spaced, a DIP switch or front panel configuration option – typically called Auto-LF – must be turned off.

Occasionally, the converse of the above may be experienced; in other words, each line of output is overprinted on the previous one. If this occurs, it's the *software* that should be reconfigured, not the printer.

The other common problem that can occur is when the first line of each successive page starts a couple of lines further down the paper. This may be either a software or a hardware configuration problem. The printer itself must be set up to the correct page length for the paper being used – typically 66 lines for standard 11 inch continuous stationery. If doing form feeds from the printer's front panel causes the paper to throw to a new page correctly, then the page length is probably correct.

Some software packages form feed by keeping a count of the number of lines printed, and sending the appropriate number of line feeds to get to the head of the next page. They do this because, if you use different sizes of paper, it's often easier to change the form length in the software rather than alter the printer configuration. If the software thinks that the page length is different to what it actually is, this will cause the problem described.

Occasionally, the form length can be correctly set and printing still begins further and further down each page. This usually happens when the printer is set to skip over the perforations of fan-fold paper. What happens is that, when the printer is two lines from the bottom of the page, it inserts two extra line feeds, so that there is a small margin at the top and bottom of each page and nothing is printed across the perforations. The PC software knows nothing of this, and merrily prints extra line feeds as if nothing had happened. The solution is to disable the skip over perforations. The alternative – reducing the form length in the software configuration – is only satisfactory if the form length in the *printer* configuration will always be set correctly. Otherwise, the perforation skip will continue to conflict with the software, and there will be unwanted blank lines appearing on each page.

11.14 Diagnosing Problems

It's usually clear if a problem is of a mechanical nature. If paper isn't feeding correctly, or print quality is poor because the print head is worn or malfunctioning, the solution will entail dismantling the printer, and possibly replacing some parts. Because there are so many types of printer, it isn't possible to give a comprehensive fault-finding guide. If you decide to tackle this type of problem, you'll need to apply a certain amount of common sense. Some problems that may be encountered, and their possible causes, are outlined here:

Printer will not print:

❑ Check power to printer.

❑ Check no error condition shown on front panel.

❑ Check printer operation (self-test).

- ❏ Check software configuration (printer port selection etc.). Check you are not printing a non-PostScript file to a PostScript printer. Try printing from DOS.
- ❏ Check cable is plugged into correct socket.
- ❏ Check cable wiring, especially handshake lines.

Printer outputs rubbish; beeps, page-throws etc.:
- ❏ Serial printer: check software settings (speed, data format etc.).
- ❏ Switch off and on, to ensure buffer is cleared and default power-up settings are restored.
- ❏ Check printer control code emulation matches software settings.
- ❏ Check printer operation by performing a self-test.

Document is printed correctly, but sections of data are missing:
- ❏ Serial printer: check handshaking is enabled by both software and printer interface.
- ❏ Check handshake lines (Serial: RTS(DTR)/CTS, Parallel: BUSY) are working and cable is correctly wired.

Certain characters are consistently printed wrongly:
- ❏ Serial printer: check word length / parity settings.
- ❏ Parallel printer: check data cable for short or open circuits; check interface for correct functioning.

Line graphics characters printed incorrectly (e.g., as italics):
- ❏ Incorrect character set selected (should be IBM or PC character set). Change this from front panel or internal DIP-switches, as described in manual.
- ❏ Serial printer: interface must be set to eight data bits, no parity.
- ❏ Parallel printer: DATA7 line in cable is open circuit.

Document formatting (e.g., bold, underline) not executed correctly:
- ❏ Incorrect control code emulation set.
- ❏ Font cartridge not present.

Pound sign not printing:
- ❏ Incorrect character set selected. Change this from front panel or internal DIP switches.
- ❏ Check software configuration.

❑ Incompatible software.

Top of each page starts further down (or up) the paper:

❑ Check page length set correctly (in both software and hardware).

❑ Disable skip over perforations.

Paper jams or feeds incorrectly:

❑ Check paper feed path is free of obstructions.

❑ Check continuous stationery feeds freely and straight into printer.

❑ Pinch rollers require adjustment.

Print is faint on parts of the paper:

❑ Ribbon worn.

❑ Ribbon is not winding on; check that it is properly seated in its mounting and the ribbon drive wheel is engaged.

❑ Laser printers: toner low or unevenly distributed. If the latter, this may be corrected by removing the toner cartridge and rocking it from side to side.

Summary

This chapter began by looking at the parallel interface and how it works. It's fast and requires little configuration. However, parallel interfaces will only work over short distances.

We described the different types of printer available. Dot matrix printers are cheap and reliable but give relatively poor quality. Ink jets are slightly more expensive to buy, and more expensive to run, but give good quality and are quiet in operation. Laser printers are the most expensive to buy and give the best quality of all, but can only handle cut sheet paper. Daisywheel printers use typewriter technology to give good quality, but are slow and noisy in use. They are being replaced by ink jets and lasers. We described some basic preventive maintenance procedures for printers. These are best carried out at the same time as consumables – such as ribbons or toner cartridges – are replaced.

The chapter went on to look at the problems that can occur when a printer is in use. Most are caused by one of two things: incorrect interfacing or configuration. We looked at some common problems and likely solutions. The chapter concluded with a diagnostic check-list.

12

Tools and Techniques

In the preceding chapters, we looked at each major PC component and peripheral in turn. We saw how they work, what can go wrong, and what you can do about it. However, there isn't much you can do that doesn't require tools of some sort. In this chapter, we'll look at the tools you'll need to use to be an effective PC troubleshooter. We'll also look at some that you'll find useful if you want to do more than just deal with basic faults.

While everyone knows how to use a screwdriver, there are some tools and techniques you may not have used before. This chapter will show you how to use a test meter, chip inserters and extractors, and a soldering iron. It isn't essential that you have or use any of these things. But if you do, you'll increase the range of repairs and upgrades that you can perform.

12.1 The Technician's Toolkit

Some tools are essential if you want to be able to service and upgrade PCs. If you have to buy them, bear in mind that it's worthwhile investing in good quality tools. They'll last a lifetime, and help to make the job easier.

As a basic minimum, you'll need to be able to remove the system unit case, and insert and remove expansion cards and other items. You'll also need to be able to configure jumpers and switches either on cards or on the system board. You will probably be expected to carry out memory upgrades from time to time, and to change a power supply, or replace a diskette drive. Almost certainly, you'll need to be able to wire up mains plugs and test fuses and cables for electrical continuity.

To carry out these tasks, you'll need a basic toolkit consisting of the following items:

- ❏ Flat bladed screwdriver – 1/8 inch blade
- ❏ Flat bladed screwdriver – 1/4 inch blade
- ❏ Phillips screwdriver – small
- ❏ Phillips screwdriver – medium
- ❏ Phillips screwdriver – large
- ❏ TORX screwdriver – T10
- ❏ TORX screwdriver – T15
- ❏ Tweezers
- ❏ Chip inserter
- ❏ Chip extractor
- ❏ Needle nosed pliers
- ❏ Wire cutters
- ❏ Wire stripper
- ❏ Small volt-ohm meter.

Flat bladed and Phillips screwdrivers are essential for almost any task. The TORX screwdrivers are needed if you have to dismantle PCs from certain manufacturers such as Compaq. If you don't have any machines that use these special screws, you can get by without them.

You'll find tweezers useful for setting jumpers, and for retrieving screws that drop into the works! Pliers will do a similar job, especially where a stronger grip is needed. They will also be needed to attach push-on connectors, wire up data cables, and hold parts while soldering. Wire cutters and strippers are necessary to prepare mains cables for attachment to plugs, and for the manufacture of data cables. A chip inserter and extractor will be wanted when you perform memory upgrades and replace faulty integrated circuit chips. A volt-ohm meter will allow you to make continuity tests, and many other diagnostic measurements.

A range of other tools and materials may be useful, depending upon the work you intend to carry out. These include:

- ❏ Wire crimping tool
- ❏ Soldering iron and stand

- ❏ De-soldering braid
- ❏ Compressed air can
- ❏ Small vacuum cleaner
- ❏ Cleaning materials, e.g., Safeclens and Safewipe
- ❏ Diskette and Tape Drive cleaners
- ❏ RS-232 'Breakout Box'.

It can be invaluable to be able to make up data cables. Serial cables can be wired in all sorts of ways. Finding a commercial source for one with both the right connections and the required length can be difficult, especially if – as often happens – the cable is wanted yesterday! A crimping tool is probably the best way of producing custom leads. You can buy special kits containing a plug body and crimp-on pins. The pins are crimped on to the individual cores of the cable, and then pushed into the plug body with the aid of pliers.

A soldering iron shouldn't be regarded as essential, as all the electrical connections you will routinely be required to make use push-on connectors. Repairing circuit boards by replacing soldered-in components is not a cost-effective activity. Even trained service engineers will replace a board containing faulty components, rather than try to repair it. However, soldering isn't a difficult skill to learn, and there are occasions when it will come in handy. If you use a soldering iron, you'll find de-soldering braid, or a solder sucker, useful in removing excess solder from joints.

Cleaning materials and compressed air are handy for removing dust and dirt from a machine, and making it look as good as new. You can also get small hand-held vacuum cleaners. These are very useful for removing dust from motherboards and from inside keyboards. Read/write errors in diskette and tape drives are often caused by dust and magnetic oxide deposits on the head. They can be prevented by regular use of special cleaning kits.

A *breakout box* is a device that is inserted in line between two serial devices, such as a PC serial port and a printer. It allows the wiring configuration of the cable to be readily altered using jumper leads. This is helpful in diagnosing wiring faults, and in finding the correct wiring configuration to be used prior to making up a cable. More sophisticated versions have LED lamps which light up showing the signals on the cable. These can be very useful in some situations. The use of a breakout box was described in Chapter 9.

12.2 Software Tools

To be fully equipped, you'll need software tools as well as the conventional hardware variety. These should include diagnostic and test programs, and utilities to enable you to edit batch files, format disks, examine the configuration of a machine, back-up and recover data files and so on.

Diagnostic programs were discussed in Chapter 2, and some are described in more detail elsewhere in the book. You'll probably form your own ideas about which utilities are worth acquiring. There is a wide choice of commercial toolkits, many of which perform similar functions. Which to buy is often a matter of personal taste. However, a good basic toolkit will probably contain something like the following:

Utilities Disk:

❑ Small text editor: TED, SED, JET etc.

❑ Check configuration: DOSMAP, DOSINFO, MACHINFO, INFOPLUS

❑ Disk clean utility: CLEAN

DOS Disk:

❑ A bootable DOS disk, containing:

CONFIG.SYS	COUNTRY.SYS
KEYBOARD.SYS	KEYB.COM
FORMAT.COM	FDISK.COM
DEBUG.COM	SYS.COM
BACKUP.COM	RESTORE.COM

Disk Utilities:

❑ Norton Utilities

❑ Test Drive

❑ HDTest

Diagnostics:

❑ Check It

❑ BASIC Diagnostics given in this book

Anti-Virus:

❑ McAfee SCAN, NETSCAN and CLEANUP

Some of the programs mentioned above are commercial. Others are public domain or shareware. If you don't know where to obtain the latter, a disk containing many of the PD and shareware utilities described in the book, along with the BASIC programs given in the preceding chapters, is available from the publishers. Details are given in Appendix 7.

12.3 Test Meters

A volt-ohm meter is an extremely useful piece of test equipment, and should be part of every technician's toolkit. It can be used for testing fuses, though for this task a simple continuity tester would be adequate. However, the test meter can do a great deal more. The resistance ranges can be used to check continuity, but they will also show if a high resistance path is present. The DC voltage ranges can be used, amongst other things, to check the output of power supplies. You can use the AC ranges, if you are careful, to check the mains supply voltage, if this is suspected of causing problems. Figure 12.1 shows a volt-ohm meter being used to check a fuse, and the output voltage of a battery.

select resistance range
short probes together
adjust for zero ohm reading

then measure resistance of device

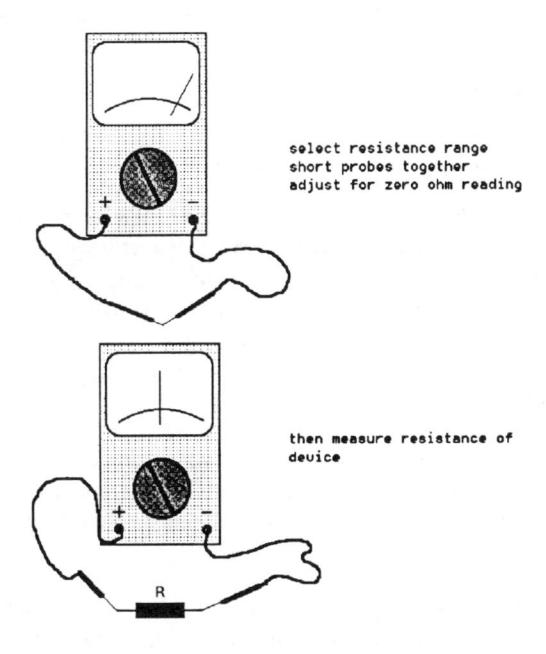

Figure 12.1a: Using a volt-ohm meter – Checking continuity/resistance

select voltage range greater than expected voltage before taking a measurement

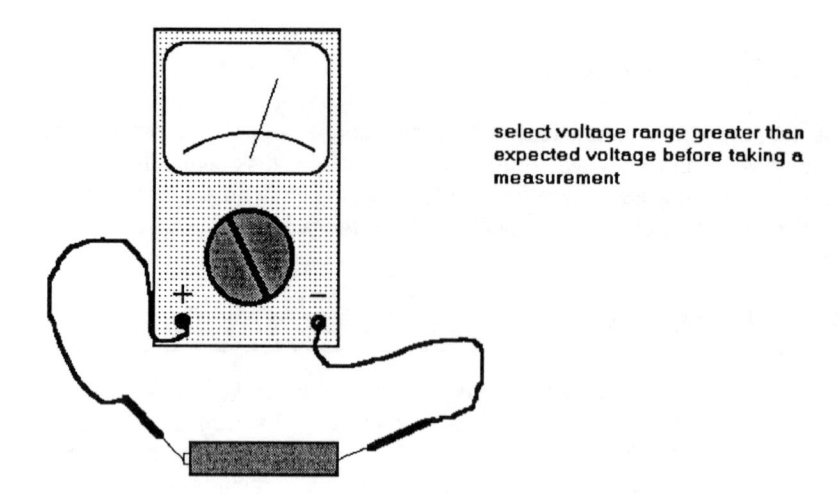

Figure 12.1b: Using a volt-ohm meter – Measuring voltage

To check a fuse, you use a resistance range. First, connect the two test probes, then adjust the meter to read zero resistance using the control provided. Then hold the probes, one at each end of the fuse. If a zero ohm reading isn't obtained, the fuse is faulty.

To check a battery, set the meter to a DC voltage range where the maximum is greater than the expected battery voltage. Then attach the probes to the battery contacts. Take care to observe the correct polarity. The voltage can then be read from the meter scale.

A volt-ohm meter need not be expensive. However, it's worth investing in a good quality one with overload protection. When you check voltages, it is good practice to always start on the least sensitive (highest voltage) setting. If you get into this habit, you're less likely to damage the meter movement by using too low a range, and sending the meter needle banging against the end-stop. However, mistakes do happen. An overload protected meter is more resistant to abuse, and will therefore pay for itself in the long run.

When deciding which test meter to buy, you have a choice between an analogue or digital readout. Which to go for is largely a matter of personal preference. However, to check out PCs, you won't need the additional precision that a digital meter provides.

Some test meters are auto-ranging. This means that they will automatically select the appropriate sensitivity range for the measurement being made. However, you'll pay quite a bit more for this facility.

12.4 Chip Removal and Replacement

Although you'll probably never have to repair PC circuit boards by replacing IC chips, you may occasionally have a need to remove and install integrated circuits. You may want to replace a faulty memory chip identified by a diagnostic program, or simply install extra memory in a machine. To remove a socketed IC without damaging it, you will need to use a chip extractor. Similarly, inserting ICs into sockets is immeasurably easier if you use a proper chip inserter.

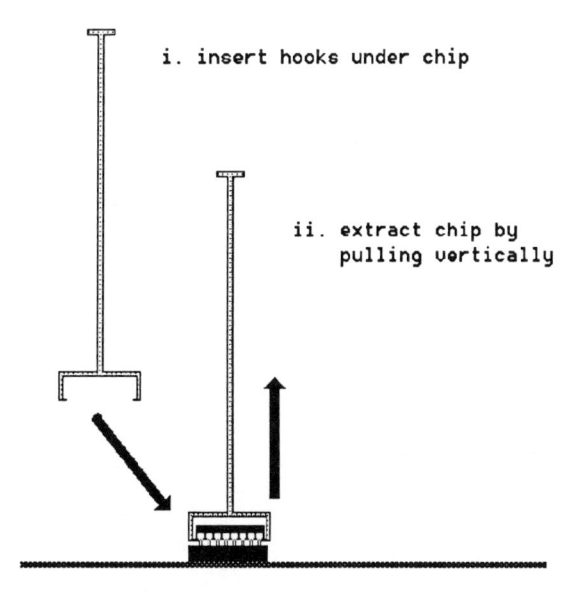

Figure 12.2a: Removing IC chips

Figure 12.2(a) shows how a chip should be removed, using an extractor. The tool has two tongues. These are hooked, one under each end of the chip. Holding the board with one hand, the chip is then extracted by gripping it with the tool and pulling vertically. This ensures that the legs aren't damaged on removal, should you later want to reinsert the chip.

If you don't have an extractor, ICs can be removed by carefully levering them out of their sockets using a small screwdriver. However, it's almost impossible to avoid bending the legs when using this method, and it should be avoided unless the chip is going to be discarded.

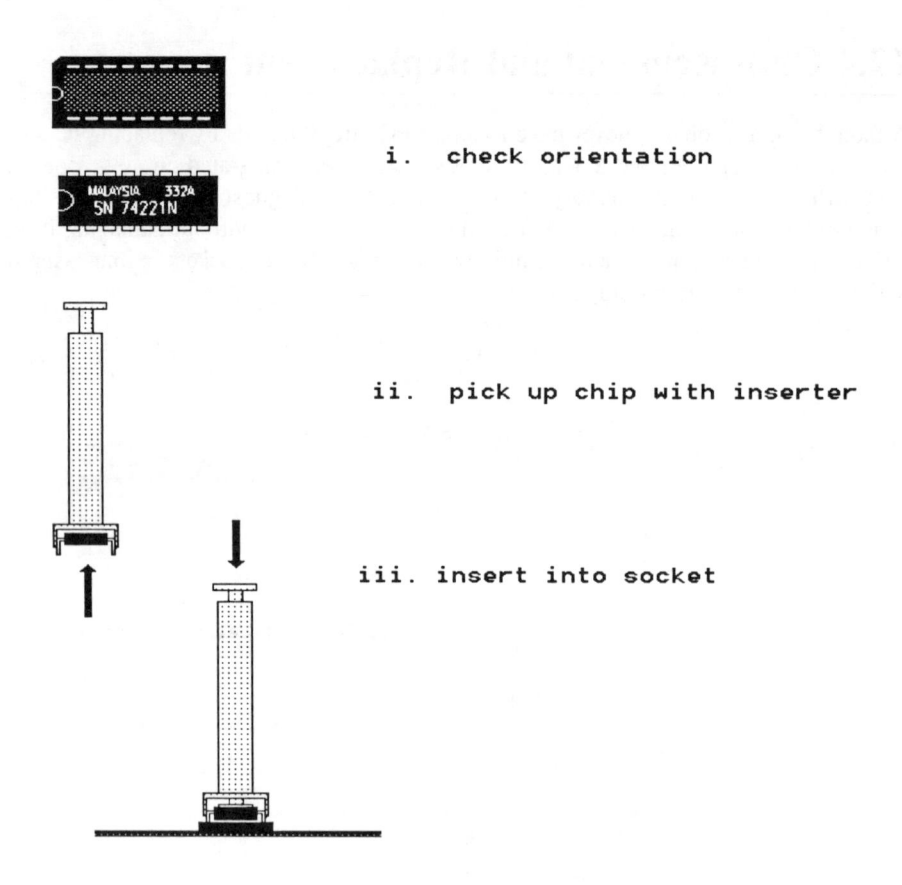

Figure 12.2b: Inserting IC chips

Figure 12.2(b) shows how to install IC chips using a chip inserter. First, press the component into the inserter, so that it is held by the spring pressure of its legs. Then hold the chip over the socket. You must take care to ensure that it is held the right way round. You insert the chip into the socket by pushing down on the spring-loaded plunger of the inserter. After removing the tool, check that all the legs have gone into the socket, rather than over the edge of it. Give the chip a final press down with the thumbs (without placing excessive stress on the board) to ensure that it is correctly seated.

It isn't wise to try to install ICs without the proper tool. Chips are manufactured with the legs slightly splayed, so they won't line up with the rows of contacts in the socket. Without an inserter it is difficult to ensure that all the legs go into the socket. Bending the legs manually so that they fit the socket is impossible to do without handling the chip excessively. This increases the risk of damage due to static electricity.

Even small static charges can destroy the ICs used in microcomputers. When handling ICs it is important to take precautions to minimise the risk of this occurring. Chips are usually quite safe while they are mounted in a circuit board. The connections to the other components help static to drain away harmlessly. However, if you touch a pin of an IC with a charged finger during handling, the static can destroy part of its internal circuitry and render it useless.

As a safeguard against static, it's a good idea to use an anti-static mat when handling ICs. Keep the chips in the anti-static container that they came in until you are ready to install them, and avoid touching the pins while handling them.

12.5 Soldering

Soldering isn't difficult, and will often enable you to carry out repairs that couldn't otherwise be dealt with. It's important to have the right soldering iron. If it's too large, it will be difficult to avoid getting blobs of solder everywhere, and you could easily damage components by overheating. If it's too small, you'll have trouble getting the parts and solder hot enough, and will end up making joints that are prone to break. An iron of 25W rating with a 2.5mm bit is ideal. A rechargeable iron is useful, because you can use it in locations that aren't close to a mains outlet.

Here are a few soldering tips that you should remember:

❑ Always use thin multi-core solder.

❑ Keep the bit clean and tinned at all times. You'll find a stand with a built-in sponge, which you can keep moistened with water and use to clean the bit, a useful accessory.

i. clean the bit and apply a little solder

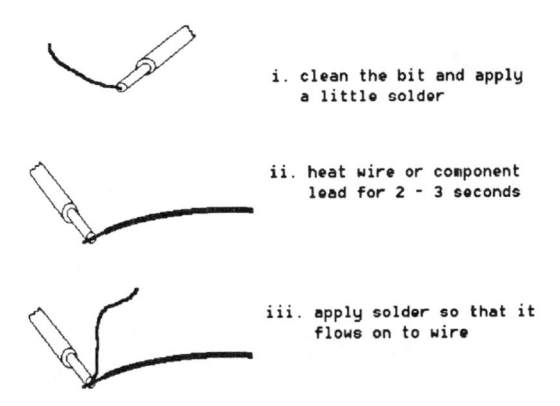

ii. heat wire or component lead for 2 - 3 seconds

iii. apply solder so that it flows on to wire

Figure 12.3a: Using a soldering iron – Tinning a wire ready for soldering

❑ When you first switch the soldering iron on, allow it a couple of minutes to reach to full working temperature. (Rechargeable irons heat up rapidly, so you switch them on just for the time they are needed.) When the bit is hot, *tin* it by applying a little solder to the tip.

Before joining two wires, or a wire and a pin on a connector, each part should be tinned. Figure 12.3(a) shows how this is done. First, tin the soldering iron bit. Then hold the bit to the part being tinned, and wait a couple of seconds for the part to reach the same temperature as the bit. Apply a little solder to it. It should flow easily. If not, the iron or the part aren't hot enough yet. Once the solder has flowed on to the part, remove the bit and allow the part to cool. You should see a bright silver covering of solder.

i. clean the bit and apply a little solder

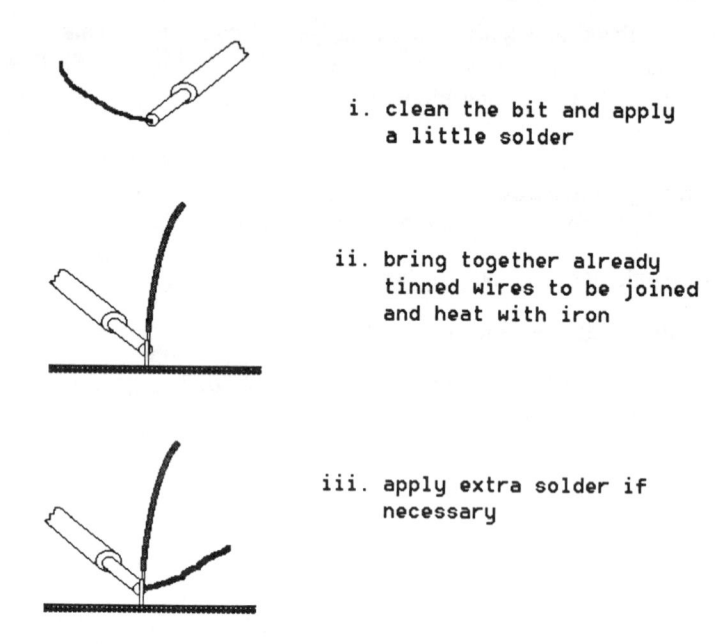

ii. bring together already tinned wires to be joined and heat with iron

iii. apply extra solder if necessary

Figure 12.3b: Using a soldering iron – Making a soldered joint

To join the two tinned parts, simply hold them together, using pliers if necessary, and apply the tinned soldering iron bit, as shown in Figure 12.3(b). There will often be sufficient solder already there to bond the parts together. If not, a little more may be applied. Remove the iron, and hold the parts still until they have cooled sufficiently for the solder to solidify. Test the joint by tugging on one of the wires.

A common mistake is to apply the solder to the part at the same time as the bit is brought into contact with it. What happens then is that the solder melts, but the part itself doesn't reach a sufficiently high temperature. The molten solder solidifies around the wire but doesn't bond to it. This is called a *dry joint*. It's a common cause of faults in electronic equipment.

12.6 Replacing Soldered-in Components

Generally, it isn't worth trying to repair circuit boards by replacing components that are soldered in. It's hard to be sure what the fault is without an extensive knowledge of electronics and specialised digital test equipment. And even if you're certain what the trouble is, it's difficult to remove a soldered-in part from the board without special tools. However, sometimes you may have an old board for which you cannot get a replacement. You may be convinced that you know where the fault lies. If you're determined to try to repair it, there's an old serviceman's trick you can use.

A soldered-in IC is difficult to remove, because you've got to melt the solder round 14 or so legs simultaneously before you can pull it out. On computer PCBs, it's even more difficult, because the board holes are plated through, so each leg is held by solder right the way through the board, from top to bottom. If you're certain that a chip is faulty, and you have a replacement to hand, the trick is not to unsolder the old chip at all.

Using a miniature pair of side cutters, hack out the faulty chip by cutting through the legs close to the chip body. Take care not to damage any tracks on the surface of the circuit board while you're doing this. With the old chip out of the way, tidy up by trimming the remains of the legs so that you are left with a neat row of stumps. Then solder the new chip to the stumps of the old one, taking care to ensure that you put it in the right way round. It may not be the neatest way of repairing a board, but it's quick, easy and it works!

12.7 Spares

If you're going to be carrying out servicing jobs on PCs you'll need a small stock of spare parts. They will be needed not only as replacements for those that fail, but also to substitute for suspect parts as an aid to fault diagnosis. The size of your parts stock and what it should contain will depend on the number and range of models of PCs that you wish to maintain.

The three items that fail most often, and which are normally dealt with by replacement, are power supplies, diskette drives and hard disks. If your PCs are genuine IBM or some Far Eastern clones, IBM pattern power supplies can be used. They can be purchased at low cost, and will fit without difficulty. Replacement power supplies for other PC compatibles, which use their own unique design, will have to be purchased from the original manufacturer. These are usually more expensive.

Diskette drives are generally standard, and readily available from many sources. There's no need to worry about replacing a faulty drive with one made by a different manufacturer. The only consideration may be the colour of the front bezel. However, some 3.5in. high-density drives will not work properly with certain BIOSes, so it is worth checking compatibility before buying.

Hard disks are expensive. If you would need a range of different types to cover all the machines that you may be asked to repair, you may be reluctant to stock an example of each. Cheaper hard disks are generally more prone to failure, so it's certainly worth keeping the odd spare. To cater for the occasional failures of more expensive drives, the solution may be to identify a supplier who can provide replacements rapidly when needed. Even with hard disks, it isn't essential to replace one with another of the same type. As long as it fits the machine physically, matches the controller, is supported by the BIOS drive table, and has a large enough storage capacity, there isn't usually a problem replacing a drive with a different model.

Monitors and keyboards occasionally fail, so it may be worthwhile to carry a spare stock of one of each. It isn't essential for them to be an exact match for the machine, especially if they are only to be used on a temporary basis while the original is repaired or an exact replacement obtained.

Failures of boards such as disk controllers and display adapters are much less common. The practicability of keeping spares depends on the number of different types in use. Again, with many machines it may be acceptable to substitute an equivalent board, not necessarily from the same manufacturer, if a fault occurs. Serial and parallel adapters are cheap. They are worth holding in stock for ready availability when a user needs an extra I/O port.

You'll need memory chips more often for upgrades than for replacement. Different machines may use different types of chip, so you'll have to keep a stock of different types. Many suppliers offer memory upgrade kits at low cost. Delivery is usually rapid once the order has been received. So it probably isn't worth holding memory chips in stock, unless prices start to rise, and you want to stock up while they're cheap.

12.8 When to Call in the Professionals

No matter how experienced you become in fault finding and fault repair, some jobs are best put in the hands of the manufacturer or a specialist maintenance organisation.

Some manufacturers at the top end of the PC market have been reluctant to allow anyone other than qualified manufacturer-trained engineers to service their machines. If unauthorised work has been carried out they may say that the warranty is void. So if a fault develops while a machine is still under warranty, it's best to leave the repair to an authorised engineer.

Even if the machine is out of warranty, it's important to be able to recognise what you can and can't reasonably hope to achieve. Some faults are difficult to find without specialised test equipment. If resources are limited, it makes sense to concentrate on being able to fix the most common faults quickly and efficiently, and leave the more esoteric problems to the specialists.

Many PCs are now sold with three months to a year's on-site maintenance included in the price. If this is the case, call in the service engineer. It doesn't make sense to spend time repairing a fault when you've already paid for someone else to do it.

Some types of fault should always be left to the experts. Monitor faults, particularly those in colour monitors, are a prime example. A colour monitor operates at extra high tension (EHT) voltages as high as 25 kilovolts (25,000 volts), or even greater. These voltages can be present inside the unit even after it has been switched off. EHT voltages are *lethal*. There are special techniques and precautions that need to be learned, to work safely with this level of voltage. Teaching them is beyond the scope of this book. If a monitor problem needs something more than the adjustment of those controls that are accessible from outside the case, it should be left to a qualified service engineer.

Apart from the danger of electrocution, you need specialised test equipment to service and align monitors. Monochrome and older low-resolution colour monitors (such as CGA or EGA monitors) can often be repaired at reasonable cost by a local TV repair shop. Modern high-resolution monitors are best shipped back to the manufacturer for repair.

Circuit board faults are also something that usually can only be rectified by a specialist repairer. You need special equipment to remove soldered-in and surface-mounted components, and these are used increasingly in modern board designs. It's impractical to hold stocks of even the most commonly used integrated circuit chips, and buying them in one-off quantities can be expensive. Finally, finding which component is faulty would be impossible in most cases without access to manufacturers' hardware level technical documentation and expensive test equipment such as a digital storage oscilloscope.

12.9 Types of Maintenance Cover

If you decide to use a third party to maintain some of your equipment, it's possible to waste money or time by choosing an inappropriate contract. Most computer maintenance companies offer a range of support contracts to meet the differing needs of their customers. The cost goes up in inverse proportion to the length of time in which they guarantee to repair a fault. Don't be misled if a contract stipulates a time – say eight hours – to respond to a fault. *Respond* is not the same as *repair*. If an engineer turns up within the specified time to see that the machine is broken, then goes away and only returns a week later with the needed spare part, he is still acting within the terms of the contract.

Guaranteed repair contracts are expensive. With this type of contract, the service company would be expected to provide a replacement machine, if the original could not be repaired within the specified time. One reason why you are reading this book is probably that you wish to save money by eliminating the need for outside maintenance contractors. But there may be a few machines for which it is prudent to arrange maintenance cover. Immense problems may be caused if vital network file servers are down for more than a couple of hours. You may not be able to guarantee a repair within this sort of time-scale, without having a complete spare machine sitting waiting to be installed at a moment's notice, and this would be expensive. It makes a lot of sense to let a specialist service company, with its greater resources, take the responsibility for the upkeep of critical equipment.

At the other end of the scale, if you have many PCs to support, it could be worthwhile taking out a contract with a maintenance company to take faulty equipment from a central collection point once a week and return it, repaired, a week later. This would let you save money by repairing the simpler faults yourself, and enable you to get the more difficult faults fixed for you at reasonable cost. It would also be a useful backup for those times when everything goes wrong at once.

Summary

In this chapter we looked at the tools that you need to carry out servicing and support tasks on PCs. Some basic tools, such as screwdrivers, are essential no matter what you intend to do. Others, like a soldering iron, can often be useful, but if you want you can get by without them. We also looked at the software tools you need to deal with PC problems. They include DOS boot disks, backup software, anti-virus programs and diagnostic utilities. You need these on each size of diskette, and the disks should be write-protected.

We went on to look at some techniques that you could benefit from learning. They included using a volt-ohm meter, soldering, and removing and replacing memory chips. We examined the problem of deciding what spare parts should be kept in stock if you want to carry out your own servicing. There are still some circumstances in which it makes sense to use a specialist maintenance company. We concluded by looking at the types of maintenance contract that you can have.

13

Installation and Use

IBM PCs and compatibles, and their peripherals, are very reliable. They will operate for month after month without a single failure. But it's wise not to take things for granted. If you give some thought to the environment in which a PC is installed, and take care of it during use, many potential problems will be avoided.

This chapter examines the things that can be done to prevent – or at least reduce the likelihood of – serious faults occurring. We'll look at the factors to be considered when choosing its operating environment. We will discuss the problems that can be caused by the power supply to the computer, and how they can be eliminated. Finally we'll highlight ways in which users can prolong the life of their PCs by taking a little care when using them.

13.1 The Operating Environment

Large mainframe computers require a temperature controlled, air conditioned environment in which to operate. Their complex electronic circuitry generates a lot of heat. The reliability of the vast number of interconnections would be adversely affected by excessive humidity and dust. Often, mainframes also require a specially filtered power supply.

The first microcomputers were designed as machines for use by hobbyists. They were intended to be used in a normal home environment. Business microcomputers were developed from these pioneer machines. The technology used in this equipment was not much different from that employed in other consumer electronics products. Microcomputers were expected to operate reliably without the need for special operating conditions.

Modern micros, such as the latest PC compatibles, use improved technology. They offer better reliability because they use fewer components and generate less heat. These machines are even less fussy about their surroundings than their predecessors. Nevertheless, anything will work better and longer in a good environment. It's worthwhile taking care that the conditions in which a PC is expected to operate are as good as they can be in the circumstances.

PCs are happy in conditions that are also ideal for their operators. People work better in surroundings that are clean, quiet, dust-free, cool, and neither too damp nor too dry. Taking a little trouble over the working environment should ensure fewer problems with both humans and machines.

13.2 Ambient Temperature

Excessive heat harms electronics. All electronic components consume power, and some of this is given off as heat. If you've ever taken the cover off a PC system unit immediately after it has been used, you'll probably have noticed that some components, particularly the ICs, get quite warm.

All electronic components have a finite life. Their life is reduced as the operating temperature increases. The ambient temperature in which a PC is run is therefore important. The cooler the air that is sucked through the case by the fan, the greater the heat that can be dissipated.

Apart from increasing the risk of component failure, excessive heat can cause other problems. The operating characteristics of electronic components change with temperature. Given the dozens of ICs, each containing thousands of transistors, plus all the other parts in a typical PC, if it gets extremely hot there's a good chance something will malfunction. Some devices – power supplies for instance – actually contain protection circuits designed to shut down if the operating temperature exceeds a certain level.

Changes in temperature cause expansion and contraction. All components warm up when they are switched on, and cool down when they are switched off. This warming and cooling causes expansion and contraction, which in turn creates mechanical stress. This causes a problem with ICs that are installed in sockets rather than soldered to the circuit board. Over a period of time, the expansion and contraction makes the legs of the IC *walk* out of the socket. Eventually, one of the pins will make only an intermittent connection with the socket, and a fault will appear. This problem will occur to an extent on any machine in which socketed chips are used. But the cooler it can be run, the smaller the expansion that will take place, and the likelihood of this fault occurring will be reduced.

Extreme cold, though less likely to be experienced in the home or office, should also be avoided. Cold will encourage condensation to form. This can cause oxidation of many metal surfaces in connectors and IC sockets. In time, this will result in an unreliable electrical contact.

If a machine has been left in extremely cold surroundings for a period, it should not be switched on until it has had time to warm up to room temperature. The resistance of electrical components decreases with temperature. This increases the current that is drawn. It's possible that the increased switch-on surge that would result could blow a fuse or cause other, more serious damage.

PCs would never have become so popular if they had to operate in an air conditioned environment. But they shouldn't be subjected to extremes of heat. For example, a PC should not be located on a desk by a window that is at some time of day in direct sunlight. On a summer's day the temperature could easily exceed 100 deg F. Also to be avoided is placing the machine beside a radiator. The temperature experienced by the machine may be much greater than that felt by the operator seated a couple of feet further away.

One important point that shouldn't be overlooked is that the ventilation slots in the system unit and monitor casing must not be obstructed. If sufficient space isn't provided behind the system unit, the fan won't be able to operate at full efficiency. Similarly, the slots in the top of the monitor casing are there to allow heat to escape by convection (some monitors also have fans) so the monitor should not be used as a repository for papers and manuals.

Most PC fans have an option of two speeds. If a machine is to be used in a warm location, it may be advisable to check that the fan is on its highest speed setting. As a health check, the temperature of the air expelled from the rear of the system unit should be just perceptibly warm. If it's significantly hotter than the ambient temperature, some of the components inside the PC are probably running very hot, and the fan speed should be increased.

13.3 Humidity

Excessive humidity can be harmful to computer equipment. This can be a particular problem if temperatures drop to a low level. If condensation forms, this can lead to a variety of problems, including the surface oxidation of metal parts such as electrical contacts, and the breakdown of insulation materials in power supplies and monitors. Fortunately, humidity at levels high enough to cause harm isn't generally found in most home or office environments. However, you should expect a higher incidence of faults in PCs used in tropical environments.

Too little humidity, which can often be caused by central heating systems, or during very hot, dry weather, can create problems with static electricity. We will discuss static later in the chapter.

13.4 Dirt and Dust

If it's essential to use a PC in a dirty or dusty environment, there's little that can be done. However, an accumulation of dust does nothing for the reliability of a computer. Regular cleaning should be carried out in direct proportion to the extent of the problem at each location.

One of the best indicators of the amount of dust in the atmosphere is the monitor. Computer monitors, particularly colour monitors, are great attractors of dust. This is due to the static charge that develops on the screen. If you put your hand close to the screen, you can feel the hairs on the back of your hand being pulled towards the CRT. You may experience a crackle of static. This static acts like a magnet for dust, which then either sticks to the screen or gets sucked into the system unit.

It's amazing how much dust can get into a PC system unit. This is because of the cooling fan, which makes the PC act like a vacuum cleaner for any dust in the vicinity. Most PC fans work by blowing air out of the rear of the system unit. Air may enter via any ventilation slots provided, as well as through other convenient apertures such as the diskette drive slots.

Dust inside the system unit can cause problems in several ways. It builds up inside diskette drives. This can foul up the mechanism. Even worse, it transfers itself to the diskettes themselves, causing read errors and a host of other problems. Dust adheres to the circuit board components, reducing their ability to dissipate heat. It builds up on plugs and sockets, where chemical substances carried by the dust can cause the contact surfaces to tarnish. This will eventually result in unreliable connections. Finally it can get into the fan motor bearings, where it could ultimately cause the fan to seize up and burn out.

If a PC is to be operated in a dusty environment then the main thing that you can do is to increase the frequency of the preventive maintenance checks, so that it's cleaned more often. However, you can reduce the extent to which dust gets inside the system unit by carefully choosing its situation.

The modern trend towards floor standing tower style system units has not helped with regard to the dust problem. A lot of dust gets kicked up by feet, and there is generally more dust under a desk than on it. Most office cleaning staff are not particularly conscientious in their use of the vacuum cleaner!

It's important to be particularly careful with network file servers. These PCs are often kept in a quiet corner of an office and run for months at a time, often 24 hours a day. Then, when the time comes to reconfigure the operating system, or run some diagnostic software, you find that the machine won't read the diskette due to the amount of dust that has built up inside the drive. If file servers can be housed in a dust-free environment, it's sensible to do so.

There are a few high-powered PCs that boast a smoked-perspex cover over the diskette drives. No doubt this idea originated in the design office rather than the engineering department. Nevertheless, these covers will provide useful protection against dust.

Keyboards can be vulnerable to the effects of dirt and dust, though by their nature they are also prone to collect other things such as biscuit crumbs and cigarette ash. Over a time, an accumulation of these things can impede the operation of the keys, and cause them to jam.

Keyboards should be regularly cleaned as part of a preventive maintenance programme. However, where one has to be used in a particularly dirty environment, an additional level of protection may be desirable. You can buy a flexible, transparent plastic membrane, which fits over the keys. This will protect the keyboard against dirt, dust and liquids, and still allow the keys to be used easily. Despite what the advertising literature claims, it's unlikely to be acceptable to a touch typist. But if a PC is to be used in a dirty environment such as a factory shop floor or a warehouse, it could be worthwhile considering the use of such devices.

As we've seen, dirt and dust will both cause problems if they build up inside a machine. However, dirt will also accumulate on the casing. Most PCs are beige in colour, like the original IBM PC. This colour seems to have been chosen to show up dirt at its worst! A grubby computer is unpleasant to use, and is less likely to be treated well by its operator. A regular programme of cosmetic cleaning may have the effect of reducing the number of faults reported, and will help to maintain the resale value of the machine.

13.5 Shock and Vibration

PCs are quite robust. Even so, there is a limit to what they will put up with. Constant vibration will cause chips to work their way out of sockets, and connectors to come loose. That's why the Army purchases special rugged computers that can withstand being moved around in military vehicles not noted for their smooth ride.

Shock and sudden impact can also be harmful. Hard disks are particularly vulnerable to the effects of shock. Even the act of putting a computer down on a desk can cause harm to some hard disks, if the heads aren't parked. Computers that are designed to be moved around – laptops and portables – mostly use drives which are self-parking.

Moving, or even jogging a hard disk while it is working can cause serious damage and loss of data. Therefore it's important to ensure that a PC isn't placed in a situation where it can easily be knocked.

Users have been known to move a PC while it's switched on, never mind bothering to park the heads. They only do it once, if much work was lost! It's a good idea to attach a sticker to a machine to remind the user of the procedure to adopt when moving it. This may seem like overkill, but if one hard disk is saved, the effort will have been repaid.

If a PC is to be installed in a location where knocks and vibration are unavoidable – such as alongside a factory production line – then consideration should be given to using special industrial PCs. Companies like Texas Microsystems build PCs engineered to military specifications, with shock-mounted disk drives and power supplies with 100,000 hours mean time between faults. Such machines can be expected to withstand harsh environments much better than those intended for normal office use.

13.6 Static Electricity

As people move about a room, they build up an electrical charge. The extent of this depends upon a number of factors: what they are wearing, the type of floor covering, the humidity level in the atmosphere and how conductive are the shoes they are wearing. Normally a static charge will dissipate after a person has remained still for a few seconds. But if someone walks quickly across a room on a dry day and then touches something that is electrically grounded – a door knob, or the casing of a PC – then it's quite likely that they will experience an electric shock.

Shocks from static electricity are unpleasant, but harmless to the individual. However, they can cause memory corruption and system crashes to occur to a computer. If people experience static shocks when touching metal objects in a room, there is a static problem in that room, and steps should be taken to minimise it.

Carpets are some of the worst culprits for generating static electricity. Certain types of seat cover can also cause static problems. A charge is generated as the operator shifts in his or her seat. Cheap furnishings and floor coverings are more likely to cause static problems than those of good quality.

Anti-static sprays may be used to treat carpets and reduce the build-up of static electricity. Anti-static mats can also be placed under the computer, and under the operator's chair. These should be electrically grounded. This should stop the operator generating a charge by shifting position while working at the computer. In dry atmospheres, you may need to install a humidifier to alleviate the problem.

Static electricity can be a more serious problem for support staff and others who need to work on PCs with the covers off. Whereas static will be discharged without causing any permanent damage if you touch the case of a machine, if an electronic component is touched when a static charge is present it can easily be destroyed. You can take precautions to prevent this from occurring by working on an anti-static mat, and using a wrist strap grounded to the chassis of the machine. However, it isn't always convenient to do this. If a few simple procedures are adopted, and always followed, the risk of damaging components through static discharge will be eliminated.

First, always touch part of the metal chassis or something else that is grounded before touching a circuit board or any other part of the machine. This will ensure that any static is discharged harmlessly to earth. Secondly, avoid touching the electronic components or the edge connectors when installing, removing or configuring circuit boards. Avoid touching the pins of ICs such as memory chips when performing upgrades, and keep boards and components in their anti-static packaging when not in use.

13.7 Mains Supply

Personal computers are designed for use in an ordinary home or office environment, and are intended to be run from the normal AC mains. However, the quality of the mains supply can vary from place to place, between home and office, between city and country, even between offices in the same building. In some locations, the supply quality can be so poor as to have an adverse effect on the operation of computer equipment.

Large mainframe computers are so complex that a tiny glitch in operation could crash the whole system, wrecking the work of perhaps hundreds of users. These systems employ special filtering circuits to protect the hardware against the effects of small fluctuations in the mains supply. Micros are far more tolerant of mains irregularities. However, if the supply quality is very poor, problems can still occur.

There are three main categories of mains disturbance: high voltage spikes, low-level noise and distortion of the mains waveform, and incorrect voltage levels and *brownouts*. Any one of them, or even all three, may affect the supply to a particular building. A further problem can be caused by frequent power failures.

13.8 Voltage Spikes

Voltage spikes on the mains can cause memory corruption and system crashes. They frequently occur when items such as kettles, fridges and electric fires are switched on and off. Other office equipment can also cause this type of mains disturbance, though appliances that draw a large current, such as kettles and fires, are the usual culprits.

To explain the effect, it's necessary to use a little school physics. The mains wiring in a building has similar electrical properties to the ignition coil in a car. It has inductance, capacitance and resistance. These properties are greater the further away you get from the ground, and from the source of the mains.

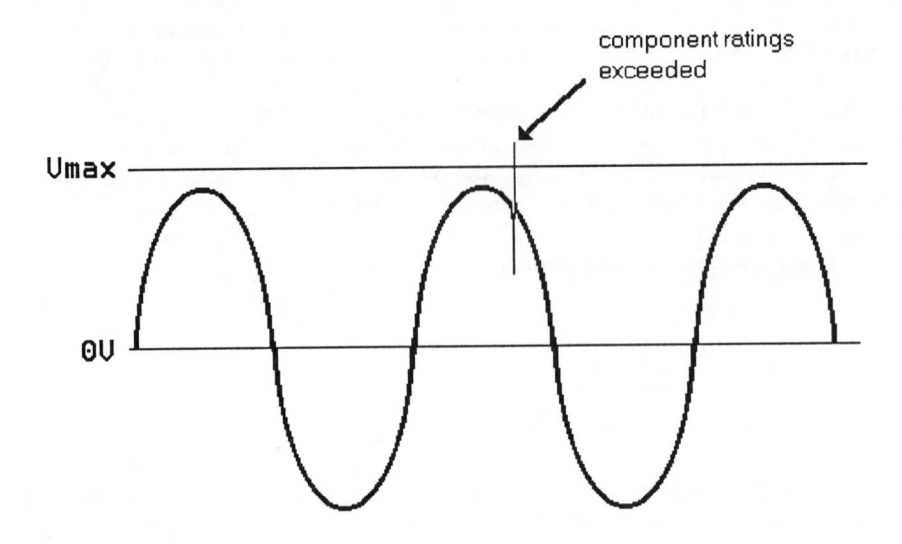

Figure 13.1: Mains voltage spikes

When a device is switched on and off, instead of a clean stepwise increase or decrease in the current through the mains wiring, you get a damped high-frequency oscillation, as shown in Figure 13.1. The frequency of this oscillation depends on the inductance and capacitance present in the mains wiring. The voltage amplitude can be large if the resistance in the mains circuit is relatively high.

The oscillation only lasts for a fraction of a mains cycle. If viewed on an ordinary oscilloscope, it appears as a spike. In some circumstances the peak voltage attained is such that it isn't filtered out by the power supply's filtering circuits. It appears as a blip on the DC voltage lines supplying the PC's electronic circuits, and can cause memory to be corrupted and the system to crash. It's even possible for the spikes to be large enough to cause power supply components to fail.

Voltage disturbances caused by switching equipment on and off will be present on any mains supply. The conditions that determine whether such disturbances will be so severe as to cause equipment malfunctions are complex and difficult to analyse. However, the topmost floors of high rise buildings are particularly prone to this type of problem.

13.9 Noise and Distortion

The waveform of the AC mains should ideally be a pure sine wave. However, in a typical office environment, where many items of electrical equipment may be in use, the actual waveform can be far from sinusoidal.

As we have seen, PCs and many peripherals use switched mode power supplies. These power supplies present a non-linear load to the mains. Current is only drawn during the high voltage part of the power cycle. If many switched mode supplies are running from the same mains circuit, the distortion of the waveform can be readily observed on an oscilloscope.

Switched mode power supplies operate by switching the mains voltage at a high frequency, so as to obtain a regulated voltage at levels used by the PC electronics. Some high-frequency energy is reflected back into the mains wiring where it appears as noise.

A typical office environment includes electro-mechanical devices such as photocopiers and printers. These present a widely varying load on the mains depending on what they are doing: sitting idle, printing or feeding paper. The load variations can cause small-scale disturbances and low-frequency noise to appear on the mains supply.

Noise and distortion tend to be most evident in locations that are also experiencing problems with spikes. In themselves, it's unlikely that noise and distortion will cause operational problems. However, it's as well to be aware of the types of disturbance that can occur, and to appreciate that the mains supply isn't something you can simply take for granted.

13.10 Low or High Voltage

Computer power supplies are designed to operate at a certain nominal input voltage. Those designed for use in the US and Canada expect a 110 VAC input. In most of Europe a 240 VAC input is standard. In other countries 220 VAC is used. Equipment should have a power supply designed for the input voltage used, and manufactured to comply with the appropriate electrical safety standards.

Switched mode power supplies are inherently tolerant of voltage level variations. Most products will perform satisfactorily over a range from −40% to +10% of the nominal input voltage. It's unlikely that constant voltage levels outside this range will be experienced from a normal domestic or office supply. However, some areas may be prone to power failures, or to momentary dips in the voltage that make the lights flicker. Rural areas supplied using overhead power lines are among those places most likely to be affected.

A power cut can cause a lot of inconvenience to a PC user. A power interruption of less than a second can cause a PC to reboot. Word processor and spreadsheet users will lose all the changes they made since the last time they saved their work. Database users may lose any updates. Worse, the database files may be corrupted and require a time-consuming file reconstruction to take place before the system can be used again. Files that weren't properly closed can wreak havoc with the DOS file system, causing lost clusters and other problems to appear. For network file servers the problems can be even more severe.

13.11 Dealing with Supply Problems

You need specialist equipment to test the quality of the mains supply. However, the geographical location of the equipment, and any previous history of unexplained malfunctions or power supply failures, will give an indication of the likelihood of problems occurring. You can then consider providing some protection.

Special *surge protector* plugs can be purchased in electrical and computer stores. These provide a limited degree of protection against power spikes. Similar protection can be provided by wiring an inexpensive metal oxide varistor (MOV) of the appropriate value across the live and neutral leads of the mains plug. The MOV has a high resistance at normal mains voltages. However, at higher voltages, the resistance falls rapidly, so that spikes are attenuated.

In practice, the effectiveness of surge protector plugs is very limited. If voltage spikes are causing a problem, the only real cure is to fit a power conditioner. This is a shoe-box sized unit that plugs into the wall outlet, and has two or three mains outlets of its own. The box contains circuitry that filters the mains and effectively prevents spikes and noise from getting through.

You can buy power conditioners in various sizes, to suit the equipment you want to connect to them. Where several PCs and peripherals are clustered together, you can save money by supplying them from a single, larger unit with multiple output sockets.

For protection against power interruptions you need an *uninterruptible power supply* (UPS). This is a device that, like the conditioner, is connected between the mains socket and the computer equipment. During normal operation, mains power is passed straight through the UPS to the computer, usually with the addition of some filtering. The UPS contains batteries, which are continually charged by the mains. It also contains some electronics called an *inverter*. This can convert the low voltage DC output from the batteries into a high voltage, AC supply.

When a rapid drop in voltage is sensed by the UPS, a relay switches over to the inverter circuitry, which starts generating an AC voltage. Depending on the power drawn and the capacity of the UPS batteries, a PC can continue to run for from a few minutes to perhaps half an hour. This enables the user to save his work and carry out an orderly shut-down of the system if the mains isn't restored during that time.

UPSs are available in a range of types and sizes. Some of the cheaper ones generate a square wave output rather than a sinusoid like the mains supply. This is acceptable for powering the switched mode power supplies used by PCs, but not other equipment. The type of UPS described in the previous paragraph is called an *off-line* UPS, because the inverter only comes on-line when a power drop is detected.

An *on-line* UPS is one in which the computer is powered by the inverter all the time. The advantage of this type of unit is that there is no switch-over delay, but the cost is higher as the components used in the inverter must be rated for constant use. On-line UPSs may be needed for minicomputers and other equipment which may be upset by the brief interruption of power – of a few milliseconds duration – when an off-line unit switches over. PC power supplies generally have sufficient reserve capacity and filtering to withstand this interruption, so the additional cost isn't justified.

13.12 Wear and Tear

Like any machine, a computer will last longer and work better if it's treated with care. We've seen how environmental factors can affect the reliable operation of a PC. However, the way in which it is used can also affect the chances of faults occurring.

Switching on can be traumatic for computers. The power supply has to provide a surge of power as capacitors in the equipment charge up to their working voltage, and the motors in disk drives spin up to operating speed. The filament in the cathode ray tube of the monitor has to heat up from ambient to working temperature. There's a sudden flurry of activity, as the machine does its power-on tests, searches for the bootable system disk, and executes the start-up batch file. If fuses, power supply components, CRTs or indeed any part of the PC is going to fail, switch-on time is a likely moment.

To prolong the life of a PC, therefore, minimise the number of times it's switched on and off. In an office, switch it on the first time you need to use it, and switch it off when you go home at night. Avoid switching off and on during the day. The only exception to this would be if the machine runs very hot, either through poor ventilation or because of very hot weather. In these circumstances, the risk of damage through overheating could be greater than that caused by switching the machine off and on.

Leaving a machine switched on for long periods while it isn't in use can harm the CRT. If the same picture is displayed for long periods, it can get burnt onto the phosphor coating on the display tube. This is more of a problem with green monochrome monitors than with colour or paper-white displays, but it can occur with any type of screen when bright characters are used.

Fortunately, there's a simple solution. Most monitors have a readily accessible brightness control. If you turn down the brightness when the system isn't in use, the screen won't be harmed. If this isn't possible, then you can use a piece of software called a screen saver. This will blank the screen if no keys are pressed for a predefined period. Pressing a key immediately restores the display. Some utilities display a short message to remind the user what has happened. Others display a moving picture, such as fish swimming in a tank, since moving pictures won't burn onto the screen.

Carelessness and abuse of the equipment can be a significant source of problems. There are several basic points of good practice that computer users should observe:

- ❏ Try to avoid smoking or eating while operating the computer. This leads to ash and crumbs getting into the keyboard, which will eventually cause keys to stick.
- ❏ Diskettes should be kept away from dust and dirt, and stored in their sleeves when not in use.
- ❏ They should also be handled correctly. Take care to avoid touching the recording surfaces. This will help to preserve the data, as well as preventing dust and grease from getting inside the drive mechanism.
- ❏ There is no need to be heavy handed when using a PC. Fingertip pressure is all that is needed to insert a diskette in the drive, and the drive handle should only be turned gently.
- ❏ Keyboards don't need to be pounded.
- ❏ Avoid pulling on cables. If trying to disconnect a lead, pull on the plug, not the wire.

Unfortunately, there's a limit to the extent to which users can be educated in this sort of thing. If people are inherently ham-fisted, there isn't a lot you can do about it.

13.13 The Importance of Backups

No-one who has ever had to deal with a problem that turns out to be a hard disk that is terminally dead (in other words, not capable of resurrection) enjoys having to explain to the user that any work done since the last backup was taken has been completely lost. It's particularly unpleasant when the last backup turns out to be weeks or months ago. The look of disbelief, followed by anguish, isn't something that is easily forgotten.

There are many ways to back up the contents of a hard disk. For smaller disks, backing up to diskette is a simple and cheap solution. The standard DOS BACKUP and RESTORE programs are too slow to make disk backups an attractive proposition. However, commercial programs such as FastBack Plus or the Norton Backup are very quick, enabling a 20 Mb disk to be backed up in a few minutes. Selective backups can be performed. This means that only the user's files need to be copied to diskette, not the software, which is normally unchanged after its initial installation.

For larger disks, tape streamers are the best solution. Low cost streamers cost about £250 ($250 US). Tape streamers are fast, but they can be unreliable, so it's important to check that a backup is good by verifying the tape afterwards. Whenever a planned restore is to be made – for example, when upgrading to a larger hard disk – it's good practice to have two backups on hand, in case one or two files on the first copy prove to be unreadable.

Backing up isn't a subject that falls strictly within the area of support and servicing, but it's so important that users should be reminded about it all the time. Having an up-to-date backup can turn the problem of a dead hard disk from a major trauma to a minor inconvenience. It's also an important safeguard against virus infection. More about computer viruses will be found in Chapter 16.

Summary

You can take the first steps to ensuring that a PC has a trouble-free life even before it has been removed from its box. If you take care to select a suitable operating environment – free from dirt and dust and extremes of temperature and humidity, and with a clean, reliable mains supply – you'll experience fewer faults.

If you treat a PC with care during its life then this will also reduce the number of problems, especially mechanical failures. Regular backups will ensure that loss of work is minimised if the hardware, particularly the hard disk, becomes unserviceable.

14

Preventive Maintenance

One of the keys to long life and reliable operation of computer equipment is regular preventive maintenance. However, it's an aspect of owning or supporting PCs that is often ignored.

There's an old saying: *If it ain't broke, don't fix it*. Like most old sayings, there is some sense in it. If you're careless when carrying out preventive maintenance (PM), it's possible to disturb something and cause a fault that would not otherwise have occurred. But this isn't a reason for not doing preventive maintenance. On balance, PM should prevent more problems than it causes. As we've already seen, dust and dirt can get into even the best cared-for equipment, and will inevitably cause problems if left to build up unchecked. It's unrealistic to expect a PC to provide reliable service for year after year without any kind of attention.

Preventive maintenance tasks fall into two categories: those that can be performed by the user, and those that should be carried out by a support technician or engineer. Perhaps the most important factor to be considered in designing a PM programme is that it shouldn't be so onerous that it doesn't get done at all. Look at the owner's manual of your car. It probably says that daily, you should check the operation of the lamps, horn, indicators, wipers, washers and seat belts, and look under the car for signs of a fluid leak. To do these checks would only take a couple of minutes, but how many car owners actually do them? Well, the same applies to PCs.

Of course, cars can cause accidents if they aren't correctly maintained. The consequences of using a badly maintained PC are less serious. A PC preventive maintenance programme should be based more on what can realistically be done, rather than what would theoretically be desirable. The programme suggested in this chapter may not be realistic or appropriate in some circumstances. Where equipment is used in particularly harsh environments, for example, it may be necessary to increase the frequency of PM checks, or to introduce additional procedures. The recommendations in this chapter should be tailored to produce a PM programme that best fits the needs and circumstances of your own particular situation.

14.1 Weekly Maintenance

IBM have a lot to answer for, when they decided to make the case of the PC beige. There are few worse colours for showing the dirt. No one would disagree that it's more pleasant to use a clean machine than a grubby one. A clean PC is likely to be treated better by those who use it, and will command a higher resale price when it's time to upgrade. Weekly maintenance therefore centres around keeping the machine clean. Usually, it will be carried out by the user.

The weekly PM check-list consists of the following tasks:

❑ Back up all data

❑ Clean the PC, monitor, keyboard and any attached device such as a printer

❑ Check all leads and cables to see that they are fully pushed home, and that the cable itself is securely gripped where it leaves the body of the plug (see Figure 14.1).

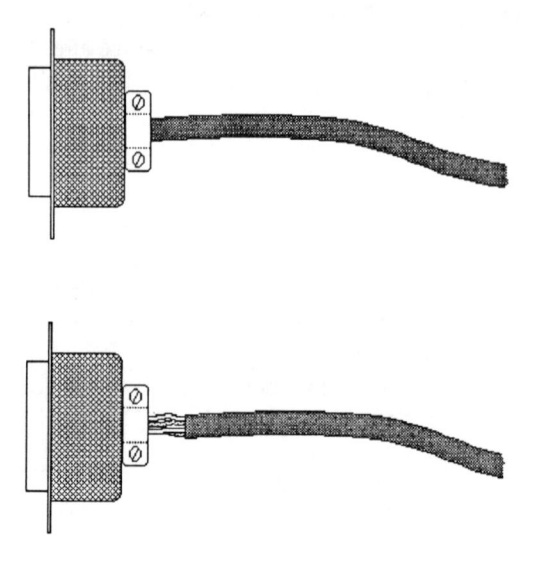

Figure 14.1: Checking plugs and cables. Top – OK; bottom – insecurely gripped

You can buy suitable cleaning materials in a variety of forms from most PC consumables suppliers. You can get foam cleaner in aerosol cans. Spray a little of the foam onto a clean, lint-free cloth. Use this to clean the system unit case, the monitor and, with care, the keyboard. Never spray the foam directly on to the case – where it might get through ventilation slots into the works – nor on to the keyboard.

Foam cleaner is effective but use it with care. You may also have trouble finding clean cloths in an office environment. A more convenient method of cleaning the hardware is to use special lint-free tissues impregnated with cleaning solution. These are usually supplied in individually sealed sachets, e.g., Texwipes. If you clean the equipment regularly, you should find that one will be sufficient to do both a PC and an attached printer.

Many PC operating problems are caused by cables. Mains leads get pulled half out, and make an intermittent connection if the cable is moved. Data cables get stretched. Then the cable outer pulls free of the cable grip, the thin wires inside the cable end up taking the strain, and eventually one breaks. Check cables for damage, and repair or replace them as necessary.

We discussed backups in the previous chapter. Taking backups should be part of the normal use of a PC. Unless the machine is only used occasionally, backups should be taken daily. However, in some situations it may be appropriate to include taking a full backup as part of the PM routine.

14.2 Six-monthly Maintenance

In the previous chapter, we saw how deposits of dust and dirt can build up inside a PC, and that the expansion and contraction causes socketed IC chips to walk out of their sockets. Therefore, it's advisable to carry out a more thorough preventive maintenance at less frequent intervals. Six months is a reasonable period to elapse between PM checks in most situations.

A six-monthly PM is conducted as follows:

❏ Clean the casing of the PC and monitor

❏ Clean the keyboard

❏ Check all leads and cables to see that they are fully pushed home, and that the cable itself is securely gripped where it leaves the body of the plug

❏ Power up the PC and clean the diskette drive(s) using a commercial diskette head cleaner

❏ Park the hard disk heads (if required) and power down

- Disconnect all cables from the PC and remove the system unit cover
- Clean out any deposits of dust
- Undo the retaining screw of each expansion card, remove the card (taking care to observe anti-static precautions), reseat any socketed IC chips, replace the card
- Check all internal cables are fully pushed home
- Replace the system unit cover, leads and cables, and test the machine.

At the six-monthly check you should clean the keyboard more thoroughly. Before using the cleaning foam or wipes, clean out the dust and debris from inside the keyboard casing. A miniature vacuum cleaner is ideal for this task. Hold the keyboard inverted while hoovering round the keys. This will remove most of the dust without requiring you to dismantle the keyboard.

Diskette drives can suffer from two problems during normal use: dust and dirt getting into the mechanism, and a build-up of magnetic oxide on the head. You may clean drives either before or after the system unit has been disassembled. Some diskette drives allow good access to the moving parts if the system unit case is removed. In dusty environments, it may be advantageous to blow out dust using compressed air before cleaning the heads. However, you shouldn't use the miniature vacuum cleaner to remove dust from within the drive mechanism, as there is a risk that you could disturb the sensitive head alignment.

You should clean the read/write heads of a diskette drive using a special cleaning kit. These generally consist of a diskette jacket containing an absorbent and slightly abrasive cleaning element in place of the usual recording surface, and an aerosol canister of solvent. To use the head cleaner, spray a small amount of solvent onto the cleaning element through the large aperture in the jacket. Then insert the diskette into the drive in the normal way. The drive should be activated for about 30 seconds by running DIR or CHKDSK, and answering *Retry* at the *General Failure Error* messages that will occur. Alternatively, you can use a special head cleaning program. This moves the head around and ensures that any oxide contamination that may have built up on the surface is scrubbed off. Don't use the diskette drive for a couple of minutes after cleaning. This will allow any residual cleaning fluid to evaporate away.

While the system unit cover is removed, take care to observe precautions against static electricity. This means discharging any static by touching the chassis of the PC with a finger or the tool in use before touching any of the components. If you've ever experienced static shocks at that location then it's probably not a good place to carry out maintenance on the machine.

Removing dust from inside the case is a job that must be accomplished with care. If it has built up between the expansion card connectors, then you can't remove it with the expansion cards in place. However, if you remove the cards, it's important to avoid letting dust fall into the connector slots themselves. If there's a lot of dust inside a PC, the best procedure is to clean out as much as possible with the cards in place, then remove them and give the cards and motherboard a final clean.

Normally, there's no need to disconnect cables (e.g., drive cables) from expansion cards. Ease the connectors off about half way, then push them back. This will clean the contacts and ensure a good connection. Check the other end of each cable as well. The edge connectors used on 5.25in. disk drives (both hard and floppy disks) are prone to work loose, and can easily be pulled off accidentally while manipulating other cables. It's worthwhile checking that they are all pushed home before closing the case. Power supply cable connectors are usually a pretty tight fit, and can normally be left alone.

When expansion cards are removed, be careful not to touch the edge connector contacts. If oil or dirt picked up on the fingers gets on to the gold plated contacts, it will cause poor electrical connections later on. If the edge connectors do require cleaning, special electrical contact cleaner may be used. Failing that, use a cotton swab soaked in pure alcohol. You can also use a pencil eraser, but make sure to wipe or blow away any fragments of rubber from the card before it is reinserted. Never clean the edge connectors with anything abrasive such as fine emery paper. This would remove the thin gold plating, resulting in poor electrical contact with the expansion bus connectors.

Socketed chips – such as memory or ROM chips – on the motherboard or on expansion cards should be pressed into their sockets to ensure a good connection. If you feel significant movement, it's likely that thermal expansion and contraction has caused the chip to start easing itself out of the socket. Eventually, one of the pins would make a bad connection, and a fault would occur. If the chips are on the motherboard, press firmly on each one with your thumb. A cracking sound may be heard as the legs are pushed further into the socket. Don't use excessive pressure. This would cause flexing of the motherboard, which might damage it. To reseat chips on expansion cards, first ground your hand to the chassis to discharge any static, then sandwich the chip and board between your thumb and forefinger and squeeze.

Expansion cards should be put back in the same slots from which they were removed. Some cards are fussy about which slots they will work in. Keeping them the same will ensure that no unexpected problems occur.

Once you've reassembled the PC, test it to check that no problems have been introduced. You can add a professional touch to the job by affixing a sticker to the back of the machine showing the date that the PM check was carried out. This concludes the six-monthly preventive maintenance.

14.3 Backup Batteries

Depending on the make and model of PC, there are a couple of other jobs that can be built into the PM checklist. One of these is the replacement of CMOS backup batteries.

All AT class machines, and many XT clones, contain a battery-backed system clock. ATs and Amstrad XTs also hold certain configuration details in battery-backed CMOS RAM. The backup batteries of these machines eventually run out, causing the loss of the clock and setup information. It may be worthwhile to preempt the failure of these batteries by replacing them as part of the preventive maintenance programme.

Several models of PC use AA-size dry cells for their backup batteries. They are cheap, readily obtainable and usually easy to install. On Amstrad PC 1512s and 1640s they are accessible from outside the case, underneath the monitor. They seem to last almost one year. Amstrads will work without the batteries, but the date and time will need to be reset each time the system is switched on.

Most ATs use a lithium battery to backup their CMOS RAM. Lithium batteries typically last for four or five years. The exact pattern of battery used varies from machine to machine. On an AT, the CMOS holds details of how much memory the system contains, the hard disk and diskette drive types, and which drives are bootable. Loss of this data will prevent you from using the machine.

Lithium batteries are quite expensive. However, from a support point of view, it would be beneficial to forestall battery failure and replace it once it is, say, three years old.

14.4 Reformatting Hard Disks

Some hard disks, particularly those found in the older and cheaper PC compatibles, tend to drift out of adjustment after a while. What happens is that you start to get the occasional read error, or the system sometimes fails to boot up the first time it's switched on. If the problem is ignored, data may eventually be lost or corrupted, or it may become impossible to read the disk at all. This was discussed in more detail in the chapter on hard disks.

The problem is common to low-cost drives using stepper motor head actuator mechanisms. It usually becomes apparent after the drive has been in regular use for about a year. When it starts to occur, back up all the data. Then perform a low-level format, followed by repartitioning and DOS formatting the drive. The data can then be restored.

If you have PCs that use drives which are prone to this problem, there's a lot to be said for the idea of reformatting them periodically as part of preventive maintenance.

However, it's a job that takes at least a couple of hours. You must decide for yourself which machines would benefit from this, and how often you need to do it.

14.5 Printers

Being partly mechanical, printers need periodic maintenance even more than PCs. This maintenance should have the following objectives:

❑ Clean out dust and paper fragments from the mechanism

❑ Check paper feed path is free of obstructions

❑ Check parts that wear out (e.g., print head) and replace if necessary

❑ Clean external casing.

Because printers require a certain amount of attention at fairly frequent intervals to replace consumables – ribbons, ink or toner cartridges – PM should be geared to the cycle of replacements. This has the benefit of relating the frequency of maintenance to the amount of use a printer receives. Every fourth ribbon, ink or toner replacement is probably a suitable interval for most machines.

The mechanics of different printers vary greatly, and so will their maintenance requirements. The manual will suggest maintenance tasks that should be carried out periodically, and the list of PM checks for each printer should be based around these.

Printers were discussed in greater detail in Chapter 11, together with a generic preventive maintenance schedule, so we'll say no more about them here.

Summary

Regular preventive maintenance will help to maintain the value and appearance of equipment, and reduce the likelihood of breakdowns. However, a PM programme must take account of what people can reasonably be expected to do, otherwise it won't be done at all. A schedule based on a weekly clean and check carried out by the user, and a more thorough clean and service at six-monthly intervals, should prove to be both practical and effective in most situations.

15

Configuration and Tuning

To get the most out of a PC you should take a little time to put some thought into how best to set it up. Although PCs have more power and memory than ever before, software has increased in size and sophistication and is written with ease of development and maintenance rather than speed of execution in mind. So performance is still an issue.

The starting point for optimising the configuration of any PC is the two files CONFIG.SYS and AUTOEXEC.BAT. These control the way DOS is set up, and specify the utilities that you want to be loaded. Other performance factors include how the system memory and hard disk are used. All these things can affect the overall performance of the machine.

Many software add-ins, including commercial, shareware and public domain utilities, can be used to improve the performance of a PC running under DOS. There are far too many such programs to describe them all here. However, we'll look at some examples and show the benefits that they can provide for the PC user.

15.1 Booting the System

Most PC configuration options are things that are determined at start-up. It's useful to understand exactly what happens when the machine is powered on.

When a PC is started up, the processor begins by executing an initialisation procedure stored in the BIOS ROM. This procedure first performs the POST checks described in Chapter 2. If these are successful the system then looks for a diskette in drive A:. If this isn't found it will check for hard disk C:. If neither of these are present then an

IBM PC will jump into ROM BASIC. Others will display a message asking for a system disk to be loaded.

Assuming a disk is found, the system will load into memory the contents of the *boot record* – the very first sector on the disk – and then execute it. If the disk is a diskette that wasn't formatted as a system disk, the boot sector contains a small piece of code that displays the message *Non-system disk or disk error* .... However, assuming the disk does contain a bootable copy of DOS, the boot sector code will cause the system to look in the disk's root directory, and check for the presence of two files: IBMBIO.COM (IO.SYS for generic MS-DOS) and IBMDOS.COM (MSDOS.SYS). If present, the code loads IBMBIO.COM (IO.SYS) into memory and transfers control to it. The system then loads in the second file, IBMDOS.COM (MSDOS.SYS), sets up various system tables, checks what devices are present in the system and initialises them. Next, it searches the root directory for a file called CONFIG.SYS. Certain settings, buffers and device drivers are set up depending on the values held in this file. Default values are used if the file isn't found or particular values aren't specified.

At this point DOS executes the command processor. Unless a parameter in CONFIG.SYS has been used to specify a different path or an alternative command processor file, this must be in the root directory, and be called COMMAND.COM. COMMAND.COM loads and runs the start-up batch file AUTOEXEC.BAT which is used to set any environment strings and run any utilities needed.

15.2 Optimising CONFIG.SYS

The file CONFIG.SYS is used to specify various options to be used by the operating system when it's loading. It must be in the root directory, and may be a hidden file. Some of the options can have a significant effect on the performance of the system. Although they are all documented in the DOS manual, examples of the most important commands are given below.

```
SHELL=C:\DOS\COMMAND.COM C:\DOS\ /P /E:320
```

If no SHELL parameter is specified, DOS will expect to find COMMAND.COM in the root directory, and will load it leaving a space for (in most versions) 160 bytes of environment strings. SHELL allows the path to the command processor to be explicitly stated. In the example, COMMAND.COM will be loaded from C:\DOS.

The second parameter defines the value of the COMSPEC environment variable, which is automatically created by DOS. COMMAND.COM has two parts: a permanent part and a transient part. The transient part can be overwritten by applications, to give them extra memory. On return to DOS after an application terminates, the permanent part of COMMAND.COM checks to see if the transient part is still there. If not, it reloads it from the pathname specified in COMSPEC.

For some reason, DOS doesn't use the full pathname given in SHELL's first parameter to create the COMSPEC path. If a second parameter isn't given, COMSPEC is set to the root directory: A:\COMMAND.COM for a diskette or C:\COMMAND.COM for a hard drive. If you've used SHELL to tell the system to use the copy of COMMAND.COM in the DOS directory, and deleted it from the root to keep things tidy, you'll get an *Invalid COMMAND.COM* error message whenever you exit an application and the command processor's transient portion has been overwritten. Use the second parameter to overcome this. Alternatively, since COMSPEC is an environment string, you can set it using a SET command in AUTOEXEC.BAT if you wish.

The /P switch tells COMMAND.COM that this copy of it is the *primary* command processor – in other words, the first one loaded. This does two things: First, it forces the command processor to stay in memory even if an EXIT command is typed. Second, it causes AUTOEXEC.BAT to be run.

The /E switch specifies the amount of space to be reserved for environment strings. Many software packages use these strings to allow you to set various options in the software. The default is 160 bytes, which is often not enough. In DOS versions 3.2 and below, the space is given in units of 16 bytes (i.e., /E:20 would reserve 320 bytes), whereas in DOS 3.3 and later the actual number of bytes is used.

```
FILES=20
```

This parameter sets the number of files that may concurrently be open. If not present, a maximum of 8 is allowed, of which five are standard devices used by DOS. Most software requires more than three open files at one time, so this parameter should always be present. A value from 8 to 255 may be specified. 20 is about right for most people, though if you are running several programs under Windows, a larger number such as 30 may be better.

```
BUFFERS=30
```

This parameter specifies the number of buffers that DOS uses to hold information read from disk. Increasing the number of buffers can greatly increase the performance of a PC. Many disk accesses, such as directory searches, constantly refer to the same sectors of the disk. Once read into a buffer, they can be reread instantly from memory, instead of having to be read again from disk.

The number of buffers used by default, if this parameter is omitted, varies depending on the type of system and the version of DOS. On early versions the default was 2 for an XT and 3 for an AT. This is far too low for good performance. Bear in mind, though, that each buffer takes 528 bytes of system memory. Early DOS machines had only 64Kb of memory, so they couldn't afford to have too many buffers! DOS 3.3 with 512Kb or more of RAM will allocate a default of 15 buffers. If the memory can be spared, performance gains will usually be seen if the number is increased to 30. However, if you're using a disk cache, you can reduce the buffers to about 8 or less, and let the cache do most of the work.

```
COUNTRY=044
```

```
COUNTRY=044,437,d:\path\COUNTRY.SYS
```

This parameter is used to specify the country-specific options to be used, such as date and time formats. US and Canadian PC users need not worry about it. The second example is valid in DOS 3.30 and above, which includes support for *code pages*. The examples given are for use in the UK.

Code pages were introduced because the standard IBM character set does not include all the characters, such as currency symbols and accented letters, used in many countries of the world. Each code page contains a slightly different character set, in which some characters – mainly the line graphics – are replaced by these national characters. Users of EGA or VGA monitors can load a special device driver using the command:

```
DEVICE=C:\DOS\EGA.CPI
```

which supports switching between standard and national code pages. This takes about 6K bytes of memory.

Few software packages use code pages, since to do so would make them incompatible with earlier versions of DOS. Unless the installation instructions for a package specify that particular code page settings must be used, it should be safe to forget them altogether. Software packages that use a graphics display, such as Microsoft Windows or Framework III, handle the display of different national character sets themselves, anyway, so code pages are irrelevant and a waste of memory.

```
BREAK=OFF
```

This parameter controls the frequency with which DOS checks whether the Break key (Control/C) has been pressed. If a PC is being used for debugging software that may on occasions get stuck in a loop, it's worth setting BREAK to ON, the default condition, so as to be able to stop the looping program. If BREAK is OFF the system only checks for the Break key during keyboard, screen or printer I/O. Reducing the frequency of Break checks should result in a slight improvement in performance.

```
STACKS=0,0
```

```
STACKS=32,128
```

The STACKS command is used to specify the number and size of stacks that are to be allocated for use by interrupt service routines. Stacks are used as workspace by programs. The first parameter specifies how many stacks should be provided, the second, their size in bytes. If none are allocated, the normal system stack will be used. This is quite sufficient for most ATs, and will result in a saving of almost 2Kb of memory compared with the default of 9 stacks.

If insufficient stack space is available, a stack overflow error will occur, and the machine will hang. This can sometimes happen if devices that cause frequent interrupts, such as communications, network or tape streamer interface cards, are in use. Amstrad PC1512 and PC1640 systems are particularly prone to this problem, and on these machines, the command shown on the second line should be included. Under Windows 3, some 80386 systems may crash in 386 Enhanced Mode if zero stacks are allocated. If this occurs, revert to the default setting.

```
FCBS=1
```

This command sets how many files can be opened at a time, using file control blocks (FCBs). FCBs are the method that DOS version 1 used for handling files. Almost no current software uses them, but the facility is retained so that very old programs may still run. The default value used is 4. Specifying a value of 1 will cause no noticeable problems, and save a further 1Kb of memory.

In many PCs, which have little in the way of expansion cards and no additional memory, the parameters given above are all that need to be present in a CONFIG.SYS file. Later versions of DOS, especially DOS 4, have many more options. Some of these take up valuable extra memory, while contributing little in the way of extra functionality. The automatic installation procedures used by DOS 4.0 and above invoke far more options than most users actually need. A significant amount of memory may be reclaimed by paring down CONFIG.SYS so that it contains only the commands mentioned above, plus any essential device drivers.

15.3 Device Drivers

A device driver is a special type of program that is loaded at boot time and forms an integral part of the operating system. It's loaded by specifying in CONFIG.SYS a line in the form:

```
DEVICE=d:\path\devdrvr.sys {parameters}
```

where the parameters are optional. Some device drivers are needed to be able to use particular hardware add-ins in a PC. These are usually provided by the hardware manufacturer. Others are supplied as part of DOS, and are used to configure the system in a particular way. Some common ones are described below.

ANSI.SYS

DOS provides some device drivers as standard. ANSI.SYS is one that makes the PC screen and keyboard emulate an ANSI terminal. This allows special sequences of characters – known as *escape sequences* because each starts with an escape character – to be used to position the cursor, set foreground and background colours and control the appearance of the screen.

In the early days of the IBM PC, software manufacturers wrote their programs for generic MS-DOS. ANSI.SYS was the only method provided by DOS for positioning text and using colour. Without it, all you could use was a scrolling monochrome Teletype-like display. So packages had to use ANSI escape sequences, and required that ANSI.SYS be loaded. This was done using the command:

```
DEVICE=d:\path\ANSI.SYS
```

Nowadays, software is written specifically for the IBM PC. Programs use PC BIOS functions or write directly to the display hardware to achieve snappy screen performance. All the screen attributes can be directly manipulated in this way, so ANSI.SYS is no longer needed.

The big disadvantage of ANSI.SYS is that it is slow! It slows normal DOS output by about a factor of 10, because every character written to the screen must be checked to see if it's part of an ANSI escape sequence. It's probably around 100 times slower than direct screen output. It also takes up several kilobytes of memory. Don't load it unless a software package specifically demands it.

RAMDRIVE.SYS

RAMDRIVE.SYS (VDISK.SYS in DOS 4) is another device driver that's provided with DOS. It allows you use some of your extended or expanded memory as a *RAM disk* – an area of memory that can be treated exactly like a disk drive.

RAMDRIVE takes four parameters. The first specifies the size of the RAM disk in kilobytes – the default is just 64Kb. The second is the sector size in bytes. This has a default of 128. The third is the number of root directory entries – the default is 64. A fourth parameter specifies what type of memory is to be used: /E uses extended memory, while /A causes EMS expanded memory to be used. To set up a 360Kb RAM drive in extended memory, therefore, you'd need to include the following parameter in CONFIG.SYS:

```
DEVICE=d:\path\RAMDRIVE.SYS 360 512 64 /e
```

The advantage of using a RAM disk is that it can be accessed almost instantaneously. Programs and data can be read from or written to it in a fraction of a second. However, it is volatile. Anything written to the RAM disk will be lost the instant the power goes off. So any newly-created files must always be copied to conventional disk storage for safe keeping before switching off the machine. An unexpected power failure will result in files in the RAM disk being lost.

A good use for a RAM disk is to hold programs and read-only data files. Many software packages have several overlay files that are loaded into memory when a particular function of the package is invoked. There can be a noticeable delay when these files are loaded, giving sluggish performance. If you copy the program and overlay files to RAM disk at start-up, and run the software from there, you'll notice a significant increase in speed. However, the benefits of RAM disks have been eroded by the improved access speed of most modern hard disks.

A RAM disk can be useful in low-cost laptops that only have one diskette drive. At boot-up you can create a RAM drive. Then you can copy the application software into it and run it. This will allow you to replace the diskette with another, which you can use to store data.

DRIVER.SYS

DRIVER.SYS was mentioned in Chapter 7. Its main function is to inform DOS of the characteristics of additional (more than two) or non-standard diskette drives.

It also has another use. On a PC with a single diskette drive, you can refer to the drive as both A: and B:. This means that it's possible to copy from one diskette to another by copying from A: to B:, and swapping the source and target diskettes when prompted by the operating system. On a PC with two drives of different types, if you want to copy from one diskette to another of the same type, you have a problem. If you try COPY A:thing.txt A:, DOS will inform you that you cannot copy a file to itself.

DRIVER.SYS can be used to associate another drive letter to an existing drive. It takes several parameters which are fully described in the DOS manual. For example:

```
DEVICE=d:\path\DRIVER.SYS /D:0 /F:7
```

will associate the next free drive letter to the 3.5in. high density diskette drive normally referred to as drive A:. Then, should you want to copy files from one 1.44Mb drive to another, you can use the command COPY A:thing.txt D:. DOS will then prompt you to insert the source and target diskettes at the appropriate time, using the two drive letters A: and D:.

15.4 DOS 4.0 and Expanded memory

Some CONFIG.SYS options in DOS version 4 allow you to use expanded memory for certain things, such as disk BUFFERS or a RAM disk. This is invoked by including an /X switch in the parameter line.

Disk buffers and RAM disks are more useful the larger they are. Using expanded memory allows them to be much larger than if they were confined to conventional memory – if sufficient RAM is fitted – and frees up more memory for applications. However, DOS 4.00 had many bugs that could lead to system crashes if the /X option was invoked. Basically, DOS 4.00 failed to identify clearly that it was using expanded memory, so other applications tried to use the same page frames as DOS, with disastrous results. These bugs were fixed in DOS version 4.01.

In DOS version 5, a more sophisticated method of memory management is used. Disk buffers will be loaded above base memory if the DOS=HIGH command is used, so the /X option is no longer needed. Memory management under DOS 5 is described later in this chapter.

15.5 Optimising AUTOEXEC.BAT

AUTOEXEC.BAT is, of course, the batch file executed automatically by COMMAND.COM when the system is started up. Its function is to run any programs – particularly memory-resident utilities – that are needed as part of the basic system set-up, and to set any environment strings such as the search path. The exact contents of AUTOEXEC.BAT will vary depending on what the PC is to be used for. However, some things are appropriate to almost every system, and these are discussed below.

```
PATH={first search dir};{second search dir}; ...
```

The first command in AUTOEXEC.BAT (apart from ECHO OFF if you want to suppress the display of commands to the screen) should set the PATH environment string. This is used to specify what directories DOS will look in to find executable files, whenever a program is run. When a command is given that isn't an internal DOS command, the operating system will search for a COM, EXE or BAT file of the same name. DOS always searches in a particular order. First, it looks in the current directory, then the first directory named in the PATH, then the second directory and so on. So the order in which directories are listed in the PATH will affect the speed with which DOS will find a program. For best performance, put the directories containing the most frequently accessed programs at the start of the PATH string.

```
PROMPT=$p$g
```

The next command should set the command prompt to show the current drive and directory. The default DOS prompt only tells you the drive letter, not the current directory. Working on a hard disk with only a C> prompt to tell you where you are is like working in the dark. Unless you use the cd command all the time you can't tell what directory you are in, which is a recipe for disaster. The PROMPT string takes just a few bytes of environment space, and makes DOS much more user-friendly.

```
SET COMSPEC=d:\path\COMMAND.COM
```

If you haven't used the second parameter to the SHELL command in CONFIG.SYS to specify the location of the command interpreter, and it isn't in your root directory, you must set COMSPEC to its full pathname. Otherwise, you'll get an *Invalid COMMAND.COM* message when you exit an application that overwrote the transient portion of the command interpreter.

```
SHARE /NC
```

If your system has large disk partitions (greater than 32Mb) under DOS 3.31 or DOS 4, then you must load SHARE. SHARE does two things. First, it provides protection against files being opened concurrently by two applications. In a network environment this could easily happen, possibly with disastrous results. On a network, applications must open files specifically in a sharing mode if other programs are to be allowed simultaneous access to them. SHARE provides support for this.

However, even on a standalone PC, SHARE is needed for its secondary function. It provides a workaround for the problem that FCBs – the method of file handling used mostly by very old programs – are unable to handle logical sector numbers greater than 64K. In a large disk partition, the sector numbers can exceed this. If SHARE isn't loaded, you run the risk of disk corruption, because sector numbers are truncated to 16 bits. They will wrap round to zero once 65535 has been reached. So you could overwrite the disk's directory and other files with data intended for sectors higher than 64K.

If DOS detects a large disk when it is loaded it attempts to load SHARE itself. If it can't locate the program, a warning message is displayed. SHARE can be loaded manually in AUTOEXEC.BAT. The /NC switch turns off the file sharing checks. These checks should cause no harm on a standalone system, but some programs open the same file more than once, and this will cause file sharing violation error messages to appear.

In DOS version 5, the problem with FCBs is taken care of by DOS itself, so SHARE need only be loaded if file sharing protection is required.

```
CHKDSK
PAUSE
```

Next, the batch file should run the CHKDSK utility to check the integrity of the file system, and pause to allow the user to read its output. If there are any lost clusters or other problems it's essential they are spotted and dealt with before they have a chance to cause serious problems. I have seen a hard disk that seemed perfectly OK until one day a corrupt file was noticed. When CHKDSK was run, almost half the files on the disk were found to be destroyed. The problem was traced back to something that happened two or three weeks earlier. Running CHKDSK regularly should prevent this from occurring.

The flaw in the idea of using CHKDSK as a routine check of the file system, is that it relies on the user spotting when errors are reported. This problem wouldn't exist if CHKDSK terminated with a non-zero error code if errors were found. A batch file could then test this, and put up an appropriate message. But current versions of CHKDSK don't do this, so you'll have to rely on the user.

```
SCAN C: /a
```

PC viruses are very prevalent these days. It's a good idea to include a daily virus scan in the start-up procedures. In the example above, the shareware McAfee SCAN utility is shown, though there are many other products that do a similar job.

It isn't ideal to test for viruses from within AUTOEXEC.BAT. A boot sector virus could have already installed itself by the time the batch file is run, and then hidden its presence from the virus detector. The safest way to check for viruses – which are discussed in more detail in the next chapter – is to boot from a write-protected system disk and run the virus scanner from that. However, few users are going to bother to do this on a regular basis. Running a check in AUTOEXEC.BAT is the next best thing.

15.6 Keyboard Utilities

In most countries outside the US and Canada, the keyboard layout used differs slightly from the standard one that the PC BIOS knows how to handle. The KEYB utilities are provided to cater for this. For example, in the UK, AUTOEXEC.BAT may contain one of the following commands:

```
KEYBUK

KEYB UK

KEYB UK,437,d:\path\KEYBOARD.SYS
```

The first form of the command is used where a separate utility is provided for each national keyboard layout. It's normally used under DOS 3.2 or earlier, though some PC manufacturers provide separate utilities with later versions of DOS as well. With DOS 3.3, Microsoft introduced a single, parameter driven utility, which used either of the second or third forms of the command.

For a program that only has to change the ASCII codes produced by half a dozen keys, KEYB is something of a leviathan. It seems to grow with every new version of DOS, and currently takes something in the region of 10Kb of valuable memory. One feature of KEYB is that you can switch to the default US keyboard layout by pressing Ctrl/Alt/F1, and then revert to the national layout again by pressing Ctrl/Alt/F2. Not many people know that, and I suspect that few would have a use for it even if they did.

Microsoft's keyboard utilities can cause a few problems. Certain unusual key combinations aren't passed through to the BIOS, such as Ctrl/Alt/+ and Ctrl/Alt/- which are used to toggle the processor speed on some clones, or Ctrl/Alt/S or Ctrl/Alt/Esc which can be used to call up the SETUP utility in some BIOSes. Some versions of KEYB.COM left interrupts disabled for too long while processing keystrokes, and can cause problems with communications software.

Windows 3 users who can put up with having a few mismatched keys during the times when they are using old-style DOS programs can dispense with keyboard converters altogether, because Windows does its own key remapping.

PC keyboards have an auto-repeat feature, which IBM called typematic. When you press and hold down a key, after about half a second the key will automatically repeat at 10 keystrokes a second.

```
100 REM === LISTING 15.1 - SPEED UP 'AT' KEYBOARD ===
110 DATA 176, 243, 230, 96, 185, 255, 255, 226, 254, 176, 230, 96, 205, 32
120 INPUT "Enter initial delay in quarter seconds, [1 - 4]: ",I%
125 IF I%<1 OR I%>4 THEN 120
130 INPUT "Enter repeat rate, 0=fast 31=slow, [0 - 31]: ",R%
135 IF R%<0 OR R%>31 THEN 130
140 OPEN "O",#1,"KEYSPEED.COM"
150 FOR K%=1 TO 10: READ J%: PRINT #1,CHR$(J%);: NEXT K%
152 PRINT #1,CHR$(I%*32-32+R%);
154 FOR K%=1 TO 4: READ J%: PRINT #1,CHR$(J%);: NEXT K%
158 CLOSE #1
160 END
```

The repeat rate of AT type keyboards is programmable. The default is slow, so it's a good idea to run a utility to reduce the initial delay and speed up the repeat rate. You can include this in AUTOEXEC.BAT. Listing 15.1 is a BASIC program that you can use to create a utility called KEYSPEED.COM. Run the BASIC program and enter the initial delay and repeat rate required. Then run KEYSPEED.COM. Once you're happy with the responsiveness of the keyboard, copy KEYSPEED.COM to your utilities directory, and include a line to run it in AUTOEXEC.BAT.

XT keyboards can also be speeded up. There are both commercial and PD utilities that will do this. However, it's much more difficult to do, and these utilities may cause conflicts with the applications software. KEYSPEED.COM has no effect on XT keyboards.

15.7 Using Expanded Memory

One of the most difficult aspects of setting up PCs is memory management. It's a complex subject. The best solution will depend on the machine itself and the type of applications that will run on it. We'll start by looking at the basic principles of memory management.

The only form of additional memory that XT-compatible systems can support is expanded memory. This comes on an expansion card and must be used with a device driver that is included in CONFIG.SYS.

The most important configuration option for expanded memory is the selection of the page frame. As explained in Chapter 1, expanded memory is memory that is outside the address space of the 8088 and 8086. However, the hardware associated with the card can switch four 16Kb *pages* of RAM into a 64Kb page frame located within the PC memory map. Most machines have an unused area between the display adapter memory and the system ROM that can be used for this purpose. It's essential to ensure that the page frame area chosen really is unused, or system crashes and other problems will occur. If you can't find an unused 64Kb, perhaps because of the presence of other memory-mapped I/O cards in the machine, some conventional memory below 640K may have to be sacrificed to make room for it.

Once you've established the area to use, configure the card to the appropriate base address using a jumper. The device driver line in CONFIG.SYS will probably require a parameter specifying this address. You must insert this device driver before any others – such as RAM drives or disk caches – that expect expanded memory to be present.

Expanded memory cards can be used in 80286 and 80386 machines. These processors can also use extended memory. On the more modern 286s and all 386s and above, expanded memory can be created using a special device driver that converts extended memory into expanded memory. The device driver – for example, EMM386.SYS – must be included in CONFIG.SYS. A parameter to the device driver specifies the page frame base address. You can also reserve some extended memory for use by applications that use it instead of expanded memory.

These days, most hardware supports the Lotus-Intel-Microsoft 4.0 Expanded Memory Specification (LIM 4.0 EMS). This is more flexible than the earlier EMS specification in the way that memory can be configured. It allows *backfilling*. This is a feature that enables whole sections of memory below 640K to be swapped with expanded memory. A large backfill area permits multitasking software such as Desqview and real mode Windows 3 to operate more efficiently.

LIM 4.0 memory isn't restricted to just one 64Kb page frame. Nor does the page frame need to occupy a contiguous block of memory. Any unused areas of the memory map can be used to hold EMS pages. The greater the number of pages available, the more efficiently software can run. However, you must still avoid areas of the memory map used by devices. The device driver must be given parameters to tell it the areas to be excluded. For example, if there is an I/O card using the region from D0000 to D3FFF (hex), you must exclude it in the device driver parameter line, or conflicts will occur. You can also specify that areas like the video buffer for EGA and VGA graphics can be used by the memory manager, if it's known that this won't conflict with the applications running on the machine.

15.8 High and Upper Memory

One of the main reasons for using a memory manager is that it gives you ability to move device drivers and TSRs – such as keyboard and network drivers – into memory above 640K. Third-party products that can do this include HeadRoom from Helix Software, QEMM-386 from Quarterdeck Office Systems, and Qualitas' Move 'em and 386 to the Max. This facility has also been incorporated into DR DOS and MS-DOS version 5. With a little effort, you can often obtain over 620Kb of conventional memory free, even when network drivers are loaded.

Now that AT class machines are the standard for business use, more applications programs require the use of extended memory. The BIOS functions for using extended memory are crude, and provide no way for applications to tell if blocks of memory are in use by other programs resident in the machine. To overcome this problem, Microsoft introduced the *Extended Memory Specification* (XMS). This is supported by extended memory managers such as HIMEM.SYS.

XMS gives applications access to several functions in addition to those provided by the AT BIOS. These include the ability to use Upper Memory Blocks (UMBs) and the High Memory Area (HMA). UMBs are blocks of memory between 640Kb and 1Mb that are unused by devices. High memory is the 64Kb block of memory located just above the 1Mb threshold, which can be used even in real mode. Device drivers and TSRs can be loaded into UMBs and the HMA, instead of conventional memory. XMS memory is used by much of the latest software, including Microsoft Windows 3 when running in Standard or 386 Enhanced modes.

Obtaining the optimum memory configuration can be difficult and time-consuming. Most third-party products include a utility – such as Qualitas' *Maximize* – that analyses your system memory usage and recommends the configuration to use. Sometimes you can improve on the suggested configuration, but usually only after a good deal of fiddling around. Some device drivers and TSRs run more slowly when loaded in high memory, so it's worth checking the performance of a system before finalising the memory configuration.

15.9 DOS 5 Memory Management

MS-DOS version 5 is the first version of MS-DOS to include memory management features. These can deliver substantially more conventional memory, particularly for users of 80386-based machines. However, 8088s and 8086s, many older 80286s and any machine with only 640Kb of RAM will not obtain any benefits.

If you have a suitable machine, the first step is to ensure that your CONFIG.SYS contains the lines:
```
DEVICE=C:\path\HIMEM.SYS
DOS=HIGH
```

These lines are usually added to the configuration file when DOS 5 is installed. They tell DOS to load the XMS memory driver, and then to use high memory to load parts of the operating system. This will typically free up 40Kb of base memory.

The next step is only applicable to users of PCs with 80386 processors and better. This is to add the line:

```
DEVICE=C:\path\EMM386.EXE
```

after the HIMEM.SYS line, but before any other device drivers are specified. You can add the switch `/NOEMS` if none of the programs you run need EMS memory. You should also change the DOS= parameter so that it reads:

```
DOS=HIGH,UMB
```

This tells DOS to maintain links with upper memory blocks in high memory. It can then load device drivers and programs into these blocks using the DEVICEHIGH and LOADHIGH commands.

EMM386.SYS uses about 8Kb of conventional memory. However, you can get this memory back, and more, once you start loading device drivers and TSRs high. Finding the best order to load the device drivers and TSRs is a matter of trial and error.

To load a device driver high, you simply change the DEVICE= command in CONFIG.SYS to DEVICEHIGH=. To load a TSR high, insert LOADHIGH before the program name. DOS doesn't report an error if it is unable to load the program high, it just loads it in ordinary memory instead. So, to see where the program has gone, and how much memory remains, you should issue the command:

```
MEM /C
```

and then examine the results. If you haven't managed to get all your device drivers and TSRs to load high, you may need to change the order in which they are loaded, to make the best possible use of your high RAM. However, certain device drivers must be loaded in a particular sequence, while others may not work properly in upper memory, so it's a good idea to make changes one at a time, and test the system between each change. On many systems, it will be possible to obtain more than 620Kb of free memory for DOS, after all the device drivers and TSRs have been loaded.

15.10 Managing TSRs

TSRs, so-called because they use the DOS *terminate and stay resident* function to remain in memory after control has been returned to the DOS prompt, are essential to most people's use of a PC. Programs that are TSRs include well-known applications such as Borland's SideKick, network drivers, printer control utilities and keyboard enhancers.

TSRs can cause problems. You can install so many of them that not enough memory is left for standard applications to use. Also, TSRs hook themselves into various system interrupt routines. Sometimes they can conflict with each other, and with normal programs, to cause odd malfunctions and even system crashes. Some TSRs are only required by a particular application. For example, a mouse driver is only needed by programs that support the use of a mouse. However once loaded, it can be difficult to remove a TSR. It then takes up memory that could be used another program.

If lack of free memory is becoming a problem then on a 386, as we've seen, you can move TSRs into high memory. However, there are other possible solutions. There are commercial utilities – such as Pop Drop Plus or Above Disc – that allow TSRs to be removed from memory, or rolled out to disk or expanded memory, ready to be reloaded when needed.

A cruder solution is provided by two public domain utilities named MARK and RELEASE. These can be used to remove TSRs permanently from memory when they are no longer required. You run MARK before the TSRs that will later be removed. It saves the state of the interrupt vectors at the time it's loaded so that they can be restored once the TSRs have been removed by RELEASE.

```
: Example batch file showing use
: of MARK and RELEASE
MARK
: now load TSR program
NETBIOS
: load program which requires TSR
NETCOMM
: call RELEASE to remove TSR
RELEASE
```

Listing 15.2: Using MARK and RELEASE

Usually, MARK and RELEASE would be run from a batch file. A typical example would be to use them to control the loading of NETBIOS, which is needed for many applications that communicate over a network. An example batch file is shown in Listing 15.2.

Another public domain program that can be used to install and remove both TSRs and device drivers from the command line is LOADSYS. This also has the ability to load programs – including COMMAND.COM – into memory above 640K. It has a vast range of options, which are explained in the documentation file that accompanies the program. The options to be used must largely be determined by trial and error. LOADSYS is very much a tool for the expert, and won't be discussed in detail here.

15.11 Disk Partitioning

Hard disk performance can be affected by the way it is partitioned and the way the directories are structured. Often, under DOS 4 and above, a large disk is simply partitioned as a single drive C:. On the other hand, under DOS 3.30 it is frequently allocated as a succession of 32Mb partitions, plus one small one to use whatever space remains. However, intelligent partitioning of a disk can yield some useful benefits.

Under versions of DOS earlier than 5, you should only use disk partitions larger than 32Mb if you need to have room for a very large file. If you don't have any files that big, it's more efficient to divide the disk up into several smaller partitions.

Large partitions waste space. DOS allocates disk space to individual files in units of one *cluster*. (Under DOS 4 and above they're called *allocation units*, which amount to the same thing.) The size of a cluster varies, depending on the size of the partition and the version of DOS. Typically, it is 4Kb for partitions less than 16Mb (which is very wasteful of small hard disks), 2Kb for 16 – 32Mb, and 4, 8 or 16Kb above that. A cluster is the smallest unit of disk space that DOS can allocate, so a small batch file 50 – 100 bytes in length could actually be using up to 16Kb of hard disk space. From a disk utilisation point of view, between 16 and 32Mb is the optimum size for a disk partition.

The problem isn't as great with disks formatted under MS-DOS version 5. DOS 5 uses a cluster size of 2Kb for partitions of up to 128Mb. From 128 to 256Mb the cluster size is 4Kb. Above that, it goes to 8Mb.

Large partitions have another disadvantage: they increase the disk access time. The clusters that make up a file, and the files within a directory, can be kept anywhere within a partition. For example, the first cluster might be located at cylinder 3, the next at cylinder 603, the one after that at cylinder 10 and so on. The drive heads have to move back and forth all over the disk to read the whole file. The further they have to move, the longer it takes, so performance suffers. Even if the disk isn't fragmented, and files occupy contiguous blocks of clusters, individual files and directories can be scattered all over the disk.

Suppose you decided to allocate several partitions, each for a particular purpose. Your DOS programs and general purpose utilities are located in the first partition C:. Word-processing software and the directories containing your word-processing files are located together on a small partition D:. A spreadsheet program and directories containing spreadsheet files are in another partition E:. Now, whichever activity you are engaged in, all the files you need, both program and data files, will be contained within one partition. The partition occupies a clearly defined portion of the disk. All the drive head movements will be contained within that area of the disk, so the average access time will be improved. Structuring a hard disk like this is also tidy. It keeps related files together, and may be more convenient when it comes to taking backups.

15.12 Directory Structure

Within a partition, the directory structure can also affect performance. Most file paths are specified starting from the root. Directories are just like files. To find them, DOS must look in the root, and search serially through the files it contains until it finds the entry for the first level subdirectory file. Then it reads this file, looking for the next directory level (if the file is nested several levels deep) or the program or data file specified.

This search mechanism works best if the disk is structured in a certain way. Because DOS reads through each directory from start to finish when it searches for a file, directories should not be allowed to become too large. It's better to divide large directories up into several smaller ones, each containing a proportion of the files. This will reduce the time taken to find a file, and help to deliver better performance. Since almost all file searches begin at the root, this should be kept as clear as possible. Apart from files that have to be there, like CONFIG.SYS and AUTOEXEC.BAT, it should contain nothing but directories.

15.13 Defragmentation

While optimising the partitioning and directory structure of a disk is a good idea, it will only give a small improvement in performance. Another technique that can speed up disk accesses is *defragmentation*.

When a file is created, the clusters that hold the data can be written anywhere on the disk. DOS allocates unused clusters to files in such a way that they tend to occupy space released by files that have previously been deleted. If the deleted files were smaller than the one being written, it's inevitable that the new file will be stored in several chunks. In other words, it will be fragmented – it won't occupy a contiguous area of the disk.

Another type of fragmentation is where individual files within a directory are scattered all over the disk. This can also adversely affect performance. For example, when it loads a program, DOS must first read the directory to find where the program file is. Then it must move the heads to this location to read the contents of the program file. When it is executed, the program may read a configuration file to find out some user-specified settings. DOS must read the directory again, to find the location of the configuration file on the disk, then go to that location and read the file into the program's buffer. If the directory, program and configuration file are located at widely separated parts of the disk, a lot of head movement will be needed, and it will seem to take a long time. If all three files are next to each other, hardly any head movement will be needed and access will be much faster.

The effects of fragmentation can be minimised by partitioning the disk as described earlier, but fragmentation within the partition will still occur. The solution is to run a *defragmenter*. This is a program that can move all the clusters belonging to a particular file into a contiguous area, and collect together all the files in a directory into one part of the disk. One of the best known defragmenters is Speed Disk, part of the Norton Utilities package. Besides defragmenting files and collecting them together, Speed Disk can arrange the files in a particular order – specified by the user – so that directories come first, followed by executable programs, then overlay files and so on. This will reduce the time taken by DOS's linear searching of directories.

Speed Disk works by moving clusters of data around the disk, updating the directory and FAT entries to show their new location. The program can be interrupted safely by pressing Escape. Nevertheless, there is a risk of a corrupted disk if an involuntary interruption occurs due to a power failure. It's cautious, but wise, to take a full backup of your disk before you run Speed Disk.

A full optimisation may take half an hour or more, depending on the size and speed of your hard disk. However, the results are worth the effort. While the performance gain is only small, the reduction in disk head movement is very noticeable, and must inevitably result in increased life for the drive.

15.14 Disk Caches

If you seek further improvements in disk drive performance, one solution may be to install a disk cache. This may be thought of as a large buffer in memory used to hold a copy of the most recently used blocks of data from the disk. These blocks include the directories, programs and data files that have been most recently accessed.

Though a hard disk may hold hundreds of files, the number of files actually accessed when a particular task is carried out is usually quite small. Many of the disk accesses that take place during a task are repeated accesses of the same files. Obvious examples are directories, program overlay files and database indexes. If the disk cache is large enough to hold sufficient of the most recently accessed blocks of data, it's likely that many disk reads will be for blocks already held in memory. If this is true, the data won't have to be read from the disk itself. The proportion of reads that are for blocks already held in the cache is termed the *hit rate*. Disk reads that are satisfied from the cache are almost instantaneous, so a disk cache large enough to give a high hit rate can produce a substantial improvement in disk performance.

To improve the hit rate, disk caches *read ahead*. In other words, they automatically read in the sectors – up to a whole track – following the one requested by a program. Then, if the program requests the next sector of the file, that sector will probably be already held in the cache. This is most often true if the file isn't fragmented. So it's a good idea to periodically defragment your disk, to get the best out of your disk cache.

When it comes to writing to disk, cache programs fall into two categories. Most use what is termed *write through*. This means that data written to the cache is written to the hard disk as well, and control isn't returned to the application until this has been completed. For disk writes, a cache can actually slow things down a little, because additional processing is required compared with a plain DOS write. However, it's the safest way to do it.

Some disk caches, such as the Norton Cache, Hyperdisk, PC Kwik and others, offer a facility known as *staged write* or *delayed write*. What this does is to return control to the application as soon as the cache has been updated. The user isn't held up waiting for the data to be written to disk, and can immediately get on with processing his spreadsheet or whatever. The cache software waits until the system is idle before writing the data to the disk itself.

Staged writes can make a PC really fly, but there's a risk attached. When a program writes a block of data, three things must be updated: the file itself, the FAT and the directory entry. All three must be consistent. If a power cut or a reboot occurs before the disk itself is updated, the FAT, directory entries and data blocks may not be in step. If they aren't, DOS won't be able to make sense of the disk, and files will be lost. Many people use cacheing with staged writes quite happily, but others have had hard disks irrecoverably trashed. From a support point of view, the benefits are probably outweighed by the risks. The performance gains could be completely wiped out by the loss of days of work, and the time spent recovering data from a corrupted disk. Use staged writes at your own risk!

The benefits of disk cacheing are becoming eroded by improvements in the performance of hard disks. The newer hard disk controllers often have their own on-board caches, and the use of a cacheing utility can actually result in poorer performance. The amount of memory allocated to a disk cache must be large – at least 512Kb – to show any significant advantage in normal use. In practice this restricts the use of cacheing to systems with significant amounts of extended or expanded memory. Older systems with slow ST-506 drives may benefit even if a smaller cache is used, but even better performance could be obtained by replacing the drive with a more modern type.

If a disk cache is installed, it's advisable to check it out thoroughly with all the software applications that are likely to be used on the PC. Most caches should not cause any problems. However, one cache I came across was incompatible with Ashton-Tate's Framework III, so be warned!

15.15 BUFFERS and FASTOPEN

The disk buffers set up by DOS according to the value of the BUFFERS command are a crude form of disk cache. They don't use any clever techniques such as read ahead or delayed writes, so the performance improvement they can deliver isn't startling. However, unlike most cacheing utilities they are free, being part of the operating system.

FASTOPEN is a utility that attempts to speed up access to files by storing their location in memory so that if the file is opened on a subsequent occasion DOS does not have to search through the directory structure to find the location a second time. It isn't actually a disk cache. In fact, it's a kludge to overcome the inherent inefficiency of the DOS file system when dealing with large numbers of files. On most PCs, FASTOPEN has no noticeable effect. However, it can cause problems with some applications. It's best avoided.

15.16 Mathematics Coprocessors

Almost every PC sports a socket for a maths coprocessor on the motherboard. Fitting one might seem a good way of improving the performance. However, the benefits depend very much on the type of work for which the machine will be used.

The maths coprocessor is a very specialised processor. It's good for only one thing: calculating *floating-point* numbers. Most tasks carried out on a PC – word processing, data storage and retrieval, business finance and so on – get by using just integer arithmetic, which the 80x86 CPU can handle quite happily. Floating-point arithmetic is primarily used for scientific work. Perhaps the most common PC application that uses it is computer-aided design (CAD). The calculations needed to work out how an object will look when viewed from different angles, which lines will be hidden and so on, can be performed up to 10 times faster by an 80x87 floating point unit (FPU).

Intel make a range of coprocessors to go with their CPUs. The 8087 is used with the

8088 and 8086, the 80287 is for use with the 80286 and so on. Like CPUs, FPUs are rated according to the clock speed at which they can operate. An 8MHz 8087 is needed to run with an 8MHz 8086; a 25MHz 80387 to run with a 25MHz 80386. However, the 80287 runs at two-thirds the CPU's clock speed. The faster the FPU, the higher the cost. 80387s are expensive, so you should be sure that the software you use needs one before spending your money.

PC coprocessors are made by other manufacturers besides Intel. Many high-performance systems have a special socket for a Weitek coprocessor. Cyrix and IIT produce devices that are pin compatible with the Intel parts. These manufacturers claim that their products are much faster than Intel's. In practice, the difference is slight. Some new coprocessors, such as the Weitek, give better performance only if used with software specially written to take advantage of their unique facilities. Most software only supports the standard Intel devices, so no benefits are gained.

The actual performance increase gained by fitting an arithmetic coprocessor is likely to be less than expected. Even CAD applications spend more time drawing lines than they do calculating, so only a fraction of the claimed 10 times speed improvement will be seen overall. Whether it's worthwhile fitting an FPU or not depends entirely on the software to be used. Packages that don't mention a need for an FPU, or merely say that it is supported if fitted, probably won't benefit from it. If the package actually *recommends* that a coprocessor is fitted, then you'll probably see an improvement in speed.

15.17 ROM Shadowing

Many systems provide the option to shadow the BIOS ROM. This is usually a function of the chip set used on the motherboard, and was discussed in Chapter 4. The access time of ROM is significantly slower than that of RAM, so whenever the CPU is fetching instructions or data from ROM – when it's performing BIOS functions – it executes extra wait states. In other words, it has to run more slowly. Shadowing causes the contents of the ROM to be copied into RAM. The BIOS routines are then executed from RAM, allowing the processor to run at full speed all the time.

In practice, the benefits of ROM shadowing are doubtful. BIOS functions are performed roughly twice as quickly when held in RAM. However, in a normal program, the proportion of the time spent executing BIOS routines is quite small, so the performance gains are diluted accordingly. Programs that use the BIOS to output text to the screen – mainly DOS itself and some utilities – are noticeably snappier if the EGA or VGA BIOS is shadowed. However, most software packages bypass the BIOS and handle their own screen I/O to get the best performance, so the benefits of shadowing are negligible. One graphics benchmark that was tested showed an improvement of six per cent. This might sound worth having, but in practice you're unlikely to notice it. Nor does shadowing the system and the hard disk controller BIOS deliver any perceptible improvement in performance.

ROM shadowing is rather like some performance-tweaking gadgets you can buy for cars. It may improve the benchmark results by a whisker, and it may give you the contented feeling that you have the hottest PC in the office, but the practical effects are more illusory than real.

15.18 Configuration Problems

There are an almost infinite number of ways that a PC can be configured. Consequently, the potential for configuration-induced problems is almost limitless. Fortunately, most of the problems that are encountered are quite commonplace. A selection of the most common problems, with possible solutions, are given below:

System displays *Invalid COMMAND.COM*:

❑ DOS is unable to load or reload the command interpreter. Check the COMSPEC environment variable. Either there is no COMMAND.COM at the specified path, or it's from a different version of DOS to the one from that the system was booted.

System displays *Out of environment space*:

❑ The number and length of strings used in SET commands exceeds the space allocated. Specify a larger value in the SHELL= parameter in CONFIG.SYS.

System halts with *Fatal stack error*:

❑ Use the STACKS command in CONFIG.SYS to increase the number and/or size of stacks provided.

Program prints square brackets, arrows and other characters before meaningful text on the screen; jumbled screen layout:

❑ Program requires ANSI.SYS device driver to be loaded.

UK keyboard: pound sign key gives hash character; @, quote and backslash keys misplaced:

❑ Keyboard driver KEYBUK.COM or similar isn't loaded, or incorrect version for keyboard is being used.

Applications or TSRs do not respond to hot key combinations (e.g., Ctrl/+):

❑ Key combinations not being passed to application. Remove KEYB, KEYBUK or other keyboard enhancers.

❏ Conflict with other TSRs. Remove one by one until culprit is found.

Applications or device drivers requiring expanded memory are unable to use it:

❏ Memory manager (e.g., EMM.SYS) not installed before application or device driver is loaded.

Disk file access is slow:

❏ Too few BUFFERS specified.

❏ Files are fragmented.

❏ Too many files in directories.

❏ Incorrect disk interleave (see Chapter 8).

❏ Possible hard disk controller fault.

Application unable to open files:

❏ Check that files exist.

❏ Check file attributes.

❏ Check parameters that may be used to specify file paths.

❏ Try increasing FILES= parameter value in CONFIG.SYS.

File corruption and/or system crashes with programs that use expanded memory:

❏ Memory used as EMS page frames is also used by expansion cards. Exclude these areas from use by means of parameters to the expanded memory manager.

❏ Conflict with expanded memory used for buffers etc. by DOS 4.00. Use conventional memory instead.

❏ Memory manager used is incompatible with application.

File corruption, lost clusters occurring:

❏ Application program not closing output files. System is being turned off or rebooted without properly exiting the program.

❏ Disk cache is in use, and system is being turned off or rebooted before the cache buffers have been flushed to disk.

❏ SHARE not loaded when large partitions are being used.

Summary

In this chapter we looked at how a PC can be tuned for best performance. The optimum setup is largely determined by what is in CONFIG.SYS and AUTOEXEC.BAT. Memory shouldn't be wasted by loading device drivers or programs that aren't needed. It's good practice at start-up to do a health check on the DOS file system by running CHKDSK. A virus check is also advisable.

Memory management can be problematic. The standard memory managers that come with DOS or a memory card normally provide only basic expanded memory support for applications programs. DOS 5 and third-party memory managers include support for high memory, and upper memory on 386s. These products can solve many support problems by increasing the conventional memory left for DOS. Another solution is to use utilities that can load and unload TSRs. This can free up extra memory when the TSRs aren't required.

Hard disk performance can be optimised by using smaller disk partitions and ensuring that files don't become fragmented. Disk cacheing can be used to obtain further increases in performance. DOS itself provides tools for improving file access times, though FASTOPEN is best avoided.

Installing a maths coprocessor or using ROM shadowing can improve performance. However, the amount gained is dependent on the application, and may be negligible.

16

Computer Viruses

PC virus attacks are becoming disturbingly common. Once, press reports about company computers paralysed by computer viruses could be dismissed as unnecessarily alarmist. Now, however, there can be few organisations that have not fallen victim to one of these malevolent programs at some time or other. A recent survey suggested that the proportion was about one company in four. Personal experience seems to suggest that it is, in fact, far higher.

In 1988, there were just a handful of PC viruses. They intrigued the experts. Nothing like them had been seen before. When the press found out, some sensational stories appeared. However, most of us who worked with PCs had not then seen a PC virus. Nor did we know of anyone who had. We thought it was nothing to worry about. Little did we know! By 1989, there were about 20 distinct varieties, but incidences of infection were still quite rare. By 1990, the number had grown to over 100. To date, in the summer of 1991, there are over 500 identifiable varieties. If the trend continues, the number could be well into four figures by mid-1992. This is not a problem that can simply be ignored.

However, it is important to get things into perspective. Despite the creativity of virus writers, around 95% of PC infections are caused by one of the ten most common viruses. Only 50 or so viruses have actually been found *in the field*. The others have been sent to virus experts, presumably so that their creators can show how clever they are. Of course, there's always a risk that one of these other viruses could turn up on a user's PC, but so far, the risk seems small.

In this chapter, we'll start by looking at the different classes of malicious program, and how they work. You'll learn what steps to take to protect PCs against virus attack, how to detect viruses, and how to deal with an attack if one is discovered.

16.1 What is a Virus?

A computer virus is aptly named. It's a program which attaches itself to other computer programs so as to spread from one machine to another. Its effect may be relatively benign; it may simply display a harmless message or change the colours on the screen. Or it may be destructive, corrupting data files or even wiping out the entire contents of a disk. Whichever it is, it is a nuisance, and must be eradicated before it can spread any further.

A virus is a program. In order for it to replicate itself and carry out its other activities the code of the program must be executed by the computer. The virus achieves this by modifying executable (program) files – files with a .COM, .EXE, or .SYS extension – overlay files or the boot sector of a disk, so that its own code is executed first, followed by the code of the main program. The slight extra delay on loading, before the expected initial program display appears, would not usually be noticed by the user.

Viruses may conceal copies of themselves in various locations. These include the boot sector, file allocation table (FAT), partition table, disk sectors marked as bad, program files, hidden files and data files. However, a virus would not attach itself to text or data files alone, since these are never run as programs by the computer. Program instructions, held in executable files, must be modified in order to get the code executed and activate the virus.

Most viruses, when activated, load a small part of themselves into memory. This remains resident until the PC is rebooted. The virus can then continue to infect files and carry out other activities long after the original *carrier* program has finished running.

Like its biological counterpart, a computer virus will usually wait a while – until it has replicated itself a number of times, for example, or until a specific date such as Friday 13th – before performing any malicious acts. This helps to ensure that it has spread widely before the user becomes aware of its existence.

16.2 Trojans and Logic Bombs

The term *virus* is often used to describe any computer program that has a harmful intent. In fact, only programs that replicate themselves in the manner just described are entitled to be called viruses. Other types of malicious software include the trojan and the logic bomb.

Trojans are named after the trojan horse of Greek mythology. A trojan is a program which purports to be something useful and harmless, but is really a disguise for something nasty. A classic example of this is the notorious AIDS Information Diskette, which was sent by mail to thousands of computer users chosen from a computer magazine mailing list. The program appeared to be an innocent piece of software which assessed the user's risk of contracting AIDS. However, the installation routine set up hidden files that were called from AUTOEXEC.BAT. One of these incremented a counter. After the system had been started up 90 times, the program scrambled the user's hard disk. It then displayed a message requesting that a registration fee should be sent to an address in Panama, to obtain a program to unscramble the data.

The AIDS Information Diskette was the subject of much publicity in the press. Most reports referred to it as a virus. But unlike a virus, the program did not replicate itself. It was simply a trojan horse, an attempt at extortion that fortunately did not succeed.

A logic bomb is a piece of software that has code built into it to perform some destructive activity at a predetermined time. Logic bombs have often been used by disgruntled ex-employees of a company to corrupt files or cause other damage after they have left. Since it's rare for computer management to check what code goes into a program, if the correct results are produced, it's surprising that logic bombs are not encountered more often.

16.3 Virus Prevention

Of all the types of malicious program discussed, the virus is undoubtedly the most widespread and the most worrying. PC viruses are now so common that no-one can afford to ignore the problem. To spread, a virus has to get on to a computer. So the first step in dealing with the problem must be to prevent viruses from infecting machines in the first place.

Ignoring for a moment the particular problems of networked PCs, there are only two ways in which a virus can find its way on to a system. The most common way is from software executed or copied from floppy disk. The other is from software downloaded from computer bulletin boards, using a modem.

Modems are much less common than diskette drives, so the most common way in which viruses spread is through the exchange of diskettes. A virus must attach itself to a legitimate program in order to be activated. It spreads when someone gives a copy of the infected file to somebody else. You can prevent viruses from infecting programs on diskette by physically write-protecting the diskette. You can make it more difficult for viruses to spread by never giving copies of programs to other people. So there is a lot you can do to combat viruses, simply by following good housekeeping procedures.

The licence conditions for most software packages usually state that the software may be used on one machine only. Consequently, there is rarely a legitimate reason for transferring programs from one machine to another. Public domain and shareware software is an exception, of course, and it has been unfairly blamed for the spread of viruses as a result. Another exception is the programmer who is developing programs for use by others. Programmers need to be particularly careful that any diskettes they distribute are virus-free.

Diskettes received from outside sources which may contain software – demonstration disks, magazine cover disks and so on – should all be treated with suspicion, and scanned for viruses before they are run. Even commercial packages should not be regarded as safe; I have heard of several cases in which shrink-wrapped software was found to be infected by a virus. Fortunately, reputable software companies are aware of the dangers and take stringent measures to prevent them ever occurring.

Since viruses infect program files, you should be particularly careful to safeguard master copies of commercial software packages. You should never install software from the original master disks. Write protect them, if they are not write protected by the manufacturer. Then make a copy, and write protect that. Now put the originals away in a safe place, and install the software from the copy you have just made.

It may not be possible to install some software packages from write protected disks, or even from copies, if they use a copy protection system. If you encounter this iniquitous practice then there is little you can do except complain vehemently to the supplier.

System boot disks and other diskettes containing software should always be write protected. If you can, avoid mixing data and programs on one diskette. Then disks containing software can be permanently write protected.

Extra care must be taken when downloading software from bulletin boards. Any software obtained from such a source must be treated as suspect. It should not be used until it has been checked using up-to-date virus checking software. Bulletin board systems (BBSs) can provide a lot of useful information, but it is worth bearing in mind that amateur BBSs are the main channel by which virus writers release their creations into the world. So you can't be too cautious.

Professional information services such as Compuserve, BIX or CIX exist as forums for members to exchange technical information, but they also contain software for people to download. These systems are relatively safe. Unlike amateur BBSs, the names and addresses of subscribers are known so that they can be billed every month. This would make it easy to trace who had uploaded an infected program. But caution is still advisable. Every program that is downloaded should be checked for viruses before it is run.

If viruses are quite common on business PCs, they are widespread among home computer users – they aren't as fussy about where a program comes from. Piracy – illegally copying copyrighted software – is widespread, particularly among the young. This free-and-easy attitude is conducive to the spread of viruses. Home PC users –

especially those with children who are allowed to use the PC – who regularly transfer files between their office machine and the one at home on diskette, must understand the risks, and know how to avoid them.

These days, most PCs have a hard disk. The bigger the hard disk, the greater the damage that a virus could do. So it's important to prevent a virus from getting on to a hard disk in the first place. You've already seen that there's only one way a virus can become active – by running infected code. So if you can find a way to prevent virus-infected code from ever being run, you'll be safe from viruses.

In some companies, PCs have had their diskette drives removed. Users can only run software that has been installed on their hard disk, or their network, by the PC support department. Diskless workstations are quite common on networks. However, the absence of a diskette drive would be unacceptable or impractical for many PC users. To be safe, diskette users must follow a simple rule: check every diskette for viruses before using it.

16.4 Network Security

The problems that could be caused if a virus found its way on to a network are potentially even more serious than for a stand-alone PC. Some network operating systems provide little better security than DOS itself. Many low-cost networks are designed to allow local resources – hard disks, diskette drives and printers – to be shared with any other user. The potential this offers for a virus to spread is a nightmare.

More sophisticated operating systems, such as Novell NetWare, have multiple levels of security. Individual users can be given read/write access to a restricted area of the network disk, but read-only access to the areas containing software. Supervisor level access rights can be required before write access to the software is granted.

If network security is being used, should a user run a program infected with a virus, the infection would be confined to the area of the network disk to which that user had write access. The fear that a virus could bypass the security mechanisms and travel directly from PC to PC via the network cable is unfounded. To achieve this would require at least a detailed knowledge of the network adapter hardware and communications protocols and even then it would probably be impossible.

The greatest risk would occur if the supervisor logged in – having network-wide access rights – using a PC on which a virus was active. The virus would then have the opportunity to create havoc over the entire network. In fact, only the LOGIN program would need to be infected for the virus to be able to transmit itself to every machine on the network. Every user who logged in using the infected program would immediately infect their own PC. Consequently, a supervisor should always reboot the system from a clean, write-protected boot disk before logging in unless he is positive that the machine being used is virus-free. If the supervisor is scrupulously careful, and users are given no greater access rights than they need, the risk of a virus infecting files on a network can be kept to a minimum.

16.5 Virus Symptoms

If a virus manages to infect a machine, there are many ways it can use to announce its existence. It may simply put a message on the screen, such as *Your PC is now Stoned. Legalise marijuana* which is displayed by the Stoned virus. Alternatively, strange screen behaviour may be noticed, such as text falling to the bottom of the screen character by character (Cascade), or a bouncing ball moving around (Italian). Some viruses may remain undetected until files start disappearing or being corrupted, or the disk is scrambled.

A user who is completely familiar with the way his PC normally operates might notice the presence of a virus before it gives itself away. The sort of behaviour that could indicate the presence of a virus includes:

❏ Programs taking longer than normal to load

❏ More disk activity than normal for an operation

❏ Disk accesses occurring for no apparent reason

❏ Disk volume name changes

❏ Hidden files or bad sectors appearing

❏ Changes to the size of executable files

❏ Unexpected changes to file date and time

❏ Less free memory available than usual

❏ Random, unexplained errors occurring.

Regular running of the DOS utility CHKDSK would be sufficient to highlight many of these changes to a system's behaviour. However, few users can remember how many bad sectors or how much free memory their system has. For most people, virus detection software is the safest way to ensure that a virus is detected before it has a chance to do any damage.

16.6 Virus Detection

There are three principal methods of virus detection. The first works by looking for patterns of bytes – the *signature* – which indicate that a file contains a particular virus. It has the advantage that it can be used on any disk, even one that has never been seen before. It is also fast, so running the software is not too lengthy a task. Its disadvantage is that it can only detect viruses that it has been programmed to recognise, so to remain effective, the program must be frequently updated. This type of program is called a *scanner*.

The second method of detection works by *fingerprinting* files – calculating a sophisticated checksum for each – and comparing the result with that which was obtained on a previous occasion when the disk was virus-free. The mathematics of the checksum is such that the odds are millions to one against a virus altering a file and still producing the same fingerprint. The disadvantage of this method is that it works by comparing checksums with a previous value, so it is useful for checking known disks for virus infection, but not diskettes that have come from elsewhere and have not been checked before. The checksum calculation is also fairly time-consuming. The advantage is that fingerprinting will detect any modification to a file, so any virus will be detected, not merely those that the program knows about. This category of software is known as *checksummers*.

Virus detection programs using either of these methods are available, and are essential for running periodic tests on disks. VIRUSCAN from McAfee Associates uses the first detection method and has an option, if a program switch is set, of also using the second. This combination provides an effective tool for detecting virus infection.

Anti-virus software is available which will sit in memory, and check program files as they are loaded. A small memory overhead is incurred, and loading takes longer because of the time taken to check the file. However, if the software is loaded as part of the AUTOEXEC.BAT procedure then no deliberate effort is required by the user. This is an advantage if the user cannot be relied upon to check disks manually.

The detection methods described both suffer from one major disadvantage: they can only detect virus infection after it has occurred. A third type of anti-virus program – called a *monitor* – works by warning the user whenever it detects the type of activity that would be performed by a virus: writing to executable files, tampering with the boot sector, attempts to format a disk and so on. The problem with this type of software is that there are so many ways in which a virus can go about its business that it is almost impossible to monitor them all. Many virus activities are indistinguishable from legitimate use of the PC. Consequently, the user will receive warnings every time he formats a disk, compiles a program and so on.

Most detection programs in this category assume that viruses will use DOS or BIOS function calls to carry out their tasks. Surprisingly, many viruses do use documented methods of accessing system resources. Others use more sophisticated techniques such as accessing hardware registers directly, and thereby avoid detection. Some viruses –

known as *stealth* viruses – can hide signs of their presence (such as an increased .EXE or .COM file size). Therefore it is unwise to place too much faith in the third type of anti-virus software.

No virus detection method is infallible. Virus specialists recommend that you should use all three types of detection software to provide as good protection as it is possible to get. Since most of them also make money by selling anti-virus software, one may take a cynical view of such a recommendation, although since there are deficiencies in each method of detection, it probably has some validity.

For cost-effective virus protection, the best choice would be to use a scanner, obtaining regular updates from a reliable source. Most viruses encountered are well-known and readily detected by this type of software. In a business environment, management controls, such as discouraging the use of games and software from unknown sources, will help to minimise the risks. Should the worst happen, and a virus attack occurs, an effective backup procedure will provide the final safeguard.

16.7 Dealing with a Virus Attack

If the worst happens, and a virus attack occurs or is suspected, don't panic! It's simply a technical problem that can be dealt with in a calm, logical way. Here's what to do:

Stop using the computer.

There's a small risk that any work done since the virus installed itself on the machine may be lost anyway, so there is no point in carrying on. But leave the system switched on – the next reboot might trigger some destructive action, if it hasn't already.

Call an expert.

This is one of those occasions when you can't have too much real expertise on hand. Some viruses are unforgiving of inexpert attempts to remove them. Non-technical users should not try to deal with the problem themselves.

Collect together any diskettes that have been recently used on the infected machine.

Every diskette will eventually have to be checked for the presence of the virus. Try to identify from whom each diskette was received, and to whom any were sent. This will help in tracing the source of the infection, as well as who else may be affected.

Tell others in the office that a computer virus attack is suspected.

If one PC in an office has a virus, it's quite possible that others will also have it. Tell others to make them aware of the situation. Then they can be on the alert for the symptoms on other machines, and stop exchanging diskettes with other users, until the problem has been cleared up.

If you *are* the virus expert, you'll need to put together a basic toolkit in readiness for dealing with a suspected virus attack. This should contain the following:

- *A write protected bootable DOS disk* that also contains FORMAT.COM and a disk editor such as the Norton Utilities' DISKEDIT.EXE.

- *A write protected disk containing anti-virus software.* This should contain both detection software to check for the presence of viruses, such as McAfee SCAN, and disinfectant software for removing viruses from infected disks, such as McAfee CLEANUP.

- *A write protected disk containing backup software,* together with some blank media for backing up important data files.

If the problem does seem to have been caused by a virus, rather than operator error, a software bug or a hardware fault, this is what you should do to minimise the spread, detect and then eradicate the virus:

- **If the infected computer was logged on to a network** it may be advisable to tell all users to log off, and close down the network. Whether this is strictly necessary depends on how good the security of the network operating system is. Many viruses cannot infect files on network drives. With those that can, the network security will contain the infection to areas to which the user has write access privileges. Be aware, however, that if the user of the infected machine has copied program files to part of the network disk that is shared with other users, then there is a strong possibility that the virus could have spread elsewhere.

- **Cold boot the PC using the write protected DOS disk.** This means, *switch the machine off*, wait a few seconds, then switch it on again with the bootable diskette in drive A:. Some viruses are able to survive a warm boot (Ctrl/Alt/Del) so this procedure will ensure that the virus is no longer in memory. From now until the machine is completely disinfected, you will be working entirely using software loaded from write protected diskettes. Take care that no program is loaded from a hard disk or other floppies. Make sure the PATH environment string is blank to help ensure this.

- **Use the virus checking software to check the disks that were in use at the time the virus was discovered.** Check the hard disk(s) first, if any, then any diskettes that were being used.

If a virus is found, begin the removal procedure. There is a risk with some types of virus, such as those which write to the FAT or partition table, that the data could be lost during the removal procedure. Apart from anything else, it is easy to make an irreversible error using something like the Norton Utilities. Before starting to disinfect a disk, consider what backups are available. If there is important work on the disk that has not been backed up, then it is possible to take backup copies of *text or data files only* either by copying them to clean diskettes or by using backup software, *as long as this is run from a clean, write protected diskette.*

16.8 Virus Removal

There are many ways to rid a system of a virus infection. By far the simplest method is to use commercial virus eradication software, such as CLEANUP from McAfee Associates. This program will identify and erase most of the common viruses automatically, taking just a few seconds on a typical hard disk. Because it is so quick and easy to use, this type of program can pay for itself the first time it is needed.

Some viruses are harder to remove than others. In difficult cases, automatic eradication software may be unable to deal with the problem, or may simply delete the infected file. There are some programs that have been written to remove a specific virus. Many of these are in the public domain, and are available on bulletin boards if needed.

If an infected disk contains only backed up or recoverable data or software that can be reinstalled from the original distribution disks, the fastest solution may be simply to wipe it clean using a utility like the Norton Utilities WIPEDISK, or low-level format it if a hard disk, then reformat it and reinstall the software and data. If this approach is taken, make sure when restoring data from the backup that no infected executables are restored at the same time!

A boot sector virus may be removed by cold-booting the machine from a clean DOS diskette, then using the SYS command to overwrite the boot sector of the infected disk with a new copy of the operating system. A virus which affects the FAT or partition table can frequently be removed by using a disk sector editor such as Norton's Utilities to write over the virus with zeros, then Norton Disk Doctor to recover the disk. If the disk seems unrecoverable, Norton's Unformat is quite often successful at recovering all except the root directory of the disk. Full details for running these utilities are given in the Norton Utilities manual. If you intend to try using this method of disinfection, it would be a good idea to practice first on an uninfected, fully backed-up system.

However you decide to deal with a virus infection, I emphasise again that *it is important to ensure that no virus is activated during the disinfection process*. This is achieved by switching the machine off, then booting up from a known clean, write-protected DOS disk. All utilities used must be run from write-protected diskettes, to remove any possibility that they could become infected.

If you are unsure how to remove a particular virus, the best idea is to call in a specialist. If the virus cannot be eradicated immediately, the infected machine should be immobilised and any infected diskettes locked away in a safe place until they can be made clean.

Once the virus has been removed, *check the disk again using the virus checking software*. Mark diskettes so that you know that they have been checked. At this point, you have broken the back of the problem. You can take time out to carry out a post-mortem to see how the infection occurred in the first place, and what can be done to prevent it happening in the future.

It is also a good idea to scan *all* diskettes to check that they are virus-free. It only needs a single infected diskette, currently lying forgotten in a drawer somewhere, to be inserted into a PC and run, and you will have the same problem all over again.

16.9 Virus Removal on Networks

If you think a PC network may be infected by a virus, extra special care is needed. To check the system, you should log on to the network using only known virus-free software. This may be difficult if you have an automatic login script that runs software from the network drive. Cold-boot the PC from a write protected diskette containing all the relevant network software, and use a login name that runs no login script at all.

A virus checker may take some time to run on a large network drive. With the possibility of a virus active it is obviously inadvisable for anyone to log in as supervisor with write access to all the system software. If publicly available software on the disk has become infected then the network should be closed down and you will need to proceed with great care.

16.10 Backups: The Ultimate Safeguard

The value of regular backups cannot be over-emphasised. Virus infection is just one of the possible disasters that can strike a PC. Recovery from any disaster is much less painful if a recent backup exists. If a destructive virus infects a system and wipes out the contents of the disk before it is detected, then no disinfector program is going to be able to recover the data. Your backup is your only hope of getting anything back at all.

If a virus attack occurs and no disinfector program is available, restoring the system from the most recent backup may be the only practical solution. However, if programs as well as data are to be restored bear in mind that some viruses can remain dormant in a system for a long time. It may be that only a rarely-used program is infected. Even when restoring to a newly reformatted disk, the virus check should be run again to ensure that the system is clean before considering the problem solved.

Summary

Computer viruses are one of the most serious problems affecting the use of personal computers today. Steps can be taken to minimize the likelihood of a PC becoming infected. These include:

❏ Using anti-virus software to check any diskettes received before they are used

❏ Write-protecting boot disks and others from which programs are run

❏ Discouraging the use of games and other software of unknown origins

❏ On a network, using the in-built security to ensure that users do not have write access to parts of the network disk on which software is stored.

In a business environment, it is essential to have a plan for dealing with a virus attack should one occur. This includes:

❏ Ensuring users know what to do and who to call if a virus is suspected

❏ Having virus detection and disinfection software available for use if needed

❏ Ensuring that all users take regular backups of their data.

Every PC user or technician must hope that he or she will never have to deal with a case of virus infection. Unfortunately, the chances of that hope being fulfilled are small. Maintaining a state of readiness is important, not only for your own peace of mind, but as part of the global fight to prevent the spread of this malicious software. If every PC user was prepared, and every PC protected, viruses could not survive. The harder we make life for viruses, the easier it will be for ourselves.

17

Networking

PC networks are becoming very popular. If you work with PCs in a business environment you'll have to get to grips with networking at sometime or other, if you haven't already. It is a subject that could fill a large book in its own right. This chapter will give you an overview of PC networking, and an insight into some of the technical issues involved.

Networks fall into two main classes. A typical PC network – anything from half a dozen to several hundred PCs in a single office or building – is a *local area network* or LAN. Separate LANs in different parts of the country – or even the world – can be linked together using communications lines leased from the national telecommunications service providers. This is called a *wide area network* or WAN. Another term you may come across is MAN. This stands for *metropolitan area network*, a network that is confined within a single town or city.

17.1 Determining the Requirements

People network PCs for a variety of reasons. A network allows users to share data files. It makes it possible for them to communicate with each other using electronic mail. It also makes it easier to provide a group of PCs with access to another system, such as a mainframe. Network PCs don't need to have a hard disk of their own, which can save money. A multi-user copy of a software package may be cheaper than several individual copies, which is another cost saving. Finally, it is easier to back up data regularly if it is held on a central file server instead of several separate hard disks.

However, networks are not the solution to all PC problems. Getting the network set up can be time-consuming. It will require ongoing support. Resilience becomes an issue. If one standalone PC fails out of half a dozen it is not a big problem. If the network file server goes down then nobody can access their data, which spells trouble for someone!

Though savings on software and hard disks can be made, they are unlikely to offset the extra cost of the network operating system and hardware. So a network must be justified for other reasons. It's not worth putting one in just so that a group of users can share a printer. A smart printer switch will achieve the same result much more simply and cheaply.

17.2 Types of LAN

Once you've identified a requirement, you'll have to decide on the sort of network that best meets your needs. Factors which will influence this decision include cost, the current and expected maximum number of users, and the type of work they will be doing. LAN products span a wide range of costs. As with most things, you get what you pay for. But there is no point in paying for things you don't need.

One important point to bear in mind when considering any type of LAN is that network software takes up memory. These days, it's not uncommon to come across applications which require 550Kb or more of free memory to run. That's why DOS 5 allows you to load much of the operating system in high memory. Yet many LAN drivers leave much less than that once they have been loaded. If you want to avoid the embarrassing situation in which you start up your new LAN and then find that you can't load the application you intended to run, check the memory requirements before purchasing. You may need to investigate the use of smart LAN cards, which hold network drivers on the card itself rather than in system memory.

17.3 Server-based LANs

Server-based networks offer the greatest resilience and power. These are exemplified by Novell NetWare, the most popular PC network operating system. In this type of LAN, one or more machines function as a file server. That is, their job is to store and retrieve files for the workstations on the network. Files on the file server can be accessed by workstations using logical drives. To an end user, the network drive is indistinguishable from a local hard disk, except that it has a different drive letter and its access time is slower. Under NetWare, the first logical drive often appears as drive F:.

A LAN can have other types of server. LAN workstations do not often have a direct connection to a printer. Instead, a print server is used. This is a PC which receives data to be printed from workstations on the network, and spools them out to one or more printers. Under NetWare, a file server can be a print server as well.

A comms server is a machine that interfaces to external systems, such as a mainframe.

Workstation software communicates with the comms server over the network, and makes it seem as if the user has a direct connection to the host from his or her own PC.

Network servers can be either dedicated or non-dedicated. A dedicated server cannot be used as a normal PC for work under DOS. This has some advantages. Most users have had the PC crash on them at one time or another. If this happened on the server, then any work which that server was processing for other users would be lost. In the case of a file server, files could be corrupted and data lost. On a non-dedicated server, there is nothing to stop a user crashing the machine or rebooting it, and causing the problems just described. For maximum security and reliability, therefore, a server must be dedicated to the task.

Another reason for avoiding non-dedicated servers is one of performance. Server tasks can be quite processor-intensive, and the power of a PC is limited. The user of a non-dedicated server will notice the machine running very slowly while it is carrying out work for other network users. Similarly, the response times for other LAN users will be affected by whatever the server's user is doing. The memory taken up by the server software will, in any case, reduce that available to DOS. This will limit its usefulness as a workstation. A non-dedicated server is a compromise. It should be avoided if possible.

17.4 Peer-to-peer LANs

Server-based LANs provide excellent performance, but are expensive. In particular, they require additional machines to be purchased and set aside as servers. For the less demanding, more budget-conscious user, peer-to-peer networks offer a lower-cost alternative. As the name implies, all machines on the network are equal; there are no special server devices. Each PC user can elect to share his printer, or part of his hard disk, with other users of the network. The network software usually provides facilities to enable each user to decide who is allowed access to what. Examples of peer-to-peer LANs include Artisoft's LANtastic and D-Link's LANsmart.

Peer-to-peer LANs provide a cheap way for a group of PC users to share resources, but they suffer from all the disadvantages of non-dedicated servers that have just been discussed. There is nothing to prevent a user from crashing his machine or rebooting it while another is accessing the hard disk or the printer. The responsiveness of a PC will be noticeably reduced whenever another user is sharing its resources. The LAN software will reduce the memory available for DOS programs.

The security features provided by peer-to-peer LAN operating systems are also usually fairly limited. For example, there is often nothing to stop a user from reading or deleting other people's files which have been stored on his hard disk.

17.5 Zero Slot LANs

An even lower-cost variation on the peer-to-peer LAN theme is the zero slot LAN (ZSL). ZSLs are so called because they use the serial or parallel port as the means of communication. They don't need a special LAN adapter card, so no expansion slot is taken up. They provide all the usual LAN facilities: file sharing, printer spooling and so on. However, the maximum number of workstations that can be supported is low – often as few as two – and data transfer is slow. The maximum speed that a PC serial port can achieve is 115,000bps, around a tenth of the speed of the slowest conventional LAN systems and just a hundredth the speed of Ethernet.

At the bottom end of the scale, products like The $25 Network and the shareware QuickLAN use the serial port and no other hardware to allow two or three PCs to be linked together. More sophisticated systems such as 3X USA's 3X Link-16 use special adapters that plug into the parallel port between the PC and the printer and allow up to 16 machines to be networked together. A quick scan through the pages of a computer magazine will reveal several other similar products.

The main advantage of zero slot LANs is the low cost. The biggest disadvantage is performance. Apart from the low data transfer speed over the wire, ZSLs take a lot of processing power. Because they do not use a dedicated adapter card, the PC must do all the work, and it can grind exceedingly slowly while another user is accessing the disk. All the disadvantages of peer-to-peer LANs also apply. However, as a way of linking together a few PCs which most of the time operate as standalones, ZSLs offer an attractive and economical solution.

17.6 Multi-user DOS

Though not strictly a LAN, a multi-user DOS compatible operating system such as Concurrent DOS 386 from Digital Research can often be the most cost-effective way of providing PC functionality to a small number of users. The operating system runs on an 80386-based PC, using the PC monitor and keyboard as one of the workstations. The other users use terminals, which are attached by serial connections.

The biggest disadvantage of this type of system is that, generally, terminals can only operate in text mode. The only graphics they can display are character-based line graphics. However, in 1991, Digital Research announced an upgraded version of Concurrent DOS called Multi-User DOS 5.0. This supports CGA graphics on terminals. Unfortunately, the speed limitations of a serial link make it impractical to support the higher resolution graphics standards such as EGA or VGA that are commonly used today.

For text-based applications, though, multi-user DOS can often deliver much better performance than a conventional LAN. This is because there is no LAN cable to slow the passage of data from the disk to the workstation. Data moves between the hard disk, CPU and memory at the speed of the PC bus. The processor power is shared between all users, so as the number of users increases, a gradual degradation in performance will be noticed. However, since most PC applications spend most of the time waiting for a user to press keys on the keyboard, there is usually plenty of CPU resource going idle. A modest 25MHz 80386 should be able to service four or five concurrent users without difficulty. More powerful processors would allow quite a large system to be run.

The main problem with multi-user DOS systems is that it is quite easy for a user to crash either his or her own session, or the system as a whole. One reason is software incompatibility; the processor is not running true MS-DOS, and if an application relies on a DOS feature that is not emulated exactly by the multi-user operating system, it may fail. Another is that PC applications are written for the single-user PC environment. They expect to have the whole machine to themselves. So they may access the PC hardware directly or do other things to upset the running of a multi-user system. The operating system must try to cope with this anti-social behaviour. Mostly, it does a good job, but the occasional program will crash it.

Multi-user DOS compatible systems are satisfactory when the users will only be running software that works reliably in that environment. They should not be given access to the DOS prompt, from which they could run other programs and perhaps crash the system.

17.7 LAN Topologies

One factor that will help to decide which is the most appropriate type of LAN to use is whether there is a need to connect with other systems. If there is, or is likely to be, a requirement to link with other LANs, minicomputers or mainframes, then a server-based solution is probably the best choice. This is because server-based LANs are most prevalent in a corporate environment, where networks are more sophisticated. Consequently there is a wide range of compatible products available to enable you to link the LAN with a multitude of other types of computer system.

Another decision that needs to be made is which network topology to use? Peer-to-peer LANs and ZSLs usually support just a single topology, often proprietary, so the decision is made for you. For server-based LANs like NetWare, you must make the decision. As there is an increasing demand for networks to be interconnected, it makes sense to adopt a topology that is not proprietary, and which has become a standard. Currently, in the PC networking arena, the two most widely used standards are IBM Token Ring and Ethernet.

17.8 Ethernet

Ethernet is a standard that pre-dates PCs by many years. It developed from the system used by universities to link Unix computers. Ethernet uses a bus topology, as shown in Figure 17.1. This means that the cable runs from point A to point B, and devices are connected along the way.

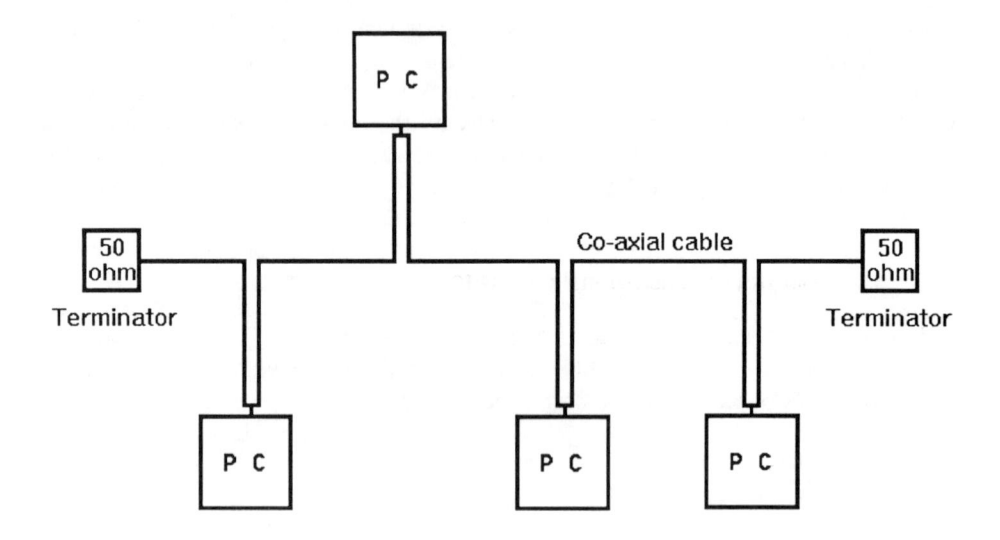

Figure 17.1: Ethernet LAN topology

Traditionally, an Ethernet bus uses co-axial cable. There are two varieties. Thin Ethernet – often called *Cheapernet* – uses thin co-axial cable such as is used for CB radio. Thick Ethernet is simply a thicker co-axial cable, and usually has a yellow PVC outer. Thick Ethernet is more expensive, but has a lower loss than Cheapernet, and so can be used for longer cable runs.

Whichever type is used, a terminator must be attached to each end of the cable. These stop the transmitted signals from being reflected back from the open ends. The reflected signals would cause interference that would seriously degrade the performance of the network.

Ethernet uses a protocol known as CSMA/CD, which stands for *Carrier Sensing*

Multiple Access with Collision Detection. This is a protocol whereby each network card listens on the net, and will only transmit if no other signals are present. If two devices start to transmit at the same time – known as a *collision* – they both stop immediately, and wait for a random period before trying again. This time, one of them will go first. The other will wait for the first one to finish before transmitting. Both messages will therefore be clearly received.

Ethernet is fast. However, as network utilisation increases, so does the probability of collisions occurring, and performance starts to drop off rapidly. In most situations, over 100 devices can be attached to the network before any noticeable degradation occurs. The big advantage of Ethernet over other network topologies is that there is a much greater choice of products that can enable you to achieve interworking with other computer systems.

An Ethernet LAN requires Ethernet adapter cards to be installed in each PC. If you use Cheapernet then the co-axial cable is brought out to the back of the PC and attached to the BNC socket on the network card using a T adapter. This makes the network more vulnerable to cabling problems. If the connection is broken – perhaps because the user disconnects the cable so as to move a PC – then the whole network will go down.

Thick Ethernet cable is more unwieldy, so it is usually run along ducting in the wall. A device called a transceiver must be fitted to the cable at any point at which a PC is to be connected. The 9-pin socket on the Ethernet card is used to link the PC to the transceiver using a drop cable. Usually, when installing an Ethernet card in a PC, jumpers on the card must be set according to whether thin or thick Ethernet is being used.

17.9 IBM Token Ring

Token Ring is a generic term for a type of network in which all the devices are connected in a ring. A signal called a *token* is passed from one device to its neighbour. A device may only transmit a message when it is in possession of the token. This protocol eliminates the problem of collisions, and so Token Ring networks do not suffer the degradation of performance that affects Ethernet when utilisation becomes high.

IBM Token Ring is a specific implementation of the Token Ring topology. Originally an IBM proprietary product, it has now been adopted as an international standard. There are not yet the wide range of connectivity products that are available to Ethernet users. However, IBM Token Ring is the ideal network to use where there is a requirement to link with other IBM computers.

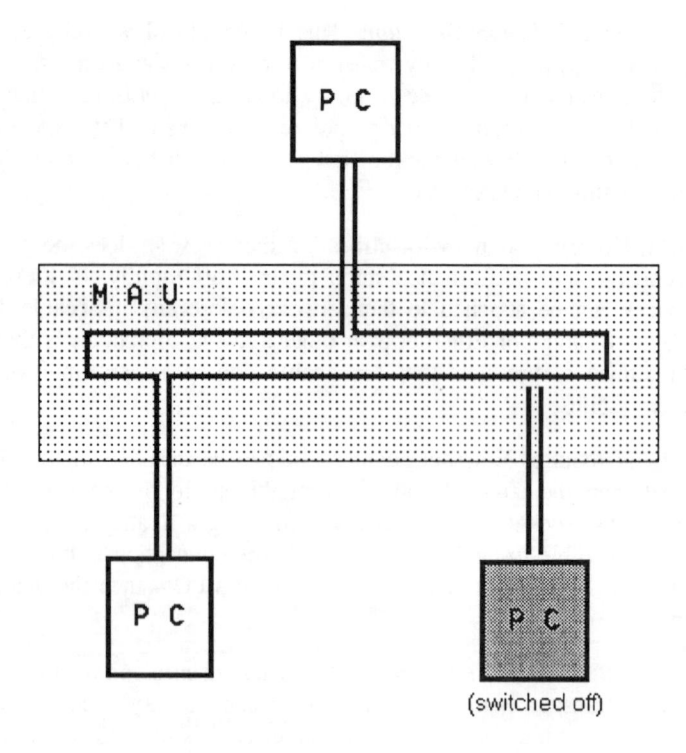

Figure 17.2: IBM Token Ring LAN topology

Superficially, an IBM Token Ring network appears to have a star, rather than a ring configuration, as shown in Figure 17.2. Each device is linked, using special IBM cable, to a box called a *Multi-Station Access Unit* (MAU). However, the cable contains both an outward and a return path. When the cable is connected to an active device, a current flows in it. This causes a relay in the MAU to switch open so that the device is included in the ring. Should the cable become detached from the device, or even damaged, the current no longer flows. The relay then closes so that the ring continuity is maintained. This gives the IBM Token Ring much greater resilience than Cheapernet.

IBM Token Ring is a good system, but it has some disadvantages. One is the relative lack of choice of products to interface it to non-IBM systems. This is not as much of a problem as it once was, though. Another disadvantage is cost. The token ring protocol is more complicated to process, and so adapter cards are more complex and more expensive. The cost of the MAU and IBM Type 1 cable is much more than a reel of Cheapernet cable, too. However, particularly for mission critical networks, the extra resilience may justify the cost.

17.10 Unshielded Twisted Pair

Unshielded Twisted Pair is not, strictly speaking, a network topology. It is a cabling system that can be used for Ethernet or Token Ring networks and many other types of data communications. UTP, unlike co-ax or IBM Type 1 cable, is not inherently good at carrying high speed data. However, it has been developed over the last few years until satisfactory results over useful distances can be achieved. Its attraction as a network transport medium is that it is thin, cheap and already in place in many buildings. Standard telephone wiring uses UTP.

UTP is more susceptible to interference than either Ethernet or Type 1 cable, which are shielded. Its installation should be left to specialists if good results are to be achieved. However, its cheapness allows buildings to be *flood wired*, so that network access points can be provided anywhere there is likely to be a desk. Given the frequency with which people move offices, and the cost of making changes to networks that use traditional cabling methods, this is a big selling point. UTP will certainly become more popular in the years to come.

17.11 Fibre Optics

Fibre optics is another data transmission medium that is increasingly found in large, high-performance networks. Because light, not electrical signals, is used to carry the data, the bandwidth is much wider than can be achieved using copper wire. Consequently, much higher data rates are possible. The loss and susceptibility to interference are very low, so long cable runs can be used. Electromagnetic radiation is zero, making fibre optics ideal for networks carrying sensitive data.

Fibre optic cable is quite expensive, and so it is mostly used as a *backbone* linking together localised copper-based LANs within a building or site. In this situation, it is unlikely to concern you as a PC user or technician. However, costs are falling, and it is only a matter of time before it is commonplace to have fibre optic cable brought out to the PC on the desk-top.

17.12 Installing LAN Cards

Apart from the cable installation, most of the work involved in setting up a LAN is specific to the LAN operating system. Little general advice can be given here. You will need to find out who the users are and what software they will require access to, and then devise a directory structure for storing the software and user data files on the disk. You'll also need to give some attention to security requirements – not just passwords for logging on, but who should be allowed to access what data. Most importantly, you will also need to decide how backups are going to be carried out.

Unless you are using a zero slot LAN, you'll need to install a network card in each PC. Network cards, like other I/O cards, have hardware I/O ports, and probably require the use of an IRQ line and a DMA channel as well. Most cards will offer several choices for each of these resources, since network cards were not something for which IBM provided reserved addresses in the PC specification. It is important to avoid using addresses that conflict with other cards in the machine, or data may be corrupted and the machine will tend to crash. Inevitably, the user will blame the network itself for this sort of occurrence. For more about card conflicts, you should refer to Chapter 4.

Once the network is up and running, you may wish to consider maximising the memory available for DOS applications. On many machines, network drivers can be loaded into high memory using DOS 5's LOADHIGH command or similar features provided by memory managers such as QEMM, 386 to the Max or LOADSYS. Alternatively, the use of network-specific memory managers such as NETROOM or LANSpace may be considered. For PCs that only need access to the network some of the time, a solution may be to de-install the network TSRs when they are not required. Chapter 15 covers the whole issue of memory management in more detail.

Summary

PC networks are popular. But they are neither cheap to buy nor easy to run, so it is a good idea to be make sure that a network is really what you need. If it is, there is a variety of types to choose from. Server-based LANs are powerful and secure, but expensive and complex to administer. Peer-to-peer LANs allow existing PCs to share resources. They don't need extra machines to be set up as dedicated servers, but they are not as reliable or as secure. Zero slot LANs are the cheapest type of network of all. However, they have limited performance and expansion potential, and are really only suitable for standalone PCs with an occasional need to access resources on other machines.

The more sophisticated LAN operating systems offer a choice of network topologies. Ethernet is very popular, and offers high performance at moderate levels of utilisation, and the widest range of options for linking to other systems. IBM Token Ring is more robust, but expensive. It offers good connectivity to IBM systems, but has more limited options to other manufacturers' equipment. Unshielded twisted pair cabling is coming into prominence, particularly as a structured cabling system that can be used for voice or data traffic. Fibre optic cable is currently used primarily for linking LANs together, but will become more widespread as costs fall.

When network cards are installed, you need to take care to avoid conflicts with other cards in the machine. Network drivers take memory away from DOS, so their presence may make memory management more of an issue.

18

Developing Your Expertise

In the preceding chapters we covered every aspect of servicing and supporting IBM compatible personal computers. We described fault-finding and fault rectification techniques, and explained the theory and practice of hardware operation. We looked at the factors to be considered when installing a machine, and outlined a programme for preventive maintenance. We also examined ways of configuring and tuning PCs, the problems of computer viruses, and provided an overview of networking. If this has all been of interest, you're probably wondering what to do next to further develop your expertise and knowledge.

18.1 Building a Toolkit

First, ensure that you have all the tools you need to carry out the tasks you expect to perform. Chapter 12 gave suggestions for what should be included in your toolkit. How comprehensive it needs to be will depend to an extent on the amount of servicing – as distinct from configuration, upgrading and troubleshooting – you will be undertaking. This is something that only you – or perhaps your employer – can decide.

You'll also need a range of software tools. Chapter 12 gave suggestions for the diagnostic software that your toolkit should include. Many specific examples of commercial, shareware or public domain programs were discussed in Chapter 2 and subsequent chapters. Many of the shareware and PD utilities mentioned are available on a disk set obtainable from the publishers; details are given in Appendix 7.

Anti-virus software is essential these days, and was discussed in Chapter 16. Whichever packages you decide to use, you'll probably need copies on both 5.25in and 3.5in diskettes. Once you've made copies, you should write protect them to safeguard against virus infection.

18.2 Making a Hardware Record

The next stage is to make a detailed record of the hardware configuration of all the equipment you will be supporting. Knowing what is inside the box will often save you from having to take the lid off. Chapter 4 discussed hardware configuration, and included an example of a form that can be used to record the details for future reference.

Even if you intend leaving the job of servicing to a maintenance contractor, it is still worth considering setting up your own schedule for preventive maintenance. This should include a health check on the hard disk. Chapter 14 suggested a programme for preventive maintenance, while more information specific to hard disks was presented in Chapter 8.

18.3 Improving your Knowledge

If you have a real interest in the technical aspects of PCs you can never know too much about them and how they work. One problem with writing a book like this is that there is not a fixed set of faults which can occur, each with a specific solution. There will always be obscure faults that are difficult to track down. That's why, throughout the book, I have explained the hardware design and how it is supposed to work, so that you can use this information to try to understand the symptoms you observe. Lists of faults and possible solutions are of little use if the problem you have is one that isn't mentioned, so only the most common problems have been given this type of treatment.

Don't think you can stop learning simply because you have read to the end of the book. There is plenty more knowledge for you to discover. Publications such as PC Magazine and Byte often contain useful technical articles explaining the operation of particular system components. Hardware reviews can also be a useful source of information. Join a user group. If it is a good one, it will have a regular newsletter which may also contain useful hints and tips from the group's PC guru.

If you have an IBM Technical Reference Manual for the PC XT or AT then this is well worth reading. Though the machines they describe are now obsolete, these manuals define the *standard* PC. They are also comprehensive and well-written, and provide much useful low-level information about how PCs work.

18.4 Going Online

Electronic bulletin boards are another invaluable source of technical information and help. They are computer systems – ranging from a single PC to a network of minicomputers – which hold messages placed there by system users. Usually, they also contain public domain and shareware programs, along with bug fixes and workarounds for commercial packages. All you need to gain access to this world of information is your PC, a modem and a comms package.

Bulletin boards can be a life-saver when you hit that impossible-to-solve problem. Just log on and type in a message describing the equipment, its configuration and the fault. Soon, often within a couple of hours, other users have logged on, read the message and replied with suggestions on how to cure it.

If you become a regular bulletin board user, simply by reading the messages posted there every day you can pick up useful hints and tips for future use. And soon, the time will come when you'll see a message from someone asking for help, and you will be the one who can respond with the solution.

There are hundreds of bulletin boards you can connect to. Most are free, run by enthusiasts as a hobby in their spare time. The disadvantage of free boards is that they rarely have a large enough user base to provide a good response to cries for help. Their primary function is usually to provide software for downloading by other home computer hobbyists. Generally, amateur boards have just a single telephone line, and when you call them, more often than not your modem will report that the line is busy.

If you're a PC support professional, you'll want to use a professional service. Undoubtedly, the best online information service is CompuServe. Though not exclusively a service for computer techies, a large part of the system exists to facilitate the exchange of technical information.

CompuServe is organised into *forums*. Each forum covers a particular topic. For PC users there are forums for hardware, communications, systems and utilities, applications and programming. There are also forums for many hardware vendors. Some software manufacturers also have their own forums. Microsoft has a number, dealing with the various applications, programming languages and operating systems that they produce. Other software companies represented include Borland, Lotus, Nantucket, Novell and WordPerfect Corp.

What makes the CompuServe forums so valuable, compared with product-specific topics on other bulletin boards, is that they are visited regularly – and usually maintained – by support staff for the products concerned. So membership of CompuServe gives you a hot line direct to the hardware or software manufacturer. If you're tired of receiving indifferent support from your dealer, this could be the solution!

CompuServe has its own communications package *CompuServe Information Manager* (CIM), shown in Figure 18.1, which is designed to make the service attractive and easy to use. It isn't intended to minimise your connect charges, though. If you spend a lot of time online, these charges can quickly mount up. However, there are ways to reduce the cost.

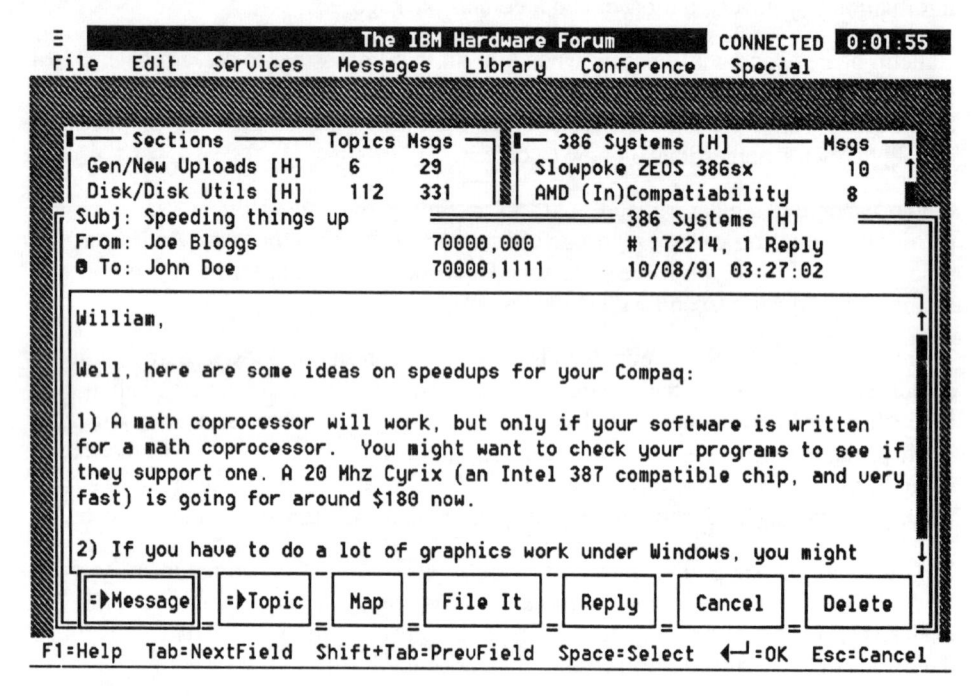

Figure 18.1: Using CompuServe Information Manager

AutoSIG is a public domain program designed specifically to access CompuServe. It will keep the time you are connected to the minimum possible. AutoSIG can be set up so that the first time you run it, it will sign on, visit each of the forums you have joined, and download a list of all the message titles or *headers*, showing the topics currently under discussion. After it signs off, you can review the list and mark the topics that are of interest, as shown in Figure 18.2.

AutoSIG will then go online a second time to download the text of the marked messages. When the program logs off again, you can browse through the downloaded messages, as shown in Figure 18.3, saving the most useful ones to disk or printing them. If you wish to respond to any message, AutoSIG allows you to create a reply offline. At the end of the browsing session, you can then go online a third time to post the replies to the appropriate forums.

```
- Marking 'WINADV' messages: 24 headers; HMN= 29513     TOP    1 - 23
  29383-   0:   FAX BOARDS                      S  5 / Enhanced Mode
  29400-   0:   Windows Enhanced/Network        S  5 / Enhanced Mode
  29344-   1:   Win386enh and Cakewalk          S  5 / Enhanced Mode
  29461-   0:   DOS trashes WINAPP font         S  5 / Enhanced Mode
  29303-   0:   Tapcis window v. full           S  5 / Enhanced Mode
  29346-   0:   Non-Win Apps                    S  5 / Enhanced Mode
  29299-   0:   Windows and DOS and Devs        S  5 / Enhanced Mode
  29300-   1:   Internal Stack Overflow         S  5 / Enhanced Mode
  29320-   0:   HELP! L123/W in enhanced        S  5 / Enhanced Mode
  29333-   1:   Disable C/A/D in Enhance        S  5 / Enhanced Mode
  29339-   1:   WIN 3.0 WINA20.386 file         S  5 / Enhanced Mode
  29360-   2:   NBW generates UAE               S  5 / Enhanced Mode
  29370-   3: M Help: Windows Crashes           S  5 / Enhanced Mode
  29380-   2:   Windows 3.0a                    S  5 / Enhanced Mode
  29441-   1:   Win3 vs CDrom                   S  5 / Enhanced Mode
  29364-   2:   Got more mem!                   S 10 / Optimization
  29352-   1:   Downloading Fonts               S 10 / Optimization
  29343-   0:   Blades                          S 11 / Shareware
  29338-   1:   Sounder Blaster - .VOC          S 11 / Shareware
  29367-   2:   Rename Upload?                  S 11 / Shareware
  29372-   2:   STABLE.ZIP Upload               S 11 / Shareware
  29392-   1:   New Windows Publications        S 11 / Shareware
  29414-   0:   COOK.ZIP                        S 11 / Shareware
      M>ark    Enter = unmark   ESCape = cancel   F10 = finished   S>ort by section
```

Figure 18.2: Marking topics of interest in AutoSIG

```
#: 13250 S2/DRDOS6                                                      96 %
    13-Oct-91  00:22:36
Sb: #13237-#DCONFIG.SYS
Fm: Andy N Other    70000,1234
To: Bob Smith       70000,4567

Bob, all my memory is Extended memory. However, via my CMOS, I'm able to
designate how much above 1mb I'd like use for EMS memory. I have set it to use
everything above 4MB. Now this may seem strange since I only have 4MB, but this
results in 384KB being used for EMS memory. This leaves me with a total of 3MB
extended. Now I've told QRAM that I want to use the entire EMS page frame (64k)
for upper memory purposes, so, in effect, I have no EMS memory that is useable
for anything. To answer your question, I have to use the EMS driver that came
with my board to map out the page frame.

Another oddity, if you will, about my system board, is that there is address
remapping/shadow RAM for BIOS, video ROM, and RAM support. The chipset is an
ACER M1207. The purported reason for the shadow RAM is to permit faster
execution of codes stored in ROM or video RAM by moving this ROM software to
local RAM. I have the option in CMOS to enable/disable all or part of this.
Evidently this movement or shadowing is done as soon as the system is powered
on and before the memory test begins. I'm not able to determine just where in
"local" RAM the ROM segments are moved; there isn't anymemory visible to me
that I can't account for in the total of 4MB.
              E>nter For More
```

Figure 18.3: Reading messages offline using AutoSIG

There are other online services besides CompuServe which are useful sources of technical information. Byte Information Exchange (BIX) – run by Byte Magazine – is another well-known example. In the UK, Compulink Information Exchange (CIX) has been established for many years. It has a loyal following of support technicians, applications developers and computer journalists among its members. Developed from the original BIX software, CIX is divided into conferences, which are equivalent to CompuServe's forums. CIX's somewhat arcane user interface contains special commands that can be used to minimise time spent online. New messages can be read into a file, which can then be downloaded and read offline.

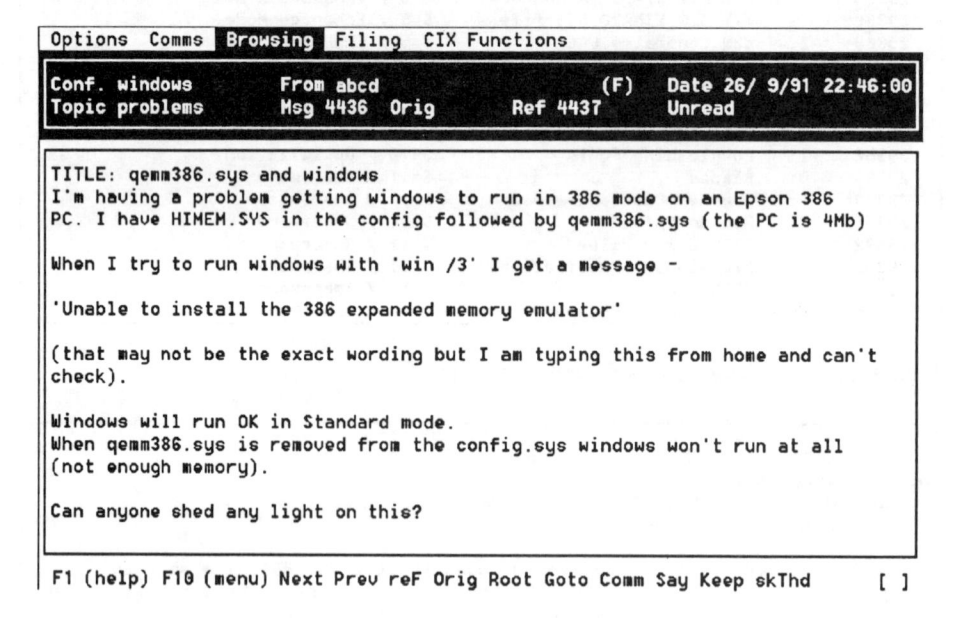

```
 Options  Comms  Browsing  Filing  CIX Functions
┌──────────────────────────────────────────────────────────────────┐
│Conf. windows       From abcd              (F)   Date 26/ 9/91 22:46:00│
│Topic problems      Msg 4436  Orig      Ref 4437  Unread          │
├──────────────────────────────────────────────────────────────────┤
│TITLE: qemm386.sys and windows                                    │
│I'm having a problem getting windows to run in 386 mode on an Epson 386│
│PC. I have HIMEM.SYS in the config followed by qemm386.sys (the PC is 4Mb)│
│                                                                  │
│When I try to run windows with 'win /3' I get a message -         │
│                                                                  │
│'Unable to install the 386 expanded memory emulator'              │
│                                                                  │
│(that may not be the exact wording but I am typing this from home and can't│
│check).                                                           │
│                                                                  │
│Windows will run OK in Standard mode.                             │
│When qemm386.sys is removed from the config.sys windows won't run at all│
│(not enough memory).                                              │
│                                                                  │
│Can anyone shed any light on this?                                │
└──────────────────────────────────────────────────────────────────┘
 F1 (help) F10 (menu) Next Prev reF Orig Root Goto Comm Say Keep skThd    [ ]
```

Figure 18.4: Using Matrix

CIX can be made easy to use. There are several offline message readers to choose from. The best is probably *Matrix*, a shareware program that can be downloaded from its own conference on CIX. An example of Matrix in use is shown in Figure 18.4.

A subscription to an online service can pay dividends. On numerous occasions, the advice I have received from other members of the service has saved me time and hence money equivalent to a whole year's connect charges. If you do decide to join an online service, I'd be happy to hear from you by electronic mail. My CompuServe ID is 100015,1242. On CIX I'm jmoss, or via Internet jmoss@cix.compulink.co.uk.

Conclusion

Servicing and supporting IBM PCs and compatibles can be interesting and fun. I hope all your equipment runs faultlessly. But if it doesn't, I hope that what you've read in this book will contribute to your success in solving the problem.

Appendix 1

Glossary of Terms

Access time: For memory, the length of time it takes the CPU to obtain a byte of data from memory once the address has been specified; for disk drives, the average length of time taken by the heads to seek to a particular track or cylinder.

Allocation unit: DOS 4 term for a cluster (*q.v.*).

Analogue: Works using infinitely variable electrical voltages.

Architecture: Used to describe a high-level view of the design of a computer system; the way the CPU, memory, I/O devices and so on are connected together to make a working computer.

ASCII: American Standard Code for Information Interchange – the standard set of characters represented by the byte values 0 to 127, used by PC compatible and other computers.

Asynchronous communications: The usual method of communication with PCs using the standard serial port; characters are sent singly, whenever they occur.

Backfilling: Technique of using the memory on an expanded memory board to replace as much as possible of the 640Kb base memory; the memory board hardware can then swap this memory in and out very quickly which improves the efficiency of multitasking software.

Bad sectors: Sectors on a disk which are damaged or unreliable, and have been marked as unusable by the system.

Base memory: The first 640Kb of memory available to DOS programs running on a PC.

Baud: Unit of measurement of communications speed – the number changes of state of the data signal per second; this usually equates to the number of bits per second.

BBS: Bulletin board system – a computer to which users can log on using a modem and leave messages for others to read and reply to; often public domain and shareware programs are available to be downloaded.

BIOS: Basic Input Output System – a set of program instructions in ROM which provide a hardware-independent interface between the operating system (usually DOS) or applications programs and the PC hardware.

Bit: Short for *binary digit*; the unit of counting in the binary numbering system, which can have the value 0 or 1; convenient for use by computers because it can be represented by a simple two-state switch – off or on.

Boot: The process by which a PC loads the operating system.

Boot sector: The first sector of a disk, which contains the partition table and the bootstrap code.

Bootstrap code: A simple loader program which is loaded by the system boot procedure, and which in turn loads the operating system into memory.

Bus: A channel for electrical signals which is used to link together all the various components inside a computer; provides a vehicle for the propagation of data, address and control information.

Byte: Smallest unit of data processed by a microcomputer, comprising eight bits; may hold an integer value from 0 to 255 or –128 to 127, or a single ASCII character.

Cache: A block of fast memory which is used to hold a copy of data stored on a slower device, so that it can be accessed more rapidly; a disk cache is used to speed up accesses to disk; fast processors often use memory cacheing since the speed of standard memory is not fast enough to allow the full processor speed to be achieved.

Cathode ray tube (CRT): Display device used in PC monitors, in which the picture is generated by scanning a modulated electron beam over a phosphor coated surface on the front of the screen.

Central processor unit (CPU): The part of a computer which actually executes the program instructions (*see microprocessor*).

Clock: An electronic circuit which beats time at very high speed and synchronises the activities of all the devices within the computer.

Cluster: The unit by which DOS allocates disk space to files; most commonly this is four or eight sectors (2Kb or 4Kb).

CMOS: Complementary Metal Oxide Silicon – this is a type of circuit which consumes very little power, and is frequently used in applications in which information is to be stored for long periods using only battery power, as in the setup data for AT class systems.

Code pages: Method provided by DOS for enabling national language characters to be displayed.

Conventional memory: Addressable memory within the 1Mb address space available to the 8088/8086 CPUs.

Convergence: The accuracy of the alignment of the three electron guns which produce red, green and blue in a colour CRT; if misaligned, white characters are fringed with primary colours.

Coprocessor: A special processor chip dedicated to the task of performing floating point arithmetic; this can provide an increase in performance for applications which do a lot of this type of calculation.

Cycle time: Length of time taken by one processor clock cycle; equal to 1/(clock speed).

Cylinder: Similar to a track, in a hard disk a cylinder represents all the tracks one above the other on each recording surface which are simultaneously accessible at one position of the heads.

Device driver: Special TSR program which is loaded permanently in memory to allow programs to use a particular device; often loaded using a DEVICE= statement in CONFIG.SYS.

Digital: Works by binary changes of electrical voltage (on/off).

DIP switch: Block of four or eight on/off switches in a dual-inline package.

Direct memory access (DMA): Process by which the system can transfer blocks of data to and from memory without the CPU needing to do the work.

DOS extender: Software which allows programs running under DOS on 80286 or better machines to run in extended memory.

Dot pitch: The distance between the phosphor dots on a colour monitor; the finer the pitch, the higher the display resolution which can be satisfactorily displayed.

Download: Process of transferring files from a remote system to your own.

Dual-inline (DIL): An integrated circuit package with two rows of connection pins, one on each side (*see also dual-inline package*).

Dual-inline package (DIP): Equivalent term to dual-inline.

Dynamic RAM (DRAM): Type of memory chip commonly used in computers which retains information only if periodically refreshed.

EMS: Expanded Memory Specification – a specification produced by Lotus, Intel and Microsoft for hardware and software to provide paged memory which is used by applications like Lotus 123 and Desqview; the latest version is known as LIM 4.0 EMS.

ESDI: Enhanced Small Device Interface – an improved version of the standard PC hard disk controller used with large hard disk and CD ROM drives.

Expanded memory: A type of memory expansion in which blocks of memory which are not themselves directly addressable by the CPU are swapped into buffers or *page frames* within the processor's address space and can be used to hold data for which there is insufficient space in conventional memory; this can be done using special hardware in an expanded memory card, or a software driver can simulate expanded memory using extended memory on an 80286 or later CPU.

Expanded memory manager: Software driver which provides functions to enable applications programs to use expanded memory.

Expansion card: Circuit card which plugs into the expansion bus connectors on the PC motherboard.

Extended memory: Memory above 1Mb which is addressable by 80286 or later processors when running in protected mode.

Firmware: Programs which have been burned into ROM.

Flow control: A method of ensuring that, over a communications link, the sending device only sends data when the receiver is ready to receive.

FM: Frequency modulation – method of recording data on to a disk by varying the frequency of magnetic pulses.

Format: The process of initialising a disk ready for use.

Fragmentation: The tendency for the clusters which collectively make up a file, and the files which make up a directory, to become scattered all over a disk.

Full duplex: Method of communication in which both ends can transmit and receive data at the same time.

Half duplex: Method of communication not often used nowadays in which only one end can transmit (and the other receive) at a time.

Handshaking: Alternative term for flow control (*q.v.*).

Hard-sectored: Disks on which the position of the sectors is determined by sector holes punched into the disk itself; such disks cannot be read in a standard PC drive.

Hayes commands: A set of commands used to give instructions to intelligent modems; each command begins with the characters AT.

High memory area (HMA): A 64Kb block of memory starting just at the 1Mb boundary which can be accessed by an 80286 or better running in real mode with the aid of a special driver.

Horizontal scan rate: The number of scan lines per second which are generated by a display adaptor at a particular display resolution.

Host: A remote computer which allows you to log on.

Host adaptor: An SCSI interface card.

IDE: Integrated Drive Electronics – a hard disk controller built into the drive itself; requires only a simple bus adapter card.

Input/output (I/O) port: Uniquely addressable location which is connected to a particular device within the computer and is used to get bytes of information to and from it.

Interlacing: A method of reducing the amount of flicker on a computer display at low vertical scan rates by scanning every other line on one pass, and then filling in the missing lines on the second.

Interleave: A scheme for distributing the logical sectors on a track so that sector n+1 is always just about to pass under the head as soon as the controller has finished processing sector n.

Interrupt: An electrical signal which is generated by a device within the computer when it requires attention from the central processor.

Interrupt request line (IRQ): A single data line used by a particular device when it wishes to signal an interrupt.

Interrupt service routine (ISR): Program instructions which are executed immediately a particular interrupt request is received; an ISR will typically save the current state of what the CPU is doing, perform some time-critical processing for the interrupting device, then restore and carry on with what it was doing before.

Interrupt vector: A single element of a table containing the start addresses of interrupt service routines, which is held so that the CPU can find where to jump to when an interrupt is received.

Jumper: Method of setting configuration options on PC boards; consists of two or more pins, which can be linked together by placing a sleeve over two of them.

Kilobyte (Kb): 1,024 bytes.

Landing zone: Track or cylinder of a hard disk to which the heads should be moved when parking them.

Large-scale integration (LSI): Technique of incorporating the functions of a number of discrete integrated circuits on one large chip.

LCD: Liquid Crystal Display – a type of display used in digital watches, calculators and laptops; favoured because it needs little current.

LIM: Lotus-Intel-Microsoft; producers of the expanded memory specification supported by most memory managers and used by many software packages.

Logic bomb: Program code which is designed to cause some destructive action when a particular trigger event occurs.

Low-level format: The process of marking sector headers on to a hard disk drive.

Megabyte (Mb): 1,000 kilobytes.

Megahertz (MHz): Unit of frequency; 1MHz is one million times per second.

Memory cycle: The process of reading from or writing to a single location in memory.

Memory manager: A program or device driver which provides EMS and/or XMS functionality and often other additional features.

Memory map: The way in which different areas of memory are used for different purposes in the design of a computer.

Memory mapped display: Method used in PC display adaptors in which the buffer holding information representing what is displayed on the screen is held in a buffer in memory which is directly addressable by programs.

Microprocessor: Large integrated circuit which is essentially a CPU on a single chip.

MFM: Modified frequency modulation – method of encoding which doubles the density of data which can be stored compared with FM.

MNP: Microcom Networking Protocol – a *de facto* standard for error correction and data compression in modems.

Modem: Acronym for *modulator/demodulator*; a device which turns digital signals into audio tones, and vice versa, to allow computers to communicate over ordinary telephone lines.

Motherboard: The main circuit board in a PC, which usually contains the expansion bus, the processor and some memory.

Null modem: Device to allow two computers to be connected using standard modem cables without a modem being present.

Original equipment manufacturer (OEM): A manufacturer who sells equipment or software made by another company under his own name.

Page frame: Block of memory below the 1Mb boundary which is used as a window for accessing swapped-in blocks of expanded memory.

Parking: Action of moving the heads of a hard disk away from the area used to store data to avoid damage to this area during transportation.

Partition: An area of a hard disk which has been designated for a particular purpose, e.g. for use by DOS.

Partition table: Part of the first sector on a hard disk, containing the starting and finishing points and other information about the partitions on a disk.

Platter: A single disk, with one or two recording surfaces, in a hard disk.

Power on self test (POST): The system tests which are performed whenever a PC is switched on.

Protected mode: Mode of CPU operation available on 80286 and later processors allowing extended memory over 1Mb to be addressed, and providing a protection system so that memory belonging to one program cannot be accessed or tampered with by another.

Random access memory (RAM): A linear array of volatile memory in which each byte can be individually accessed by means of its unique address.

Raster scanning: Method of scanning the electron beam in a CRT in which the beam scans repeatedly from left to right while moving from top to bottom to cover the entire screen surface.

Read only memory (ROM): Memory chip in which the information has been *burnt* *in* during manufacture so that it is retained even when no power is applied and cannot be overwritten by programs.

Real mode: Mode of CPU operation in which it emulates an 8086 processor and can only address up to 1Mb of RAM.

Refresh rate: Synonym for vertical scan rate (*q.v.*).

RLL: Run length limited – a way of describing data encoding methods; usually used to describe a method which uses a variable length code which allows 50% more data to be stored on a disk than by using MFM.

RS-232C: A standard for a serial interface which defines the purpose and voltage levels of the various signals used by the interface.

Scan code: Numeric code generated by the keyboard when a particular key is pressed or released.

Sector: Each track on a disk is divided into a number of sectors; each sector usually contains 512 bytes of data.

Sector header: A special code, invisible to user programs, which is used by the hard disk controller to identify individual sectors on the disk.

Sector translation: A scheme in which a hard disk having particular characteristics *pretends* to have different characteristics which are more commonly supported by existing machines.

Seek: The action of the heads in a disk drive moving from one track to another.

Seek time: The time taken for the heads in a disk drive to move from one track to the next.

SCSI: Small Computer Systems Interface – an (almost standard) interface for connecting various types of device to a computer.

Shadowing: The process of copying the contents of a ROM into RAM; since the access time of RAM is faster than ROM, wait states are not needed, so the performance of the system is improved.

Skew: Similar to interleave (*q.v.*), a scheme for staggering the logical sectors on adjacent tracks of a disk so that sector 1 of track n+1 is always just about to pass under the head once the controller has finished processing the last sector of track n.

Soft-sectored: Disks on which the size and position of the sectors is determined by the formatting software, as in the disks used on a PC.

ST-506: Standard PC hard disk interface first developed by Seagate and named after the original hard disk model which used it.

Static RAM (SRAM): Type of memory chip which retains information for as long as power is applied, without the need for refreshing, faster but more expensive than dynamic RAM.

Surface mounted device (SMD): Miniature component designed to be mounted on the solder side of a circuit board; especially suited to automated assembly.

Synchronous communications: Method of communications usually used with mainframe computers, and requiring a special interface card; characters are sent in blocks, with header and error checking information.

Timer: A device within the PC which can be programmed to produce interrupts at varying time intervals; one output from this is used to generate the memory refresh signal for the DRAM, another is used to maintain the DOS date and time.

Track: the circle described on a disk recording surface by data written there by the read/write head; each surface contains a number of concentric tracks.

Trojan: Malevolent program which masquerades as something harmless.

TSR: A utility which, when run, uses the terminate-and-stay-resident function of DOS to remain in memory, from where it can be called up over the top of other programs using a special *hot key*.

TTL: Transistor-transistor logic – a type of electronic circuit which uses 0V and 5V to represent digital 0 and 1.

Uninterruptible power supply (UPS): A device which sits between the mains outlet and the computer, containing batteries which are charged while the mains voltage is applied; if a mains failure occurs the batteries take over and generate power at the appropriate mains voltage for a period of a few minutes, allowing work to be saved and the system to be shut down.

Upload: Process of transferring data from your system to a remote one.

Upper memory block (UMB): Block of memory between 640Kb and 1Mb – on an 80386 or better system, device drivers and TSRs may be loaded into UMBs so that they don't take up valuable base memory.

Vertical scan rate: The number of complete sweeps of the CRT screen performed by the CRT electron beam in one second; this should be greater than 50Hz if perceptible and objectionable flicker is to be avoided.

Virus: A program which is designed to spread from one computer to another by attaching itself to other executable program code; such programs often attempt to hide themselves, and frequently try to disrupt the operation of the machine or destroy data.

Wait state: A single clock cycle during which the CPU does nothing except wait for an external device; needed where memory or expansion devices cannot operate at the same speed as the CPU.

Word: A unit of storage consisting of two consecutive bytes; together these can represent an integer value of from 0 to 65535 or –32768 to 32767.

XMS: Extended Memory Specification – a standard set of functions for accessing extended memory which are supported by drivers such as HIMEM.SYS allowing better use to be made of this memory under DOS.

Xon/xoff: Type of handshaking where the receiving device sends an xoff character to the transmitter when it wants it to stop sending, and sends an xon when it is ready to receive once again.

Appendix 2

Power On Self-Test Error Codes

IBM systems and some compatibles – POST error codes

00xx Miscellaneous errors
    001x   unknown error
    002x   power supply fault

01xx System Board errors
    0101   interrupt failure
    0102   BIOS ROM checksum error (PC, XT)
    0102   timer failure (AT)
    0103   BASIC ROM checksum error (PC, XT)
    0103   timer interrupt failure (AT)
    0104   interrupt controller failure (PC, XT)
    0104   protected mode failure (AT)
    0105   timer failure (PC, XT)
    0105   8042 error (AT)
    0106   converting logic test failure
    0107   Hot NMI test failure
    0108   timer bus test failure
    0109   DMA test error
    0121   unexpected interrupt occurred
    0151   real-time clock or CMOS RAM failure
    0161   system options not set: back-up battery failure
    0162   CMOS checksum or configuration error
    0163   time and date not set
    0164   memory size error

02xx Memory (RAM) errors
    0201   memory test failure – location displayed in hex
    0202   memory address failure (A0 – A15)
    0203   memory address failure (A16 – A23)

03xx Keyboard errors
    0301   stuck key – scan code of key is given
    0302   keyboard is locked

04xx Monochrome Display Adaptor (MDA) errors
    0401   memory, horizontal sync or vertical sync test failures
    0432   parallel port test failure

05xx Colour Graphics Adaptor (CGA) errors
    0501   memory, horizontal sync or vertical sync test failures

06xx Diskette drive errors
    0601   diskette drive or adaptor test failure

07xx Maths co-processor errors
    0701   maths co-processor test failure

09xx Parallel Printer Adaptor errors
    0901   printer adaptor test failure

10xx Alternate Parallel Printer Adaptor (LPT2) errors
    1001   alternate printer adaptor test failure

11xx Asynchronous Communications Adaptor errors
    1101   asynchronous communications adaptor test failure

12xx Alternate Asynchronous Communications Adaptor errors
    1201   alternate asynchronous communications adaptor test failure

13xx Game Control Adaptor errors
    1301   Game Control Adaptor test failure
    1302   Joystick test failure

17xx Fixed Disk errors
    1701   fixed disk not ready (PC, XT)
    1701   fixed disk / adaptor test failure (AT)
    1702   time out (PC, XT)
    1702   fixed disk adaptor error (AT)
    1703   fixed disk drive error (PC, XT)
    1704   fixed disk controller error (PC, XT)
    1704   fixed disk adaptor or drive error (AT)
    1780   fixed disk 0 fatal error (cannot boot)
    1781   fixed disk 1 fatal error
    1782   fixed disk controller failure
    1790   fixed disk 0 non-fatal error
    1791   fixed disk 1 non-fatal error

IBM systems and some compatibles – beep error codes

Beeps	Explanation
1 short	System operation normal
None	Power problem (or speaker defective)
Continuous	Power problem
2 short	Fault (see displayed error code)
1 long, 1 short	System board fault
Any other signal	Display fault

Systems with Phoenix BIOS – beep error codes

Fatal system board errors

Beeps	Explanation
1-1-3	CMOS read/write failure
1-1-4	ROM BIOS checksum failure
1-2-1	Programmable timer failure
1-2-2	DMA initialisation failure
1-2-3	DMA page register read/write failure
1-3-1	RAM refresh verification failure
1-3-3	Failure in 1st 64Kb of RAM
1-3-4	Odd/even logic failure in 1st 64Kb RAM
1-4-1	Address line failure in 1st 64Kb RAM
2-x-x	Single bit failure in 1st 64Kb RAM
3-1-1	Slave DMA register failure
3-1-2	Master DMA register failure
3-1-3	Master interrupt mask failure
3-1-4	Slave interrupt mask register failure
3-2-4	Keyboard controller test failure
3-3-4	Screen memory test failure
3-4-1	Screen initialisation failure
3-4-2	Screen retrace test failure

Non-fatal system board errors

Beeps	Explanation
4-2-1	No timer tick
4-2-2	Shutdown failure
4-2-3	A20 gate failure
4-2-4	Unexpected interrupt in protected mode
4-3-1	Address line failure (A16 – A23)
4-3-3	Timer chip counter 2 failed
4-4-1	Serial port test failure
4-4-2	Parallel port test failure
4-4-3	Maths co-processor test failure

Appendix 3

PC Resources

a. Memory Utilisation

Dec.	Hex.	Utilisation
0Kb	00000	
		Interrupt vector table
1Kb	00400	
		BIOS data area
	00490	
		reserved
	00500	
		DOS and BASIC data areas
	00700	
		Device drivers
		Buffers
		DOS operating system code
		TSRs
		User programs
640Kb	A0000	
		EGA/VGA memory buffer (graphics mode)
	B0000	
		MDA/HGC memory buffer
	B8000	
		Colour adaptor memory buffer (text mode)
		CGA memory buffer (graphics mode)
	C0000	
		EGA/VGA ROM BIOS extension
	C4000	
		– usually free –

	C8000	
		XT type or ESDI hard disk controller ROM
	CA000	
		Secondary XT type hard disk controller ROM
	CC000	
		Secondary ESDI hard disk controller ROM
		IBM Network adaptor
	D0000	
		– usually free –
	E0000	
		– often free –
	F0000	
		– often free –
	F4000	
		IBM ROM BASIC – often free in non IBM PCs
	FC000	
		ROM BIOS
1Mb	100000	
		Start of extended memory area

b. Hardware IRQ and Interrupt Assignments

PC and XT compatible systems

IRQ No	Interrupt	Usage
-	NMI	Memory Parity and Co-processor
0	08h	Timer
1	09h	Keyboard
2	0Ah	(reserved)
3	0Bh	Serial port COM2
4	0Ch	Serial port COM1
5	0Dh	Hard disk controller
6	0Eh	Diskette drive controller
7	0Fh	Parallel port LPT1

AT compatible systems

IRQ No	Interrupt	Usage
-	NMI	Memory Parity and I/O check
0	08h	Timer
1	09h	Keyboard
2		(used for slave interrupt controller) Note that boards jumpered to use IRQ2 will in fact use IRQ9, as the IRQ2 bus contact is connected to IRQ9, but the end result is the same, since interrupt 0Ah is stillgenerated.

3	0Bh	Serial port COM2
4	0Ch	Serial port COM1
5	0Dh	Parallel port LPT2
6	0Eh	Diskette drive controller
7	0Fh	Parallel port LPT1
8	70h	Real Time Clock
9	0Ah	(redirected IRQ2)
10	72h	(reserved)
11	73h	(reserved)
12	74h	(reserved)
13	75h	Co-processor
14	76h	Hard disk controller
15	77h	(reserved)

c. I/O port assignments

Port address range	Device
000h – 01Fh	DMA controller 1
020h – 03Fh	Interrupt controller 1
040h – 05Fh	Timer
060h – 06Fh	Keyboard controller
070h – 07Fh	CMOS real-time clock (AT)
080h – 09Fh	DMA page registers (AT)
0A0h – 0BFh	Interrupt controller 2 (AT)
0C0h – 0DFh	DMA controller 2 (AT)
0E0h – 0EFh	Real-time clock (PS/2 model 30)
0F0h – 0FFh	Maths co-processor
1F0h – 1F8h	Hard disk controller (AT)
200h – 20Fh	Game port
210h – 217h	Expansion box (PC, XT)
278h – 27Fh	Parallel port 2 (PC,XT), 3 (AT)
2B0h – 2DFh	EGA adaptor (alternate)
2E8h – 2EFh	Serial port 4
2F8h – 2FFh	Serial port 2
320h – 32Fh	Hard disk controller (XT)
360h – 36Fh	PC Network
378h – 37Fh	Parallel port 1 (PC,XT) 2 (AT)
3B0h – 3BFh	Monochrome adapter/parallel port
3BCh – 3BFh	Parallel port 1 (AT)
3C0h – 3CFh	EGA adaptor
3D0h – 3DFh	CGA, EGA, VGA adaptor
3E8h – 3EFh	Serial port 3
3F0h – 3F7h	Diskette drive controller
3F8h – 3FFh	Serial port 1

d. DMA channel assignments

PC and XT compatible systems

DRQ No	Device
0	Used by system (not available on bus)
1	-
2	Diskette drive controller
3	Hard disk controller

AT compatible systems

DRQ No	Device
0	Used by system(16 bit)
1	- (8 bit)
2	Diskette drive controller(8 bit)
3	- (8 bit)
4	Slave DMA controller input into master
5	- (16 bit)
6	- (16 bit)
7	- (16 bit)

Appendix 4

Hard Disk Data

Mfr.	Model	(Mb)	(ms)	Size	Form	Type	Hds	Pltrs	Cyls	WPC	SPT
CONNER	CP-3022	20	26	3.5		AT IDE	2	1	636		27
	CP-3024	20	35	3.5		AT IDE	2	1	636		26
	CP-3044	40	33	3.5		AT IDE	2	1	1047		26
	CP-3104	104	33	3.5		AT IDE	8	4	776		26
	CP-3204	204	25	3.5		AT IDE	8	4	1366		26
CORE	HC40	40	9	5.25	FH	ESDI	4	3	564		35
	HC90	91	16	5.25	HH	ESDI	5	3	969		35
	HC100	101	9	5.25	FH	ESDI	15	8	379		35
	HC150	155	17	5.25	HH	ESDI	7	4	1250		35
	HC150	156	16	5.25	FH	ESDI	9	5	968		35
	HC175	172	14	3.5		ESDI	9	5	1072		35
	HC310	326	18	5.25	FH	ESDI	15	8	1224		35
	HC380	376	16	5.25	FH	ESDI	15	8	1412		35
	HC650	658	17	5.25	FH	ESDI	15	8	1661		53
FUJITSU	M2225DR	32	35	3.5		RLL	4	2	615		26
	M2226D2	16	35	3.5		MFM	6	3	320		17
	M2226DR	48	35	3.5		RLL	6	3	615		26
	M2227D2	11	35	3.5		MFM	4	2	320		17
	M2227DR	64	35	3.5		RLL	8	4	615		26
	M2242AS2	45	30	5.25	HH	MFM	7	4	754		17
	M2243AS2	71	30	5.25	FH	MFM	11	6	754		17
	M2243R	108	25	5.25	HH	RLL	7	4	1186		26
	M2244E	67	25	5.25	FH	ESDI	5	3	823		6 – 65
	M2244S	67	25	5.25	FH	SCSI	5	3	823		19/35/65
	M2245E	120	25	5.25	FH	ESDI	7	5	823		6 – 65
	M2245S	120	25	5.25	FH	SCSI	7	5	823		19/35/65
	M2246E	172	25	5.25	FH	ESDI	6	10	823		6 – 65
	M2246S	172	25	5.25	FH	SCSI	6	10	823		19/35/65
KYOCERA	KC20A/B	21	65	3.5		MFM	4	2	615		17
	KC30A/B	32	65	3.5		RLL	4	2	615		26

Hard Disk Data

Make	Model									
MAXTOR	7040A	41	17	3.5	LP	AT IDE				
	7060A	65	15	3.5	LP	AT IDE				
	7080A	81	17	3.5	LP	AT IDE				
	7120A	130	15	3.5	LP	AT IDE				
	8051A	41	28	3.5	HH	AT IDE	4	2	745		28
	LXT-213A	213	15	3.5	HH	AT IDE				
MINISCRIBE	3053	44	25	5.25	HH	MFM	5	2	1024	512	17
	3085	70	20	5.25	HH	MFM	7	4	1170	512	17
	3085E	72	17	5.25	HH	ESDI	3	2	1270	512	
	3085S	72	17	5.25	HH	SCSI	3	2	1255	512	
	3130	53	17	5.25	HH	MFM	5	3	1250		17
	3130E	112	17	5.25	HH	ESDI	5	3	1250	512	
	3130S	115	17	5.25	HH	SCSI	5	3	1255	512	
	3180	74	17	5.25	HH	MFM	7	4	1250		17
	3180E	157	17	5.25	HH	ESDI	7	4	1250	512	
	3180S	160	17	5.25	HH	SCSI	7	4	1255	512	
	3212	10	85	5.25	HH	MFM	2	1	612	128	17
	3425	21	85	5.25	HH	MFM	4	2	612	128	17
	3438	32	85	5.25	HH	RLL	4	2	612	128	26
	3650	41	61	5.25	HH	MFM	6	3	809	128	17
	3675	63	61	5.25	HH	RLL	6	3	612	128	26
	6032	26	28	5.25	FH	MFM	3	2	1024	512	17
	6053	44	28	5.25	FH	MFM	5	3	1024	512	17
	6074	62	28	5.25	FH	MFM	7	4	1024	512	17
	6079	68	28	5.25	FH	RLL	5	3	1024	512	26
	6085	71	28	5.25	FH	MFM	8	4	1024	512	17
	6128	110	28	5.25	FH	RLL	8	4	1024	512	26
	8051AT	41	28	3.5		AT IDE	4	2	745		28
	8225	20	40	3.5		RLL	2	1	771	128	26
	8225AT	21	28	3.5		AT IDE	2	1	745		28
	8225XT	21	68	3.5		XT IDE	2	1	805		26
	8425	21	68	3.5		MFM	4	2	615	128	17
	8434F	32	40	3.5		RLL	4	2	615	128	26
	8450	40	40	3.5		RLL	4	2	771	128	26
	8450AT	41	40	3.5		AT IDE	4	2	745		28
	8450XT	41	45	3.5		XT IDE	4	2	805		26
	9380E	338	17	5.25	FH	ESDI	14		1224	512	
	9380S	347	16	5.25	FH	SCSI	15		1224	512	
	9424E	360	17	5.25	FH	ESDI	8		1661	512	
	9424S	355	17	5.25	FH	SCSI	8		1661	512	
	9780E	676	17	5.25	FH	ESDI	15		1661	512	
	9780S	668	17	5.25	FH	SCSI	15		1661	512	
MITSUBISHI	MR521	10	85	5.25	HH	MFM	2	1	612		17
	MR522	20	85	5.25	HH	MFM	4	2	612	300	17
	MR535-M	41	28	5.25	HH	MFM	5	3	971		17
	MR535-R	63	28	5.25	HH	RLL	5	3	971		26
SEAGATE	ST124	21	40	3.5		MFM	4	2	615		17
	ST125	21	28	3.5		MFM	4	2	615		17
	ST125A	21	28	3.5		AT IDE	4	2			
	ST125N	21	28	3.5		SCSI	4	2			
	ST138	32	28	3.5		MFM	6	3	615		17

Model									
ST138A	33	28	3.5		AT IDE	4	2		
ST138N	33	28	3.5		SCSI	4	2		
ST138R	33	28	3.5		RLL	4	2	615	26
ST151	43	24	3.5		MFM	5	3	977	17
ST157A	49	28	3.5		AT IDE	6	3		
ST157N	49	28	3.5		SCSI	6	3		
ST157R	49	28	3.5		RLL	6	3	615	26
ST177N	61	20	3.5		SCSI	5	3		
ST225	21	65	5.25	HH	MFM	4	2	615	17
ST225R	21	70	5.25	HH	RLL	2	1	667	31
ST238R	33	65	5.25	HH	RLL	4	2	615	26
ST250R	42	70	5.25	HH	RLL	4	2	667	31
ST251	43	28	5.25	HH	MFM	6	3	820	17
ST252	43	40	5.25	HH	MFM	6	3	820	17
ST253	43	28	5.25	HH	MFM	5	3	989	17
ST274A	66	29	5.25	HH	AT IDE	5	3	948	26
ST277N	65	28	5.25	HH	SCSI	6	3		
ST277R	66	28	5.25	HH	RLL	6	3	820	26
ST278R	66	40	5.25	HH	RLL	6	3	820	26
ST279R	65	20	5.25	HH	RLL	5	3	989	26
ST280A	71	29	5.25	HH	AT IDE	5	3	1032	26
ST296N	85	28	5.25	HH	SCSI	6	3		
ST325A	21	28	3.5	LP	AT IDE	4		615	17
ST325N	21	28	3.5	LP	SCSI	4			
ST325X	21	45	3.5	LP	XT IDE	4		615	17
ST351A/X	43	28	3.5	LP	AT/XT	6		820	17
ST1057A	53	19	3.5		AT IDE	3	2		
ST1057N	49	19	3.5		SCSI-2	3	2		
ST1096N	84	20	3.5	HH	SCSI	7	4		
ST1100	84	15	3.5	HH	MFM	9	5	1072	17
ST1102A	89	19	3.5	HH	AT IDE	5	3		
ST1102N	84	19	3.5	HH	SCSI-2	5	3		
ST1111E	99	15	3.5	HH	ESDI	5	3	1072	36
ST1126A	111	15	3.5	HH	AT IDE	7	4		
ST1126N	107	15	3.5	HH	SCSI	7	4		
ST1133N	113	15	3.5	HH	SCSI	5	3		
ST1144A	125	19	3.5	HH	AT IDE	7	4		
ST1144N	126	19	3.5	HH	SCSI-2	7	4		
ST1150R	128	15	3.5	HH	RLL	9	5	1072	26
ST1162A	143	15	3.5	HH	AT IDE	9	5		
ST1162N	138	15	3.5	HH	SCSI	9	5		
ST1186A	164	15	3.5	HH	AT IDE	4	7		
ST1186N	159	15	3.5	HH	AT IDE	4	7		
ST1201A	172	15	3.5	HH	AT IDE	9	5		
ST1201E	178	15	3.5	HH	ESDI	9	5	1072	36
ST1201N	172	15	3.5	HH	SCSI	9	5		
ST1239A	211	15	3.5	HH	AT IDE	9	5		
ST1239N	204	15	3.5	HH	SCSI	9	5		
ST1400N	331	14	3.5	HH	SCSI-2	7	4	1476	
ST1401N	338	12	3.5	HH	SCSI-2	9	5	1100	
ST1480A	426	14	3.5	HH	AT IDE	9	5	1474	

	Model	Cap	Access	Form	Height	Interface	Cyl	Heads	LZ	Sect
	ST1480N	426	14	3.5	HH	SCSI-2	9	5	1476	
	ST2106E	89	18	5.25	HH	ESDI	5	3	1024	34
	ST2106N	91	18	5.25	HH	SCSI	5	3	1024	
	ST2125N	107	18	5.25	HH	SCSI	3	2	1544	
	ST2182E	160	16	5.25	HH	ESDI	4	3	1453	54
	ST2209N	179	18	5.25	HH	SCSI	5	3	1544	
	ST2274A	241	16	5.25	HH	AT IDE	5	3	1747	54
	ST2383A	338	16	5.25	HH	AT IDE	7	4	1747	54
	ST2383E	337	16	5.25	HH	ESDI	7	4	1747	54
	ST2383N	332	14	5.25	HH	SCSI	7	4	1261	
	ST2502N	435	16	5.25	HH	SCSI	7	4	1755	
	ST3025A	22	19	3.5	LP	AT IDE	4		615	17
	ST3025N	22	19	3.5	LP	SCSI-2				
	ST3057A	53	19	3.5	LP	AT IDE	6		1024	17
	ST3057N	49	19	3.5	LP	SCSI-2				
	ST3096A	89	19	3.5	LP	AT IDE	10		1024	17
	ST3096N	84	19	3.5	LP	SCSI-2				
	ST3120A	107	16	3.5	LP	AT IDE	3	2	1024	
	ST3144A	130	16	3.5	LP	AT IDE	3	2	1001	
	ST3144N	126	16	3.5	LP	SCSI	3	2		
	ST4053	45	28	5.25	HH	MFM	5	3	1024	17
	ST4096	80	28	5.25	HH	MFM	9	5	1024	17
	ST4144R	123	28	5.25	HH	RLL	9	5	1024	26
	ST9025A	21	<20	2.5		AT IDE	16 max	1	1024 max	
	ST9051A	43	<20	2.5		AT IDE	16 max	1	1024 max	
TOSHIBA	MK234FB	106	20	3.5		SCSI	7	4	845	
	MK234FC	106	20	3.5		AT IDE	7	4	845	
WESTERN DIGITAL	WD362	21	80	3.5		MFM	4	2	615	17
	WD344R	41	40	3.5		RLL	4	2	782	26
	WD382R	20	85	3.5		RLL	2	1	782	26
	WD383R	32	85	3.5		RLL	4	2	615	26
	WD384R	41	85	3.5		RLL	4	2	782	26
	WD93024-A	22	39	3.5		AT IDE	2	1	782	27
	WD93028-A	22	69	3.5		AT IDE	2	1	782	27
	WD93028-X	22	70	3.5		XT IDE	2	1	782	27
	WD93038-X	32	70	3.5		XT IDE	3	2	782	27
	WD93044-A	43	28	3.5		AT IDE	4	2	782	27
	WD93048-A	43	69	3.5		AT IDE	4	2	782	27
	WD93048-X	43	70	3.5		XT IDE	4	2	782	27
	WD95024-A	22	39	5.25	HH	AT IDE	2	1	782	27
	WD95028-A	22	69	5.25	HH	AT IDE	2	1	782	27
	WD95028-X	22	70	5.25	HH	XT IDE	2	1	782	27
	WD95038-X	32	70	5.25	HH	XT IDE	3	2	782	27
	WD95044-A	43	28	5.25	HH	AT IDE	4	2	782	27
	WD95048-A	43	69	5.25	HH	AT IDE	4	2	782	27
	WD95048-X	43	70	5.25	HH	XT IDE	4	2	782	27
	WDSC8320	320	12.5	3.5		SCSI	15	8	949	48

Appendix 5

Directory of Suppliers

AMT International,
2393 Qume Drive, Tel: 408 432 0552 (US)
San Jose, Fax: 408 944 9801 (US)
CA 95131, USA.

Memory upgrades, CPU chips etc.

Atico,
1130 Burnett Ave., Tel: 415 680 8271 (US)
Suite H, Fax: 415 680 1408 (US)
Concord, Tlx: 470166
CA 94520, USA.

Memory upgrades, disk drives etc.

CD 2000,
PO Box 1061, Tel: 0753 44895 (UK)
London Road, Fax: 0753 46347 (UK)
Slough,
Berks, SL3 8RE, UK.

Hard disk drive products.

Compulink Information Exchange,
Suite 2, Tel: 081 390 8446 (UK)
The Sanctuary, BBS: 081 390 1244 (UK)
Oakhill Grove,
Surbiton, Surrey, KT6 6DU, UK.

Electronic conferencing system.

Compuserve Inc.,
5000 Arlington Centre Blvd., Tel: 800 848 8199 (US)
Columbus,
OH 43220, USA.

Compuserve Information Service,
15/16 Lower Park Row, Tel: 0800 289378 (UK)
P.O. Box 676,
Bristol, BS99 1YN, UK.

Electronic conferencing system

HyperWare,
14460 Sycamore Avenue, Tel: 408 683 4911 (US)
San Martin, Fax: 408 683 4042 (US)
CA 95046, BBS: 408 683 4923 (US)

Disk cacheing software.

JDR Microdevices,
CA, Tel: 408 559 1200 (US)
USA. Fax: 408 559 0250 (US)

All types of PC components.

Landmark Research Intl. Corp.
703 Grand Central St, Tel: 813 443 1331 (US)
Clearwater, Fax: 813 443 6603 (US)
FL 34616, USA.

Diagnostic software and tools

Loutronics,
11 Hercies Road, Tel: 0895 55399 (UK)
Hillingdon, Uxbridge,
Middlesex, UB10 9LS, UK.

Cases, PSUs, boards, monitors.

Matmos Ltd,
Unit 11, Tel: 0444 482091 (UK)
Lindfield Enterprise Park, Fax: 0444 484258 (UK)
Lingfield, W. Sussex,
RH16 2LX, UK.

Surplus parts and peripherals.

McAfee Associates,
4432 Cheeney Street, Tel: 408 988 3832 (US)
Santa Clara, Fax: 408 970 9727 (US)
CA 95054, BBS: 408 988 4004 (US)

Anti-virus software products.

Memory Direct,
33 Grosvenor Road, Tel: 0252 316060 (UK)
Aldershot, Fax: 0252 341939 (UK)
Hants, GU11 3DP, UK.

Memory upgrades for PCs and printers

MicroSystems Development,
4100 Moorpark Avenue, Tel: 408 296 4000 (US)
#104 San Jose, Fax: 408 296 5877 (US)
CA 95117, USA.

Test Drive disk diagnostic tool.

Morgan Computer Co,
64 – 72 New Oxford Street, Tel: 071 255 2115 (UK)
London, WC1 Fax: 071 436 6285 (UK)

Hardware, obsolete and bankrupt stock.

Nevada Computer Corporation,
684 Wells Road, Tel: 702 294 0204 (US)
Boulder City, Fax: 702 294 1168 (US)
NV 89005, USA.

Memory, disk drives and other PC components.

PC Power & Cooling, Inc.
31510 Mountain Way, Tel: 619 723 9513 (US)
Bonsall, Fax: 619 723 0075 (US)
CA 92003, USA.

PC compatible power supplies.

Professional Solutions Ltd,
18 Dalston Gardens, Tel: 081 206 2095 (UK)
Stanmore, Middlesex, Fax: 081 206 2096 (UK)
HA7 1DA, UK.

Systems, boards, disk drives, monitors etc.

S & S International,
Weylands Court, Tel: 0494 791900 (UK)
Water Meadow, Fax: 0494 791602 (UK)
Chesham, Bucks,
HP5 1LP, UK.
Anti-virus software, utilities.

Time Computer Systems Ltd.,
Time House, Tel: 0254 682343 (UK)
Devonport Road, Fax: 0254 664053 (UK)
Blackburn, Lancs.
BB2 1EJ, UK.
Hard disk cards.

Worldwide Computer Diagnostics Ltd.,
C2 Enterprise Business Park, Tel: 071 537 7300 (UK)
Marsh Wall, Fax: 071 515 4512 (UK)
London,
E14 9TE, UK,
Diagnostic aids

Appendix 6

Common PC Viruses

Name	Destructive?	Infects COM	EXE	OVL	Boot	Part	Increase Size COM / EXE	Symptoms	Removal
Brain (Pakistani)	N				Y		-/-	Volume label: "(c) Brain"	Cleanup, DOS SYS
Cascade	N	Y					1701/1704	Characters fall to bottom line of screen	Cleanup, Delete
Dark Avenger	Y	Y	Y				1800	Writes randomly to disk	Cleanup, Delete
Datacrime	Y	Y					1168/1280	Msg: "Datacrime Virus" Formats hard disk	Delete
Fu Manchu	N	Y	Y				2086/2080	Msg: "The world will hear from me again" and others	Delete
Italian	N				Y		-/-	Bouncing ball on screen	Cleanup, DOS SYS
Jerusalem	Y	Y	Y				1813/1808	Black box on screen, PC slows down, deletes files run on Friday 13th.	Cleanup, Delete
Joshi	N				Y	Y	-/-	Asks user to type "Happy Birthday Joshi" on Jan 5th	Backup, LLF, FDISK etc.
Nomenklatura	Y	Y	Y				1024	Randomly scrambles FAT	Delete
Spanish Telecom	Y	Y			Y	Y	3700	Msg: "Campana Anti-Telefonica"; wipes hard disk after 400th boot.	Backup data, LLF, FDISK etc.
Stoned (New Zealand)	N				Y	Y	-/-	Msg: "Your computer is now stoned"	Cleanup, DOS SYS
Vacsina	N	Y	Y	Y			1206/1353	Infected program beeps when executed	Delete
Yankee	N	Y	Y				2885	Plays 'Yankee Doodle' at 5pm	Delete

Notes:

There are many modifications of some viruses, and it is possible for a non-destructive virus to be modified to make it destructive.

Under Removal Instructions:

Cleanup indicates McAfee CLEANUP or similar anti-virus programs;

Delete indicates that the infected file may simply be deleted;

DOS SYS indicates that the SYS command may be used to overwrite a boot sector virus with a fresh copy of the operating system;

LLF, FDISK etc. means that the disk must be low-level formatted, re-partitioned with FDISK and DOS FORMATted, before reloading uninfected files from backups.

Appendix 7

Diagnostics and Utilities

A set of diskettes containing the BASIC source code given in the listings in this book, and copies of many of the public domain and shareware utilities referenced in the text, is available from the publishers. The set comprises two 5.25in 360Kb diskettes or a single 3.5in 720Kb one. Each utility is provided as a compressed archive containing all the relevant files and documentation.

The diskettes include the following utilities:

PKUNZIP.EXE Utility for decompressing the archive files on the disk.

LISTINGS.ZIP (public domain) Copies of all the BASIC listings given in the book.

SST.ZIP (public domain) System speed test - a benchmark utility.

PCINFO.ZIP (public domain) Two programs which display information about the configuration of a machine.

SHOW.ZIP (public domain) A command line utility to display various details about the system configuration.

TESTDRIV.ZIP (shareware) Utility for testing and aligning diskette drives.

FDCLEAN.ZIP (public domain) Utility for use with a diskette head cleaner.

HDTEST.ZIP (shareware) Utility for testing and recovering data from hard disk drives.

RAMTEST.ZIP (shareware) Utility for testing system memory.

MRKREL28.ZIP (public domain) Utility for allowing TSR programs which do not provide the facility themselves to be de-installed.

SCAN.ZIP (shareware) Virus scanner from McAfee Associates.

VSHIELD.ZIP (shareware) Memory-resident virus checker from McAfee Associates.

CLEAN.ZIP (shareware) Virus remover from McAfee Associates.

Note about shareware: Shareware programs are provided on a try-before-you-buy basis. They are not free software. If you wish to use the shareware utilities provided on these disks on a regular basis, you must register your copy of the software with the manufacturers. Details of how to register are included with the documentation files provided as part of each package.

Ordering Information

A disk containing all of the above is available direct from:

Sigma Press, 1 South Oak Lane, Wilmslow, Cheshire SK9 6AR, UK.

Phone: 0625 - 531035   Fax: 0625 - 536800

The current price (at June 1992) is £10 in the UK; add £1 in Europe (outside UK) or £3 (airmail elsewhere). Specify 5.25 inch (two 360 Kb disks) or 3.5 inch (one 720 Kb).

Cheques payable to Sigma Press; Access and Visa welcome – quote card number, expiry date, cardholder name and address, and delivery adddress if different

Index

386 to the Max 267

A
adapter
    8514/A display 105
    display 91, 100
    PS/2 display 104
allocation units 270
AMI BIOS 30
ANSI.SYS 260, 276
Asynchronous Comms Adapter 167
asynchronous communication 169
autodialling
AUTOEXEC.BAT 262
AutoSIG 304
azimuth misalignment 122

B
backfilling 266
backplane 2
backup 244, 289
    batteries 252
BACKUP.COM 222
bad sectors 160
BASIC 37
batteries, backup 252
beep error codes 319
BIOS 255
    AMI 30
    Phoenix 319
boot error 165
booting, system 255
boot record 256
boot sector 145
BREAK 258
break out box 178
BUFFERS 257, 274, 277
bulletin boards 302
burst mode 16
bus, system 10

C
cache
    disk 272
    Norton 273
Calibrate 154, 161
cards
    expansion 65
    hard disk 148
CGA 93, 96, 102, 103
    errors 318
change-line problems 126
Check It 31, 76, 85, 161, 176, 222
chip
    removal 225
    replacement 225
chip sets 53
CHKDSK 263
CLEAN 222
CLEANUP 223
clock 13
clusters 145, 270
    lost 277
CMOS 165
    setup 60
code pages 258
Colour Graphics Adapter (CGA)
    See CGA
COMMAND.COM 256
communication, async. / sync. 169
communications adapter errors 318
communications protocol 170
compression, data 194
COMPSURF 151
CompuServe 303
COMSPEC 256, 263
CONFIG.SYS 222, 256
conflict, memory 72
controller
    diskette drive 120
    hard disk 143, 277
corrupted diskettes 128

corruption
    directory 166
    disk file 166, 277
COUNTRY.SYS 222
CSMA/CD 296
cycle time 13
cylinder wraparound 147

D

data compression 194
Data Communications Equipment
    See DCE
Data Terminal Equipment
    See DTE
DCE 193
DEBUG.COM 222
defragmentation 155, 271
device drivers 259
devices, surface-mounted 3
Digital Diagnostics Diskette 32
DIP switches 58
Direct Memory Access 14
directories 166
    structure 271
disk
    caches 272
    error 256, 318
    hard 2, 133
    interleave 277
    large partitions 263
    non-system 256
    optimisation 153
    partitioning 270
    performance 165
    slow 277
disk boot error 165
Disk Doctor 161
diskette
    change-line problems 126
    corrupted 128
    double-density 116
    soft-sectored 115
diskette drive 113, 116
    controller 120
    errors 318
    external 131
    installation/removal 129
diskettes
    hard-sectored 116
Disk Manager 146
Disk Technician Advanced 161
display
    adapter 100
    adapter, PS/2
    laptop 95
    problems 107
DMA assignments 323

DMDRVR.BIN 146
DOS
    extenders 19
    multi-user 294
DOS 4.0 261
DOSINFO 222
DOSMAP 222
DOS v5 262
    memory management 268
DRDOS 6 163, 267
drive
    diskette 113, 116
    double-density 130
    external 131
    installation 129
    misalignment 121
    removal 130
DRIVER.SYS 261
drive table 146
DRIVPARM 126
DTE 193
dynamic RAM (DRAM) 8

E

EGA 93, 103
EGA BIOS 109
EISA 21
electricity, static 238
EMM386.EXE 268
EMM386.SYS 266
Enhanced Graphics Adapter
    See EGA
Enhanced Small Device Interf.
    See ESDI
environment variable 256
erasure, accidental 162
error
    beep codes 319
    CGA 318
    communications adapter 318
    correction 194
    disk 256, 318
    disk boot 165
    F1 110
    fatal stack 276
    game control 318
    keyboard 318
    MDA 318
    memory (RAM) 318
    maths co-processor 318
    parallel printer adapter 318
    POST 165, 317
    read/write 128, 165
    system board 317, 319
ESDI 142
Ethernet 296
Expanded Memory Manager 18

Index

expansion card conflicts 66
expansion cards 65
expansion slots 2, 11
Extended Graphics Array
   See XGA
Extended Memory Specification
   See XMS

F

F1 error 110
FASTOPEN 274
FAT 164
fatal stack error 276
FCBs 259, 263
FDISK 158, 159
FDISK.COM 222
fibre optics 299
file
   accidentally erased 162
   corruption 277
   deleted 162
   disk 166
   recovery 161
file control blocks
   See FCBs
FILES 257
flow control 173
FM 138
FORMAT.COM 222
formatting, low-level 149, 158
frequency modulation (FM) 138

G

game control adapter errors 318
General Failure Error 250

H

handshaking 173
   hardware 174
   software 174
hard disk 133
   cards 148
   construction 134
   controllers 143, 277
   data 324
   installing 156
   interfaces 140
   preparation 158
   problems 165
   reformatting 252
   removal 156
hard-sectored diskettes 116
hardware
   handshaking 174
   serial port 171
hardware record 302

Hayes command language 192
HDTEST 36, 161, 222
head
   actuators 136
   parking 137
HeadRoom 267
Hercules Graphics Card
   See HGC
HGC 103
high-density diskettes 116
High Memory Area
   See HMA
HIMEM.SYS 267
HMA 20
Hyperdisk 273
hysteresis 122

I

IBMBIO.COM 256
IBMDOS.COM 256
IBM Token Ring 297
IDE 143
INFOPLUS 222
installation 233
   diskette drive 129
   hard disk 156
Integrated Drive Electronics
   See IDE
Intel 8048 82
interfaces, hard disk 140
interleave factor 151
interrupts 12
interrupt assignments 321
Interrupt Requests 12
interrupt service routine ISR 12
invalid COMMAND.COM 276
IO.SYS 256

J

jumpers 58

K

KEYB 264
KEYB.COM 82, 222
keyboard 81
   dismantling 88
   errors 318
   LEDs 86
   reassembly 88
   shift keys 86
KEYBOARD.SYS 222
KEYBUK 264
KEYBUK.COM 276

L

landing zone 137, 145
Landmark speed 13
LANs
    installing cards 299
    peer-to-peer 293
    server-based 292
    topology 295
    zero slot 294
LANsmart 293
LANtastic 293
laptop display 95
LIM 4.0 EMS 266
logic bombs virus 280
Lotus-Intel-Microsoft 4.0 ems
    See LIM 4.0 EMS

M

MACHINFO 222
mains supply 239
maintenance
    preventive 247
    printers 253
map, memory 16
MARK and RELEASE 269
mathematics co-processors 274
    errors 318
Matrix 306
Maximize 267
McAfee Associates 288
    CLEANUP 223
    NETSCAN 223
    SCAN 223
MDA 93
    errors 318
MEM 268
memory 4
    addressing 6
    banks 52
    configuration 59
    conflicts 72
    direct access 14
    expanded 18, 261, 266, 277
    extended 15, 19
    high 267
    management in DOS 5 268
    map 16
    parity 52
    (RAM) errors 318
    upgrading 73
    upper 267
memory area, high 20
meters, test 223
MFM 139
Micro Channel Architecture 21
Microcom Networking Protocol
    See MNP

MIRROR 163
misalignment
    azimuth 122
    drive 121
    radial 121
MNP 194
mode
    real address 15
    virtual address 15
modems 183, 188
    auto-answering 189
    autodialling 189
    external 190
    interfacing 196
    internal 192
    null 199
    problems 196
monitor 91
    digital 94
    testing 97
Monochrome Display Adaptor
    See MDA
motherboard 50
    configuration 56
    connectors 53
    removal 78
    repair 78
    replacement 74, 78, 79
mouse 185
    button operation 188
    cleaning 187
    erratic movements 188
    operation 186
    pointer absence 188
    problems 188
Move 'em 267
MS-DOS 5 163
MSDOS.SYS 256
MS-DOS v5 267, 268

N

NETSCAN 223
network
    security 283
networking 291
non-system disk 256
Norton Cache 273
Norton Utilities 33, 154, 222, 288
Novell NetWare 283, 292

O

optimisation, disk 153
out of environment space 276

P

page frame 266

parallel ports 201
    circuitry 202
parallel printer adapter errors 318
parallel printer problems 210
parity error 78
parking, head 137
PATH 262
PAUSE 263
PC Kwik 273
PC Probe 32, 154
PC resources 320
PC Tools 33
performance, disk 165
performance enhancement 74
Phoenix BIOS 319
plotters 184
plugs, surge protector 242
ports
    hardware 171
    input 9
    output 9
    parallel 201
    parallel circuitry 202
    problems 175, 180
    RS-232C 167
    serial 167
POST 26, 27
    checks 255
    error 77, 165, 317
    error codes 317
pound sign problem 276
Power-On Self Test
    see Post
power supply 2, 39
    removal 47
    replacement 48
preparation
    hard disk 158
printer adapter, errors 318
printers 183, 201
    configuration problems 214
    daisywheel 207
    dot-matrix 204
    ink-jet 204, 205
    laser 204, 206
    maintenance 253
    parallel cable wiring 211
    problems 210, 213
    thermal transfer 207
processors 4
PROMPT 262
PS/2 Display Adapter 104

Q
QEMM-386 267

R
radial misalignment 121
RAM
    dynamic 8
    static 8
RAMDRIVE.SYS 260
RAMTEST 36
read/write
    error 165
    errors 128
RECOVER 162
recovering files 161
reformatting hard disk 252
RELEASE (and MARK) 269
RESTORE.COM 222
RLL 138
ROM shadowing 64, 275
RS-232C 167, 168
run length limited
    See RLL

S
SCAN 223
scan code 85
SCSI 142
sectors, bad 160
sector translation 147
segment registers 6
sensitivity 122
serial port 167
    hardware 171
    problems 175, 180
serial printers, problems 213
settings, communications 196
setup, CMOS 60
shadowing, ROM 275
SHARE 263
SHELL 256
skew 152
Small Computer Systems Interface
    See SCSI
soft-sectored diskettes 115
software
    handshaking 174
    tools 222
soldering 227
Speed Disk 272
spindle speed 122
SpinRite 154, 161
STACKS 258
static RAM (SRAM) 8
stealth viruses 286
SuperVGA 93, 96
surface-mounted devices 3
surge protector plugs 242
synchronous communication 169
SYS.COM 222

system
    bus 10
    booting 255
    crashes 277
system board errors 317, 319

T
tape streamers 245
terminate and stay resident
    See TSRs
Test Drive 222
test meters 223
timer 14
Token Ring, IBM 297
toolkit, building a 301
tools, software 222
Trojans (virus) 280
TSRs 267, 269

U
UART 171
UMBs 267
UNDEL.COM 162
UNFORMAT 164
uninterruptible power supply
    See UPS
Universal Asynchronous Rec/Trans
    See UART
Upper Memory Blocks
    See UMBs
UPS 242
utilities 222

V
V.22 193
variable, environment 256
VGA 93, 96, 104
VGA BIOS 109
Video Graphics Array
    See VGA
viruses 264, 279
    detection 284
    list of 332
    logic bombs 280
    prevention 281
    removal 288
    removal from networks 289
    stealth 286
    symptoms 284
    trojans 280
voltage spikes 239

W
Wait States 8
Windows 3 265
wraparound, cylinder 147

X
XGA 105
XMS 267